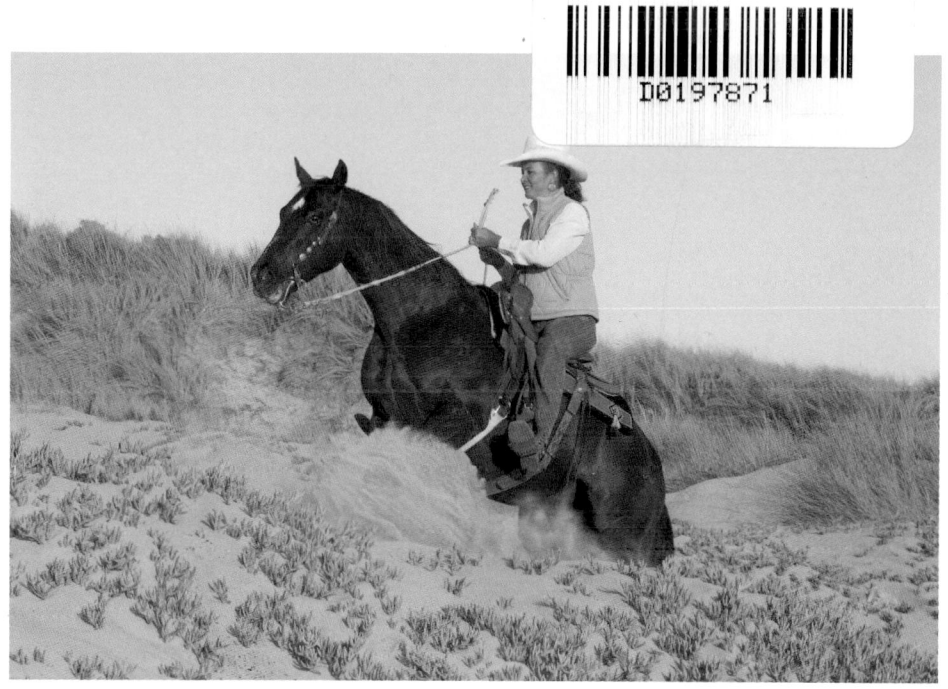

Confessions of a Compact Camera Shooter

Get Professional Quality Photos with Your Compact Camera

Rick Sammon

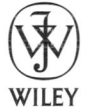

WILEY

Wiley Publishing, Inc.

Confessions of a Compact Camera Shooter

Published by
Wiley Publishing, Inc.
10475 Crosspoint Boulevard
Indianapolis, IN 46256
www.wiley.com

Published simultaneously in Canada

ISBN: 978-0-470-56507-0
Manufactured in the United States of America

10 9 8 7 6 5 4 3 2 1

For general information on our other products and services or to obtain technical support, please contact our Customer Care Department within the U.S. at (800) 762-2974, outside the U.S. at (317) 572-3993 or fax (317) 572-4002.

Wiley also publishes its books in a variety of electronic formats. Some content that appears in print may not be available in electronic books.

Library of Congress Control Number: 2009937273

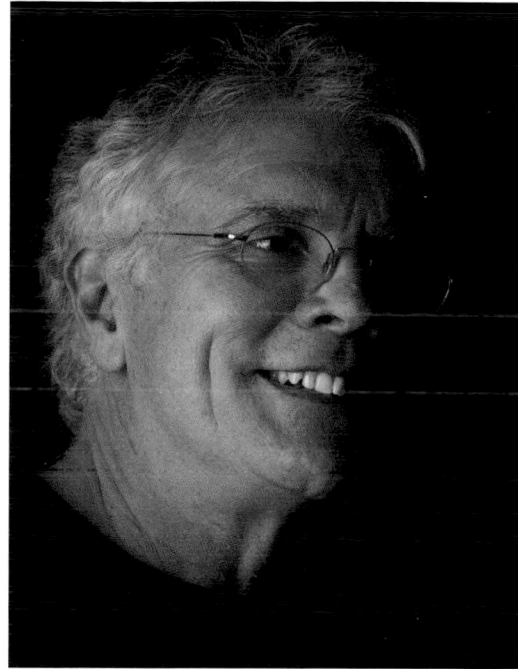

© Judith Monteferrante

Rick Sammon

Canon Explorer of Light Rick Sammon has published 36 books. All but this one, his forth with Wiley, have featured the work he's created with the help of professional digital SLR cameras.

His book, *Flying Flowers* won the coveted Golden Light Award, and his book *Hide and See Under the Sea* won the Ben Franklin Award.

Rick, who has photographed in almost 100 countries, gives more than two dozen photography workshops (including private workshops) and presentations around the world each year. Rick also hosts five shows on kelbytraining.com, and he writes for *PCPhoto* magazine.

Rick has been nominated for the Photoshop Hall of Fame and is considered one of today's top digital-imaging experts. He's well-known for cutting through lots of Photoshop "speak" and making it fun, easy and rewarding to work and play in the digital darkroom.

Rick enjoys helping photographers improve their work by presenting workshops and seminars throughout the world. He says it's a blast.

When asked about his photo specialty, Rick says, "My specialty is not specializing."

See www.ricksammon.com for more information … and photographic inspiration.

Credits

Acquisitions Editor
Courtney Allen

Project Editor
Jenny Brown

Technical Editor
Alan Hess

Copy Editor
Jenny Brown

Editorial Manager
Robyn Siesky

Business Manager
Amy Knies

Senior Marketing Manager
Sandy Smith

Vice President and
Executive Group Publisher
Richard Swadley

Vice President and Publisher
Barry Pruett

Book Designer
Erik Powers

Media Development Project Manager
Laura Moss

Media Development Assistant
Project Manager
Jenny Swisher

Acknowledgments

As you saw on the cover of this book, I get credit for writing it. And sure, I put a ton of work into it; but the truth is, I had a lot of help—just like every author. It's the same for all artists. Take Tom Cruise, for example. He gets top billing, but he has dozens and dozens of people—from makeup artists, lighting directors and set designers to acting coaches and stylists—that make him look good.

So I thought I'd take this opportunity to thank the folks who helped put together this work, as well as those who have helped me along the path to producing it, which is my 35th.

The always calm and patient Courtney Allen at Wiley was my main editor and project manager. She did a great job calming me down when things did not go as planned, and she was always patient when I was impatient. Thank you, Courtney, for all your help and understanding.

Barry Pruett, VP at Wiley, also gets a big "thank you." Thanks to my initial meeting with Barry, I have four books with Wiley and four how-to DVDs (on Canon cameras).

Behind the scenes, the following people helped bring this book to life:

Jenny Brown was my editor, making sure that what you're actually reading is what I meant to say. Like Courtney, Jenny always had a smile on her face, even when she probably wanted to kill me!

Erik Powers, designer, did a wonderful job laying out this book, compiling the text and photos into pages that are easy on the eyes. Thanks, Erik, for making me and my photographs look so good!

And of course a big thank you goes to my technical editor, Alan Hess. Alan not only checked my facts; he also added new insight to the technical side of picture making.

Thank you all for your eagle eyes and artistic flair!

Three Sammons get my heartfelt thanks: my wife, Susan; my son, Marco; and my Dad, Robert M. Sammon. For years, they have supported my efforts and helped with my photographs. Thank you for all your help and love.

When it comes to photo industry friends who have helped me with the book, I have more than a few. Rick Booth, Steve Inglima, Peter Tvarkunas, Chuck Westfall and Rudy Winston of Canon USA have been ardent supporters of my work and my photography seminars. So have my friends at Canon Professional Service (CPS). My hat is off to these folks, big time!

Jeff Cable of Lexar hooked me up with memory cards and card readers, helping me capture images for this book and my other books, too. Kelly Mondora of Westcott helped me with lighting accessories (reflectors and diffusers) that let me control the light and play with the light. What fun … Kelly and the gear, that is.

On the digital darkroom side, Adobe's Julieanne Kost, onOne Software's Mike Wong and Craig Keudell, and Tony Corbell and Ed Sanchez of Nik Software always are there to get me the latest and greatest info and software. And speaking of software, Scott Kelby of Photoshop fame gets a big thank you for just being who he is: a very sharing person.

Thank you all. I could not have done it without you …

Contents

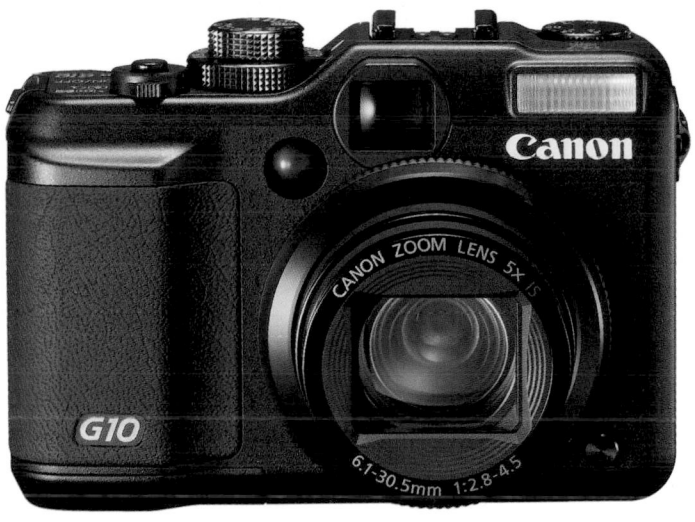

Foreword

Full-Featured Compact Digital Cameras

"Not a digital SLR" can mean superb image quality with a lot of capability.

by Rob Sheppard

For a while, the digital SLR was the ultimate imaging gear. The small, compact digital cameras had good features, but they still seemed like substitutes for the "real thing."

Compact cameras had limitations with viewfinders, restricted focal lengths, challenges with autofocus and slow responses to real-world photography.

Today, these small cameras are a distinct and important choice for any photographer. They can provide a great option for photographers who need a small, high-quality back-up camera, for photographers who need to travel light but don't want to sacrifice quality, and for photographers who just want to keep their gear simple, compact and lightweight. These cameras are well worth considering for many types of photography.

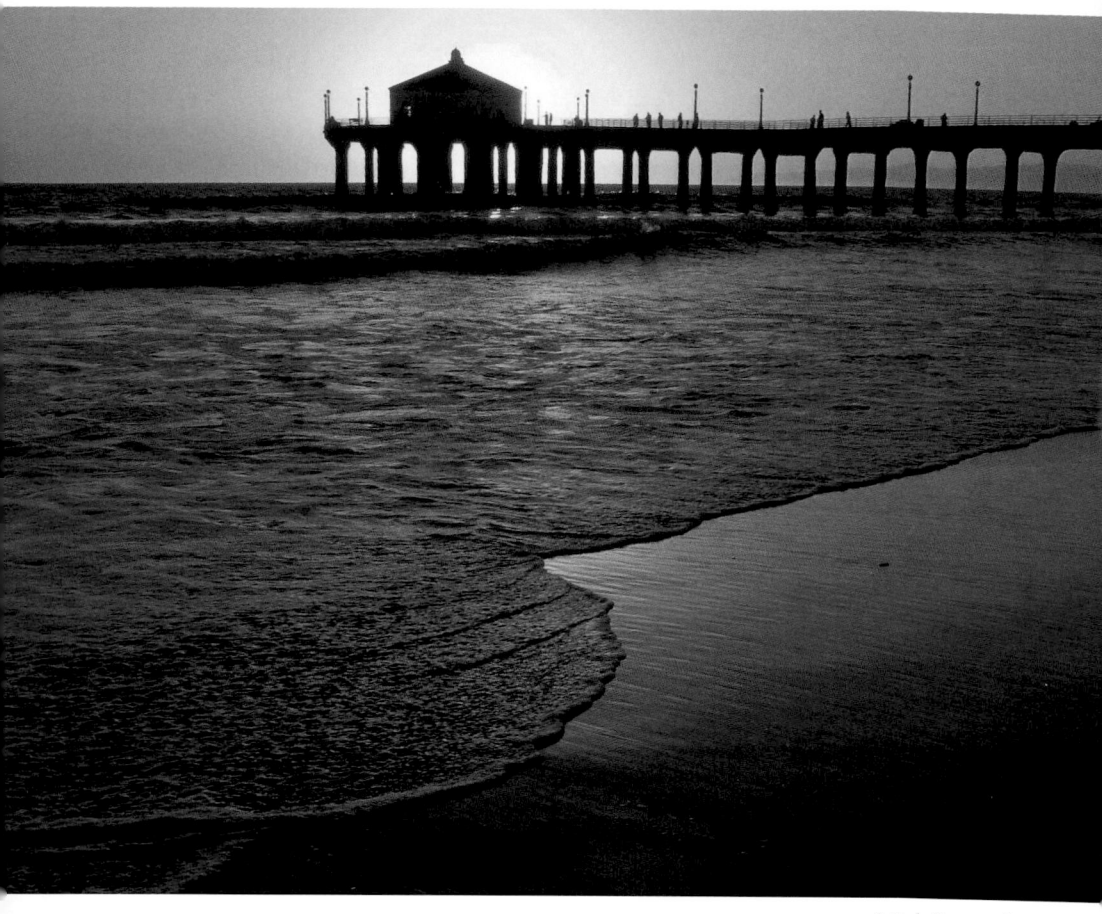

© Rob Sheppard

Point-and-Shoot is a Different Category

A lot of people call any camera that is not a digital SLR a "point-and-shoot." I want to be clear: I am not talking about point-and-shoots here. A true point-and-shoot is a camera that you literally point ... and shoot; and it can do nothing else.

Full-featured compacts have all of the controls of a digital SLR: full choice of exposure modes, both auto and manual; auto and manual focus; full control of ISO; and a complete choice of white balance.

About the only thing they don't have from a functional point of view is inter-changeable lenses. And price ... these cameras come at much lower prices than digital SLRs.

But even that has now changed with the introduction of compact cameras from Panasonic and Olympus that do offer interchangeable lenses!

Megapixels and Sensors

Megapixels are way overrated as a factor for comparing cameras. As one who's shot about every type of camera on the market today—and has made prints up to 16x20—I can tell you that nearly every digital camera now available has enough megapixels for most photographers' needs.

Anything over 8-10 megapixels will produce a decent, true-photographic quality print at 16x20 inches or smaller. So unless you need billboard-sized prints, you will be fine with the megapixels available.

That said, there is a real difference among sensors. The smallest cameras have sensors that are, predictably, physically very small. They are a fraction of the size of a sensor on any digital SLR. This means that the megapixels of a compact camera tend to be crammed into a smaller size, which can mean challenges in terms of noise, tonality and color. On some cameras, these issues are significant at larger print sizes. Yet many types of compact cameras have such state-of-the-art sensors and internal image-processing capabilities that image quality remains very high.

The largest sensors for this category of camera are found in the Micro Four Thirds cameras from Panasonic and Olympus. These sensors are identical to those found in the larger Four Thirds cameras; the micro only refers to the camera and lens size (the mount is different).

Size as a Choice

The physical size of a camera can make a big difference if you are traveling light. A compact unit may be the best option for photographers who are taking a camera along on a business trip and need to deal with airline weight restrictions. A compact camera will also help keep your gear sized down for other situations that require easy travel or even backpacking.

All of the full-featured compact digital cameras are significantly smaller—and more portable—than any digital SLR. Plus, the range of lens focal lengths in a compact camera makes them even more convenient for photographers on the move.

The big-zoom compact cameras often include focal lengths from wide-angle to extreme telephoto in a complete camera/lens package that is still smaller than a digital SLR. Even if you look at the smallest of these compact cameras, ones that fit a pocket, the camera/lens capability is usually smaller than the lens alone for the digital SLR!

Lenses and Focal Lengths

You do have *some* lens choices to make when looking at a compact digital camera. While most do not have interchangeable lenses, they do come with different ranges of focal lengths and maximum apertures.

Look for a range of focal length possibilities that will be satisfying to you. It can be frustrating to find your camera does not go wide enough or have enough telephoto power for the kinds of shots you want to take. Compare the equivalent 35mm focal lengths to get an idea of what the camera can do.

Watch out for such marketing ploys as "10X" zoom. Of course that means the lens zooms from its widest focal length to its most telephoto as a factor of ten. But what it does not say is what the specific wide or telephoto size is. If you need a strong wide-angle setting, you may discover that the 10X starts with a barely wide-angle focal length and goes to an extreme telephoto—not what you need. Always check what the real range is by looking at focal lengths, usually given in 35mm equivalents. (The actual focal length numbers will be meaningless to most photographers.)

The maximum aperture of the lens can be an important consideration as well. In order to keep lenses small for many compact cameras, manufacturers compromise on "slower" lenses—those that have reduced maximum apertures or f-stops. This is especially true for telephoto focal lengths that can be a maximum of f/5.6 or even slower. And it can be a problem if you want to do a lot of low-light, handheld photography. In this situation, the larger the maximum aperture, the better. Go with f/2.8 or, at most, f/4.

Another good thing to look for in a camera or lens is image stabilization. This is a technology that can reduce the problem of image blur due to camera movement during exposure. It is an especially important feature for big-zoom cameras, as image stabilization will dramatically increase any photographer's ability to get sharper photos with strong telephotos under a range of conditions.

If you really want the ultimate in lens possibilities, look into the Micro Four Thirds cameras from Panasonic and Olympus. These cameras have a selection of ultra compact lenses for the cameras, plus they can use any standard Four Thirds lens with an adapter.

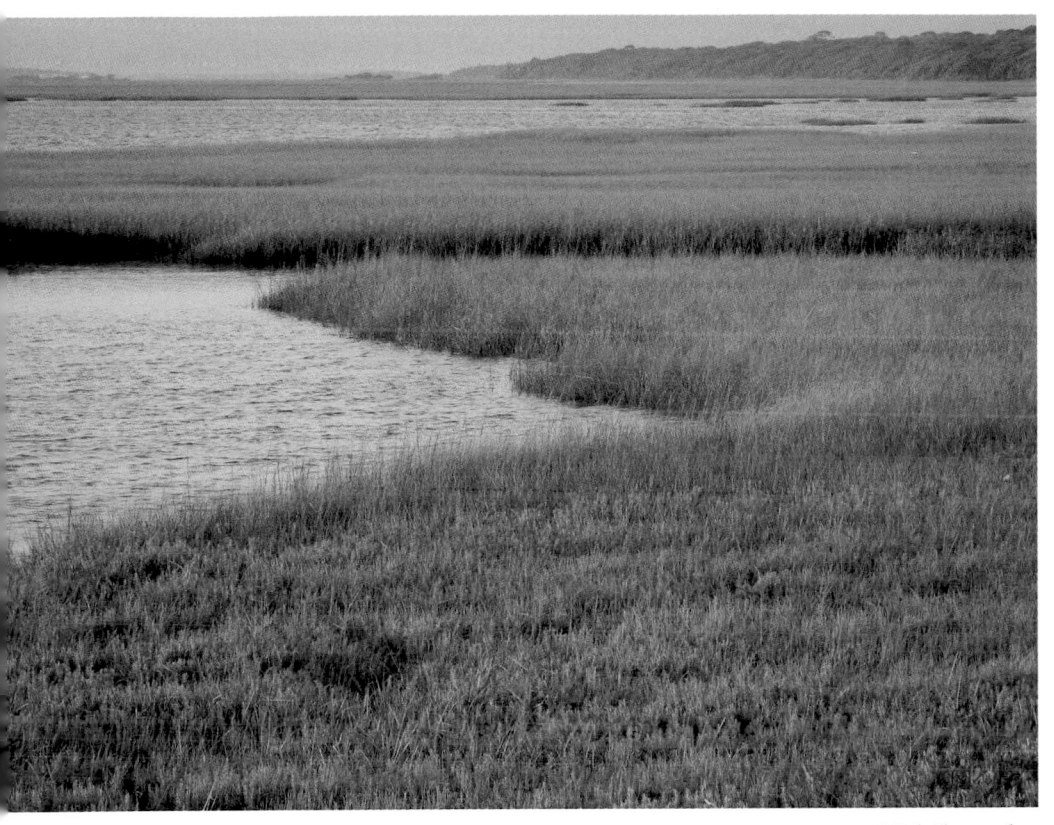

© Rob Sheppard

LCD Viewfinder

You will find a range of options for viewing your scene as you photograph. All of the cameras discussed here have a live LCD, so you can always use that. Many of them now have advanced, densely pixeled, 3-inch LCDs that give amazing visual displays. These can be well worth considering, as they do affect your experience when shooting.

Another LCD option is the tilting or swivel screen, compared to a fixed screen on the camera's back. A tilting or swivel LCD will make your camera more versatile and easier to use.

You can compare LCDs to a degree by comparing resolution. Higher resolution is usually better. However, simply looking at LCD resolution can be misleading, as there are other factors that affect LCD display. You really need to compare them at a store to see how you react personally to the display.

Many cameras in this category are now losing any other "viewfinder." It is an LCD or nothing. Luckily, the LCDs are much better now than even a year ago, but not all photographers want to be limited to only an LCD.

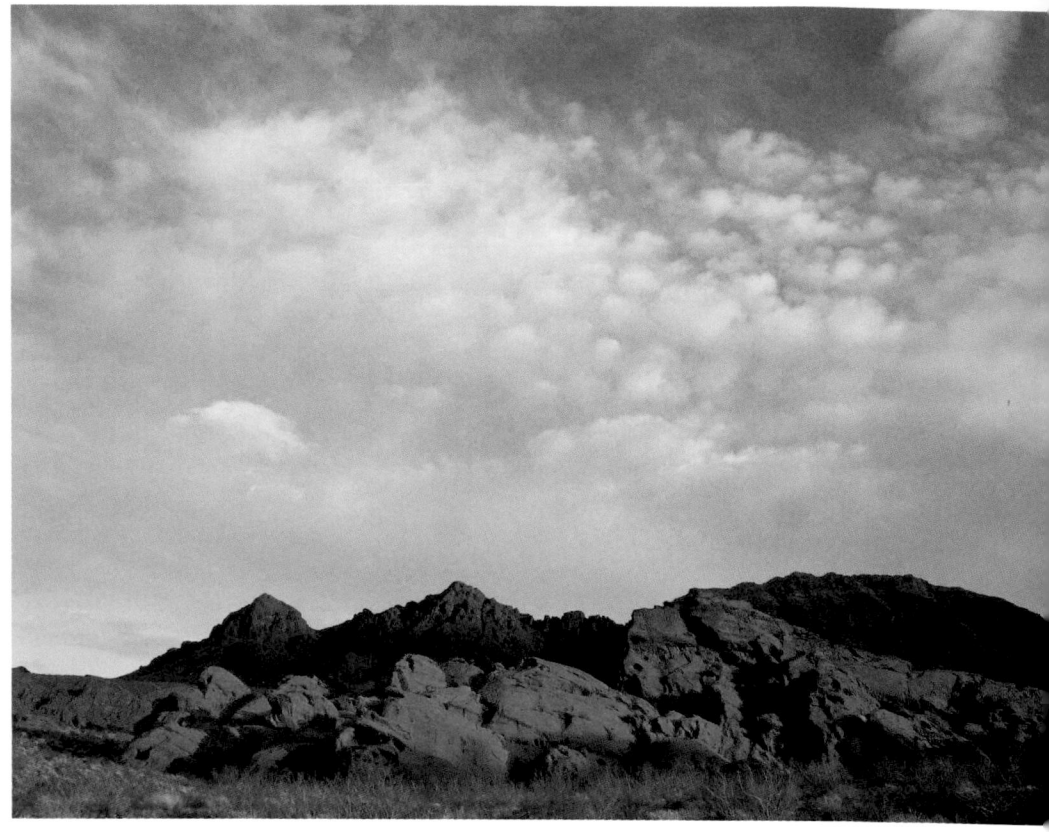

© Rob Sheppard

EVF Viewfinder

You will find an optical viewfinder on a few cameras. This is a view that is totally separate from the lens or sensor. Its advantage is that it is very bright, but it can cause framing problems with close shots. Plus everything looks in focus on a viewfinder, so you cannot tell what is sharp and what is not in the actual photo.

A common type of viewfinder for the larger zoom cameras is the EVF, or *electronic viewfinder*. This will give the camera a digital SLR-ish shape, but does not make it a digital SLR. An SLR is a single-lens reflex, which refers to a viewfinder system in which the single lens of the camera is bounced off a mirror, through a pentaprism (or penta-mirror system) at the top of the camera. Once this happens, light is "reflexed" or bent through the optical system.

An EVF viewfinder takes the signal from the sensor and displays it on a high-quality, tiny LCD that you see through the viewfinder eyepiece. This requires an extremely high resolution LCD for optimum quality.

An advantage is that you see exposure and white balance; a disadvantage is that EVF viewfinders rarely look as good as an optical true-SLR finder. You will see quite a difference among cameras in this area, so it is worth taking a look through any camera you are considering for purchase—before you buy.

Other Factors to Consider

Manufacturers put a lot of work into their cameras to make them either better for your use or more attractive to look at and handle. And I don't think it is vain for a photographer to want a camera that they enjoy holding and looking at! A camera you enjoy this way will be used more often than a camera you dislike, no matter what its features are.

If you want to use filters—a polarizing filter can be useful for a lot of outdoor photography—you need to be sure your camera includes the capability of adding a filter in front of the lens. If you want to use a larger flash than the built-in unit (because all built-in flashes have unimpressive power), to do something like bounce flash, be sure your camera choice allows you to add an external flash. Some do; many don't.

You will see a lot about very high ISO settings with these cameras. Frankly, images from a compact camera look best at ISO settings of 400 and below. High ISO settings often result in highly processed images that don't have the fine-detail that the cameras are capable of when shot at lower ISOs.

The compact camera used to be a slow machine—sometimes excruciatingly slow from push of the shutter button until the shutter actually fired. That is no longer a big problem. These cameras won't match a pro digital SLR for speed, but they will typically be as good as lower-priced digital SLRs.

In closing, we need to realize that digital compact camera technology is moving fast—very fast. No doubt, newer compact cameras will offer less noise at higher ISO settings than the compact cameras of today. And digital zooms will increase in quality. Maybe all cameras will shoot HD video. And some cameras may accept accessory lenses.

But don't wait for anticipated advancements. Get the best camera you can afford today and start the compact camera fun!

Website:
www.robsheppardphoto.com

Blogs:
www.photodigitary.com
www.seeingcreation.com

Handing Over Your Camera

No matter how basic or sophisticated your camera, here are some quick tips from Rick on how to advise the "photographer."

No matter how basic or sophisticated your camera, here are some things to tell the "photographer."

1) Don't cut off the top of my head or my toes.

2) Watch the background. Make sure there is not a tree growing out of my head and that a person I don't want in the photo is not walking behind me.

3) Don't put my head dead center in the frame.

4) Tell me when you are going to take the picture. Count to three.

5) Please take three shots.

And don't forget to say "thank you."

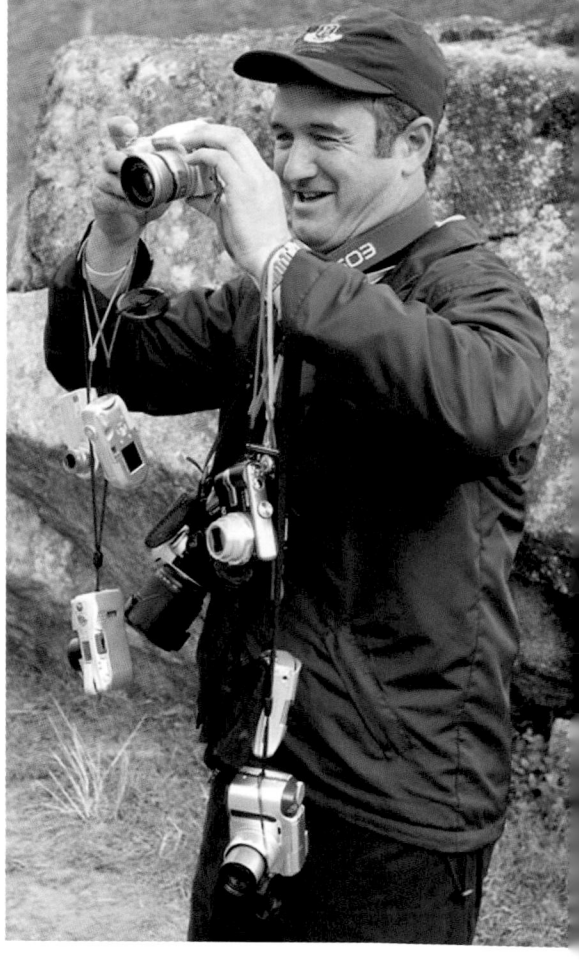

© Rick Sammon

Here are some guidelines for you to follow:

1) Set your camera on Program or Green (full auto) mode before handing it over.

2) Turn the flash on if you think there is a possibility of shadows on your face.

3) Make sure the auto focus is set.

4) Take a test shot (maybe of the person who will be taking the picture) to illustrate the kind of picture you want.

5) Make sure the shutter speed is fast enough to prevent a blurry picture caused by camera shake.

Nice … there you are!

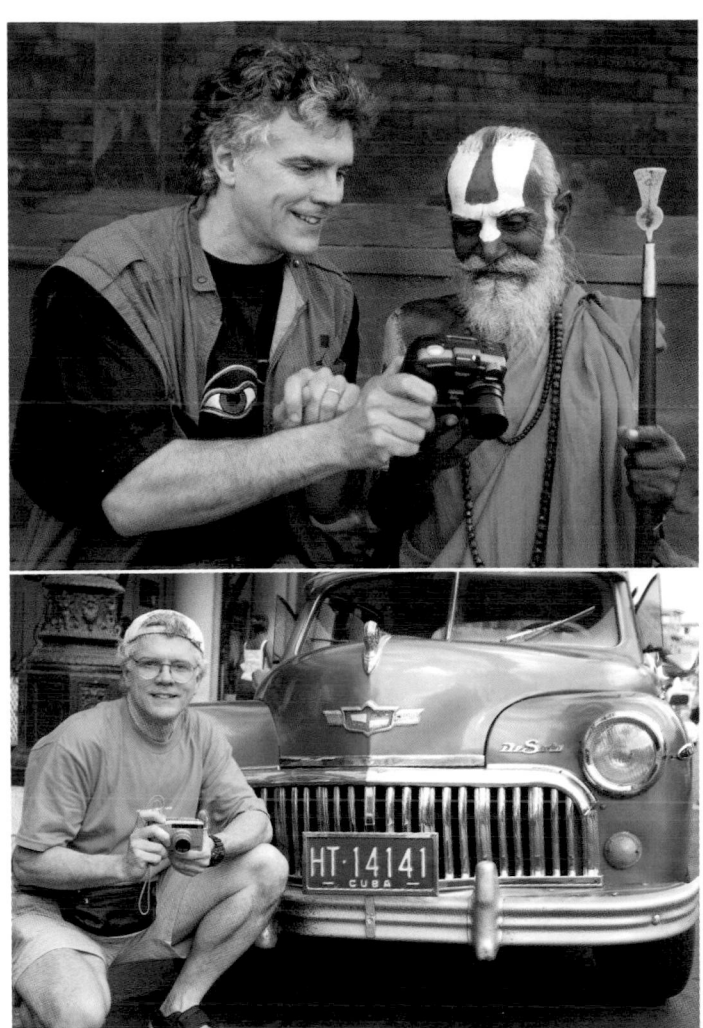

Preface

Compact Camera Photo Gallery: Believe It or Not

Believe it or not, I have been photographing with digital compact cameras for about ten years. Among numerous trips around the world, I took a compact camera to the Royal Kingdom of Nepal in 1997, India in 1999 and Cuba in 2001. I thought it would be fun to select my favorite compact camera photos from those trips; they are pictured in this chapter.

Believe It: Inspirations for a Compact Shooter

This is not a how-to chapter. Rather, it's a gallery-type chapter that's designed to inspire you take great pictures with you compact camera.

I also wanted to show you that I actually have been shooting with compact cameras for some time—in addition, of course, to shooting with my pro SLRs. Some of these pictures have never been published … and may never have been if not for this book.

So you might be asking, "Why did Rick take pictures with his compact digital camera when he had his pro SLR with him?" Well, on my trips to Nepal and India, my pro camera was a film camera. I was just getting into digital photography at that time, and I wanted to compare the results from both cameras.

India

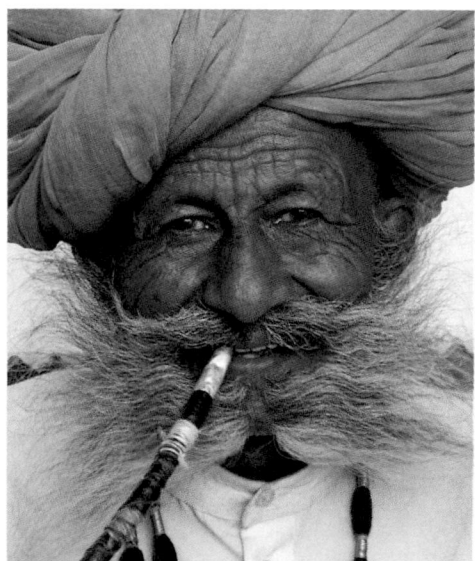 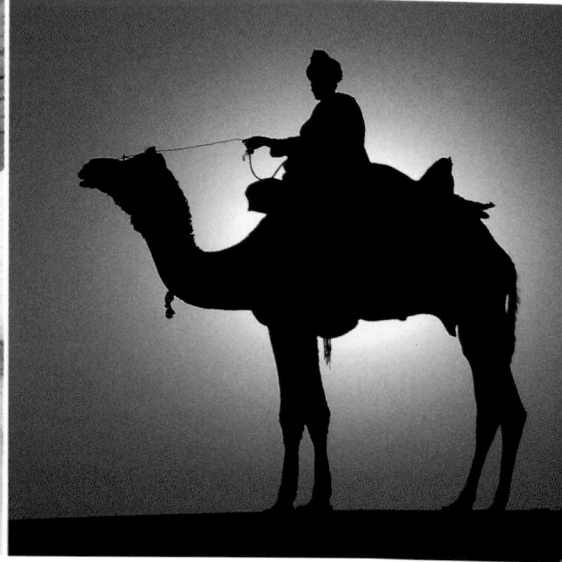

Holy Man and Camel at Sunset

Royal Kingdom of Nepal

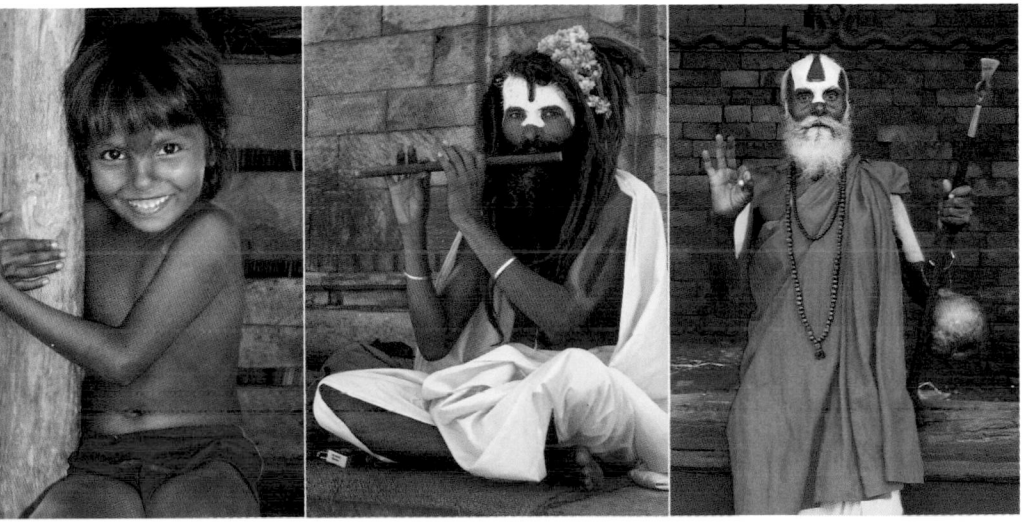

Youngster and Two Holy Men

India

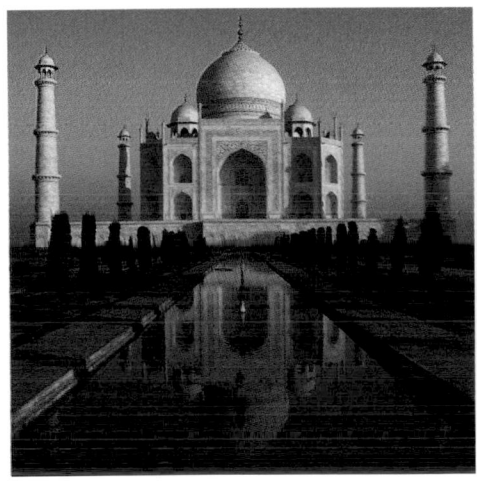 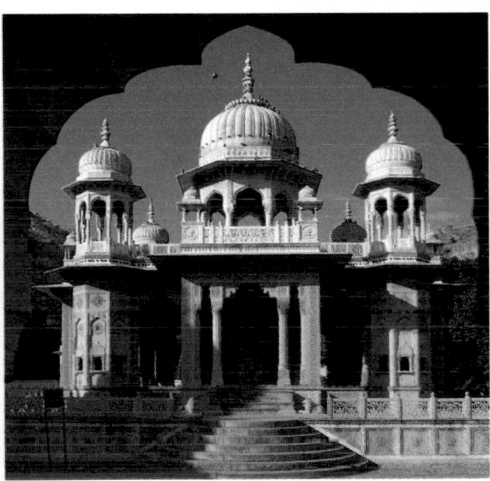

Taj Mahal and Palace

Royal Kingdom of Nepal

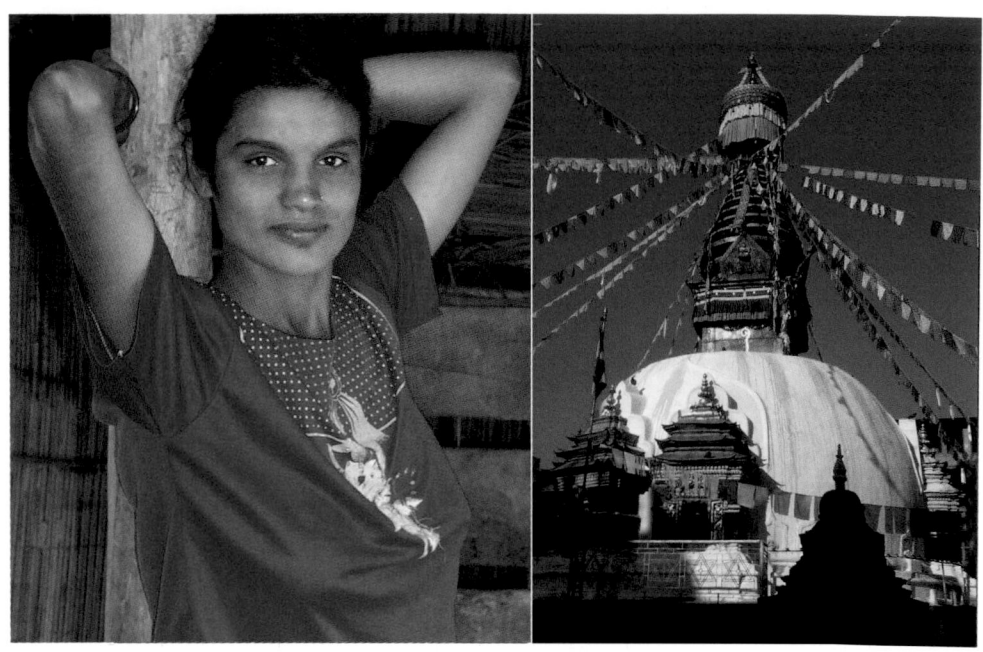

Young Woman and Stupa

Cuba

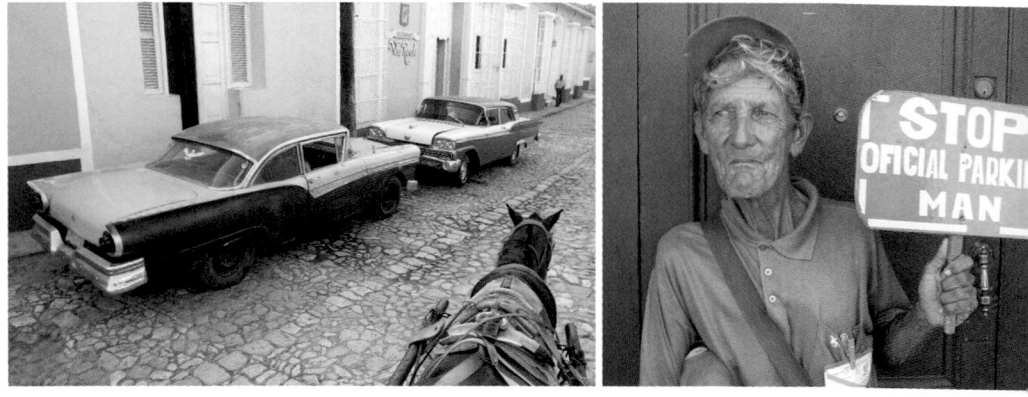

Trinidad City Scene and Official Parking Man in Old Havana

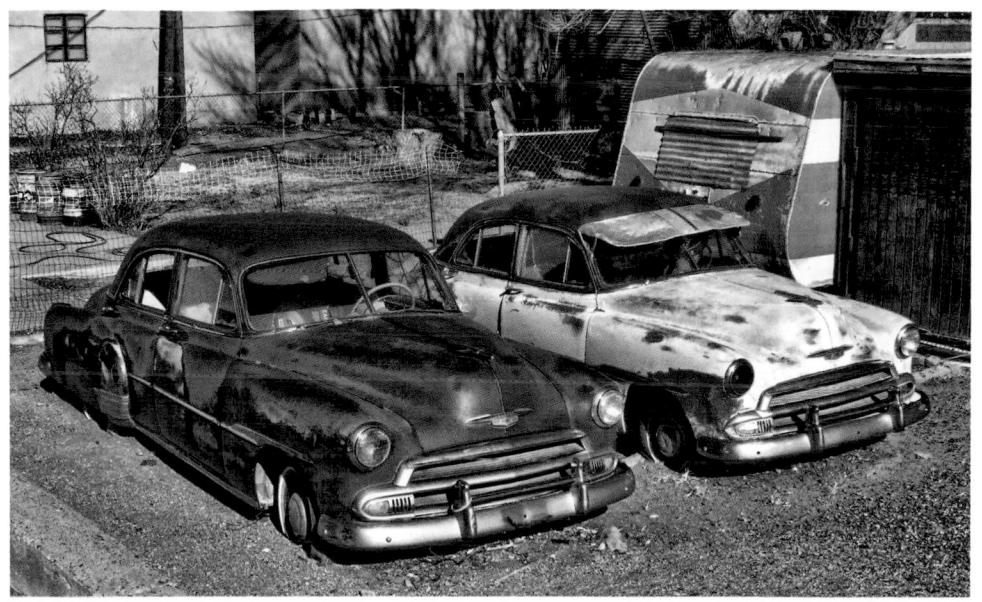

Introduction

Confessions of a Compact Camera Shooter

I took a trip to Bosque Del Apache, New Mexico. With my new Canon G10 compact camera in hand, I took a few pictures. And then I saw the results. That's all it took to convince me to write this book.

My intent is to help photo enthusiasts who shoot with compact cameras to take better pictures.

Sure, I take 90 percent of my "serious" pictures with my professional SLR cameras. After all, I am a professional photographer. But I must confess: I truly enjoy shooting with my compact camera. Not only is it fun and easy, but the results are pretty darn good! In fact, I never leave home without one.

So this chapter is my confession—one that I am happy to share with you.

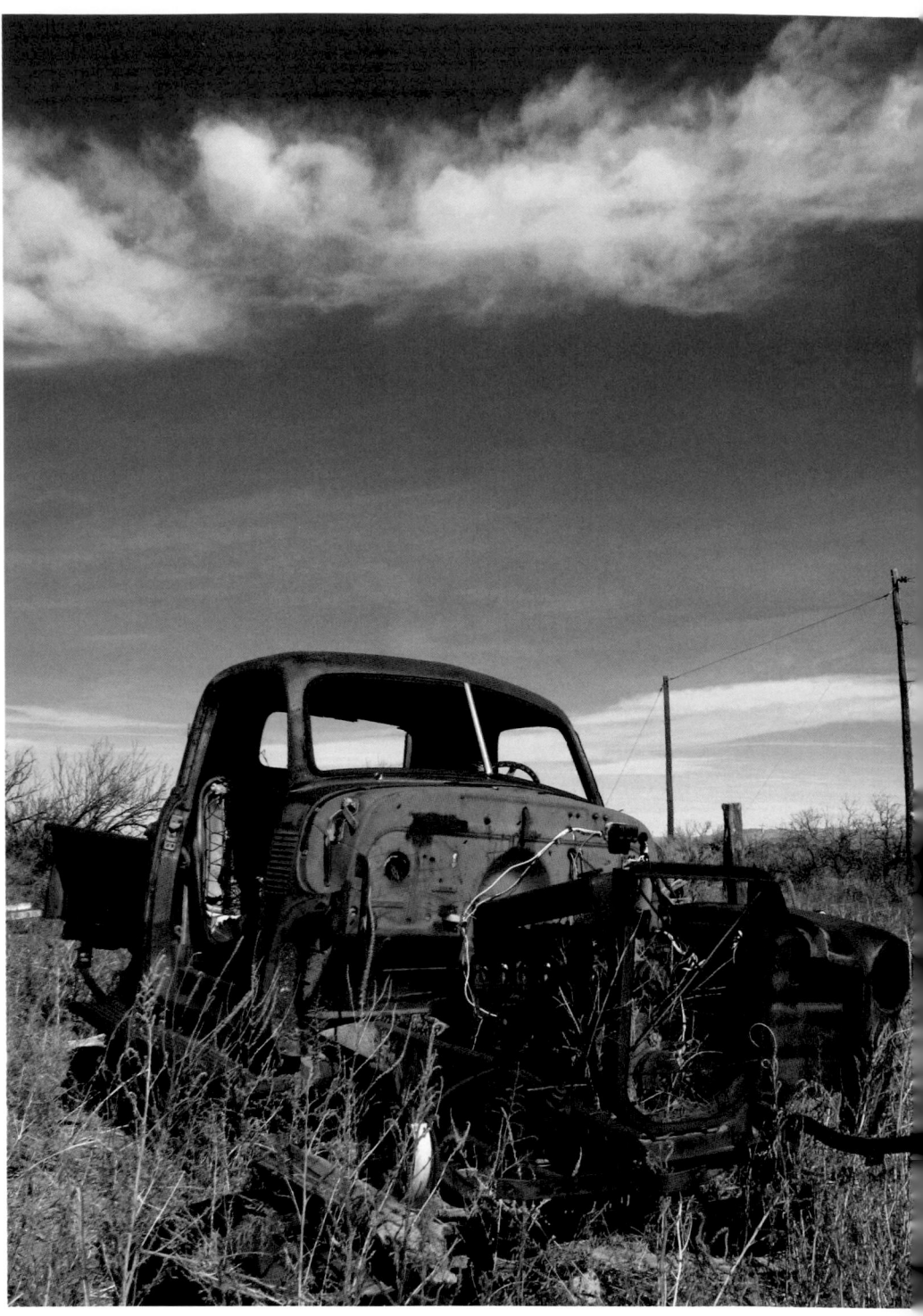

Confession

Guilty as charged. It's true. I need to make a confession: I took nearly all the pictures in this book with my Canon G10 compact camera.

I use the word *confession* sort of in jest because I am known for shooting with top-of-the-line digital SLR cameras. And with good reason; they produce knockout images in all lighting conditions—indoors and out—plus they accept more than fifty lenses and dozens of accessories that expand the camera's capabilities.

So, like some pros I know, I'd have to plead, tongue in cheek, "the Fifth" when asked about shooting with a less-than-the-best camera.

The pictures in this Introduction were shot in Socorro, New Mexico, and nearby Bosque del Apache, where I was co-leading a photography workshop with famed wildlife photographer Greg Downing for Naturescapes (www.naturescapes.net).

Why did I use a compact camera for taking important images in these totally cool locations—places to which I'd never been? Well, first, I wanted to see if I could, indeed, get good shots with the type of camera that many amateurs, including soccer moms, use. What's more, for once in my life, I wanted to just walk around and totally enjoy the experience without lugging around my forty-pound SLR backpack. Although I did have it nearby… in the trunk of my car … at all times.

So friends, here are some compact camera images along with some important info about compact cameras. I promise to tell the whole truth and nothing but the truth.

Please note that not all the camera features mentioned in this book are available on every compact camera. Check your manual to find out which ones are available on yours.

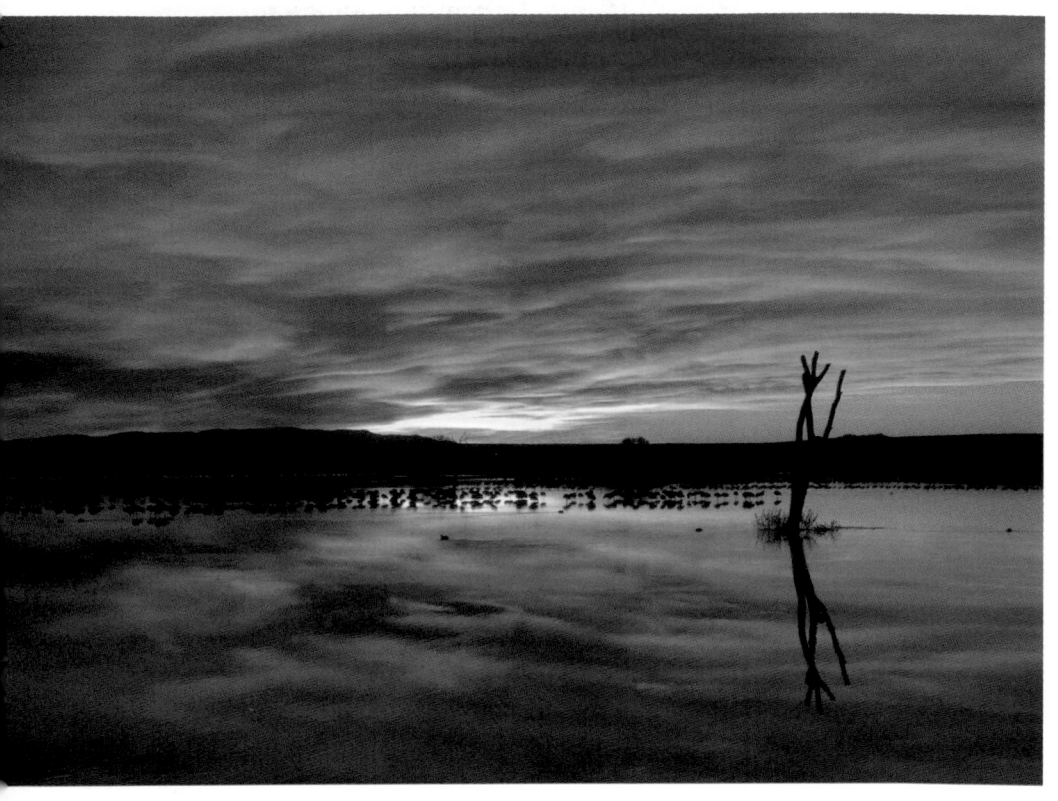

Keep It Clean

I love this shot. It's clean. By that, I mean it has very little digital noise (also referred to as *grain*). (See page 91 for a more descriptive explanation on noise.)

I took this photograph with my compact camera on the first day of the trip in Bosque del Apache. I set my camera on a tripod and set the ISO to 100, the exposure mode to Av (Aperture Priority), activated the self-timer and took the shot.

At low ISO settings, compact cameras deliver relatively low-noise images—as long as the light level is not *too* low. Noise increases in low light and at high ISO settings. And this is where digital SLRs really shine; they minimize noise in low light and at high ISO settings. But clearly, you can get nice low-light photographs with a compact unit, too. Don't worry! After all, a picture with some noise is better than not picture at all.

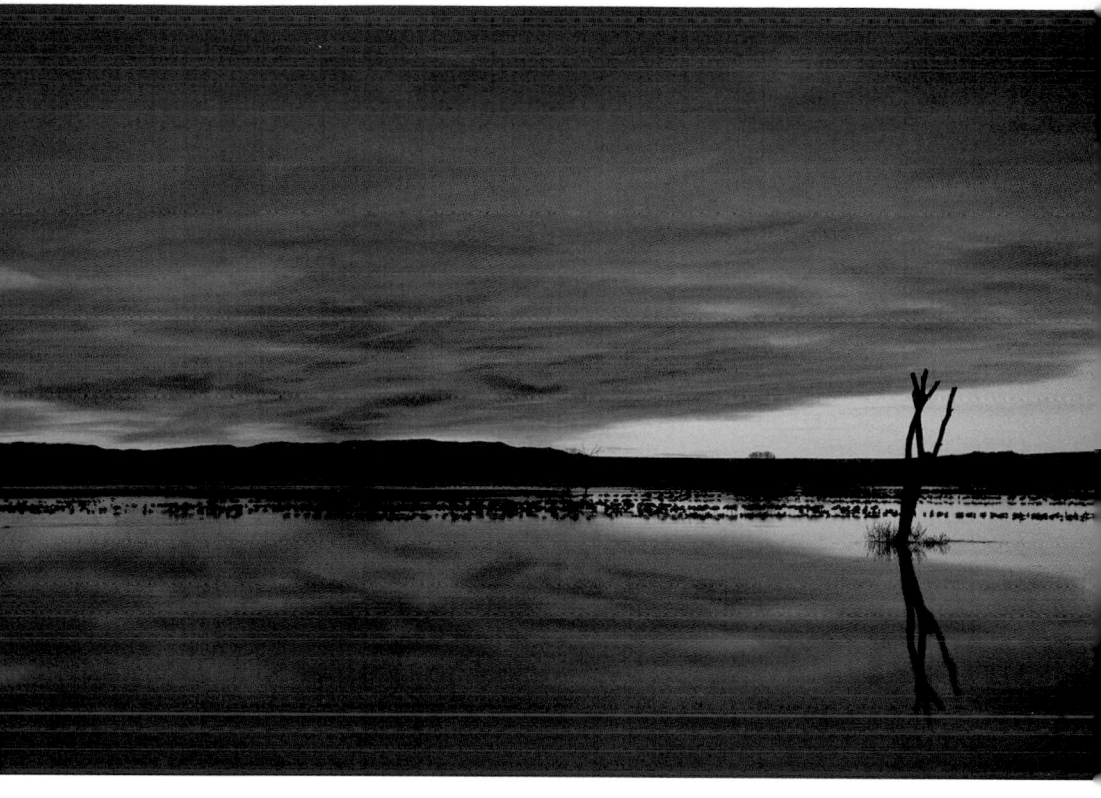

See the Difference?

I took this shot with my compact camera, too. Check out the detail and color before you read on. Take your time. Nice shot, don't you think?

Okay, I'm kidding. I actually took this shot, earlier that morning, with my Canon 1Ds Mark II (a dSLR) and 24-105mm lens, using the same settings that I used on my compact camera.

It's one of my favorite images from the shoot. It's a beautifully clean image, and I challenge anyone to see, at least on the pages of this book, any difference in image quality between this and the previous image. Challenge applies for an 8x10-inch print of each image, too.

Compact cameras can offer professional results in the hands of a thoughtful photographer.

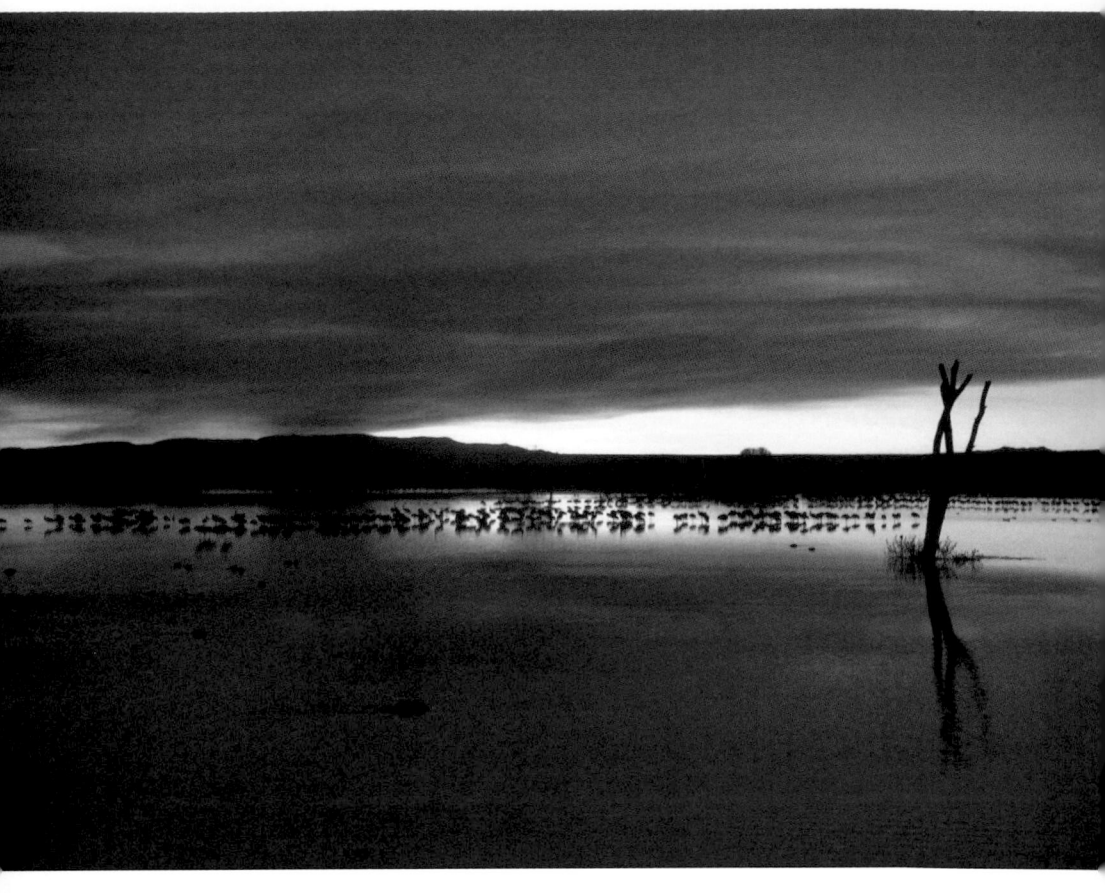

Noise

I shot this with my compact camera, mainly as a test, early in the morning of my first day in Bosque del Apache. It was a hand-held shot. I had my ISO set to 800, mainly to test the noise. That is, to see how grainy the photograph would be. You'll notice the noise in the image, but it was expected.

So one of the key differences between the two types of cameras is noise: Digital SLRs produce low-noise images at high ISO settings, while compact cameras produce noisy images at high ISO settings. However, compact cameras are getting better and better when it comes to noise, so newer models will have less noise than older models, generally speaking.

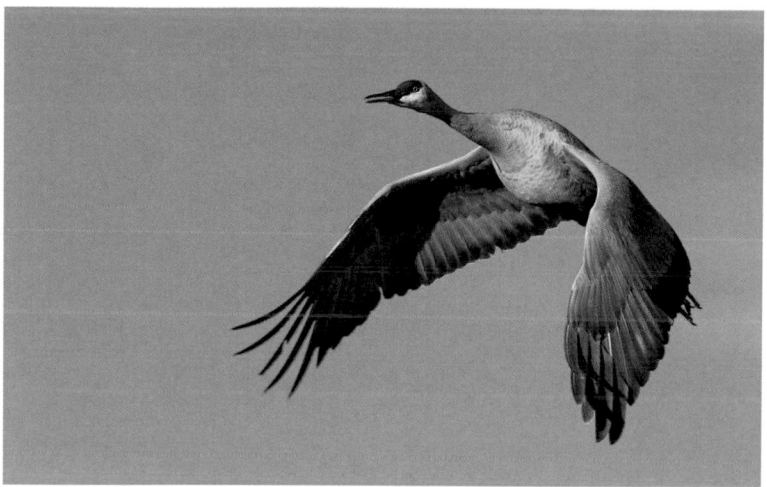

Lens Appeal

Another key difference between a compact camera and a digital SLR, and the reason I will not divorce my digital SLRs, is that I can use dozens of lenses on my digital SLRs, while my compact camera only has a built-in zoom. For this photograph, I used a Canon 400mm IS DO lens on my Canon 1D Mark III SLR.

Unlike my compact camera, my digital SLR has:

- Quick focusing capability
- No shutter lag (although the lag's not bad in the G10)
- More focusing points (and therefore greater focus accuracy in more situations)
- A higher frame rate
- A much larger image sensor for higher quality images and enlargements
- On-sensor noise-reduction feature

Perhaps what I miss most in a compact camera are very wide lens settings: 14mm, 15mm and 17mm. I especially like those focal lengths for landscapes and when shooting in close quarters indoors. And of course I miss the telephoto zooms. But you know what, when I can, I do what we did before we had zoom lenses: I zoom with my feet!

In the compact camera's defense, these more-portable units have many of the exposure modes (Av, Tv, P, M) that my digital SLR offers. They have exposure compensation, offer a histogram, and even feature an overexposure warning. What's more, most compacts shoot movies—not high-def like my Canon 5D Mark II, but movies good enough for fun and for posting on YouTube.

Speaking of YouTube, one of my Bosque del Apache movies is posted on YouTube. Check it out by typing Rick Sammon in the Search window.

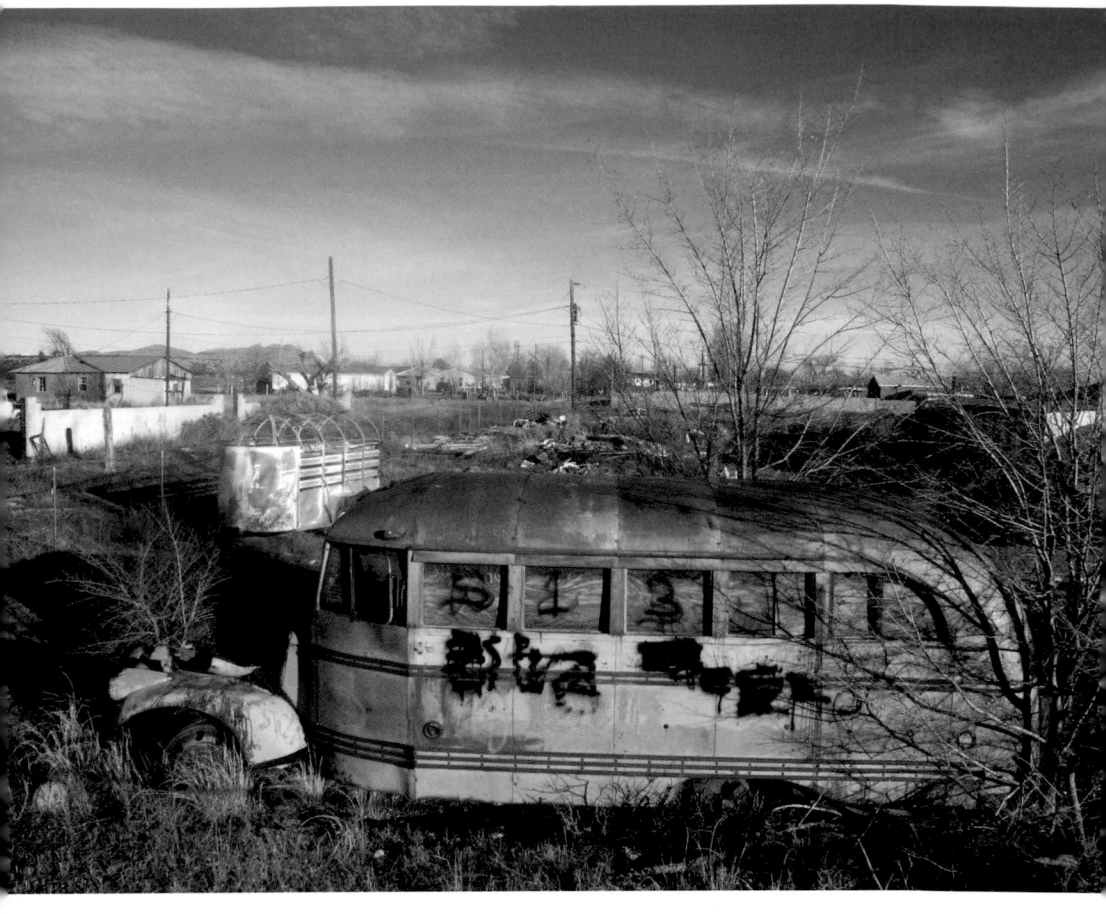

Check It Out

Here is another compact camera shot, taken in bright light. Again, my ISO was set to 100. Check out the color and detail … and sharpness … and lack of noise. I took this picture so I could compare it to the following one.

By the way, you need to know that the ISO setting basically determines the camera sensor's sensitivity to light. As the ISO increases, so does the sensor's sensitivity. Photographers typically use high ISOs in low light because it helps the camera process the limited amount of light to show the scene.

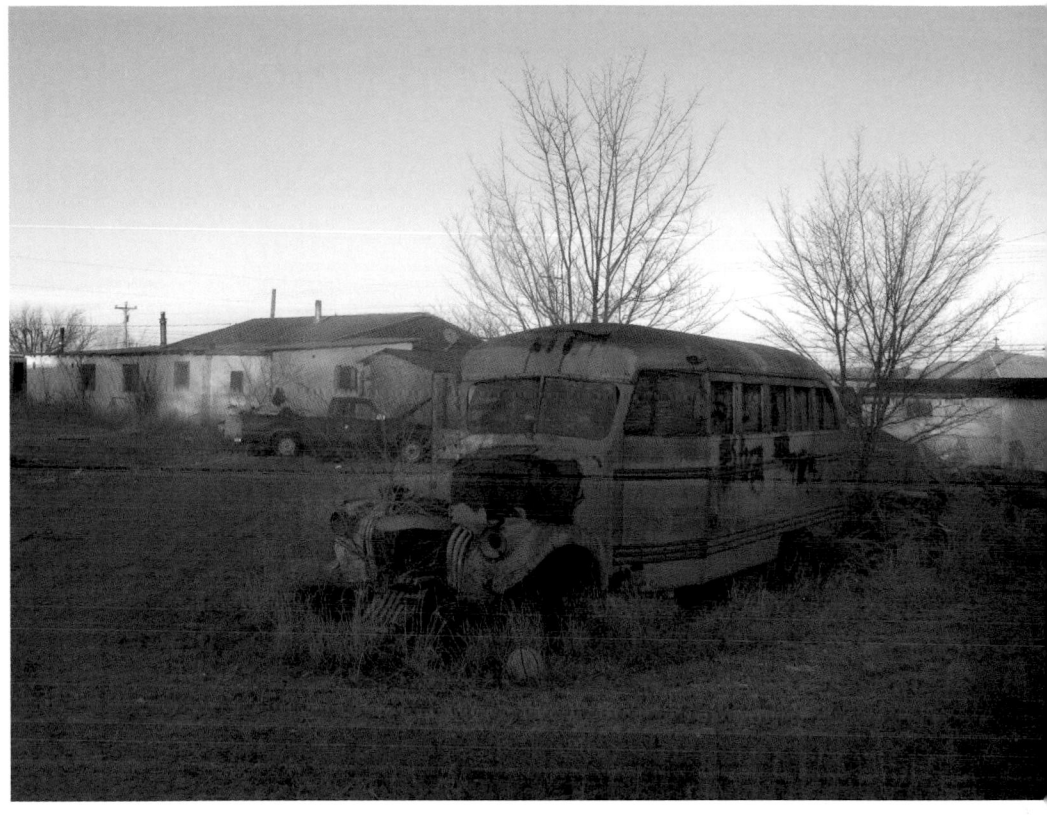

Uh Oh ...

Here is a second shot of the bus taken shortly before sunset. This time the bus was in the shade. To get the depth-of-field and shutter speed I needed, I had to set my ISO to 400. You may not be able to see the grain in the image here, but it's there in the shadow areas. Also, the picture looks a bit flat. Read on.

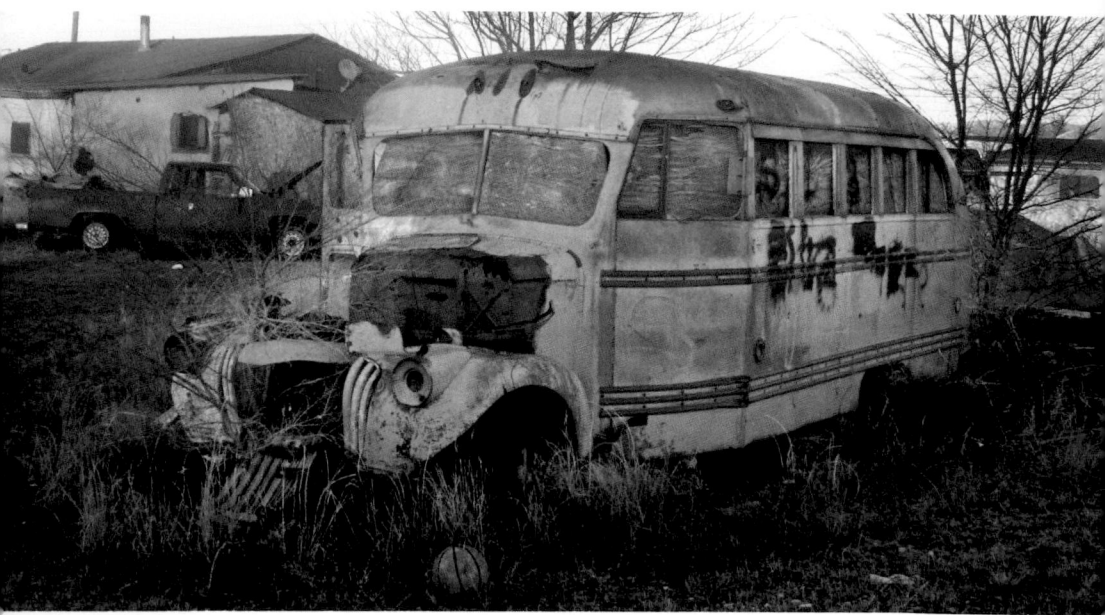

The Rescue

No problem. Photoshop Elements to the rescue! With a few basic adjustments in Adobe Camera RAW, combined with a bit of cropping, I was able to transform a lackluster shot into an image with vibrant colors. Voila!

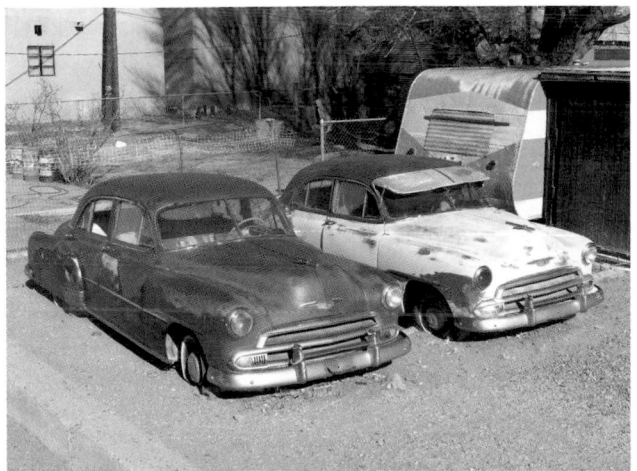

Plug In for Fun

Speaking of Photoshop Elements, rest assured that it's covered more toward the end of this book. For now though, here are two more examples, created with a plug-in called Topaz Adjust from Topaz Labs (www.topazlabs.com).

The top image is my original G10 shot.

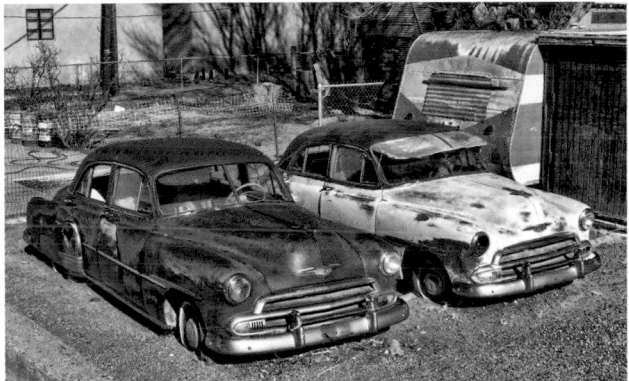

I applied Topaz's Spicify effect to boost the contrast and create the middle image.

I applied Topaz's Psychedelic effect to create the bottom image.

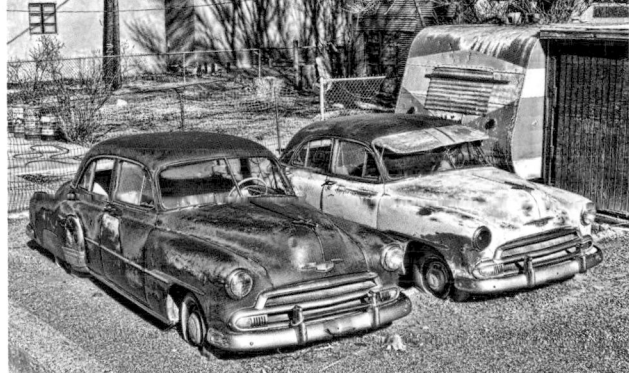

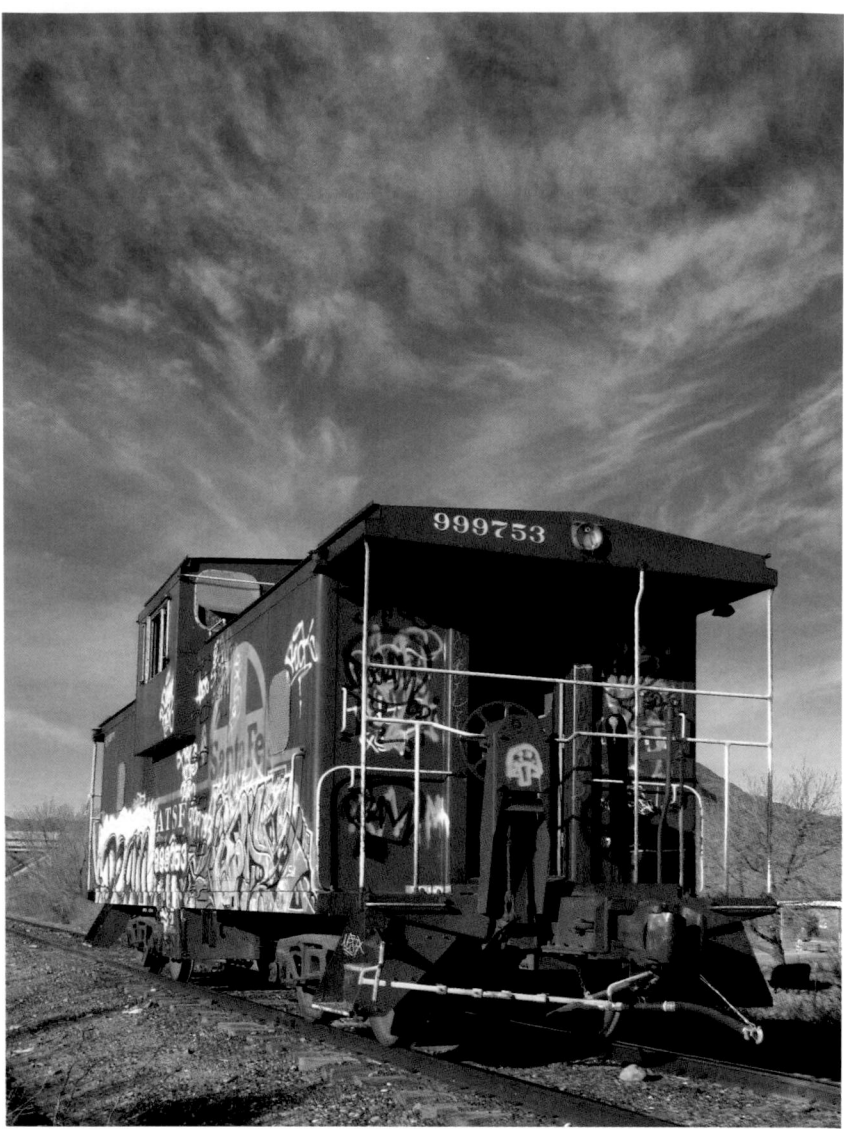

Save As ... What?

Okay, now it's time for another confession. All the compact camera images you see here were created from .... (drumroll please) ... JPEG images. That's right! Rick "RAW Rules" Sammon shot JPEGs for the first time in nine years—again to test the compact camera's capabilities.

And guess what? A few tweaks in Photoshop Elements yielded some very nice images, including this photograph of a caboose.

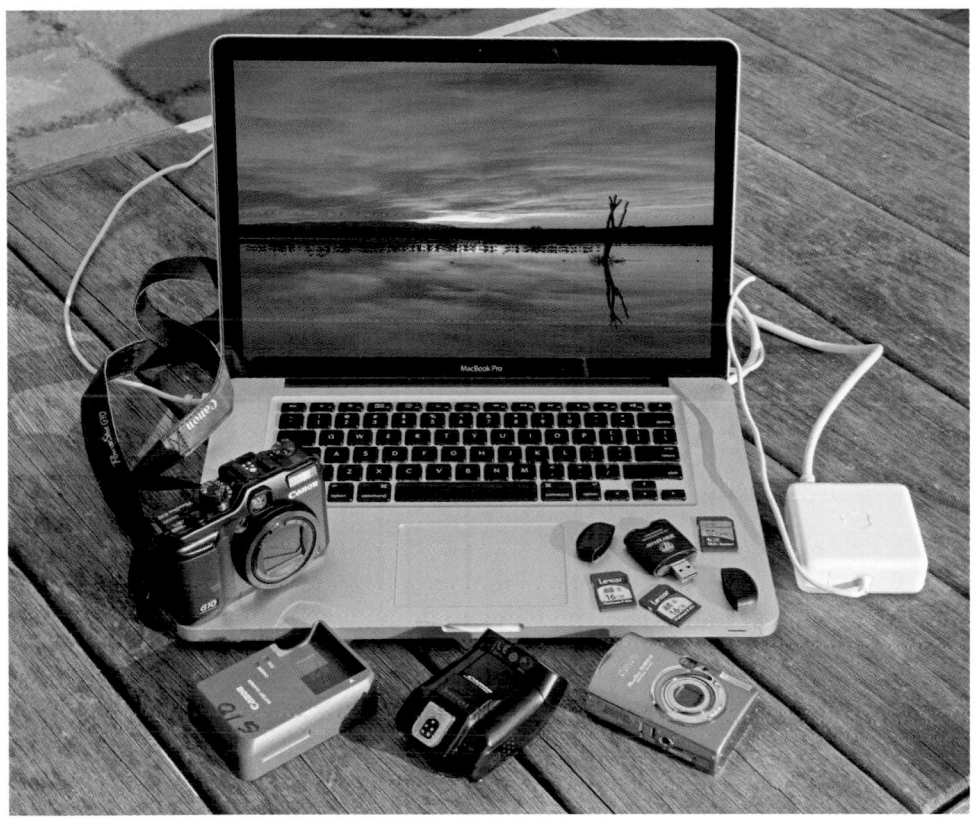

Compact Shooter's Gear Bag

Here's a look at my on-location compact camera gear. You may not need all this stuff, but I thought you'd like to see what a serious compact camera shooter takes on the road.

- Compact camera, Canon G10
- Accessory flash for added power and creativity
- IR-converted compact camera, Canon SD800 IS
- Memory cards
- Card reader
- Battery charger
- Laptop loaded with Photoshop Elements

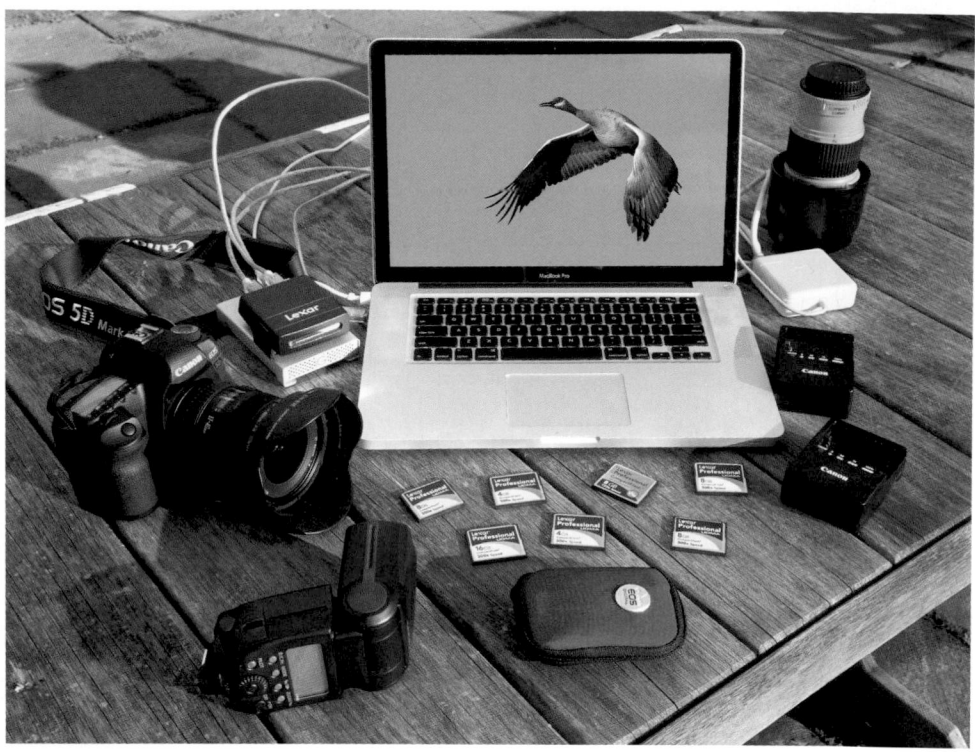

A Heavier Load

Compact cameras are the perfect choice for many photographers. However, after shooting for a while with a compact camera, some photographers want to move up to an SLR system to expand their creative horizons.

Here's a look at some of my digital photography travel gear. You may not need all this stuff, but the collection gives you an idea of the gear commitment that is usually made by serious on-location digital photographers.

- Laptop loaded with image-editing program
- Digital SLR, lenses and flash
- Battery chargers
- Memory cards
- Memory card reader
- Portable hard drive

Not shown (only prime gear in this photo): another camera body, other lenses, flash diffuser, polarizing filter, batteries for flash, extra camera batteries, surge-suppressor power strip, tripod and camera bag. Strong back on you, right?

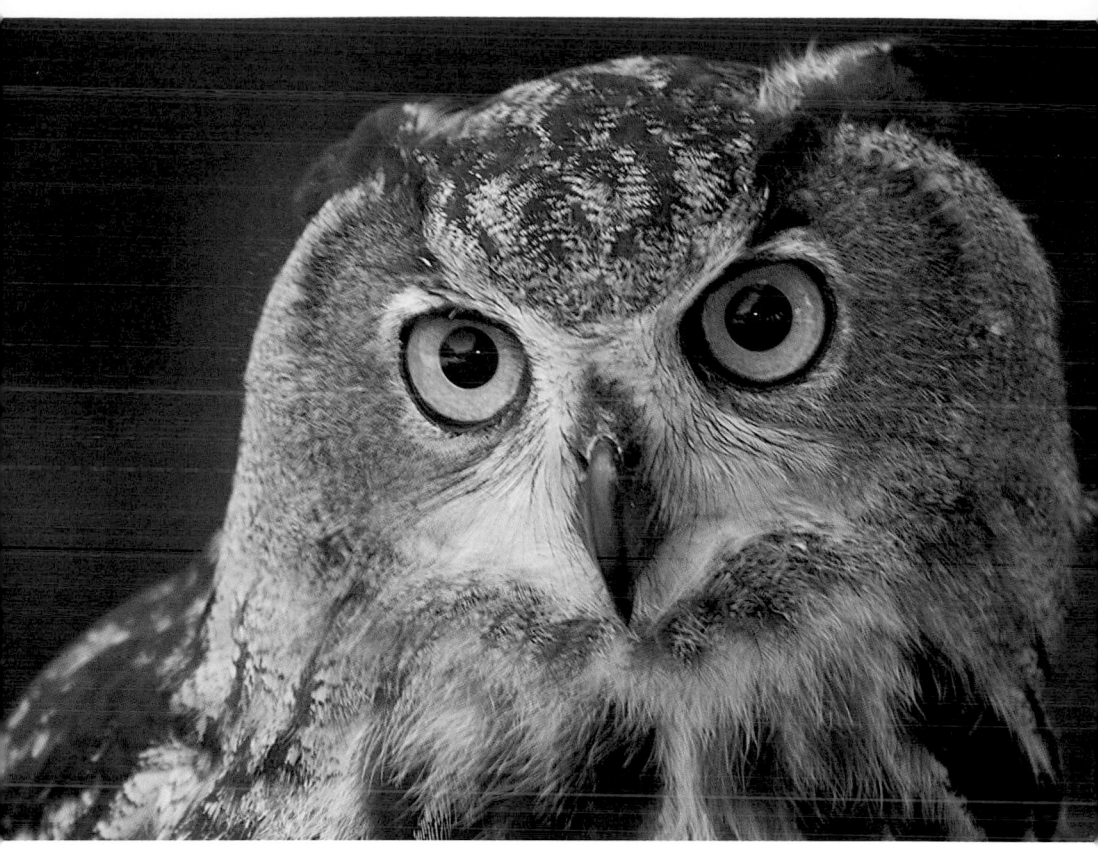

Part I

Compact Camera, Pro Results

I thought I'd start off this book will some pictures that illustrate the whole point of it. And that is: compact cameras can take pictures that rival those taken with digital SLR cameras.

So let's play a guessing game. Can you tell which pictures were taken with a compact camera and which ones were taken with a pro digital SLR camera?

You'll find the answers on the last page of this chapter, the page with the palm tree. No skipping ahead!!

People Pictures

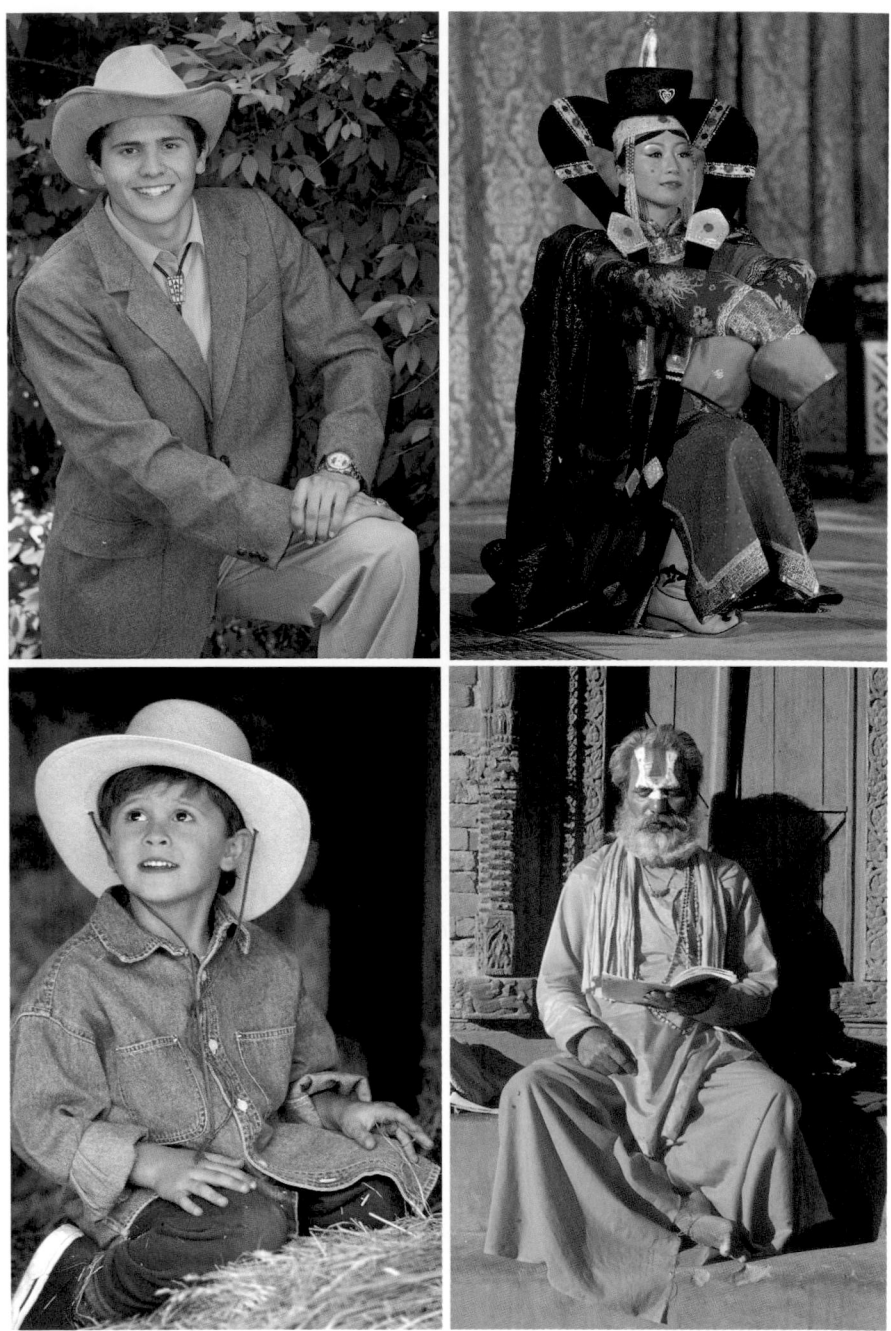

Clockwise from top left: Marco Sammon, Croton-on-Hudson, New York; performer, Mongolia; holy man, Nepal; and Marco as a child, Upstate New York.

Animals

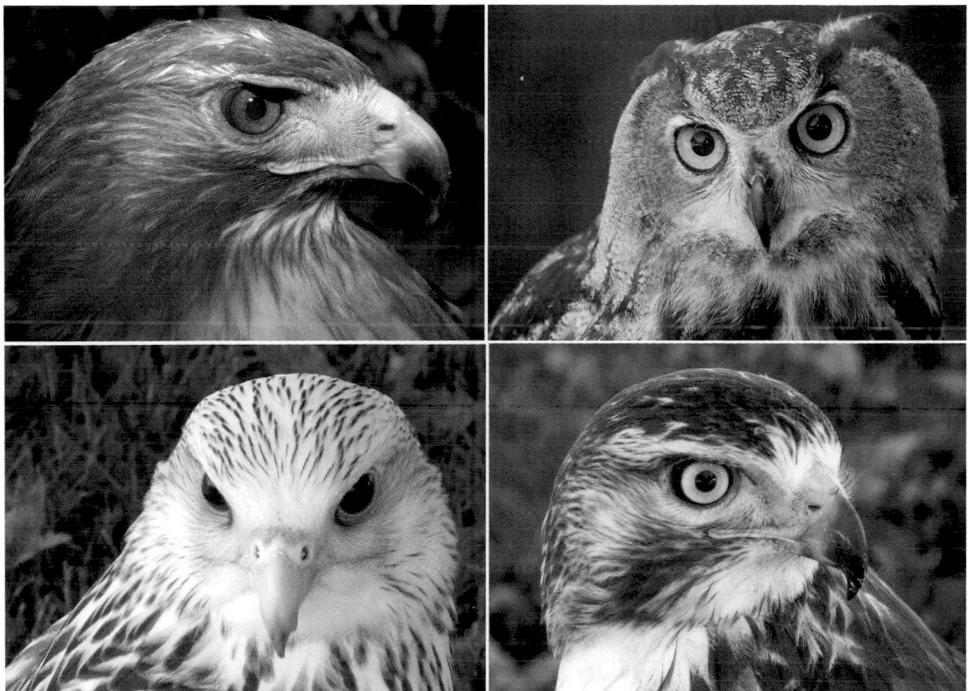

Hello compact camera friends! Here are a few people shots and a few shots of some fine feathered "friends." The guessing game continues. Guess which pictures were taken with my pro SLR and which ones were taken with my trusty compact camera.

While you're trying to figure this out, consider these tips on photographing people:

- Set your white balance to the existing lighting conditions to ensure good skin tones. (Find out more on white balance settings in Part VII.)
- Focus on the eyes.
- Your subject does not always have to be looking at the camera.
- The background can make or break a shot.

And here are some tips on photographing birds:

- Get the eyes in focus.
- Use the telephoto setting on your zoom lens to blur the background.
- See and shoot eye-to-eye.
- Take a lot pictures, as birds move their heads quickly, possibly causing you to miss more shots than you get.

Landscapes and City Scenes

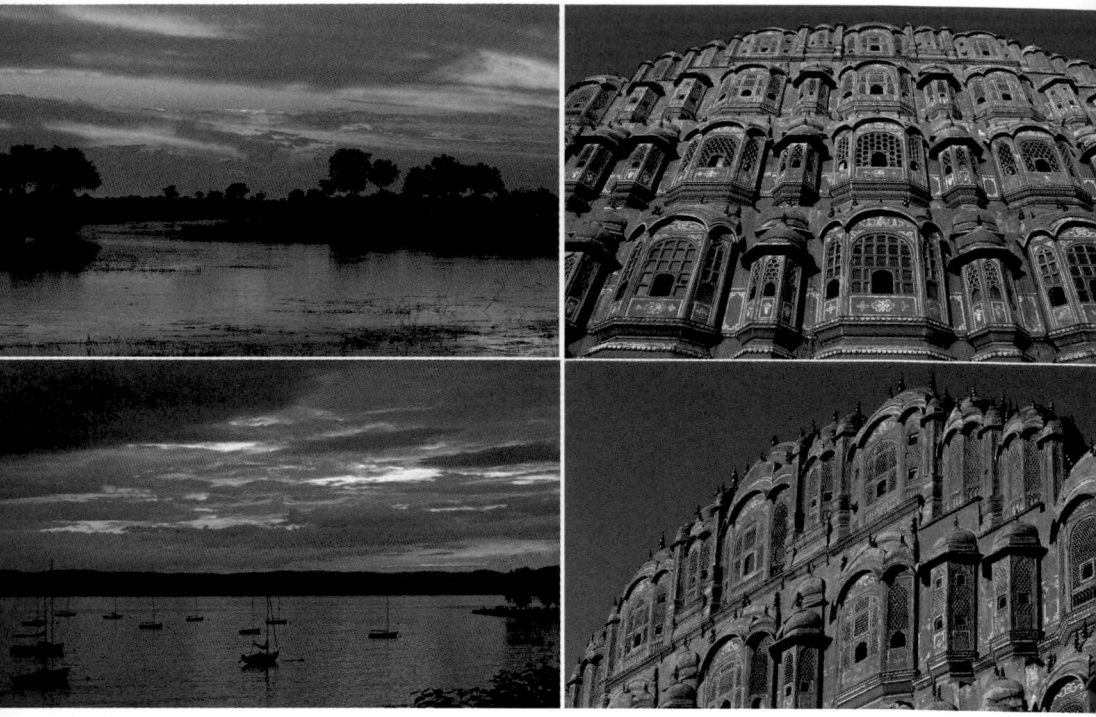

Clockwise from top left: Botswana; Palace of the Winds, India;
Palace of the Winds, India; and Croton-on-Hudson, New York.

Keep on guessin'.

I like these photographs, because they bring back fond memories—some close to home and some in a far-away location.

Speaking of memories, here's a tip to save your digital memories: Always back up your pictures in at least two places. I prefer hard drives because the write time is much faster than the write time of CDs and DVDs. I also keep one backup in my office and one in my house, just in case of fire, etc.

Again, the answers to the guessing game are on the last page of this chapter. In reading the answers, keep this expression in mind: Cameras don't take pictures, people do!

Snow and Nature

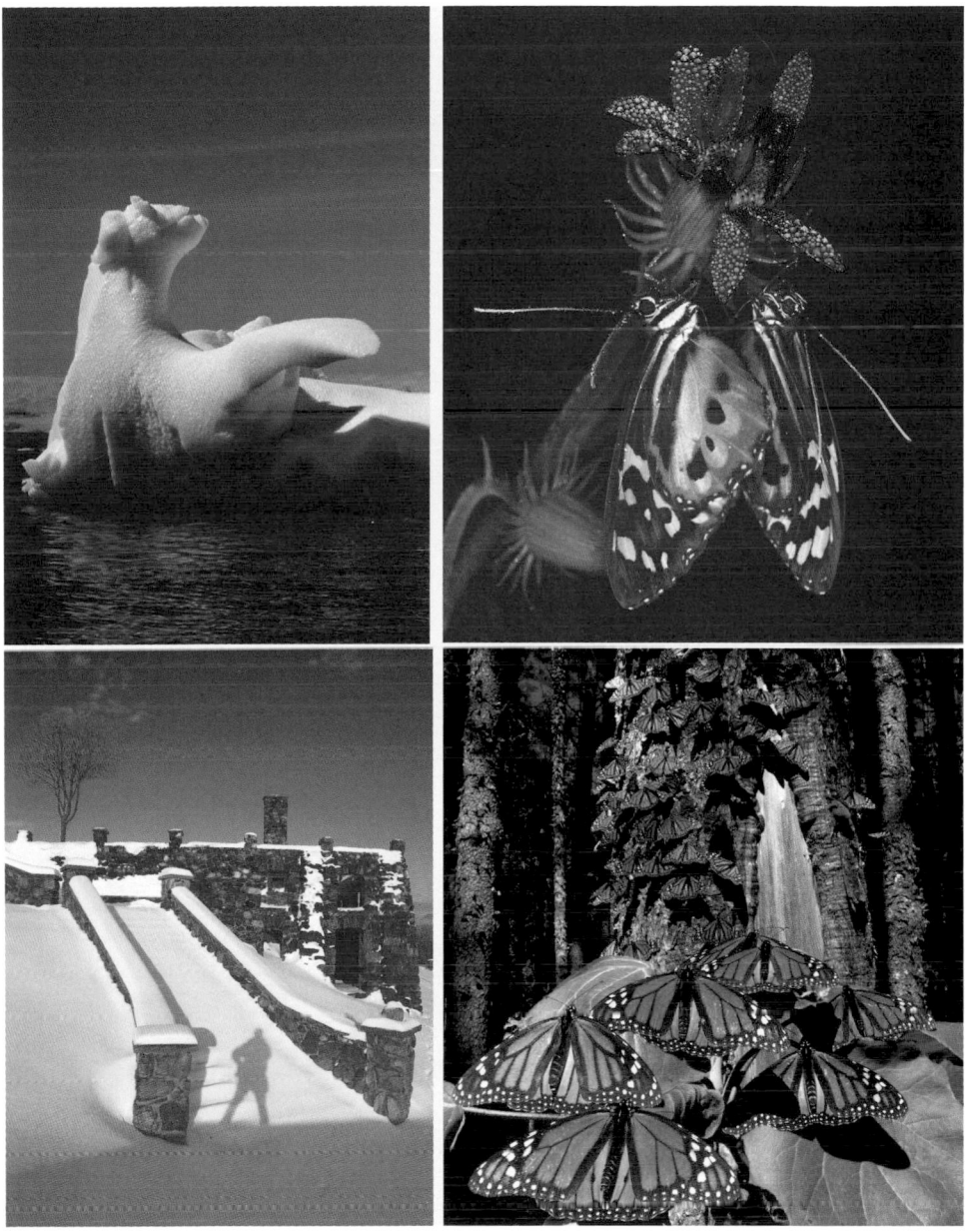

Clockwise from top left: Antarctica; Butterfly World; Coconut Creek, Florida; Michoacan, Mexico; Croton-on-Hudson, New York.

Pro Studio

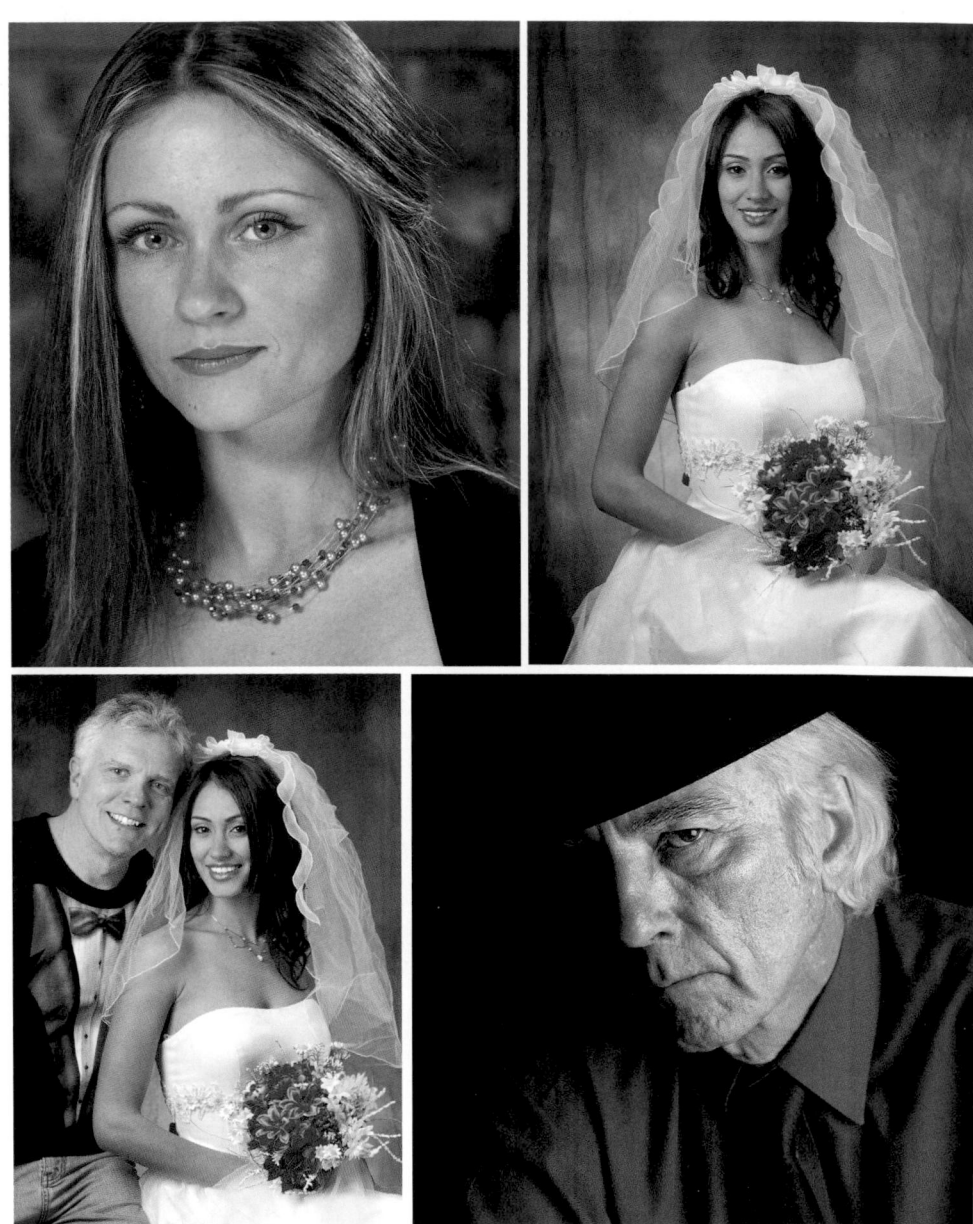

Clockwise from top left: New York, New York; New York, New York; Buffalo, New York; and New York, New York.

Tell a Story with Pictures

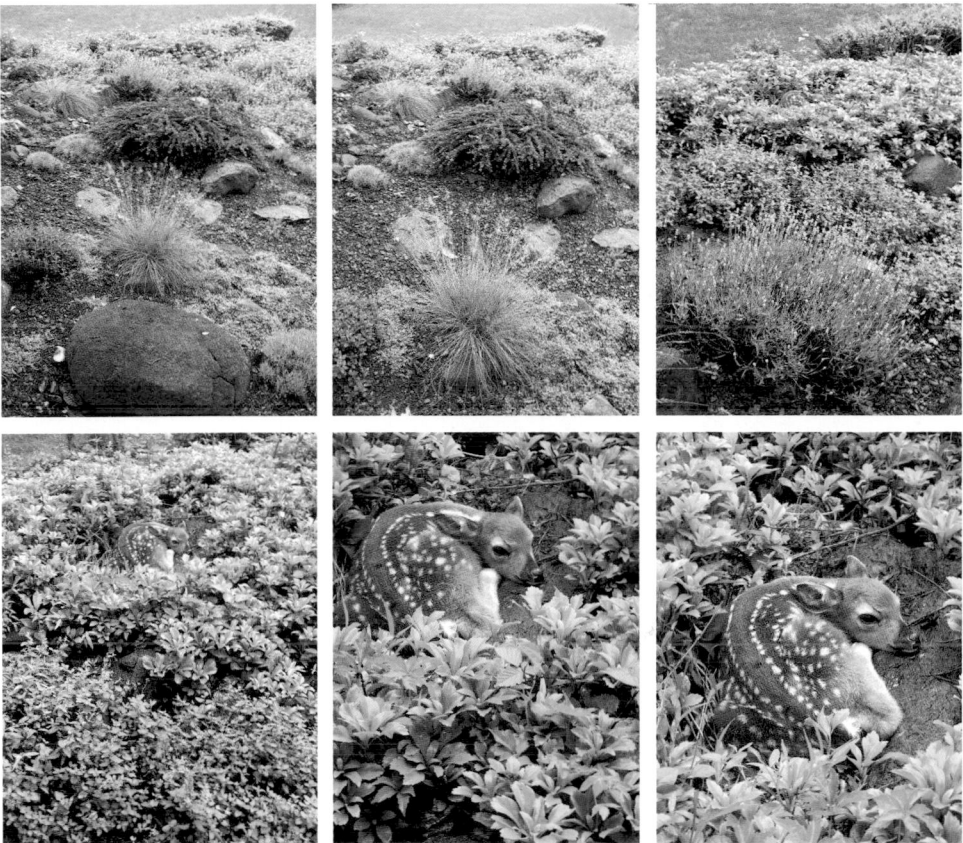

Croton-on-Hudson, New York.

How cute, right? The little fawn was resting in my backyard when I took these pictures. I was able to get this series of photographs because I approached the fawn very, very slowly. In wildlife photography, patience pays. Same is true for people photography.

Hey, I am wondering if you guessed correctly about the images on these pages. The answers are only a page turn away!

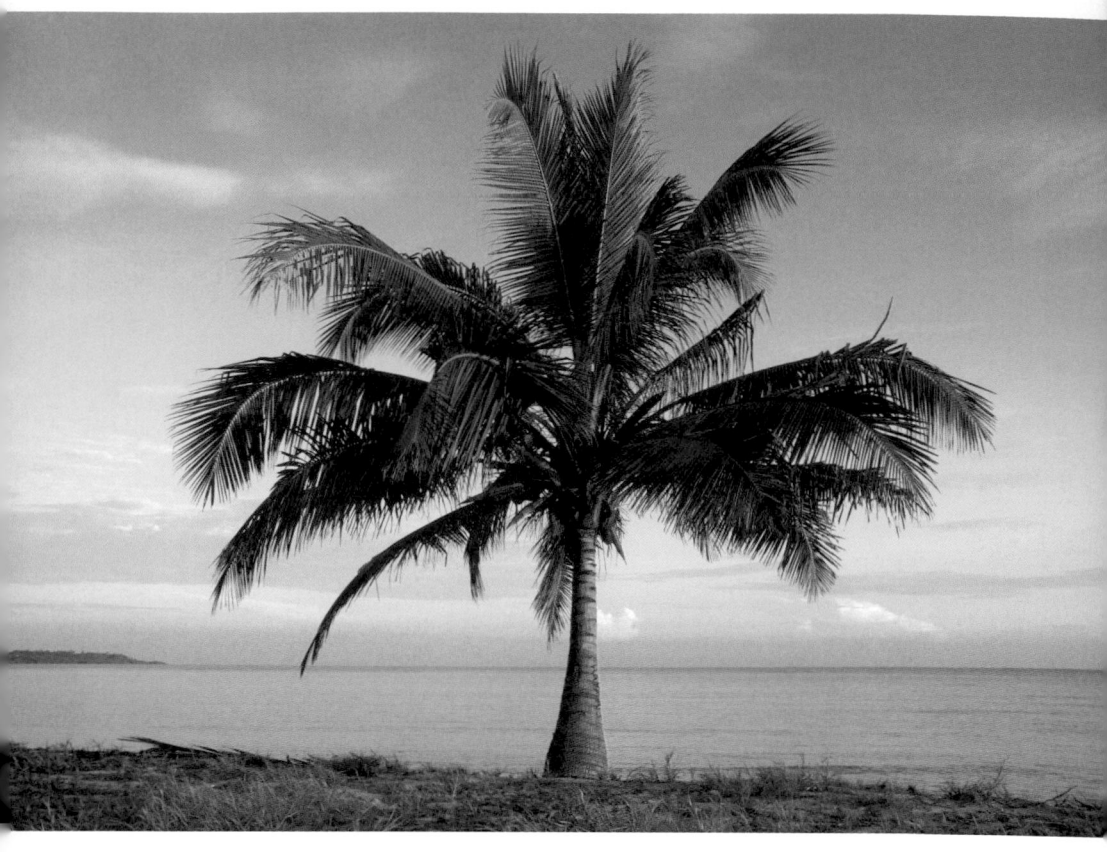

The Answers

Okay. I hope you did not skip ahead. Here's the scoop on which cameras I used for the pictures in this chapter.

The top pictures on the following pages were taken with my professional SLR camera: People Pictures, Animals, Landscapes and City Scenes, Snow and Nature, and Pro Studio.

The bottom pictures on those same pages were all taken with my compact camera.

The pictures on the Tell a Story with Pictures page were all taken with my compact camera.

What about the palm tree (Kuna Yala, Panama) on this page? Compact camera, I confess.

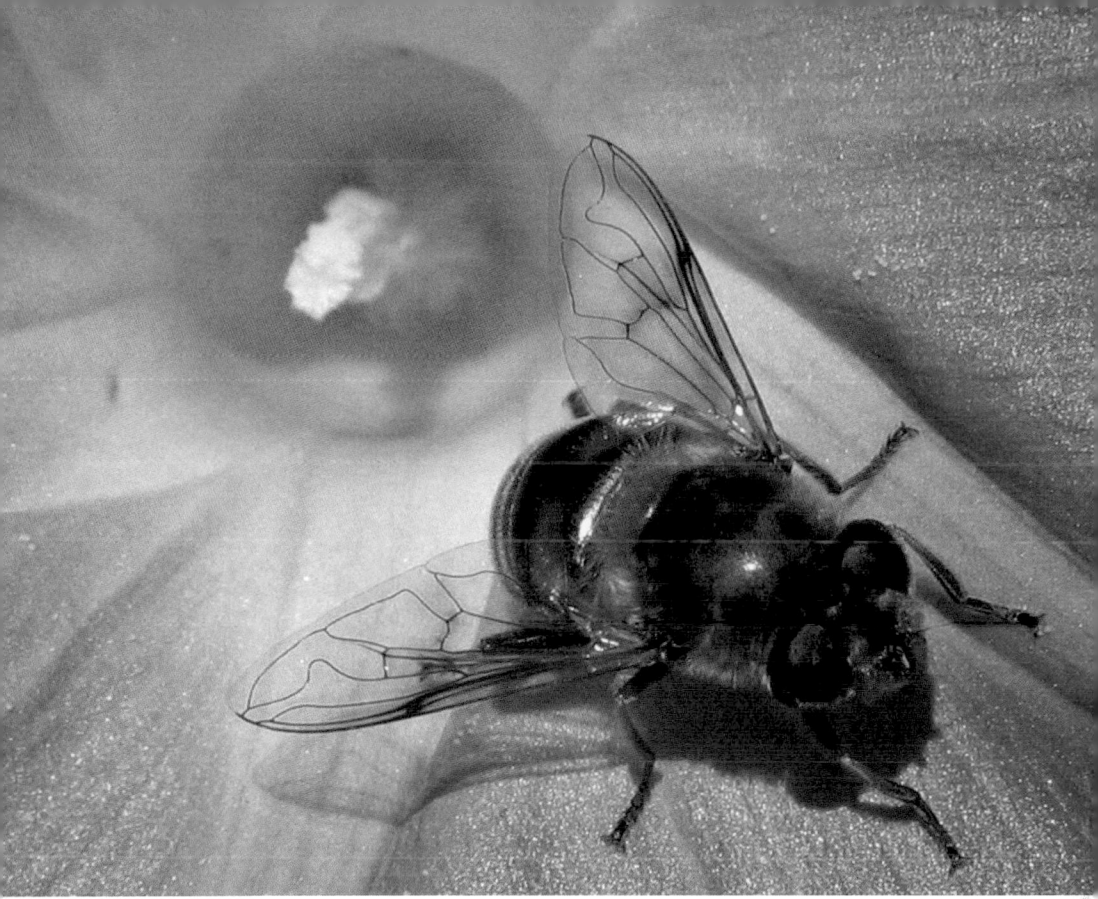

Part II

What Your Compact Camera Can and Can't Do

Compact cameras are indeed small wonders, delivering photographs that rival those taken with professional digital SLRs .... but not in all situations and conditions and not for all subjects. In this chapter you'll learn about what your compact camera can and can't do—and how to make the best of each and every situation.

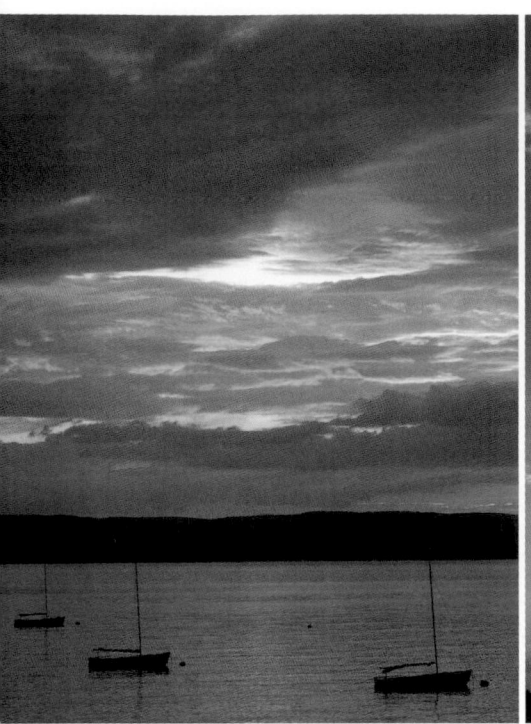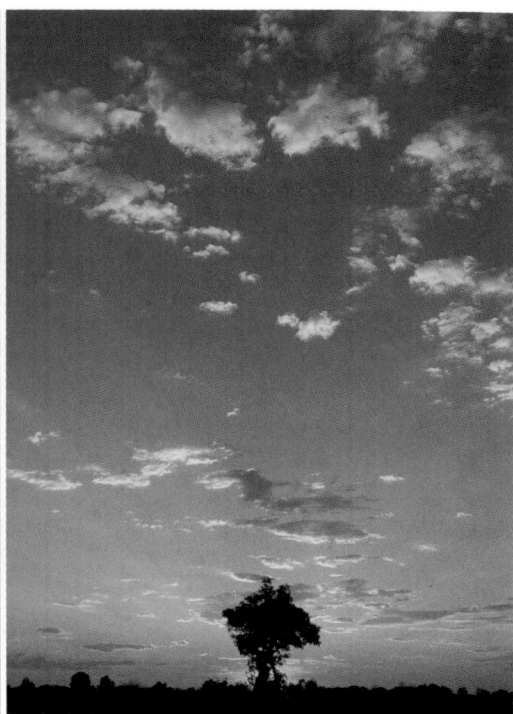

Image Quality

From a technical standpoint, a compact camera can't deliver the same quality images as a digital SLR. That's because the size of the image sensor in compact cameras is smaller than those in digital SLRs. That difference can be significant in terms of detail and digital noise (grain) when making big prints, especially if the photograph was taken in a low-light situation. The difference mostly shows up in shadow areas.

However, if you are only interested in making prints up to 16 x 20 inches or sharing your pictures on the web, you may not see any difference. What's more, you can upsize an image without losing detail (to a point) with a plug-in called Genuine Fractals from onOnesoftware (www.ononesoftware.com).

I took the picture on the left with my compact camera. I took the picture on the right with my pro SLR. While the picture on the left has more digital noise, it's still a nice picture.

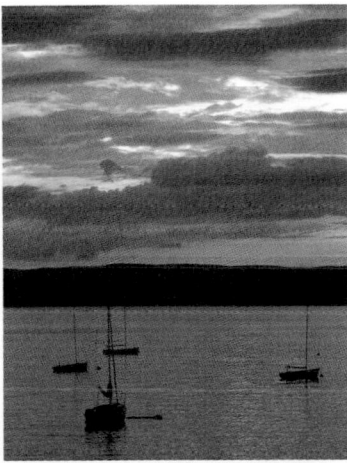
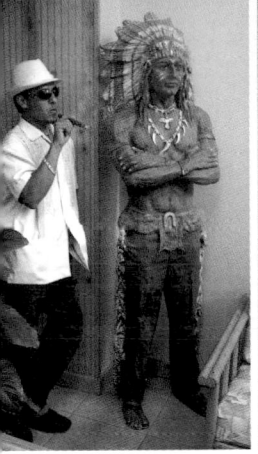
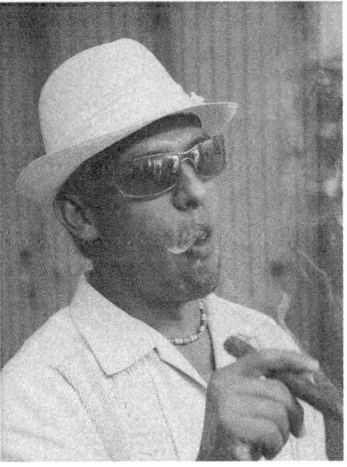

Digital Noise Difference

Digital noise is one of the major factors to consider when taking a picture—whether you're using a compact camera or a professional-quality dSLR.

My advice: Always try to select the lowest possible practical ISO setting. The lower the ISO, the less noise you'll get in your pictures.

When you set the ISO, you basically set the sensitivity of the camera's sensor—at least you can look at it that way. If the ISO is too low, you may get a blurry picture caused by camera shake.

To use a low ISO in a low-light situation, you'll need to use a tripod or other camera support. Otherwise, make sure the image stabilization feature (not available on all cameras) allows you to shoot a steady shot. A warning usually pops up on the camera's LCD monitor when the shutter speed is too low for a hand-held shot.

The two pictures on the left were taken with my pro SLR camera. The ISO was set at 400 for the top image and 800 for the bottom image.

The two pictures on the right were taken with my compact camera. The ISO was set at 400 for the top image and 800 for the bottom image. Both of these compact camera shots have more noise than the shots from my pro camera.

You will not see the noise in a picture when viewing it on the back of your camera. You may not even see it on a web site if the picture is small. However, you will notice it when you make a print that is 8x10 inches or larger.

Personally, I like to shoot the cleanest possible picture, a picture with as little noise as possible. However, if it's a choice between a picture with noise or no picture, I go for the picture with a bit o' noise.

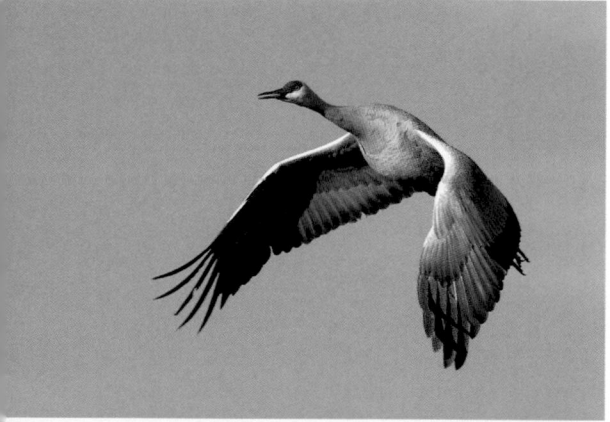

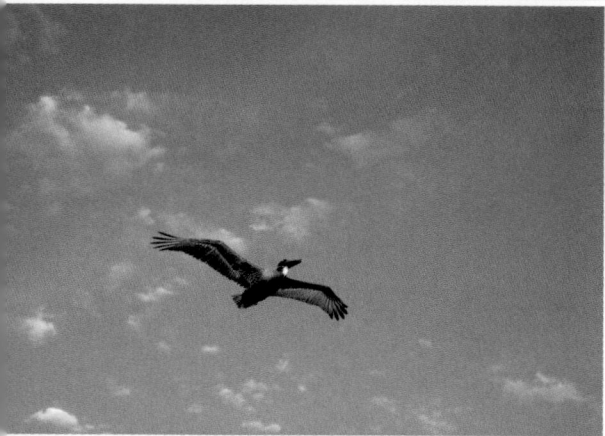

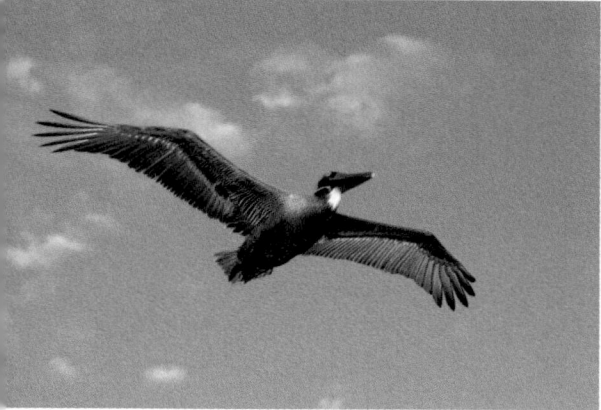

Getting Close to a Subject

Digital SLRs accept telephoto lenses that help you get full-frame shots of distant subjects. Some of these lenses cost thousands of dollars. Compact cameras have a built-in zoom with a relatively small zoom range (compared to the range you'd get with the more than fifty lenses that are available for digital cameras). Therefore, getting close to a distant subject is a limitation of compact cameras.

I took the top photograph with my pro SLR and a 400mm lens. I took the middle photograph with my compact camera with the zoom set at the longest optical setting. The pelican is fairly small in the picture.

I could have used the camera's digital zoom, but digital zooms tend to soften and pixelate an image. I also could have used an accessory telephoto converter on my lens, which would have extended the range of the zoom in the third photo. Instead, I chose to crop the image and use Genuine Fractals (mentioned earlier in this chapter) to upsize the image. Why? Because accessory telephoto converters, too, tend to soften and pixelate an image.

Sunsets—and More on Subject Size

I am sure you have seen sunset photos in which the sun is a fairly large red ball in the scene. That's not going to happen when you photograph a sunset with a compact camera.

This is because, as mentioned on the previous page, your compact camera can't get you as close to your subject as an SLR.

I took the top picture with my pro SLR. I took the bottom picture with my compact camera.

Again, you can upsize a picture in the digital darkroom (using image editing software)—to a point. The key is to envision the end result when you are looking through the viewfinder.

Speaking of which, to avoid damaging your eyes, never look directly at the sun when taking a picture.

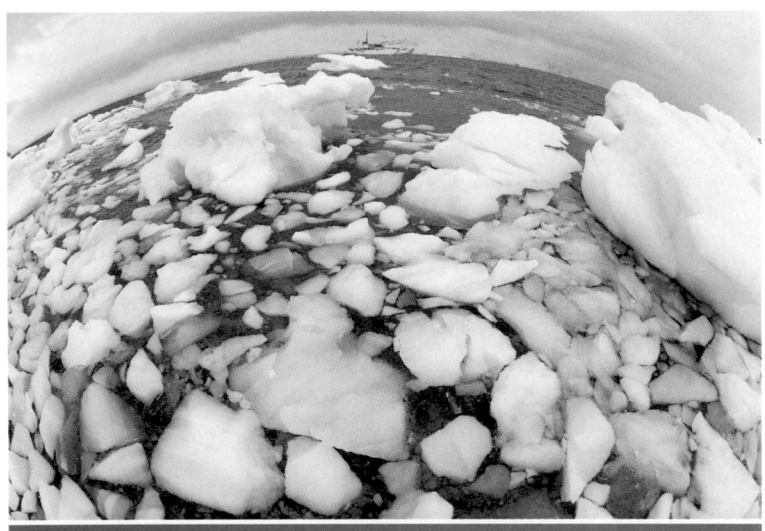

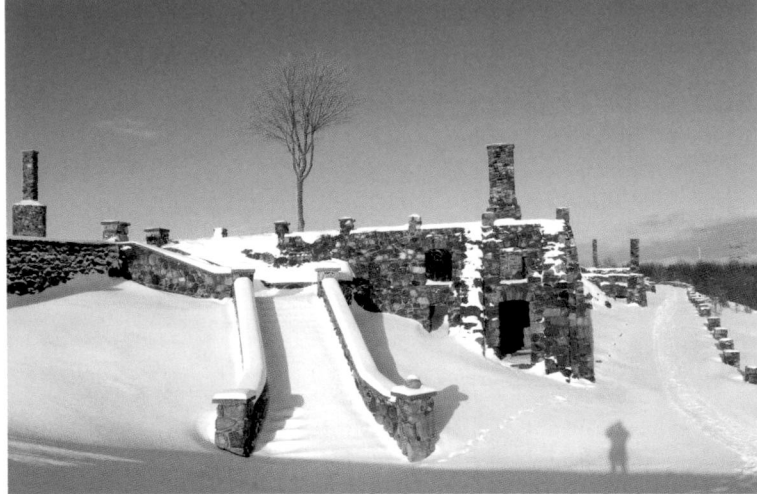

Maximum Wide-Angle View

Compact cameras can take nice wide-angle views, as illustrated by the bottom picture on this page. However, you can't get as wide of a view with a compact camera as you can with a digital SLR. This is due to the size of the sensor.

I took the top picture with my 15mm full-frame fish-eye lens on my full-frame image sensor pro SLR.

If you want a wider view than you see in your viewfinder or on the camera's LCD monitor, do what we did before zoom lenses: zoom with your feet … move back a few steps.

The curved-horizon effect you see here is not possible with a compact camera.

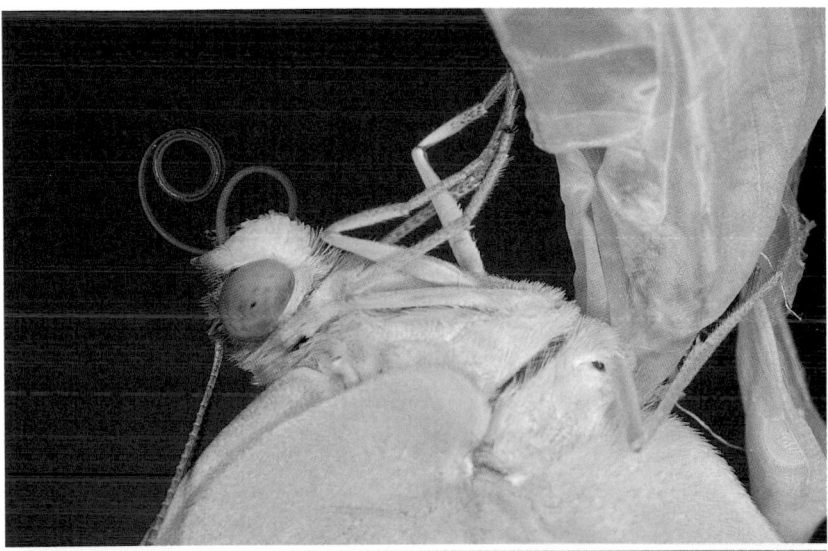

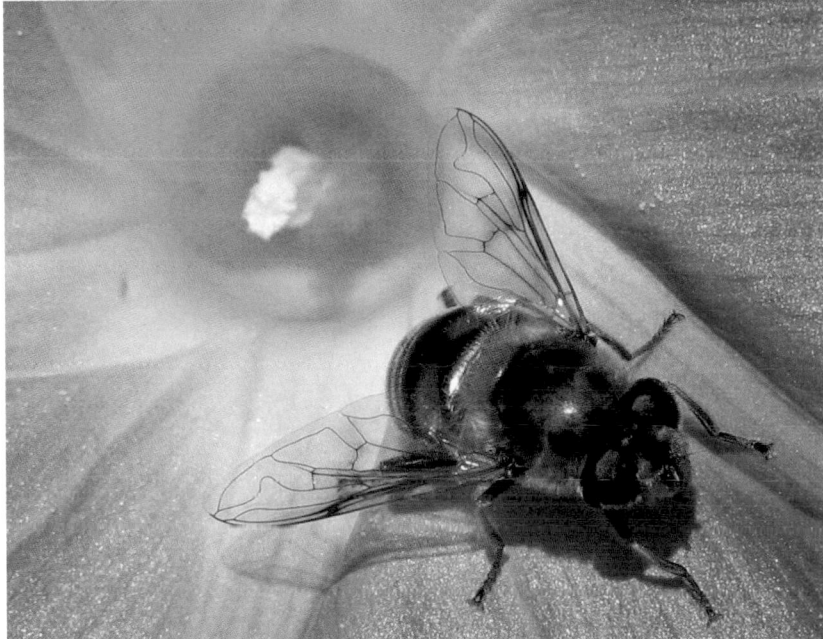

Close-ups

You can get pretty darn close to a subject when your compact camera is set to the close-up mode, as illustrated by the bottom picture that I took for a Canon brochure.

If you want to get closer, as illustrated in the top picture that I took with my pro digital SLR, then you'll need a special macro lens.

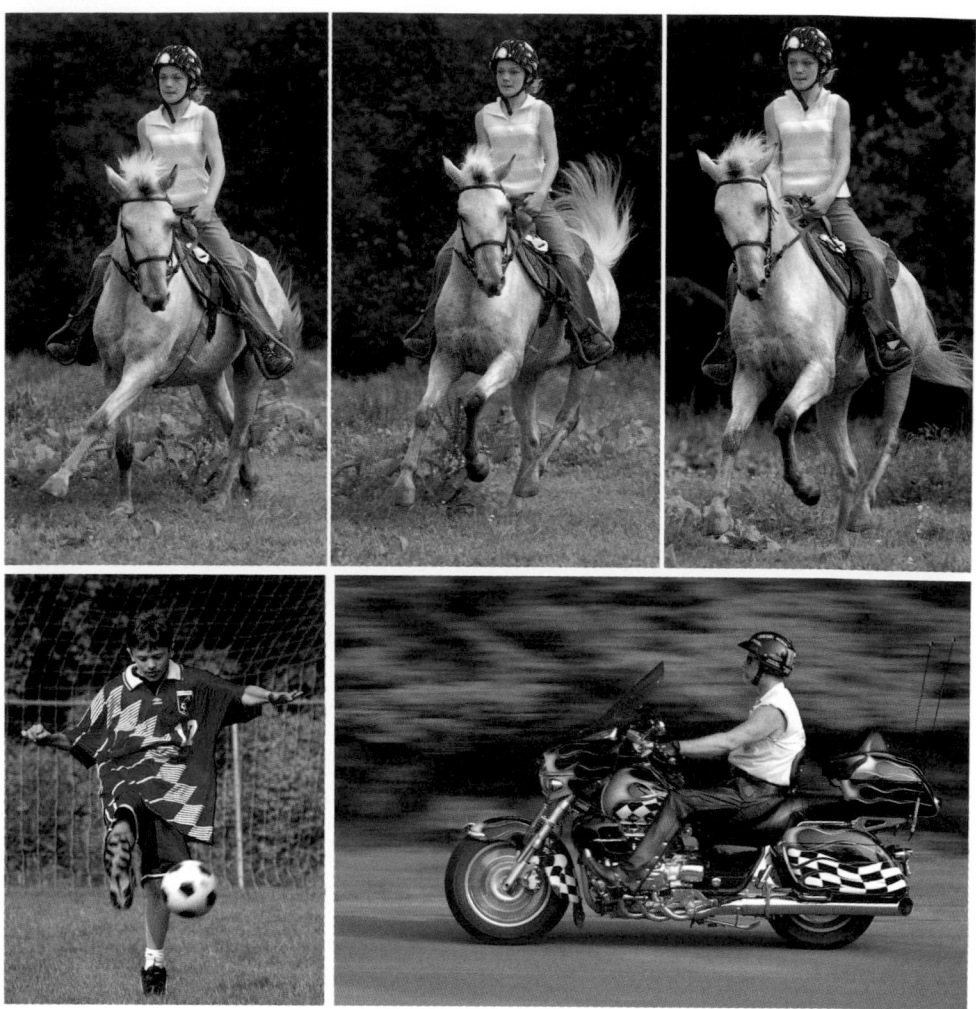

Action Sequences

Frames don't advance as quickly with compact cameras as they do with digital SLRs. A compact camera simply cannot make rapid-fire, several-frame-per-second sequences like the horse and rider shot.

But if you plan your shots, you can still get great action shots, as illustrated by my compact camera shots of my son playing soccer and the motorcycle rider.

You can get action sequences with compact cameras. It's just that there will be more space (time) between the pictures.

In addition to planning your shot, setting the ISO to HIGH or 400 or even 800 (which gives you a faster shutter speed) will help to freeze the action.

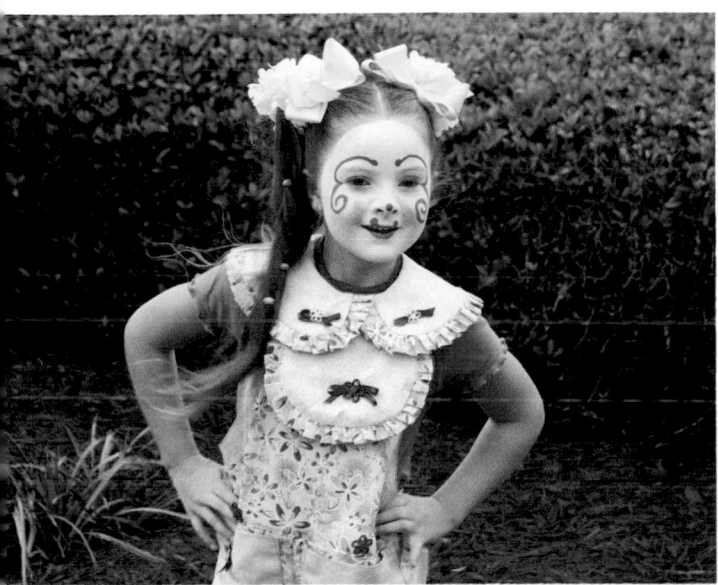

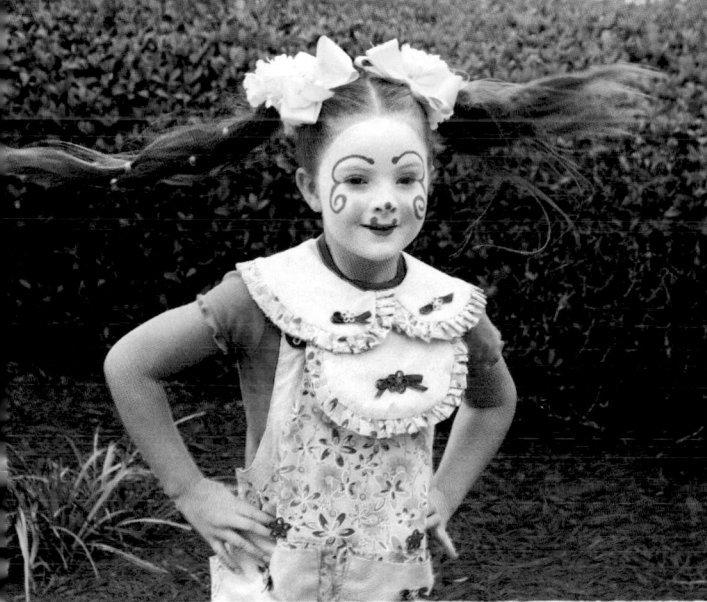

Shutter Lag

Shutter lag is the amount of time between when the shutter release button is pressed and the instant that the picture is taken. And it may be the biggest complaint among compact camera owners.

Shutter lag is common with all compact cameras, but as price increases, shutter lag decreases. This is good to know if you plan to buy a compact camera or upgrade.

Due to shutter lag, you may miss a fun action shot, like the girl twirling her pigtails pictured in the bottom photograph.

Knowing about shutter lag helps you plan for a shot, so you can actually get more dynamic images like the bottom picture.

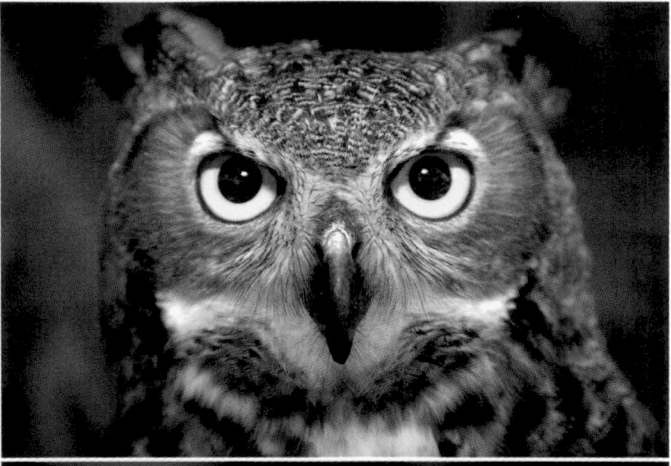

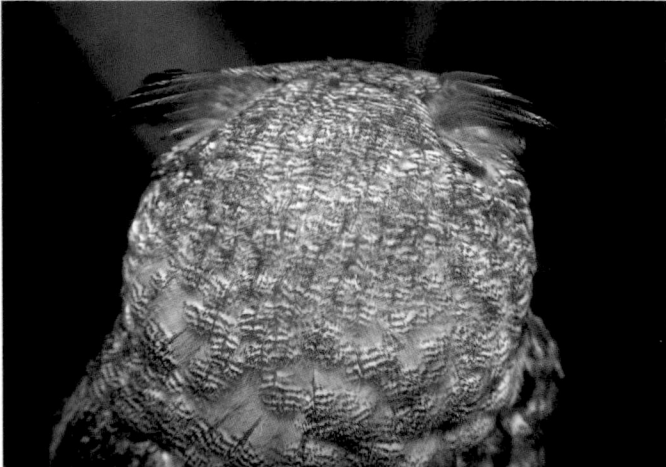

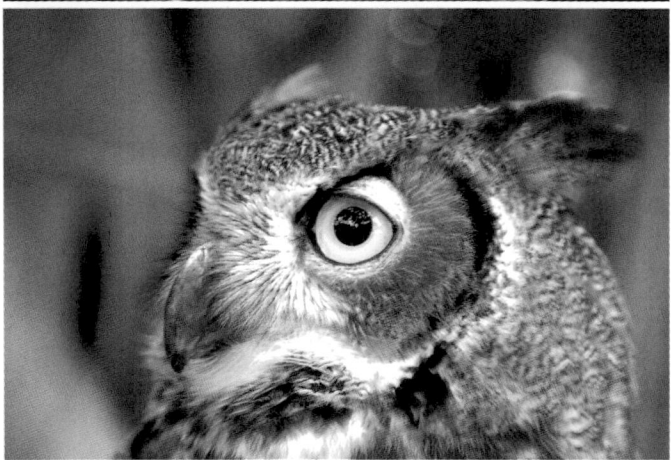

More on Shutter Lag

If you've ever tried to photograph your pet in action, you've likely already discovered this: Shutter lag also comes into play in animal and wildlife photography.

Here, too, you need to plan your shots. It's the only way to get a shot like the top photograph where the owl is looking directly at the camera—instead of shots like the bottom two pictures.

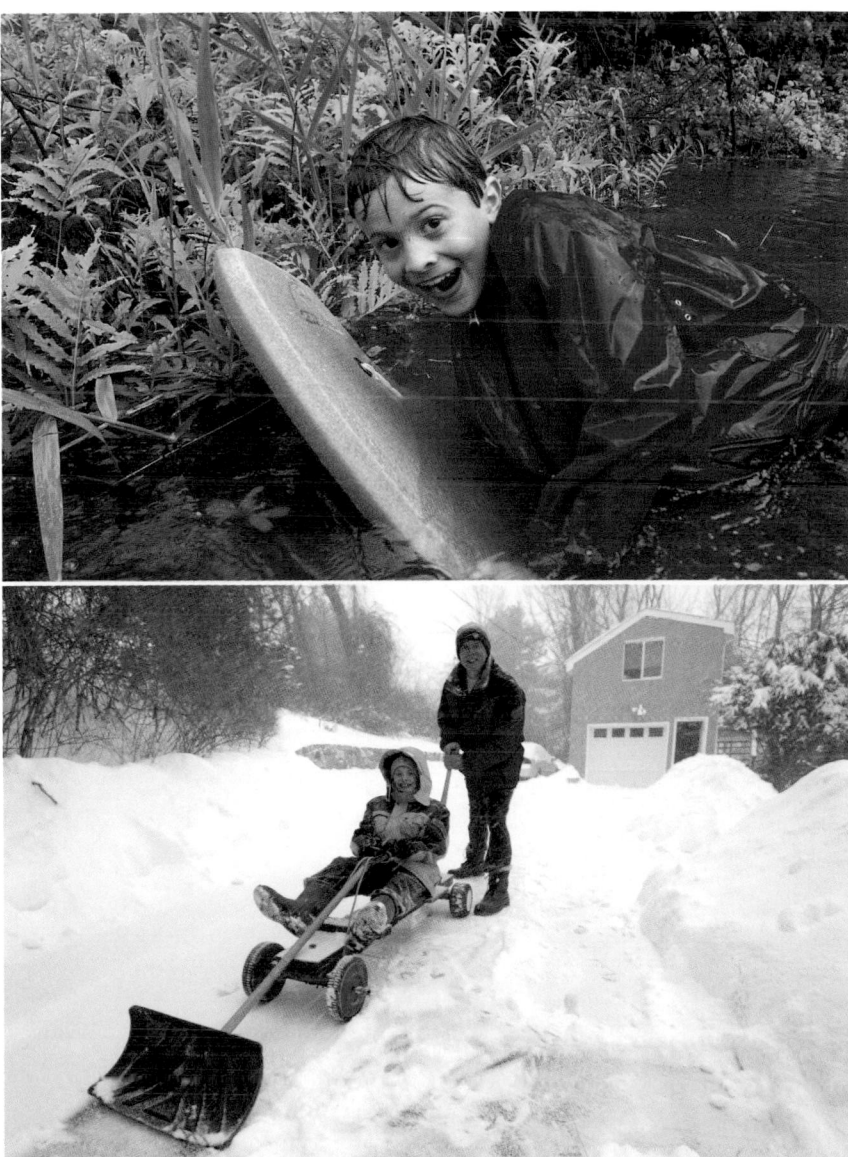

Always Ready for Fun

One thing your compact camera does have in common with a pro digital SLR is that it's always ready for fun—perhaps even more so! Some compact cameras are waterproof, making it easier to take pictures in the rain, sleet and snow.

If you enjoy outdoor sports, you may want to consider a waterproof camera or a waterproof casing for your current compact camera.

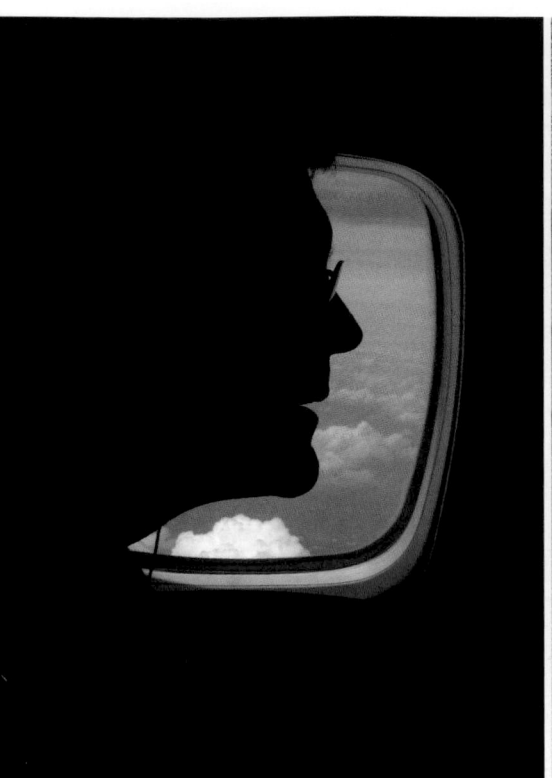 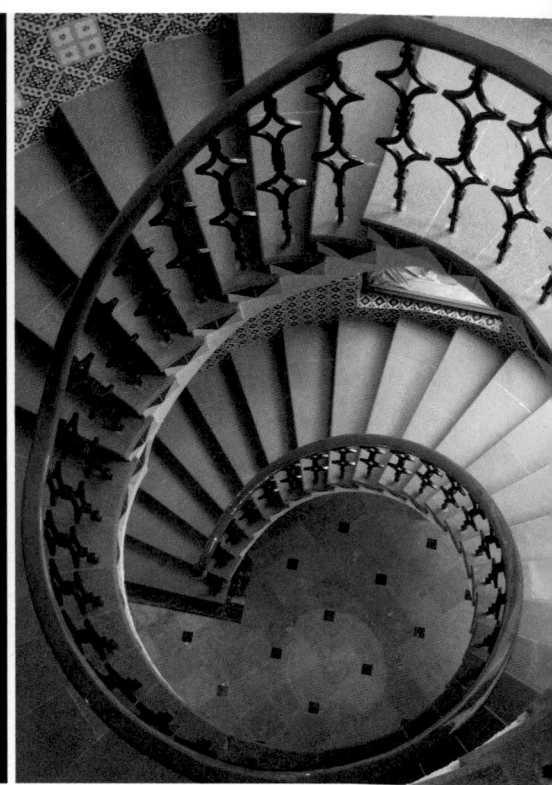

On-the-Spot Creativity

One of the things I love about my compact camera is that I can always have it with me. I never leave home without it!

Always carrying a camera means always looking for pictures … for me anyway. I find myself taking pictures with my compact camera that I normally would not consider for my SLR, as pictured here: a self-portrait taken at 30,000 feet and a winding staircase in Mexico City. What fun!

Always carry your compact camera. I guarantee that you will begin to see more creative picture opportunities.

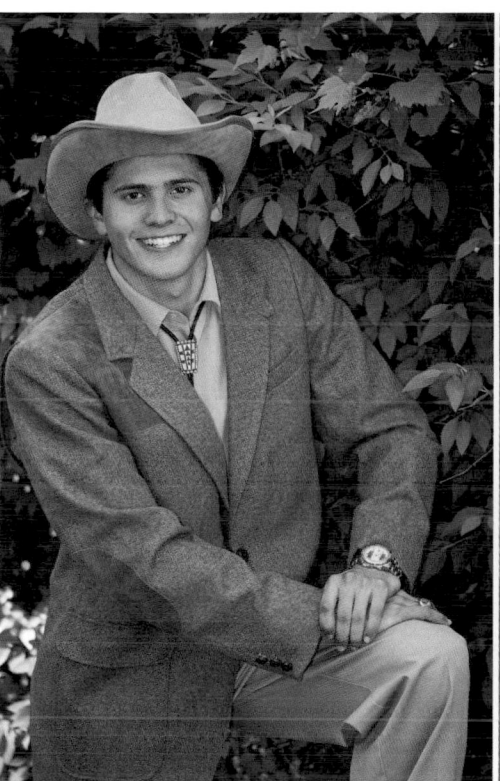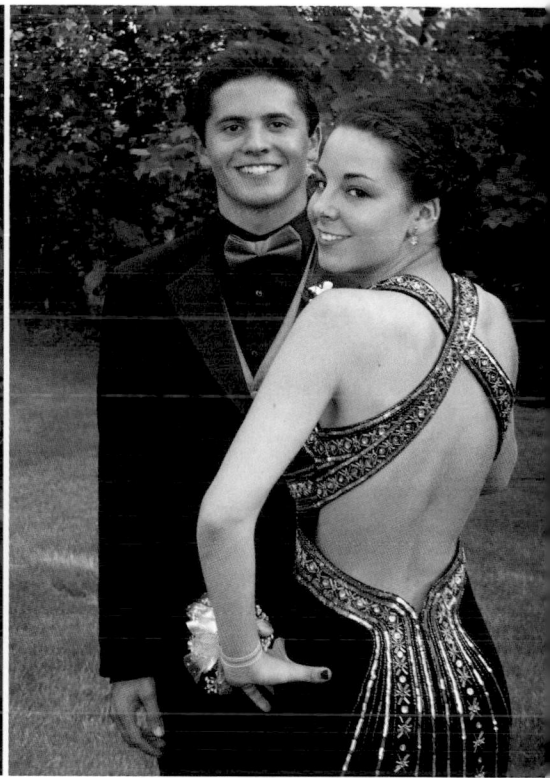

Know Your Camera

If you take away one tip from this chapter, make it this: Know what you camera can and can't do. Read the instruction manual … as well as this book.

When you know you compact camera, you can take professional quality pictures—like the ones on this page. One was taken with my pro camera; one was taken with my compact camera. Can you tell the difference? I won't confess which is which …

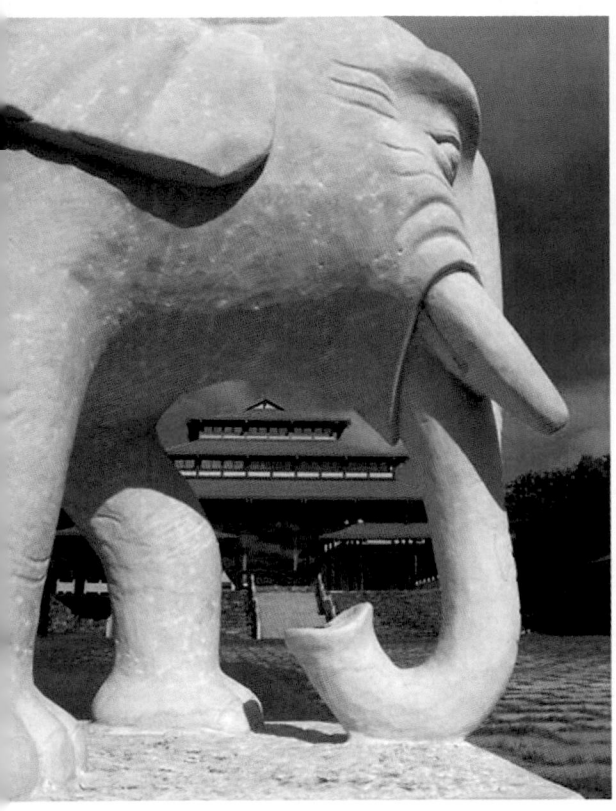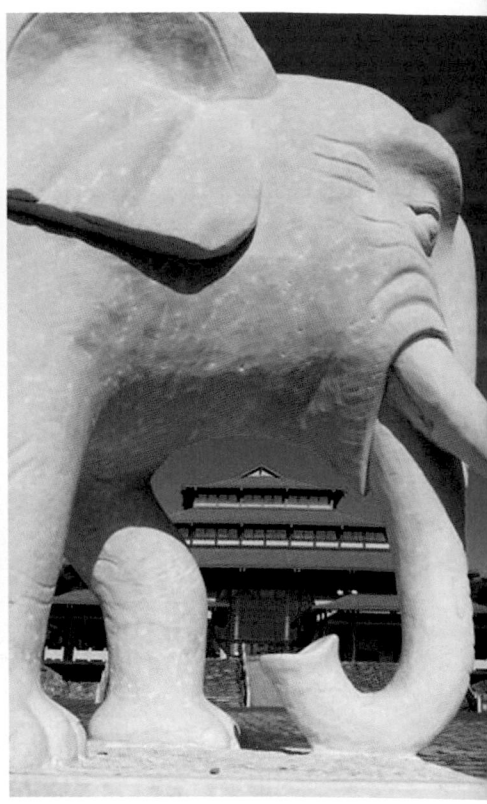

Good News!

I thought I'd end this chapter with some good news … for those of you who will eventually move up to a digital SLR camera anyway. The news is that you can use many of the techniques that I cover in this book to make great pictures with a compact camera or a dSLR. I took the picture on the left with my compact camera, and I took the picture on the right with my pro SLR. I used the same technique to get the entire scene in focus: I chose a wide-angle setting (35mm) on my zoom lens; I shot at a small aperture (f/11); and I set the focus 1/3 into the scene. Rather than think about what your compact camera can't do, think about all it can do!

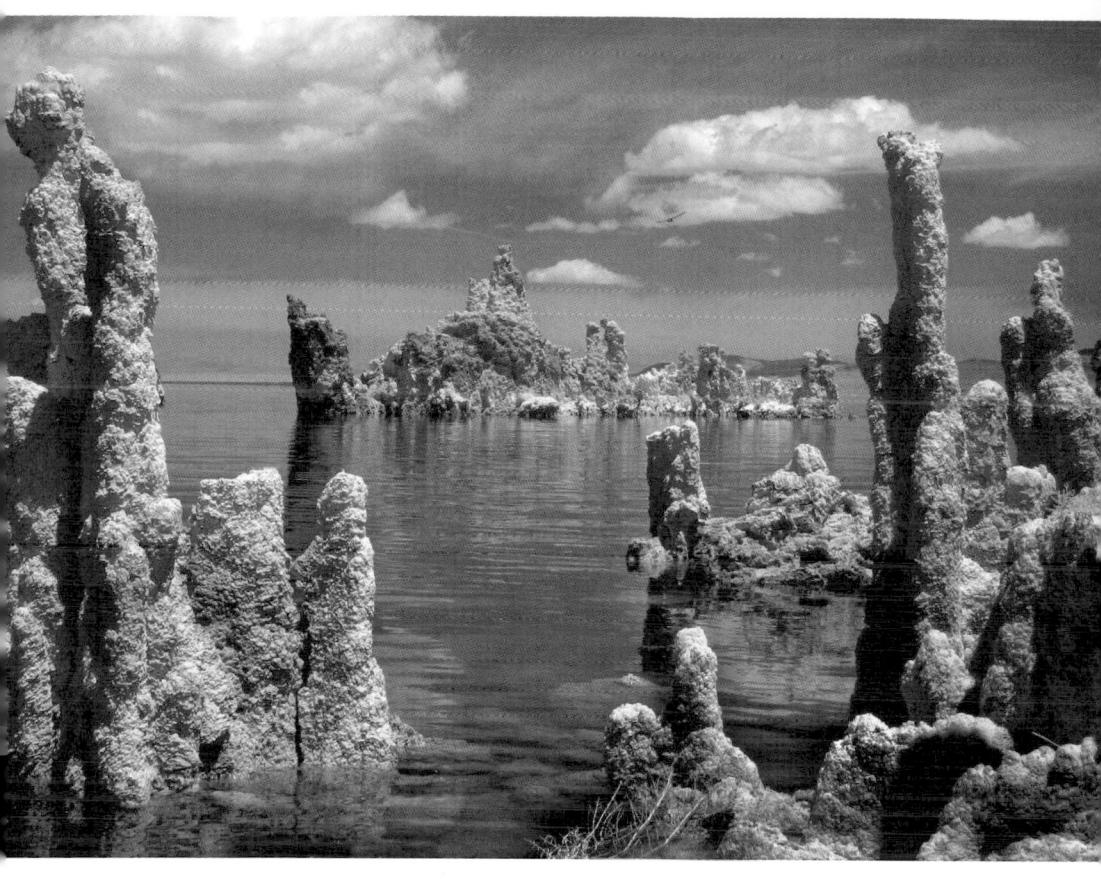

Part III

Top Tips for Great Digital Pix

Throughout this book you'll find hundreds of tips on how to get the most out of your compact camera. But for those of you who want to jumpstart your photo-learning fun, I'll share my top tips for great digital pictures before I get into specific camera features and benefits. Many of the topics in this chapter are covered in more detail later in this book.

But why wait? Let the fun begin!

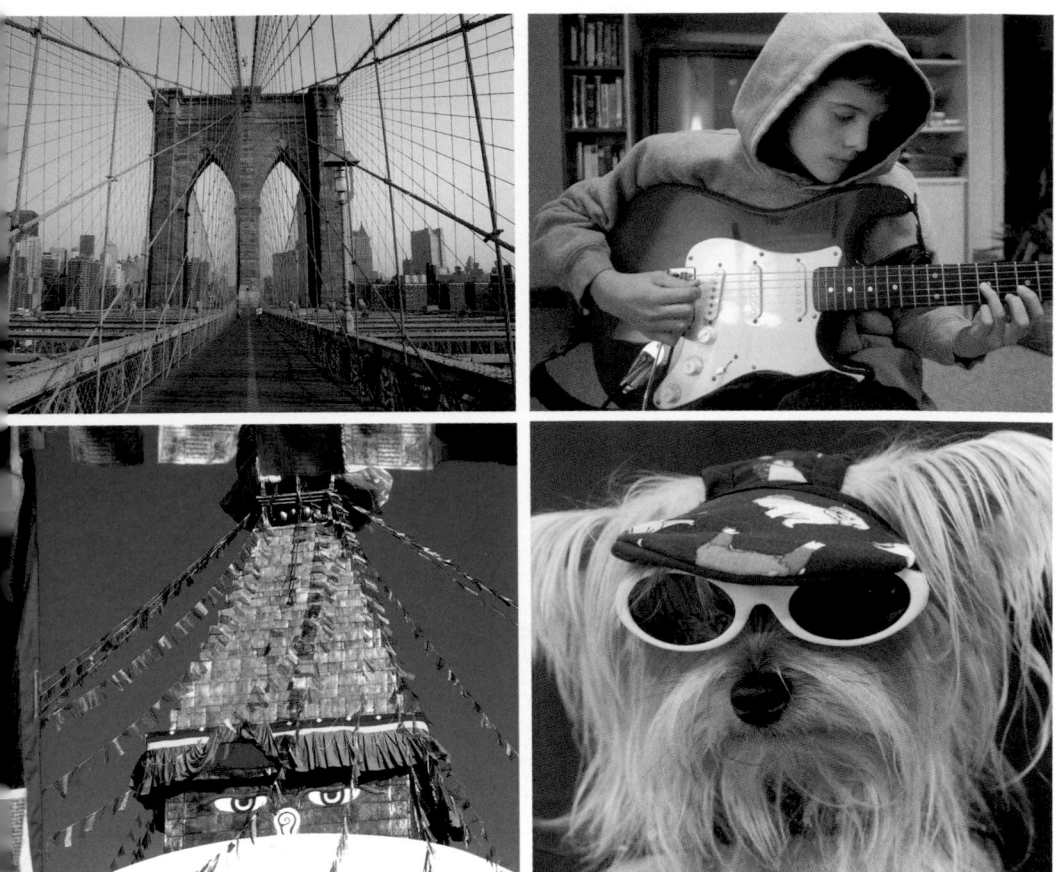

An Interesting Subject is Key

I know this sounds like a ridiculously basic tip, but it's truly fundamental. An interesting subject is one of the most important requirements in being able to make a good photograph. Even more than your tools and prowess as a photographer, the top reason that the photographs in *National Geographic* magazine look good is because the subjects—in each and every photograph—are interesting.

You need to seek out interesting subjects. They might be landmarks, landscapes and cityscapes, wildlife, people, pets or some other magnificent thing; but if you plan to show and share your work, the subject should have universal appeal. Otherwise, if you plan to take pictures for only yourself and your family, then a family member engaged in some activity is, no doubt, an interesting subject—to your family.

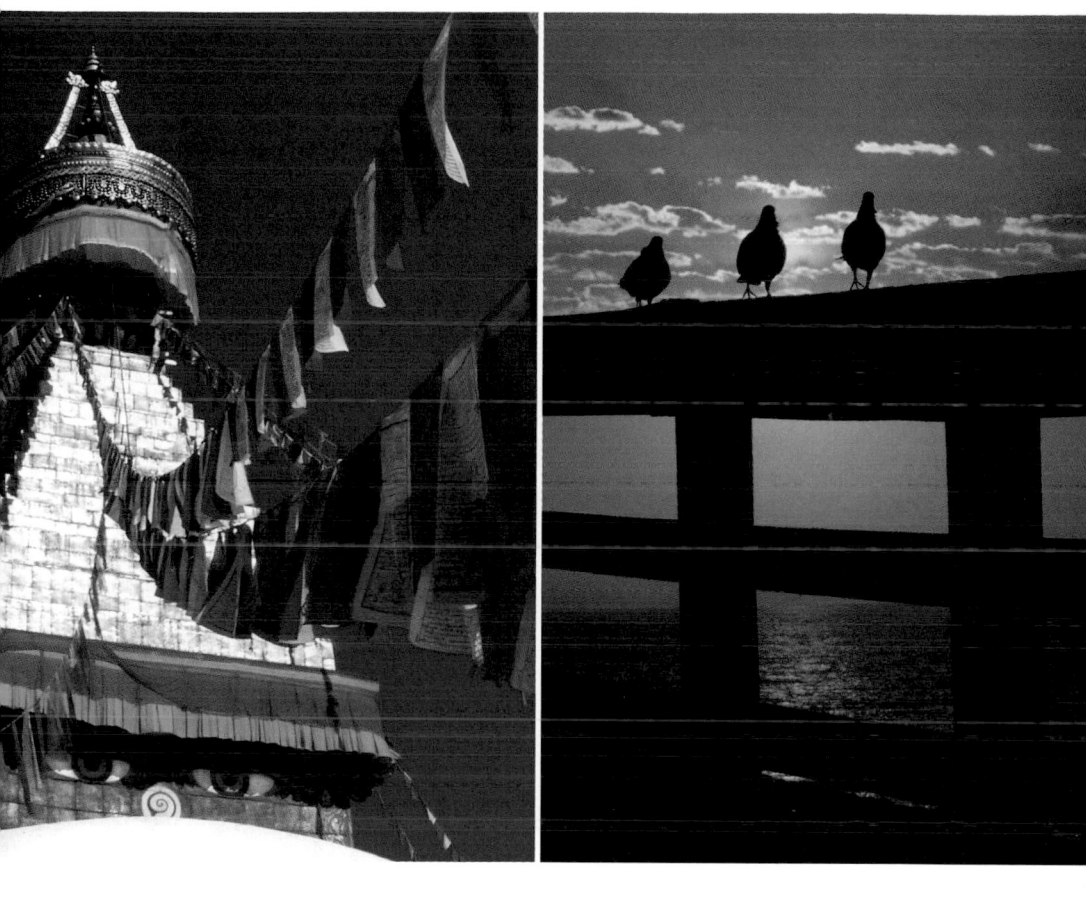

Go for Good Composition

"The name of the game is to fill the frame" is one of my top composition tips.

It means: Move in or zoom in close and cut the clutter. That's what I did for this picture of a stupa and prayer flags in Nepal.

In the sunrise picture, I did not fill the frame. Instead, I left some "breathing room" at the top of the frame. My point: Think about the rules … and then think about the benefits of breaking the rules.

Here are two more composition tips:

1) Dead center is deadly; don't place the main subject in the center of the frame.

2) Imagine a tic-tac-toe grid over the scene and place the main subject where the lines intersect.

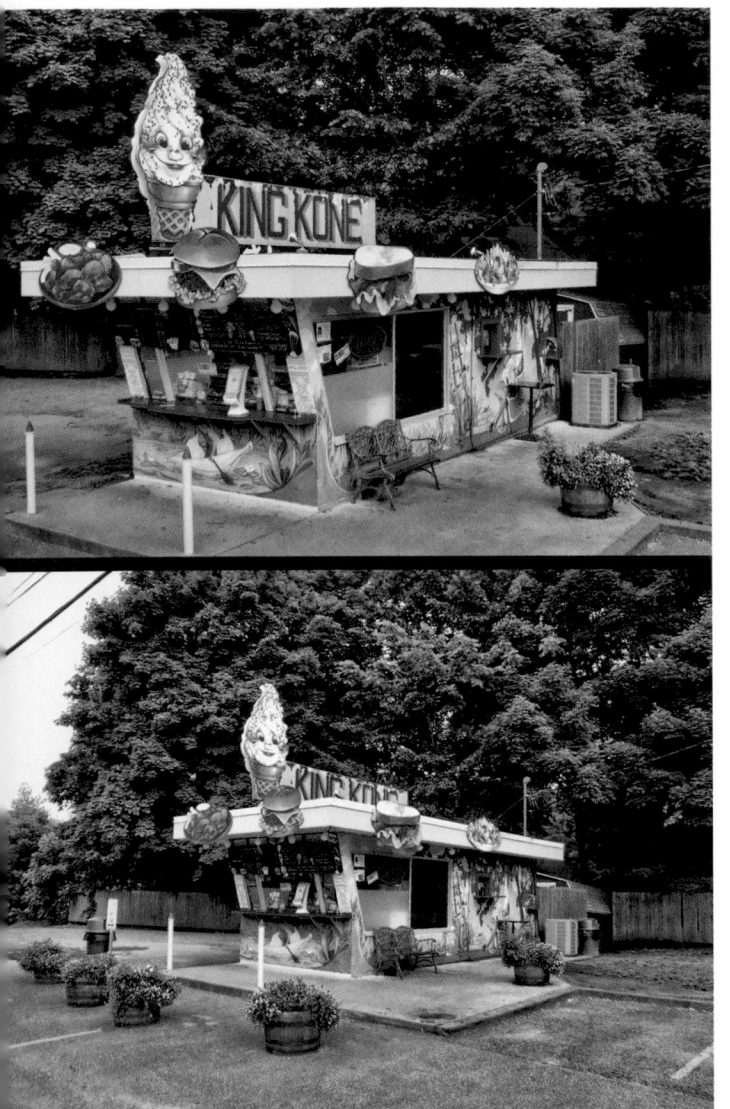

Pick an Interesting Vantage Point

Along with good composition goes a good vantage point. Your ideal vantage point may not be immediately obvious though. So when you see an interesting subject, you need to visualize how the subject will look from several different shooting positions.

A good example of this is the bottom image, which has pretty poor composition. A main issue is that you can't read the name of the restaurant, which I think is an important part of the scene. In the top photograph, you can. That's because I used a technique made famous by Ansel Adams, the most famous landscape photographer of all time. I took the shot while standing on the roof of my car.

Photographing from above, by the way, also works when photographing large groups. It's easier to see all the faces that way.

Both of these pictures were enhanced in Topaz Adjust (www.topazlabs.com), a plug-in that helps you create images with brighter light areas and darker shadow areas. Photographs with this kind of wide contrast range are called *high dynamic-range* (HDR) images. More on this effect beginning on page 197.

Focus on Auto Focusing

Just because you have an auto focus camera does not mean that the camera always knows where to focus to get the shot you want. That's why some cameras have different focus modes, focus locks and a manual focus option.

When I took the top picture, the focus was set one-third of the way into the scene (using the camera's focus lock). This ensured that the saw blade and the logger were in focus. If I had let the camera do the focusing, it would have focused on the logger; the saw blade might have been out of focus.

When I took the bottom photograph, I set the focus to manual—because I was shooting though my office window, which could have caused the camera to focus on the window rather than on the mother deer and her baby.

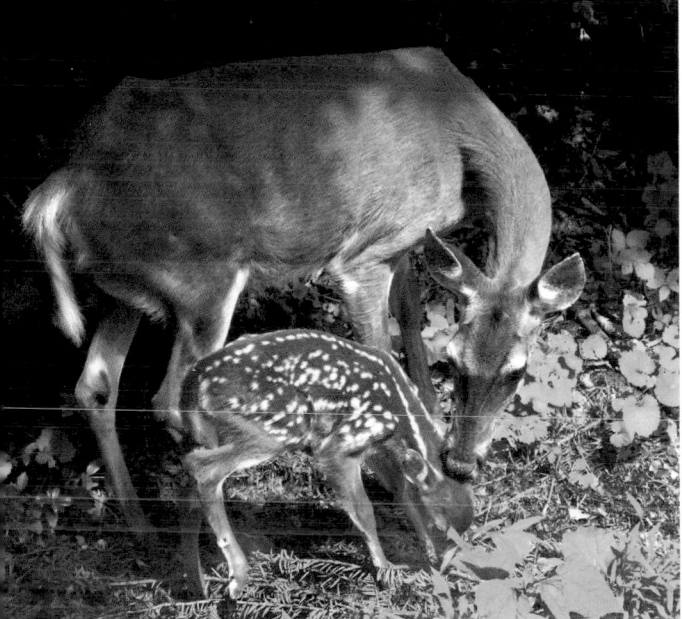

In the bottom photo, I wish the fawn's face was more visible, but I like the interaction between the mommy and baby. It makes this a fun shot to keep.

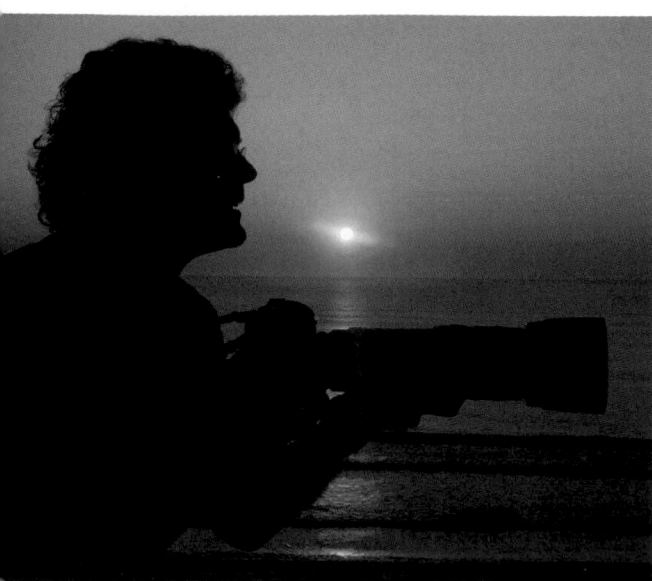
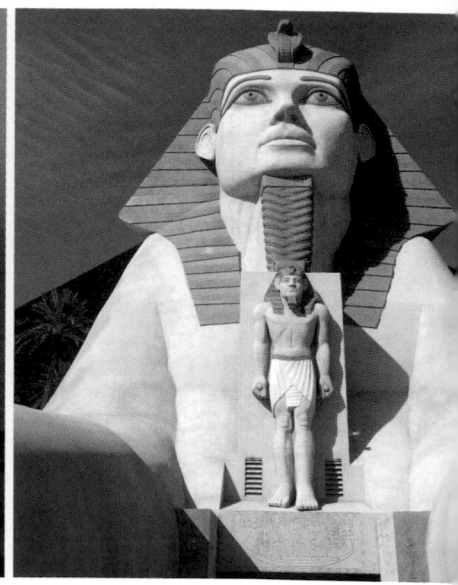

Fine-Tune Your Exposures

One of the cool features on every mid-range compact cameras is the +/- control, which allows you to increase or decrease the exposure. Sometimes that's necessary; sometimes it's a choice.

Technically speaking, when the picture on the left was taken, the exposure compensation was set at -1. This increased the color saturation in the picture and prevented the highlight area around the sun from being washed out. If that sounds too technical, think of it this way: You'll simply get a better sunset picture with your exposure compensation set at -1.

When I took the picture on the right, I set the exposure compensation at +1. This is standard practice when photographing scenes with lots of bright areas.

Take the time to fine-tune your exposures in camera, and you'll spend less time fixing your exposures in the digital darkroom.

Be Aware of the Background

The background can make or break a photograph. Therefore, it's just as important as the main subject.

In the top picture, taken in Croton-on-Hudson, New York, the background is not distracting; it complements the subjects. In the middle photograph, also taken in Croton, the background is busy; it's distracting.

But wait, the background in the bottom photograph is also busy, filled with palm trees and molas, which are beautiful hand-sewn fabrics hanging on the clothesline. Yet somehow it adds to the photograph. This image was taken in Kuna Yala, Panama.

Before you shoot, think about the background and consider whether it will add or detract from your main subject(s).

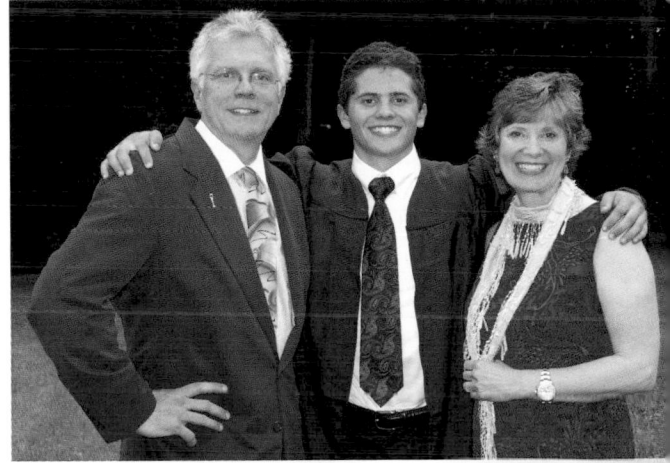

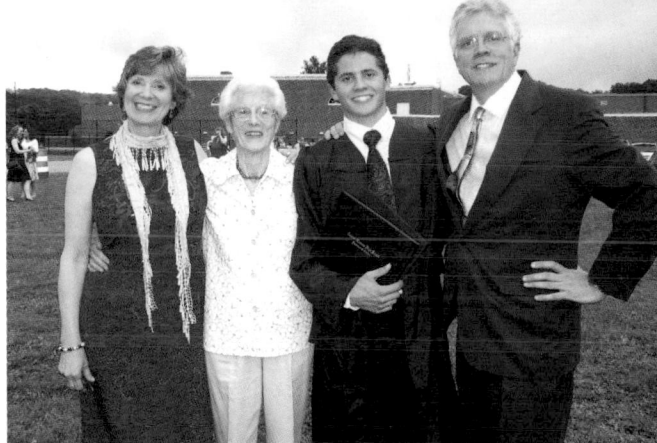

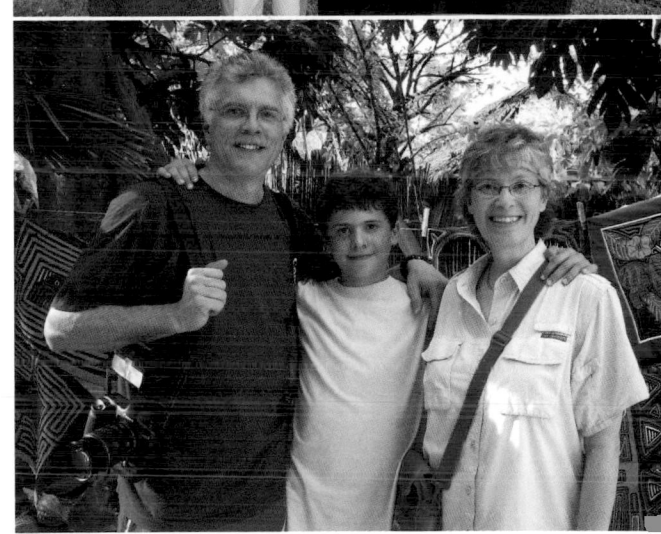

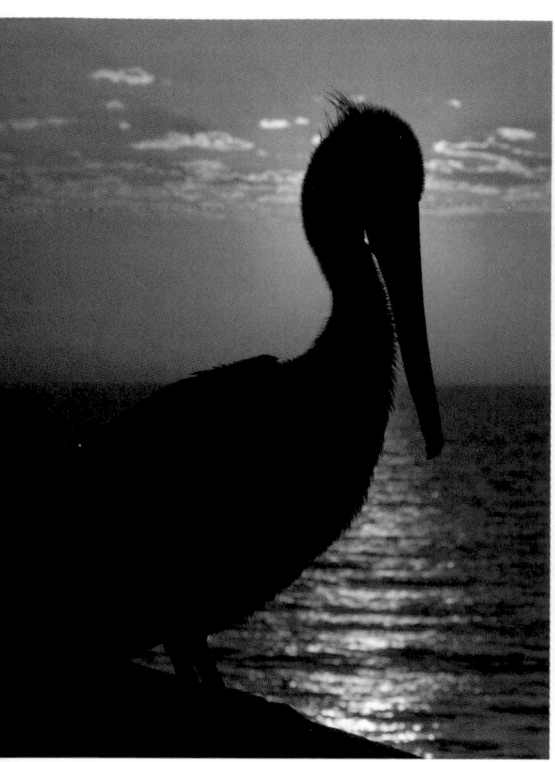 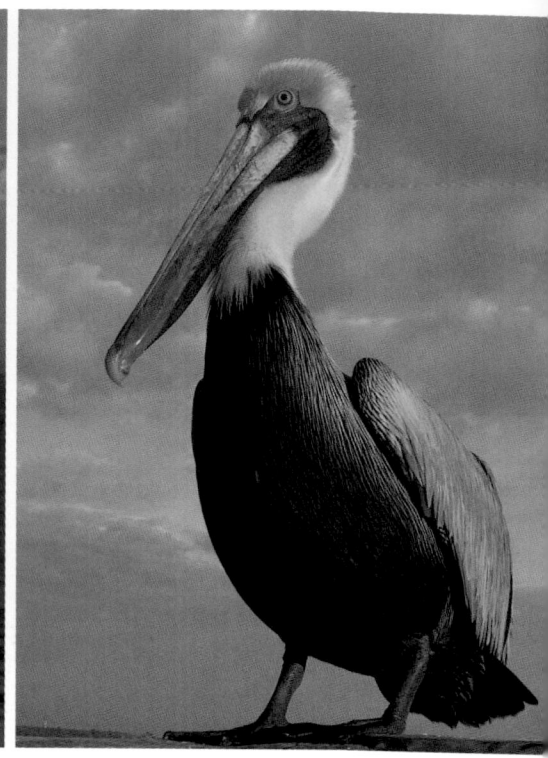

See the Light

I took these pictures within about a minute of each other while on the St. John's Pier in St. Augustine, Florida. I was only about two feet away from these peaceful pelicans. One was silhouetted against the rising sun; the other was front-lit by the sun.

In photography, we need to see the light—its direction, color, contrast range in a scene, and quality. In doing so, we can make correct decisions about exposure and camera settings, including exposure compensation, white balance setting, ISO and so on.

Both pictures were taken at what pros call the "golden hours" of early morning, which also occur during late afternoon. The golden tones of pictures taken during the "golden hours" have deeper shades of red, orange and yellow, making them prettier than pictures taken during midday, when the light is cooler.

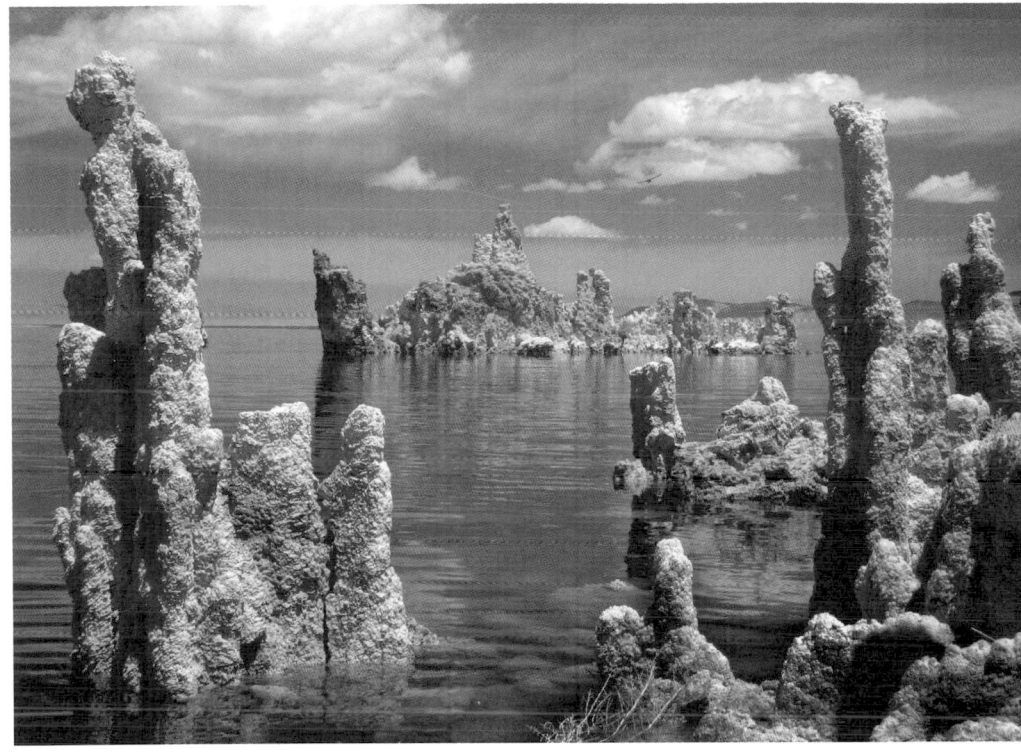

Create a Sense of Depth

We see the world in three dimensions: height, width and depth. Our cameras only see two: height and width. Therefore, it's our job to create a sense of depth in our pictures.

Basically, there are two methods for achieving depth effect. One, place a foreground element in a scene, as I did when photographing these tufas in Mono Lake, California. Two, shoot in the early morning and late afternoon when long shadows add a sense of depth to a scene.

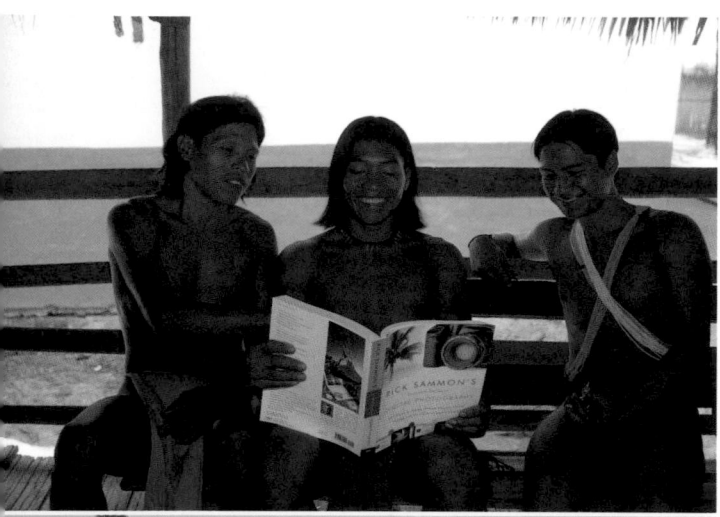

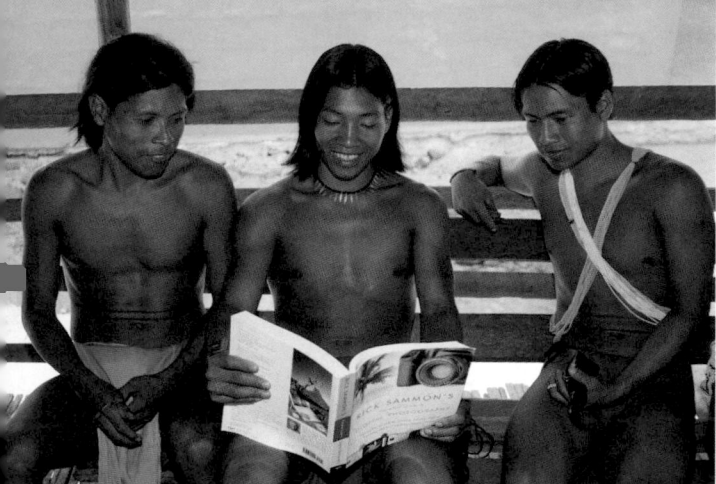

Control the Light On-Site

As I mentioned a few pages back, seeing the light is an important element in the making of a good picture. Controlling the light on-site is another.

We can control the light with a flash, reflector and/ or diffuser. The top picture shows the subjects sitting in the shade ... too dark against a brighter background. To remedy the situation, I used a flash with a diffuser for what's called daylight fill-in flash photography.

My advice for serious picture makers: Never leave home without a flash, a reflector and a diffuser.

And, hey, you don't have to spend a lot of money on a reflector and diffuser. I have a kit: Rick Sammon's Light Controller and Tote. You can pick it up for around $100.

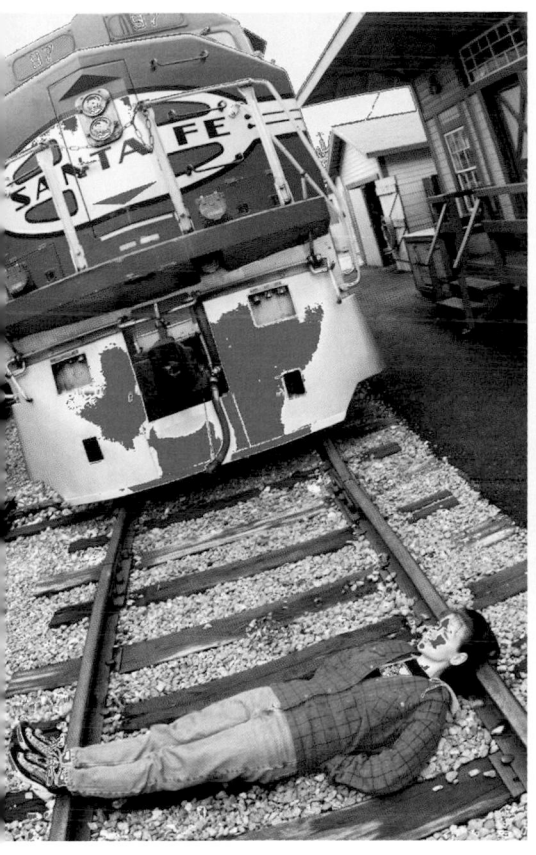 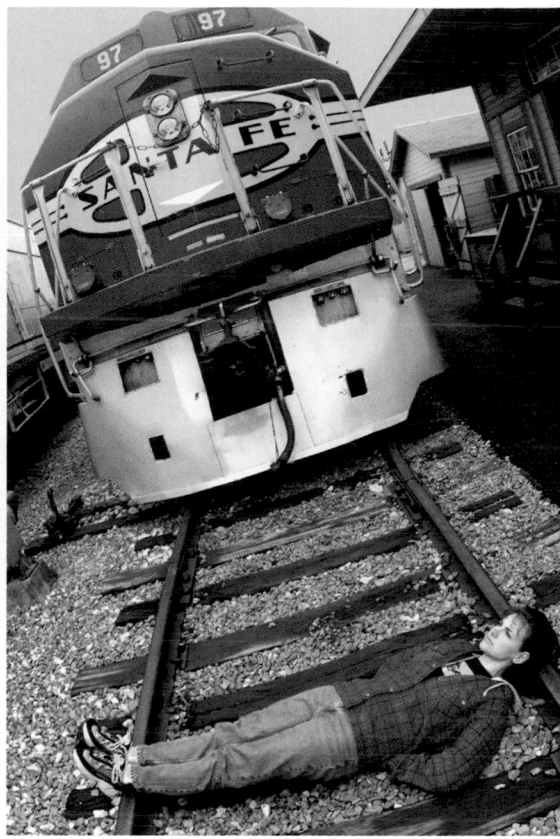

Check Your Exposures

One of the very useful features of digital cameras is the overexposure warning you get on the LCD screen when areas of picture will be overexposed and washed out.

That overexposure warning (not available on all compact cameras, by the way) can save a shot by telling you that you need to reduce the exposure with the exposure compensation (+/-) feature. If the picture is too light and the warning is flashing, reduce the exposure using the - (minus) setting.

The picture on the right is correctly exposed. The picture on the left shows the overexposed areas in red, which usually blink white on a camera's LCD monitor.

Heed the overexposure warning and you'll avoid photo washout.

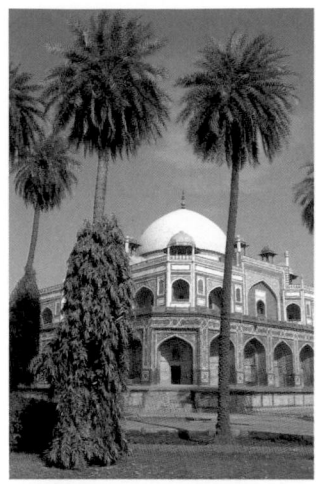
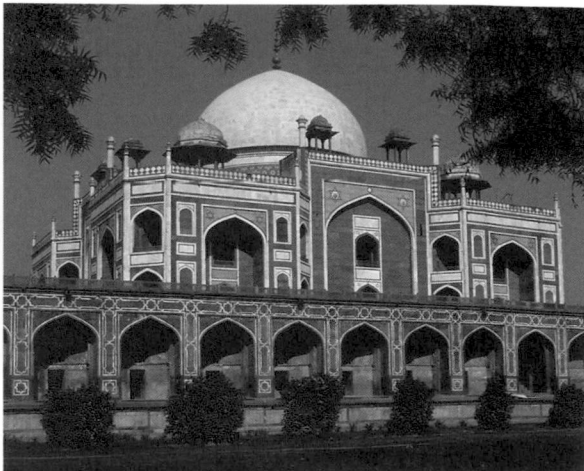
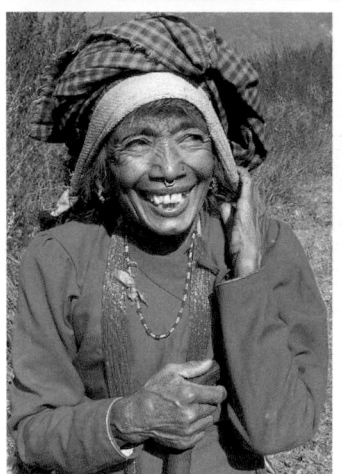
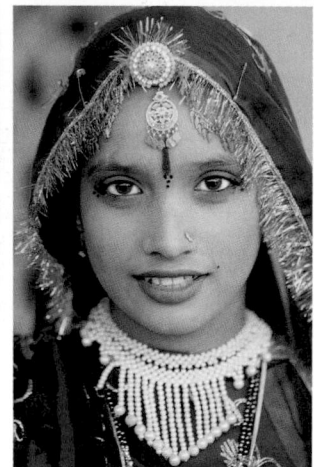
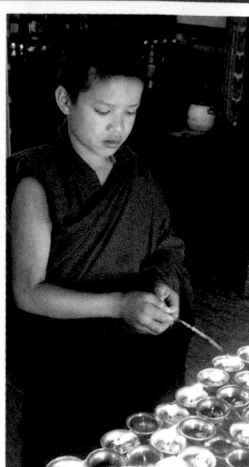

Check Your Camera Settings

Most compact cameras offer dozens of settings: white balance, picture styles, ISO, exposure modes, focus modes, metering modes, etc. Mostly likely, you'll be changing these settings from picture situation to picture situation to get the best possible in-camera photograph.

It's important to constantly check and recheck your camera settings. If you don't, you may get an off-color picture. This is the result of setting the wrong white balance, as illustrated in the picture on the top right.

Or, you may get an oversaturated picture, a black-and-white picture, or a picture with more or less depth-of-field than desired.

Remember: Check those settings!

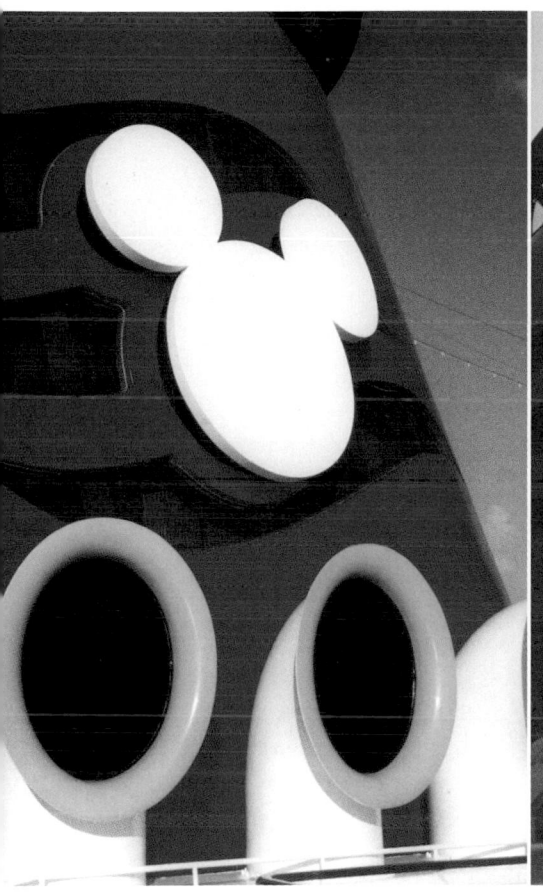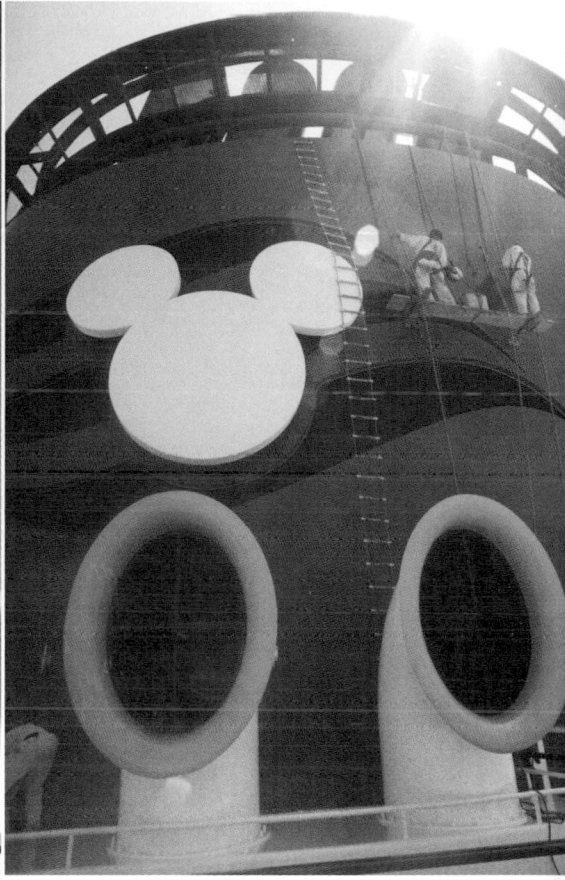

Watch for Lens Flare

Compact cameras don't come with lens hoods. This handy accessory is designed to keep strong, direct light off the lens. When such light hits the lens, it can cause *lens flare*.

On the right is an example of lens flair; it's what happens when direct sunlight hits the lens. That lens flare is the white, washed-out effect at the top right-hand part of the image.

When you are shooting in direct sunlight, be aware of potential lens flare. A simple solution to avoid this detrimental effect is to shade your lens with your hand or hat.

Subtle Lens Flare

Here are two more examples of lens flare. The lens flare (pink glow below the sun) in the sunset picture was unavoidable, because I was shooting directly into the sun. Even so, I still like the shot because it brings back a nice memory.

The lens flare in the red house shot (octagons in the left side of the frame) could have been avoided if I had shielded the lens.

Don't underestimate the importance of checking for lens flare. Clearly, I think this is important; I devoted two pages to the topic!

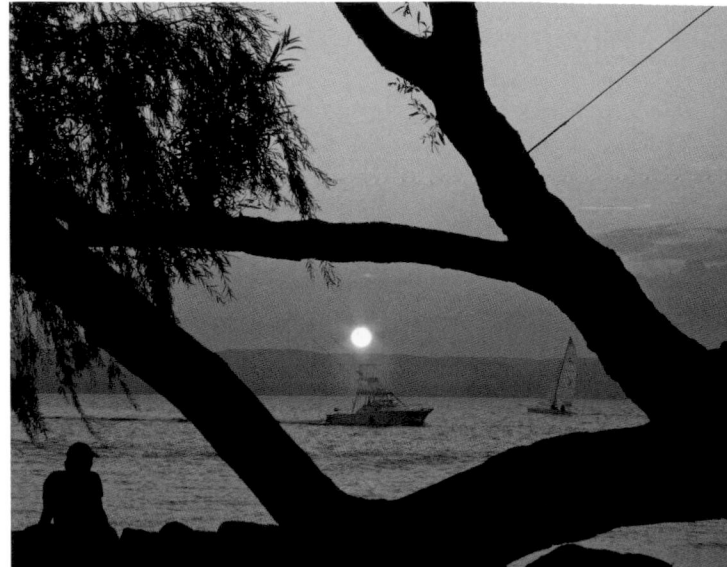

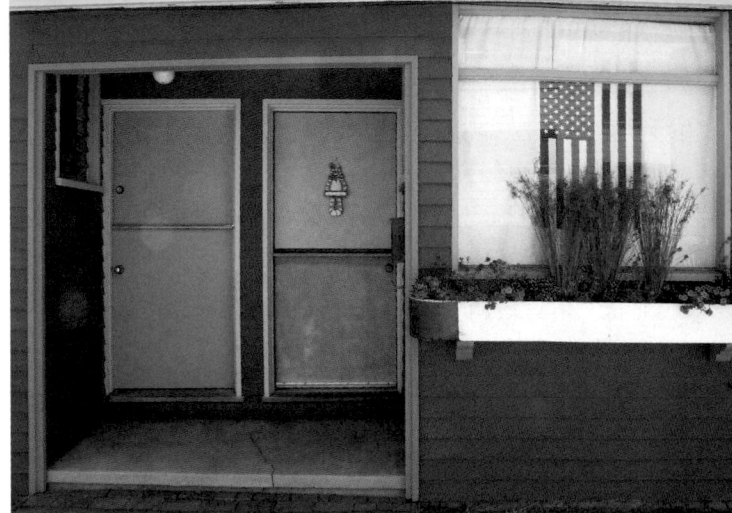

Use Your Radar

When traveling, always keep the "radar" up. This means *looking,* rather than just seeing. It's kinda like the difference between hearing music and listening to it. It changes everything.

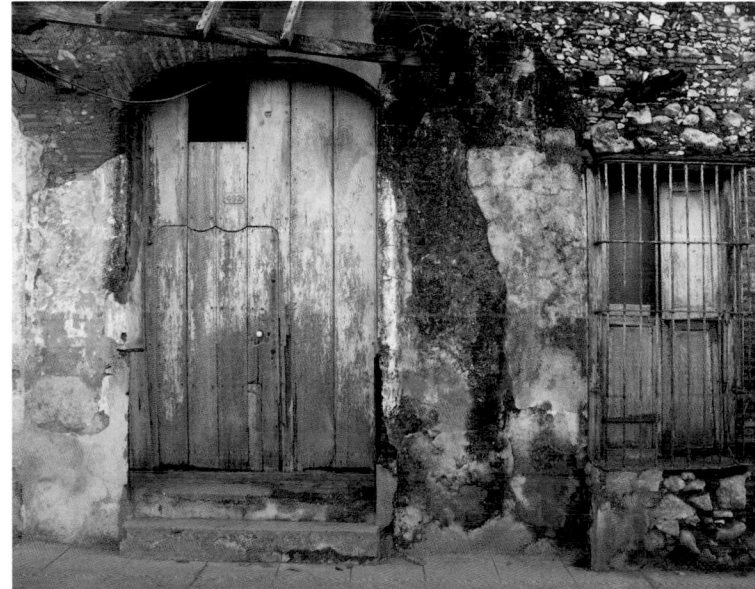

An example: While walking around the streets of Trinidad, Cuba, I noticed this wonderful wall, which made for a nice photo. Shortly after photographing the wall, I moved on. Then, about three minutes later, I noticed a horse-drawn cart coming down the street at a moderate speed. Because my *radar* was up, I saw a potential picture in my mind's eye. The

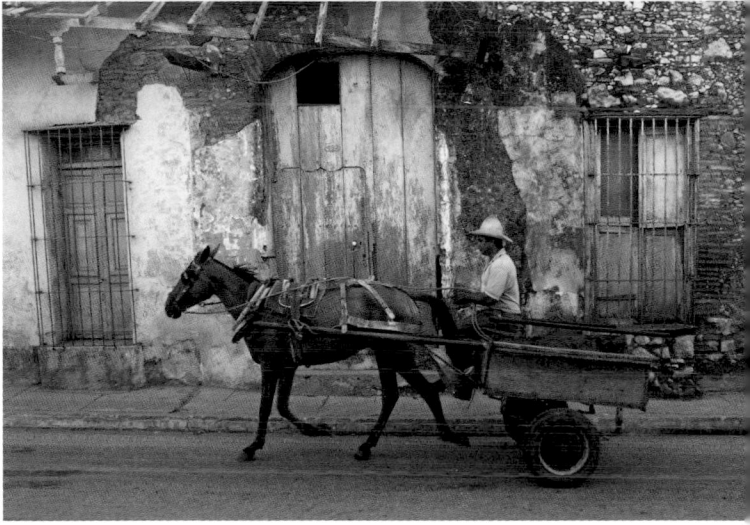

picture was the cart in front of the wonderful wall. I ran back to the wall at top speed and snapped the picture you see here—with my Canon G10 compact camera.

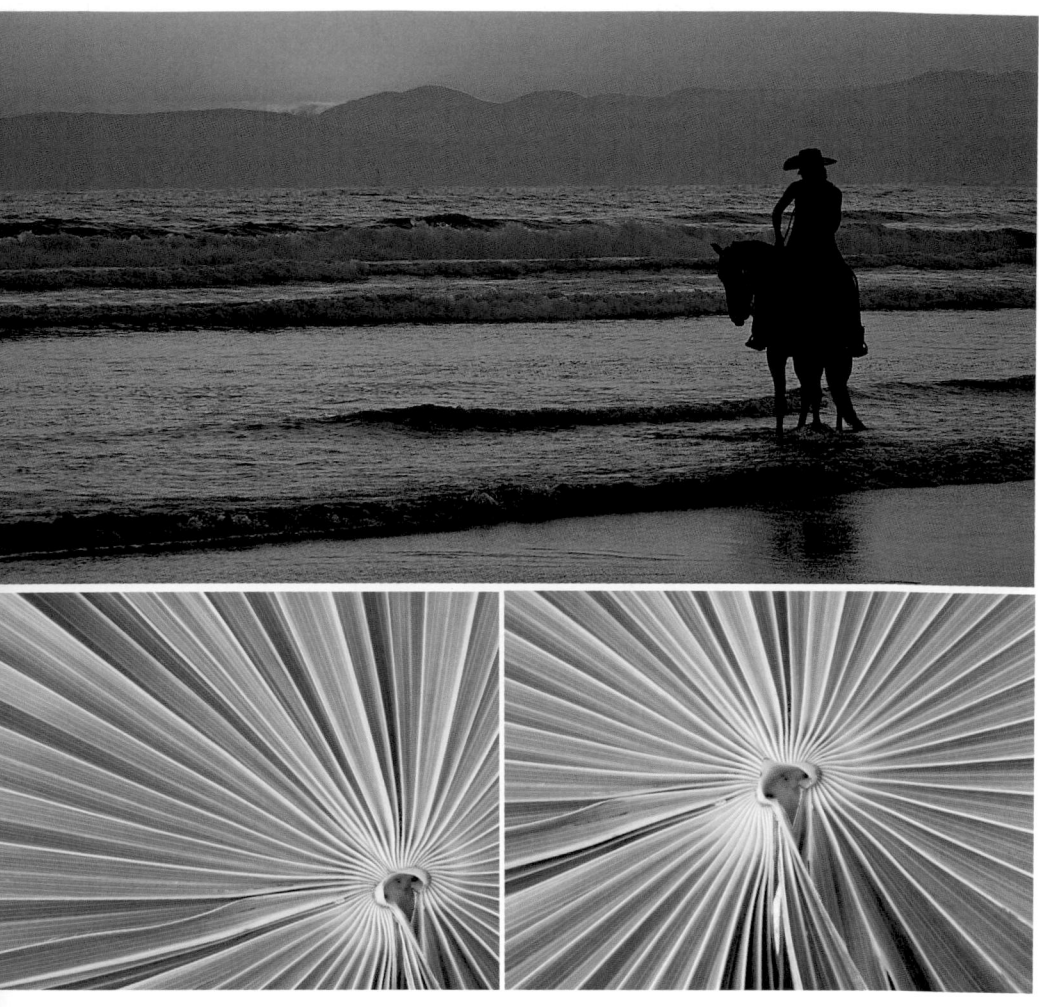

Dead Center is Deadly

When it comes to composition, placing the subject in the dead center of the frame is almost always deadly. It's much better to place the subject off center, as illustrated in the top photograph that I took of a horse and rider at sunset in Los Osos, California.

Compare the bottom two photographs. In one, your eye gets stuck on the main focus point in the center of the frame. In the other, your eye wanders around the frame.

Remember: Dead center is deadly. It's just so booooooring!

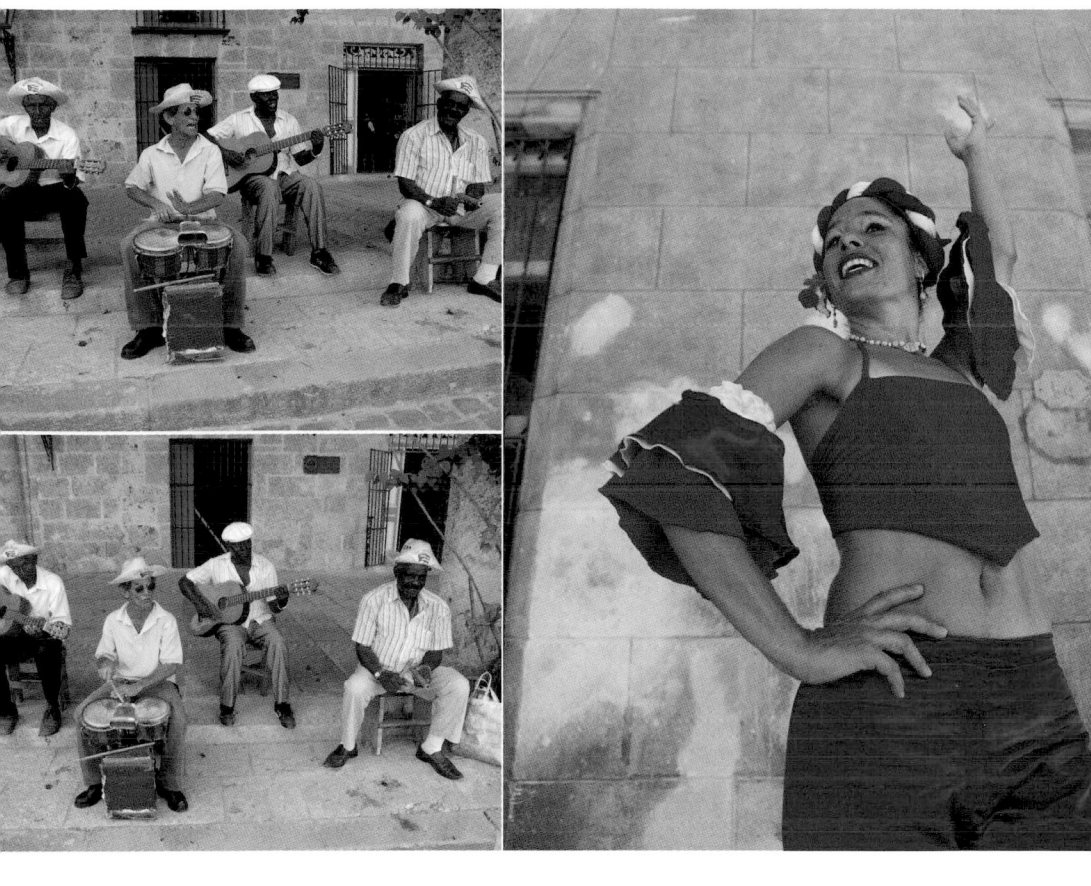

See Eye to Eye

When it comes to photographing people, I almost always try to see eye-to-eye. This means you need to get down (or up) to the subject's level. At eye level, the viewer of your photograph communicates more with your subject.

Compare these two pictures of Cuban musicians. One was taken while I was standing straight up; it looks like a snapshot. The other was taken while I was kneeling; it is a much-improved shot.

Of course, I do break that rule (as many others), as you can see by the picture of the woman performer, who was actually on stilts when I took the shot.

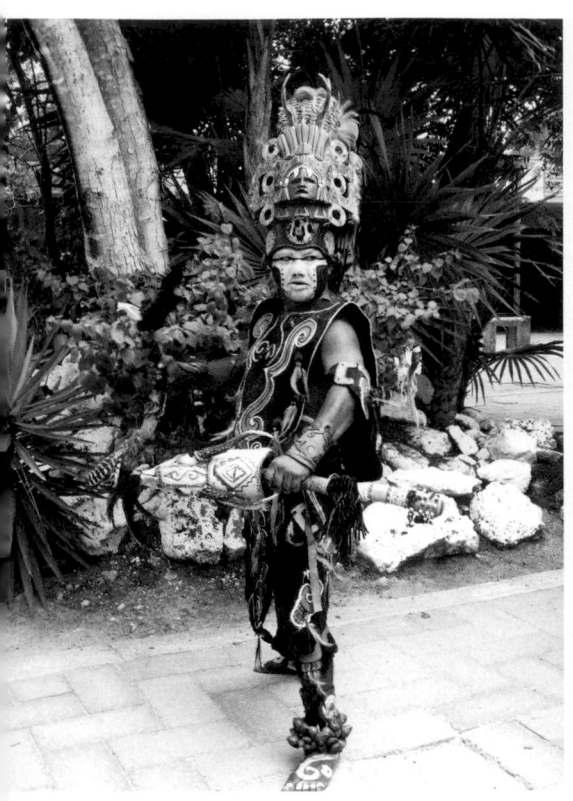 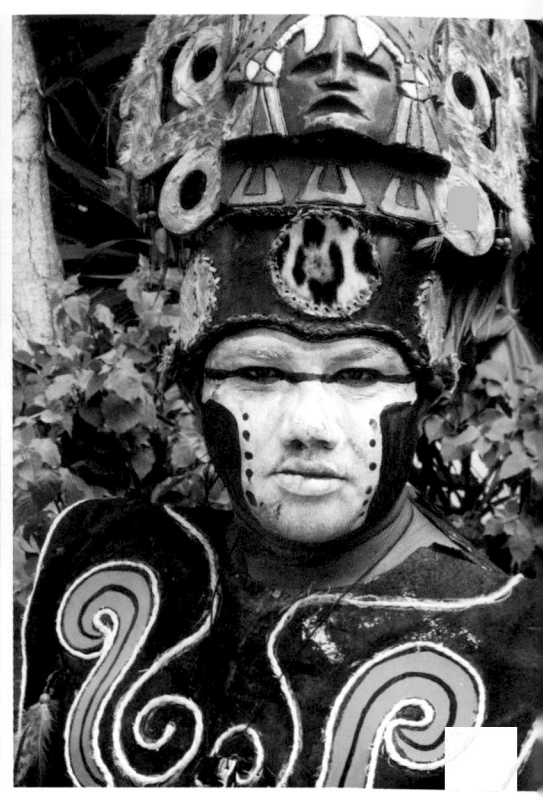

When You Think You Are Close Enough, Move Closer

This tip applies to all types of photography: people, wildlife, landscapes and so on. When you think you are close enough, move in closer. Cut the clutter, and your picture will have more impact.

I photographed this performer at a resort in Mexico. The full-length shot shows the boring location. The headshot could have been taken in a remote Myan village. All I did was move in and zoom closer to fill the frame with what I thought was the most important subject matter: the man's face and headdress.

When You Think You Are Done Shooting, Shoot More

Here's another "when you think" tip. When you think you have the shot, keep shooting. It's quite possible that you'll get an even better shot.

When I was in Cuba, I really wanted to get a nice portrait of this young woman. The posed shot, her pose, is okay… and I thought it was my best keeper. But when she looked up at her dad and gave a smile, I took another shot. That more relaxed shot is my favorite portrait from the impromptu photo sessions.

Keep shooting.

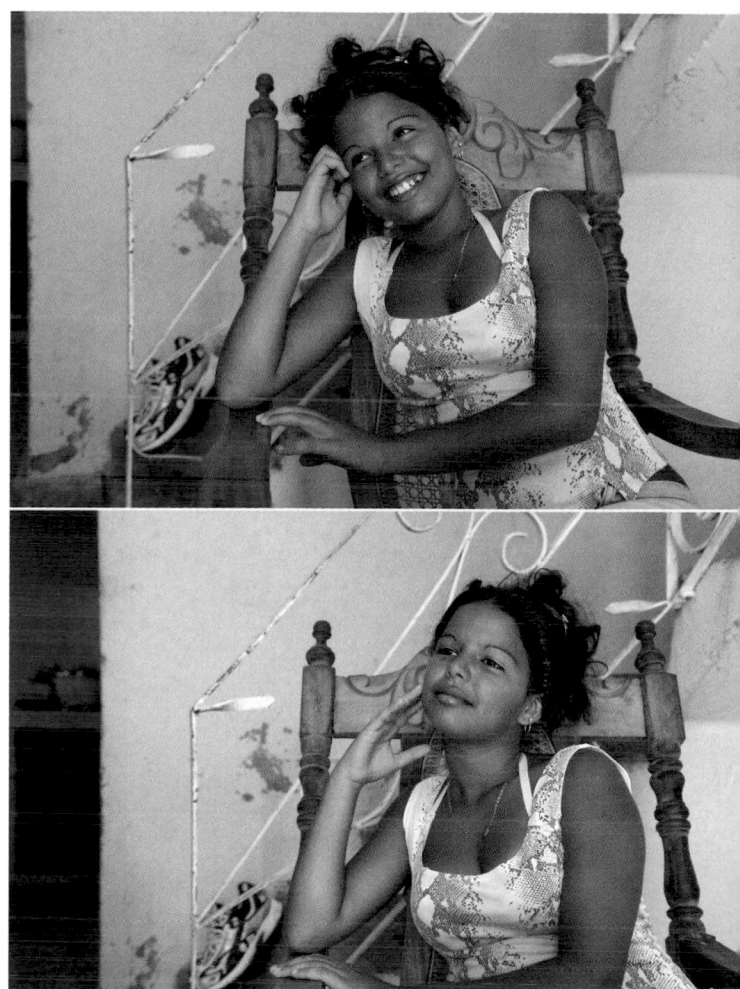

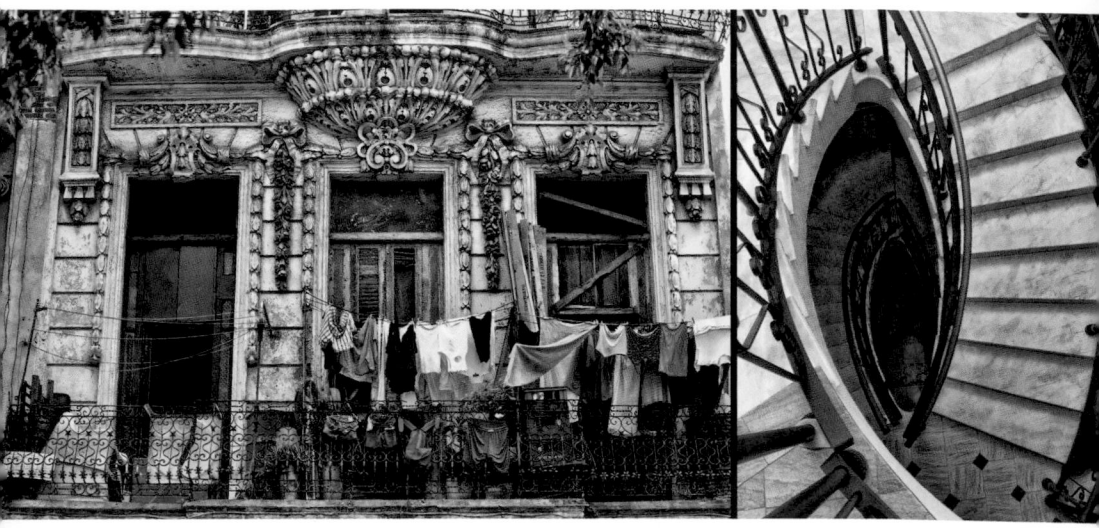

Always Look Up, Always Look Down

Whenever I teach a workshop, one of the basic tips I give is this: Always look up, and always look down. We are usually so focused on a getting a shot that is "right in front of our eyes" that we forget to look around for other pictures—and that includes looking back, too.

Both of these pictures were taken in Cuba. For the picture on the left, I looked up and shot. For the picture on the right, I looked down and shot.

Both of these pictures were enhanced with one of my favorite plug-ins, Topaz Adjust from Topaz Labs (www.toapzlabs.com). At the click of a mouse, Topaz can increase the color saturation and details in a picture. Sure, you could do the same thing in Photoshop Elements, but it would take much longer. Me? I go for the one click!

The Name of the Game is to Fill the Frame

One of the first photo tips I ever learned was, "The name of the game is to fill the frame." In other words, you want to fill the frame with interesting subjects and avoid dead (boring) space.

The top picture illustrates this technique. The bottom picture, the first shot I took in the set, has too much dead space on the right side of the image. To fill that space, I asked the hansom cab driver to pull his rig into the scene.

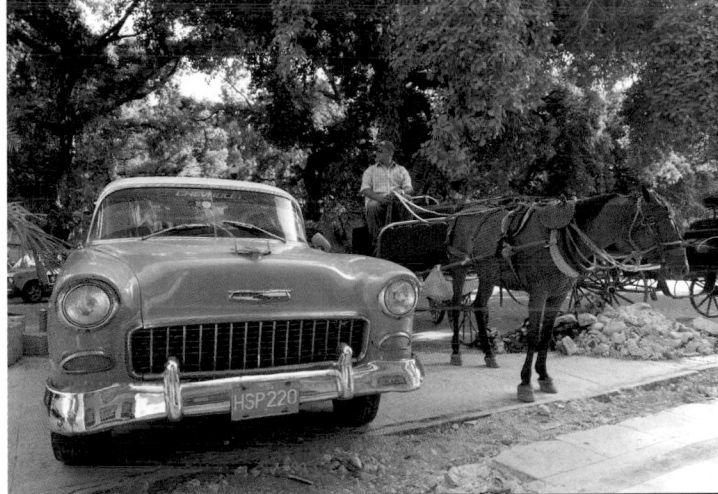

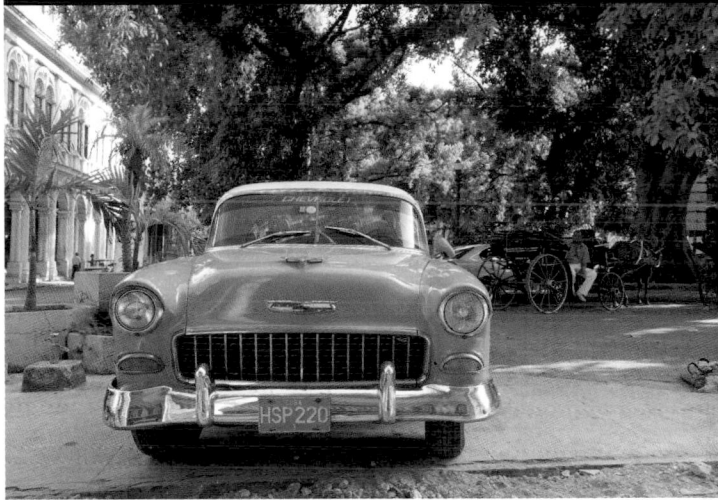

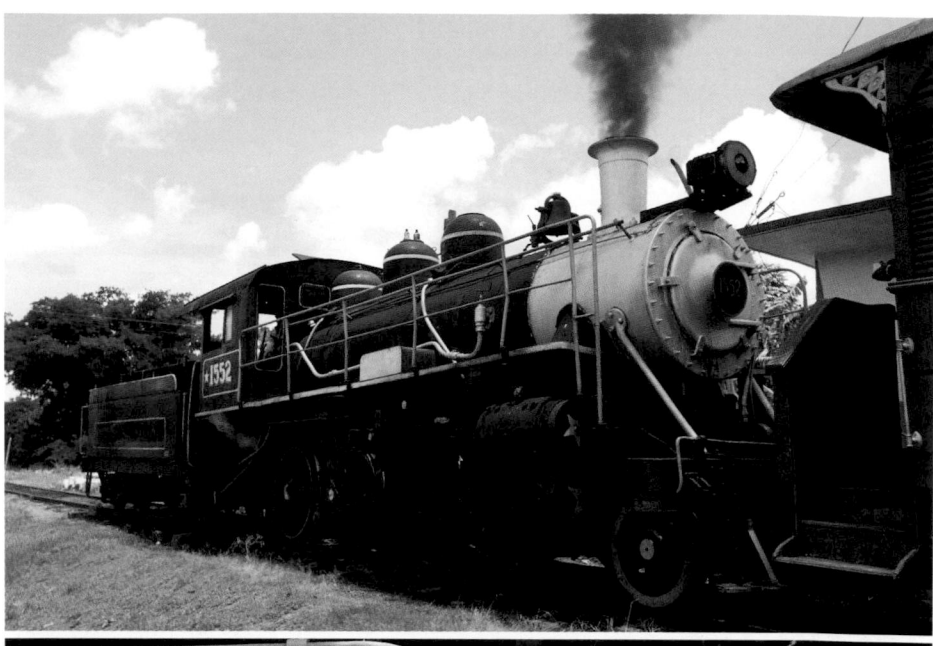

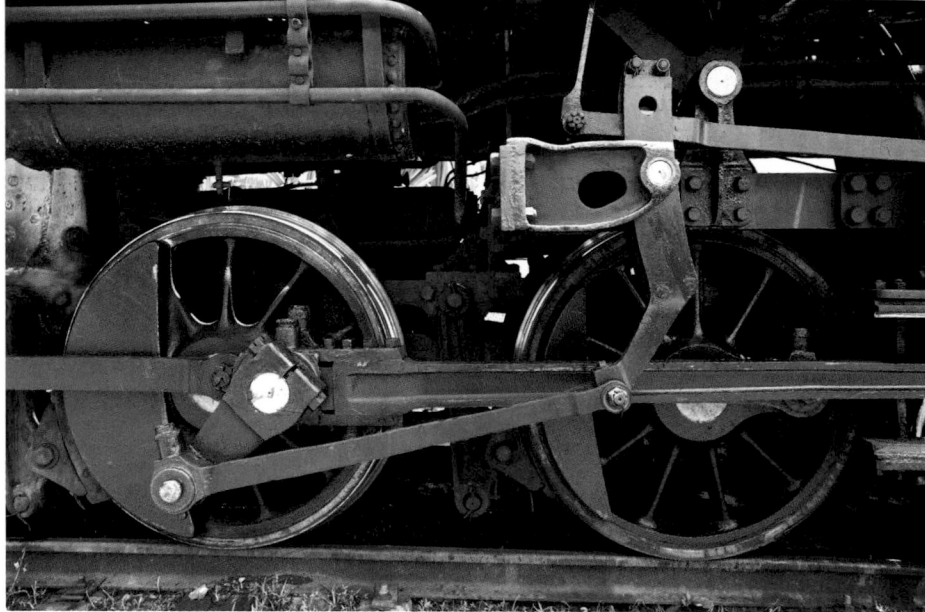

Don't Forget the Details

When you are out photographing, don't forget to capture the details of a large subject, as I did here when photographing this steam engine in Cuba. As illustrated in the bottom image, details help to tell the story of subject, and they add interest.

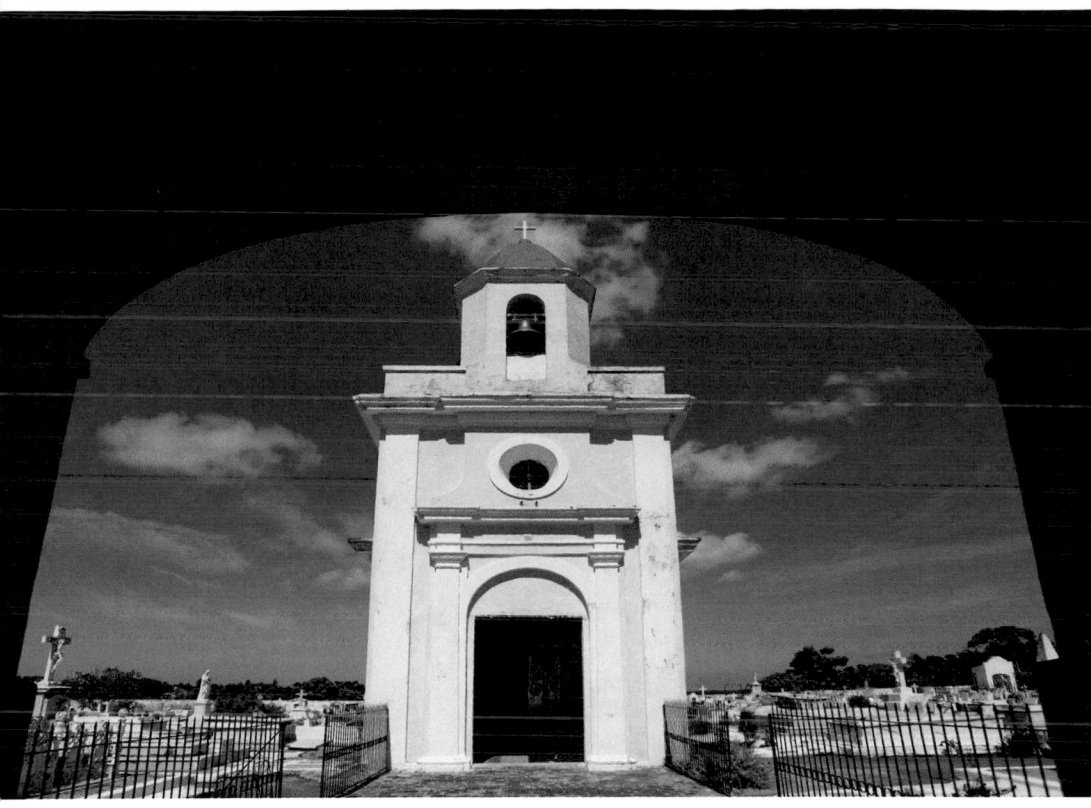

Frame It

When we frame a subject, we give viewers a special vantage for viewing a subject. Framing a scene also adds a sense of depth and dimension to a photograph, and it gives the viewer the feeling of "being there."

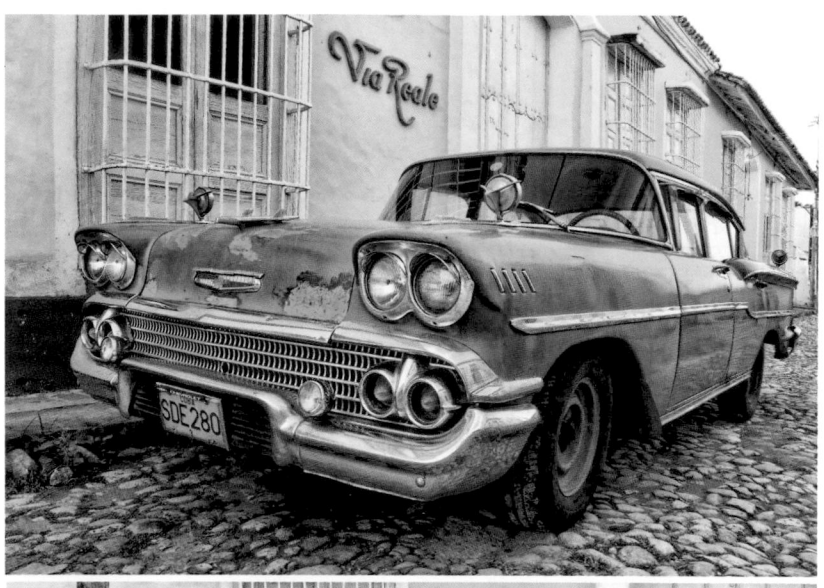

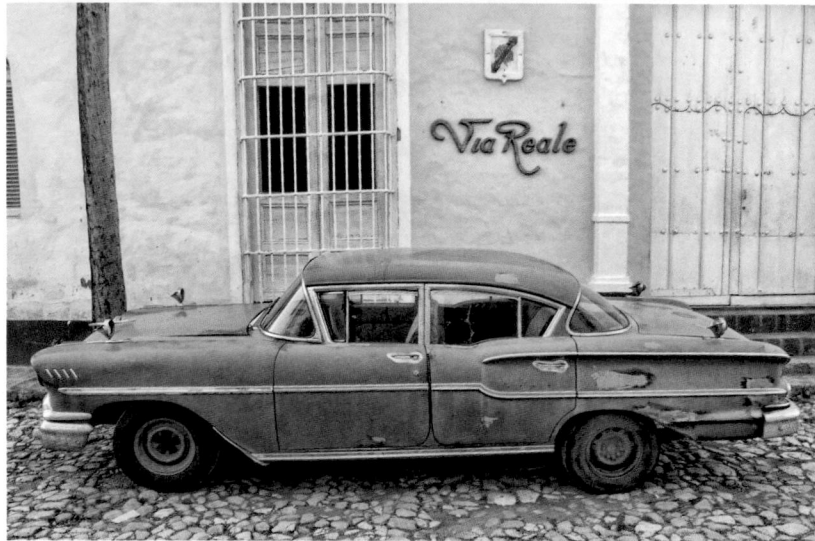

Don't Just Stand There

Most novice photographers take their pictures while standing straight up. That's okay for some shots, but it gets old pretty fast.

By simply varying your shooting height, you can turn a snapshot into a great shot, as illustrated here. Getting closer often helps, too.

Both of these pictures were enhanced with Topaz Adjust from Topaz Labs (www.toapzlabs.com). It's one of my favorite plug-ins.

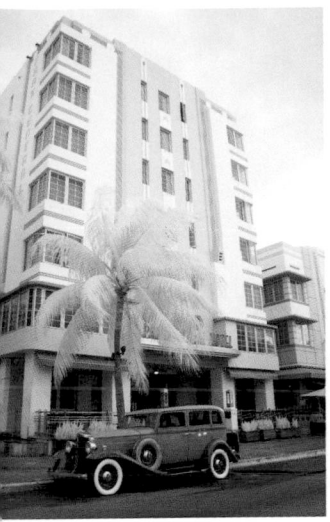 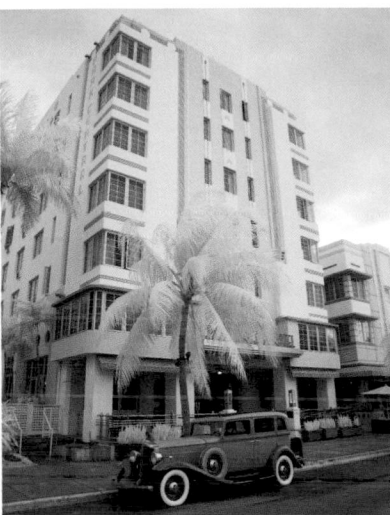 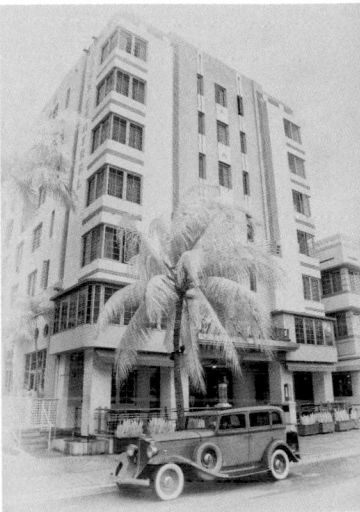

Do It In the Digital Darkroom

Previously, I mentioned Ansel Adams. One of the things he is most famous for is envisioning the end result. In his case, it was the print. In our case, it's the digital file for printing or sharing.

When you are out shooting, think about the creative possibilities that await you in the digital darkroom.

I took the original picture on the left in Miami's famed South Beach with my infrared camera. The picture in the middle is one variation, created by playing with and swapping the colors in Photoshop Elements. The picture on the right is yet another version, created with the Antique Plate filter in Nik Software's (www.niksoftware. com) Silver Efex Pro plug-in.

If you need some digital darkroom inspiration, check out www.pluginexperience.com. And of course, check out the section on Photoshop Elements later in this book.

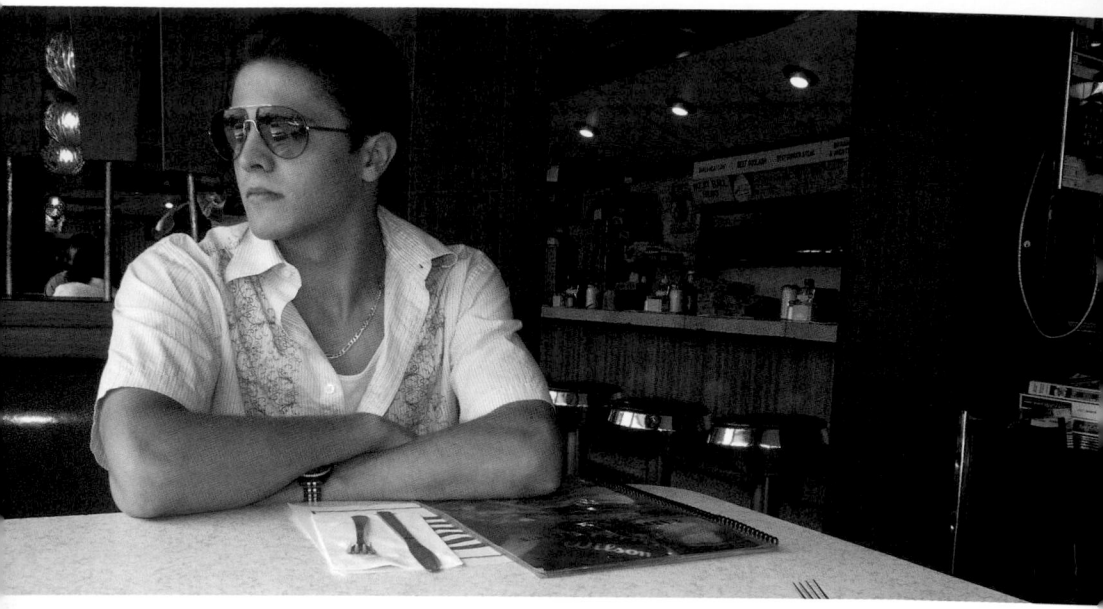

Look for Pictures within a Picture

Here's a fun and creative exercise: Look for pictures within a picture.

It's easy to spot the original image here, which I took of my son, Marco, at the "Goodfellas" diner in Queens, New York. Yes, he is trying to look like Ray Liotta. And yes, it's just a quick snapshot.

As usual, the first thing I do when I open a picture in Photoshop Elements is to experiment with cropping. I like to use this tool to improve the picture and to see if there are any pictures within the picture.

My first try at cropping is the HD wide-format image you see here. It's my favorite. However, I also like the tighter shot that shows the American flag placemat more prominently in the image. And of course, I don't think the original shot is that bad.

Have fun playing with cropping, and you may be surprised at the pictures you find within pictures.

P.S. Cropping is VERY subjective. You don't have to agree with me on my favorite choice. But if you don't, I'll be giving Ray a call …

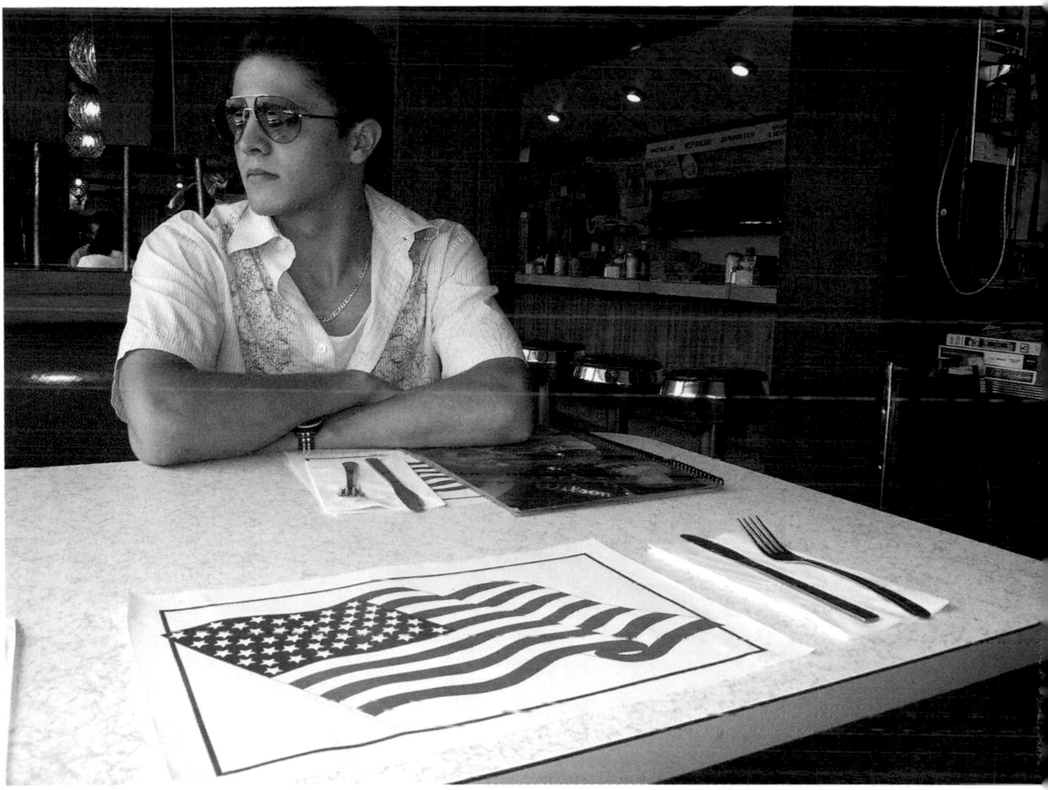

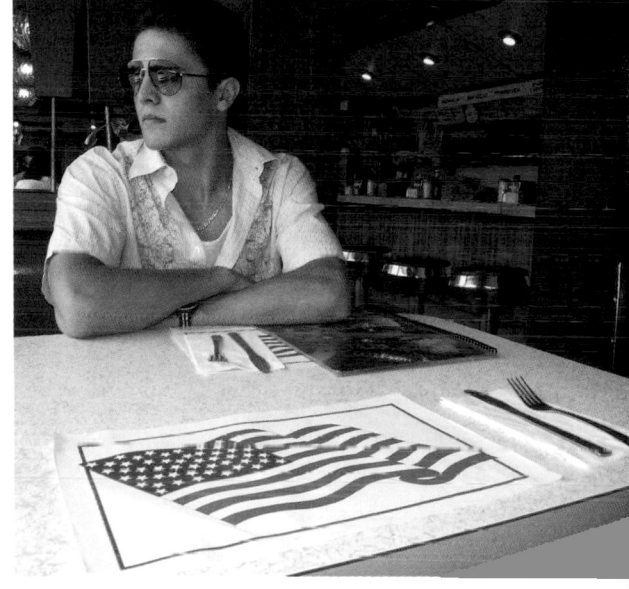

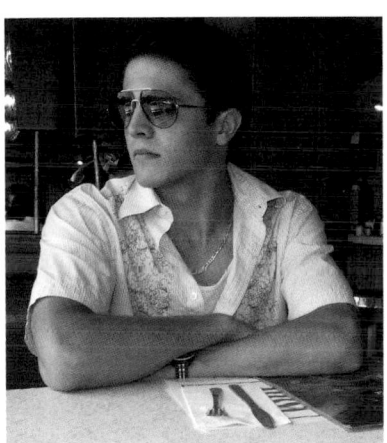

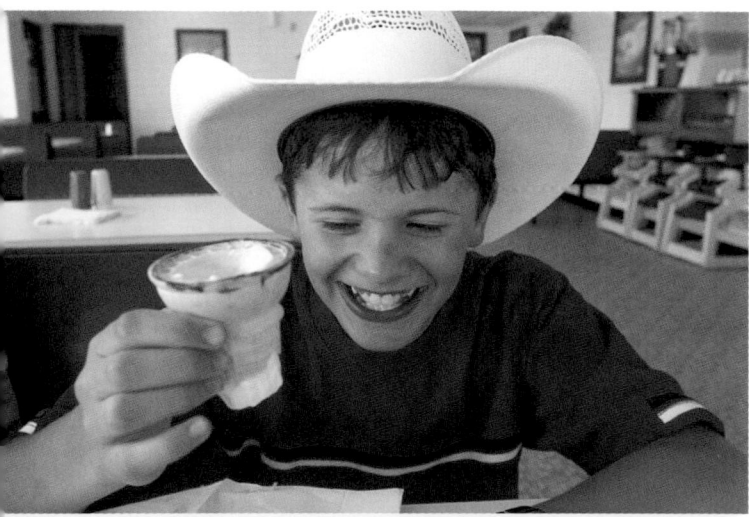

Be Ready for Fun ... and the Not So Fun

Perhaps the coolest thing about a compact camera is that you are always ready to capture the fun, as I did when my son, Marco, was enjoying the ice cream dripping out of a cone on a family vacation.

However, here's the thing: You gotta have your camera with you at all times. Compact cameras are small enough to fit in a pocket or purse. So if you actually carry one with you, it'll be there for you to record the fun ... as well as the not so fun.

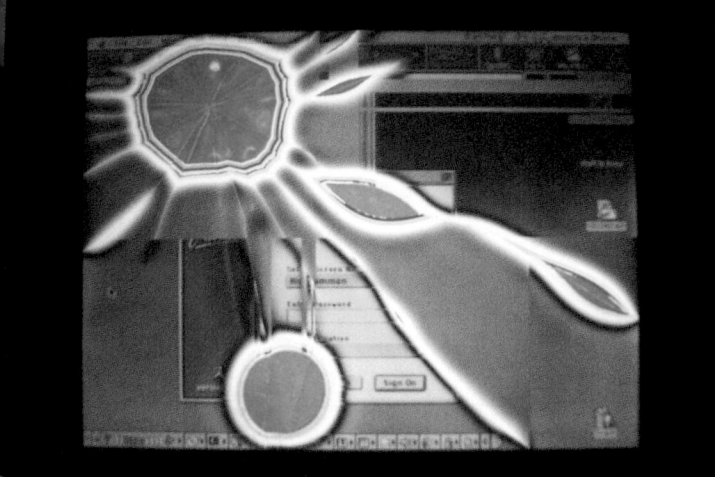

I took the picture on the bottom during the first night of one of my China workshops. It's a shot of my laptop screen, which somehow got cracked during the trip from New York to Beijing. It's a not-so-fun memory, but the photo is a good example of why it's important to pack your laptop very, very carefully.

Get in the habit of always having your camera handy. Always.

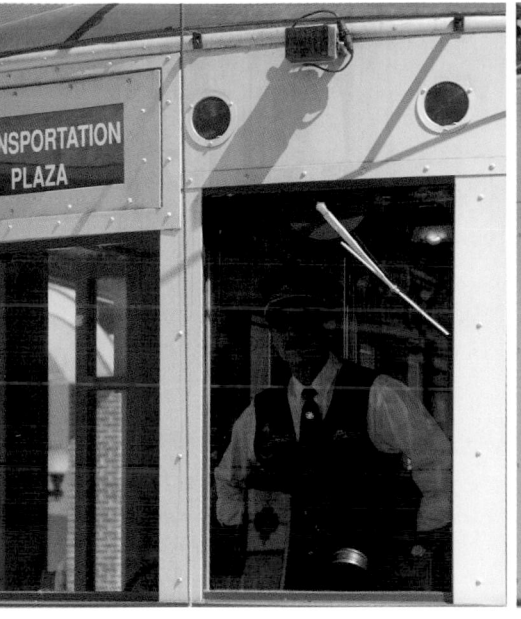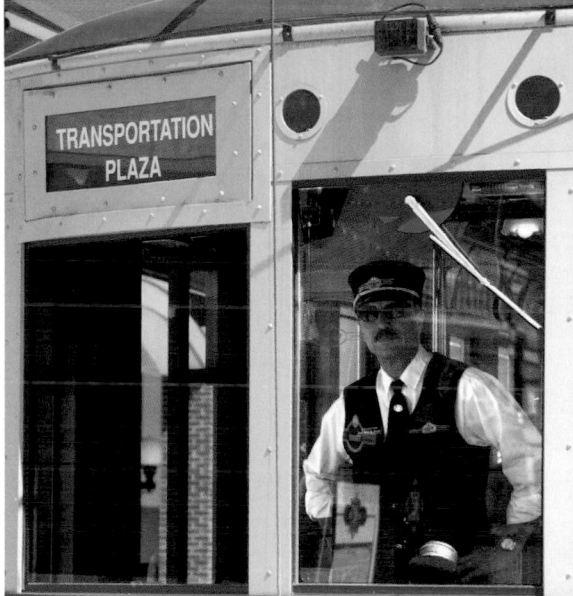

RAW Rules

Some compact cameras shoot RAW files in addition to JPEG files. If you want the most out of your picture-making experience, shoot RAW files. They have a wider exposure range than JPEGs. This means that your exposure can be "off" a bit and you can still get a good image in the end.

What's more, because RAW files have more information than JPEG files, you can pull out more from the shadows and tone down the highlights.

I rescued the shadow area of my trolley car picture quickly and easily in Photoshop Elements—mostly because I was working with a RAW file.

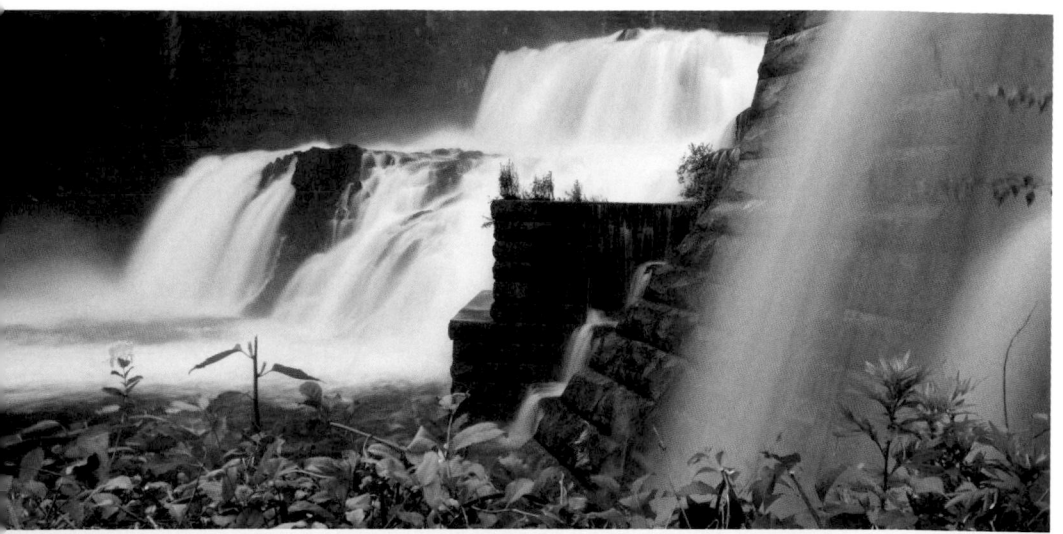

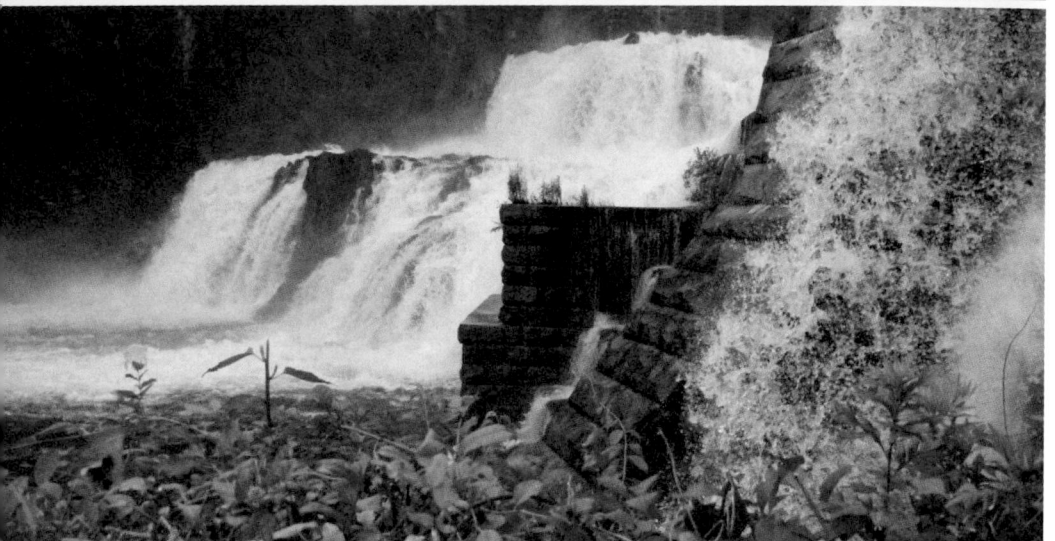

Make Pictures, Don't Just Take Pictures

Throughout this chapter, I've talked about *making* pictures as opposed to simply taking pictures. That's because there is a big difference between the two.

By creatively using your camera controls, you can turn a snapshot, like the boring photo on the bottom, into a much more creative image, like the photograph on the top. To make that picture, all I did was switch the shutter speed from 1/500 second to 1/30 second—after switching the ISO from 800 to 100 and mounting the camera on a tripod.

Always Carry a Camera

Here's perhaps the most important tip in this chapter … and maybe even the book: Always carry a camera! You just never know when a photo opportunity will present itself to you.

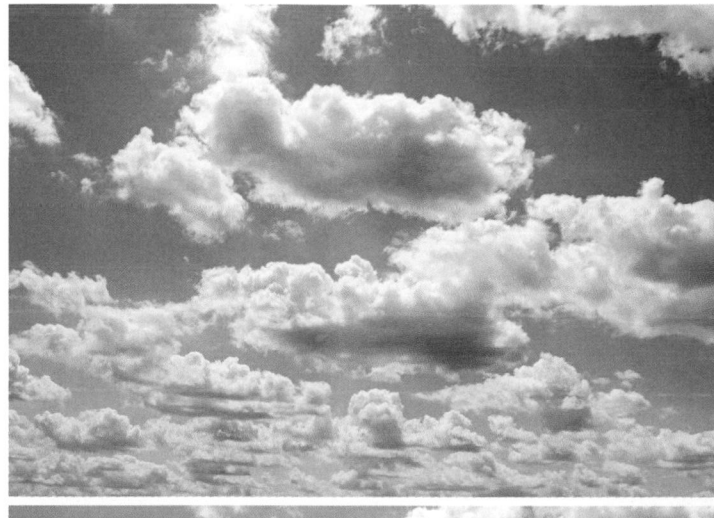

For example, I took the bottom photograph at O'Hare International Airport while waiting for a flight. I don't like that shot, but I do like the cropped and enhanced image that shows only the clouds. It's a soft and peaceful image.

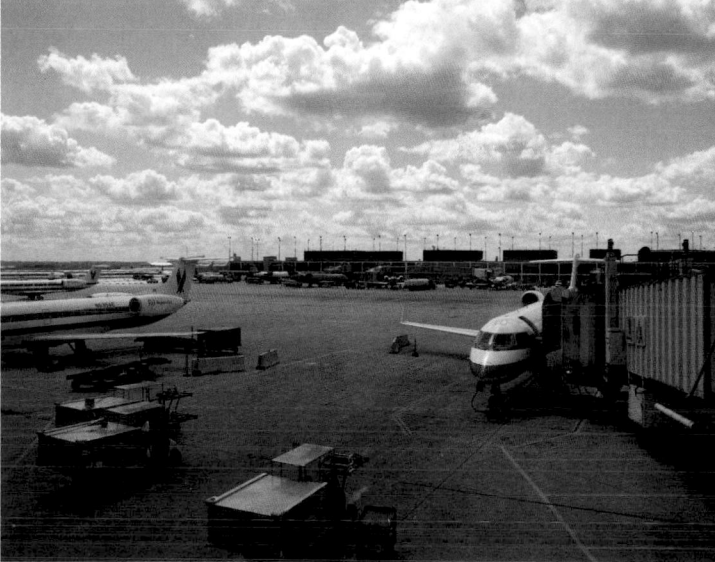

Always carry a camera, and you won't miss out on fun pictures and fun memories … although waiting for my delayed flight was really no fun at all.

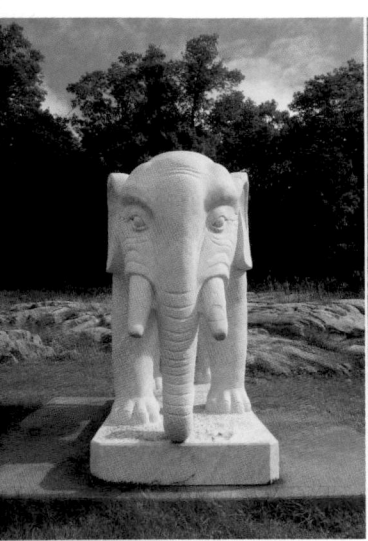 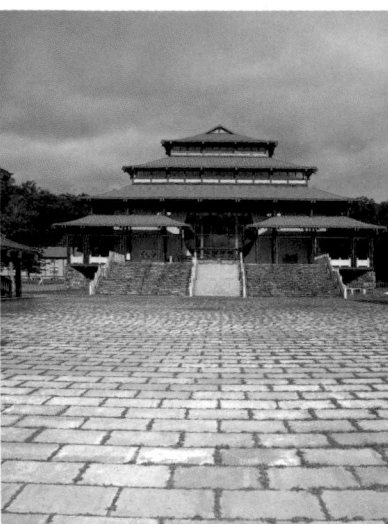 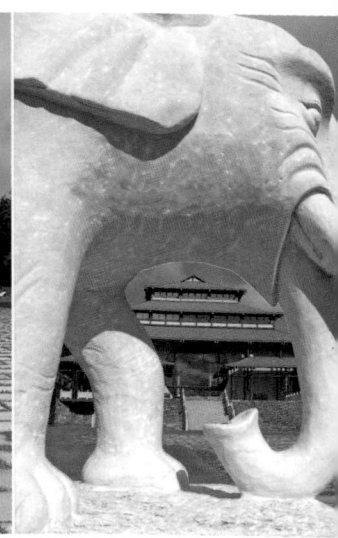

Don't Get Stuck

The middle and left pictures show interesting subjects, but the pictures themselves are boring. The picture on the right shows the same subjects pictured in one photograph. The boring aspect of the first two pictures is gone.

In the combined picture, our eyes look and move around the frame at the different objects in the scene. In the other two pictures, our eyes get stuck on the subject.

When you are composing a picture, if your eyes get stuck on a subject, your picture will probably be boring to viewers—and who wants to be boring?!

All Together Now

A successful photograph is the result of many elements coming together at precisely the right time. The elements that came together for this photograph were:

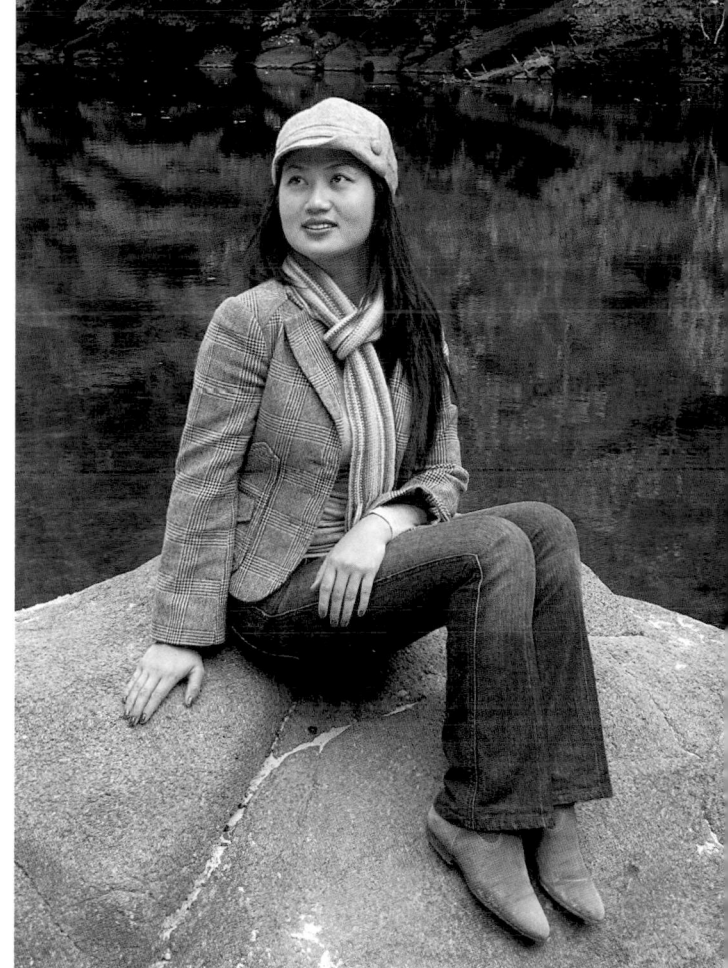

- Great location, which was scouted in advance

- Carefully chosen, plain background with no distracting objects

- Calm water, thanks to a windless day

- Nice light created by an overcast sky

- Visually appealing subject that was enhanced with a nice outfit

- Nice pose created by the subject following directions

- Good composition accomplished by not placing the subject's head dead center in the frame

- Good rapport with the subject, established in advance by making the photo session fun!

- Bit 'o luck, because all of the aforementioned elements came together

Now it's your turn. The next time you have a photo session, consider all the elements you need to make a nice photograph. And make sure they come together!

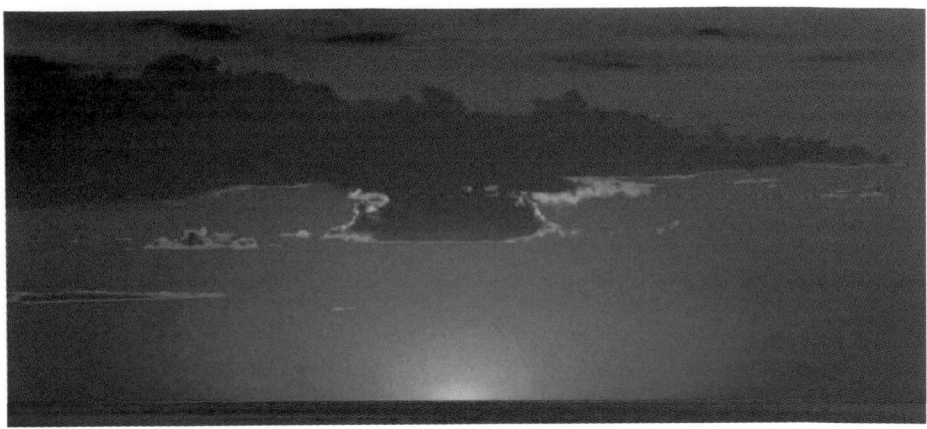

Develop Understanding

In closing this chapter, I'll share my favorite photo philosophy with you, because I think it is a very important concept for your quest to make good pictures. Perhaps, it's the most important tip in this chapter ... or even this book.

Here goes:

I hear, I forget.
I see, I remember.
I do, I understand.

In other words, you will "hear" a lot while you are reading this book, and you will probably forget some of this stuff. You will see a lot of pictures, which I hope will help you remember my tips.

Yet the real magic of photography comes when you go out and take pictures. When you just do it. That is when you understand ... and when you can have a ton of fun photographing and being creative without thinking too much about the technical side of photography.

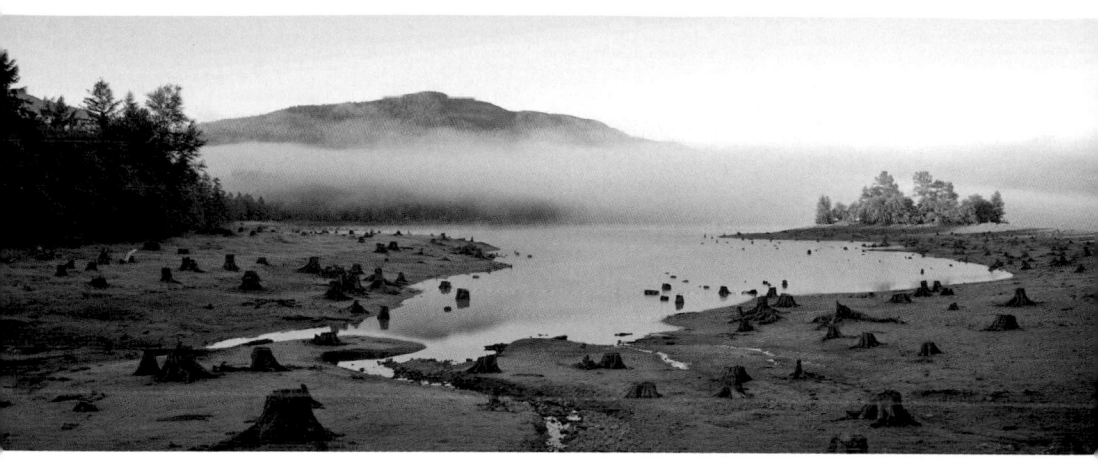

Part IV

Light: The Main Subject in Every Photograph

At first, what I am about to say will probably sound boring, but don't jump ahead. Technically, it's interesting and very important to know. So here goes: Every photograph in this book has the same main subject. That subject is *light*. No light…no photograph.

In this chapter we'll explore light—that is, how to see the light, control light during the picture-taking process, and play with the light in Photoshop Elements. When you understand these three steps, you'll make better pictures and avoid some of the common mistakes of novice photographers.

So before moving on, consider this: Famed filmmaker Orson Welles said, "You have to see a movie three times to see everything that is there."

With that, be forewarned that you may see the same lighting tip more than once in this book. It means that I really want you to "get it."

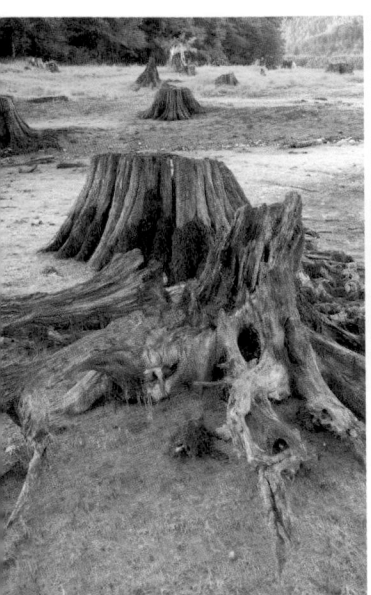 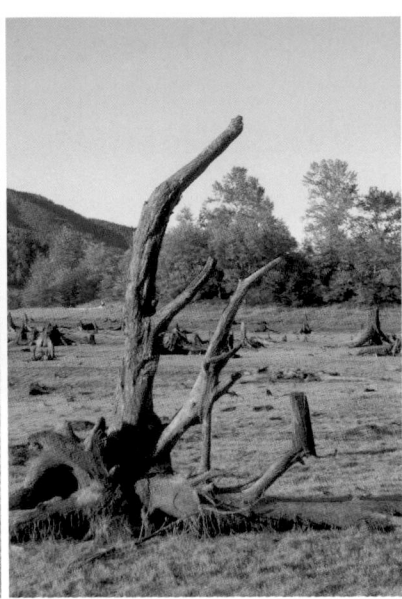 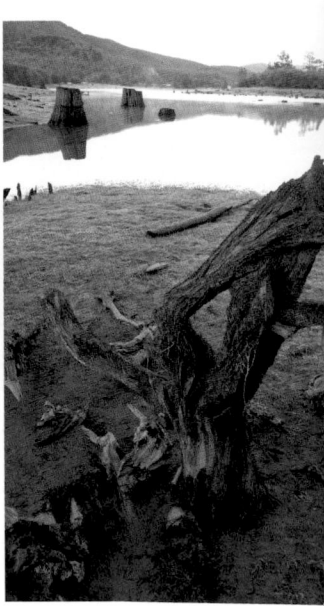

What Our Eyes See vs. What Our Cameras See

Our eyes have a dynamic range (difference in brightness levels) of about 11 f-stops. Compact cameras can only "see" a dynamic range of about five f-stops. Knowing that, you will not be disappointed when a picture of a high-contrast scene—one with dark shadows and bright highlights—does not look the same way on your camera's LCD monitor as it does to your eyes.

Here are examples of scenes that illustrate (from left to right): low contrast, strong contrast (nice contrast) and too much contrast.

Unless you are doing HDR photography, discussed later, you want to either: a) avoid shooting in high-contrast situations, or b) control the light with a reflector, flash or diffuser.

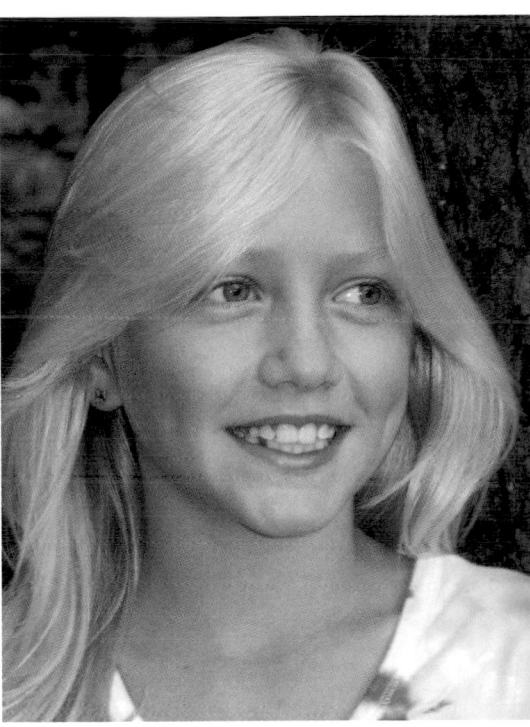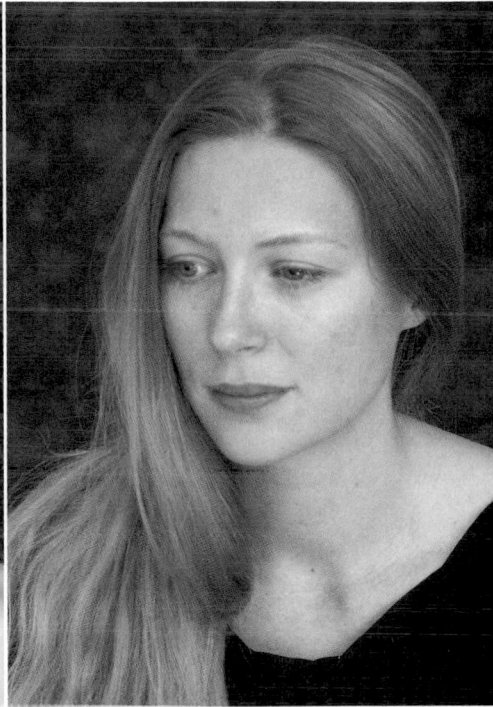

Scene Brightness and ISO Settings

To the untrained eye, subtle differences in light levels are hard to detect, although we do know and can see the difference between a bright scene and a dark scene. So just knowing that differences in light levels are sometimes too subtle to see at a glance, photographers need to change the ISO setting to accommodate the lighting conditions.

Set the ISO low when shooting in bright conditions, as illustrated by the outdoor picture on the left, and set it higher when shooting indoors in low-light conditions, as illustrated by the picture on the right.

This is especially important when it comes to compact cameras, because you always want to shoot at the lowest possible ISO for the cleanest possible, hand-held shot. That ISO may be 400 or higher indoors, but if you can use ISO 200, you will get less digital noise (which degrades image quality) in your picture.

Outdoors on a sunny day, you can probably shoot at ISO 80 or 100.

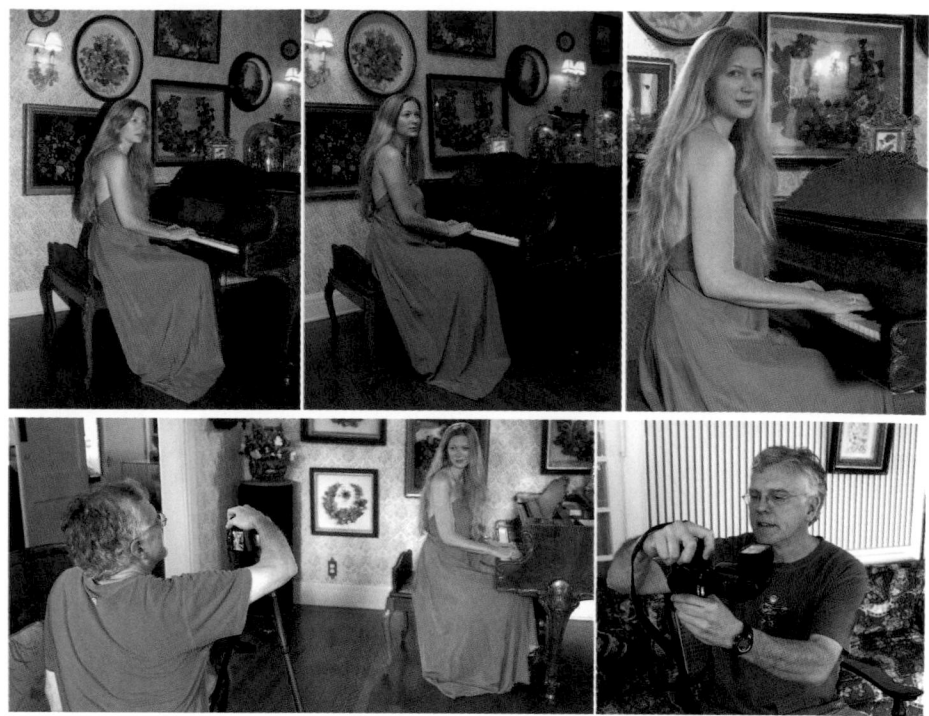

Photographing People Indoors in Low Light

When photographing people indoors in low light, you have a few options, illustrated from left to right in the top row of pictures.

One, you can set your camera to the Program mode and use the built-in flash, which will create a harsh shadow behind and next to your subject. I am sure you don't want that kind of amateurish picture.

Two, you can set your camera to the Av (aperture priority) mode, turn on all the room lights, boost your ISO to 200, set your camera on a tripod, and ask the subject to hold very still. Boosting the ISO even higher might enable you to take a hand-held shot, but your picture will have some visible digital noise—because, remember, noise shows up more in low-light situations.

Three, you can turn on all the room lights, set your camera on a tripod, set the ISO to 200 (or high), select the manual mode, dial in the correct exposure, attach an accessory flash with a swivel head, and "bounce" the light off the ceiling. Yes, much better …

Model: Chandler Strange photographed at the Alexander Hamilton House in Croton-on-Hudson, New York.

Behind-the-scenes pictures, illustrating these techniques, were shot by Susan Sammon.

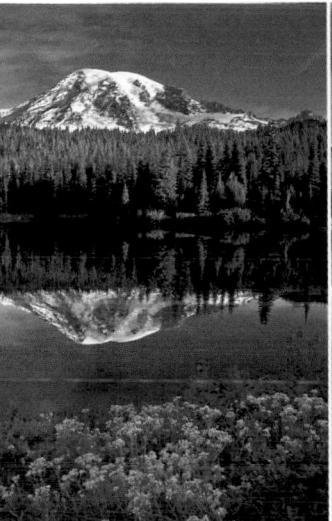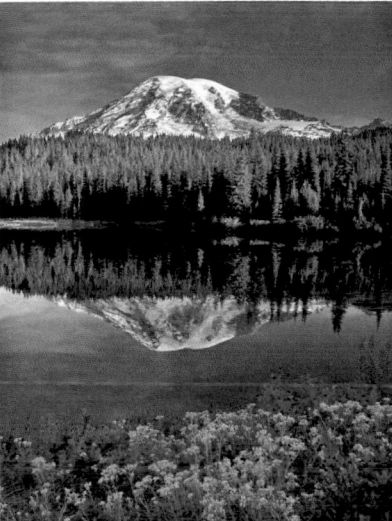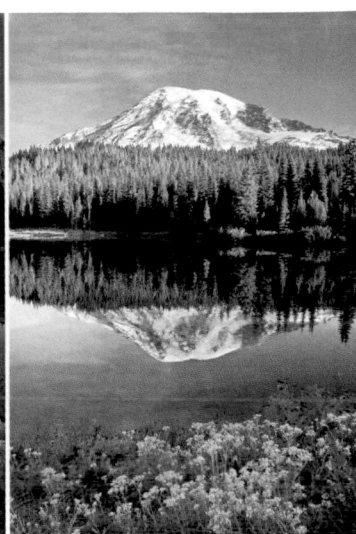

Reducing and Increasing the Light

With most compact cameras, there are two ways to reduce or increase the amount of light that reaches the image sensor.

The easiest way is to use the +/- EV (exposure compensation) control when shooting in one of the automatic modes. Set the EV to +1 to increase the light and make the scene brighter. Set the EV to -1 to decrease the light and make the scene darker.

Sometimes it's necessary to reduce or increase the light to get the shot you want. Sometimes it's a personal choice. In general though, you want to decrease the light when you think a bright area of an image may be overexposed. An example of this is the snow on the mountaintop in the middle picture. Or, you may want to decrease the light for a dramatic effect, as illustrated by the picture on the left.

The only time you want to use the + setting is when photographing at the beach or in the snow, when most of the scene is white. This situation fools the camera's meter into thinking that the scene is brighter than it really is, resulting in underexposure. On the other hand, if you overexpose a scene, it may look flat and even out of focus, as illustrated by the picture on the right.

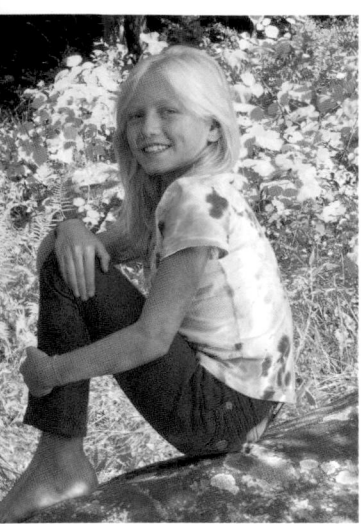 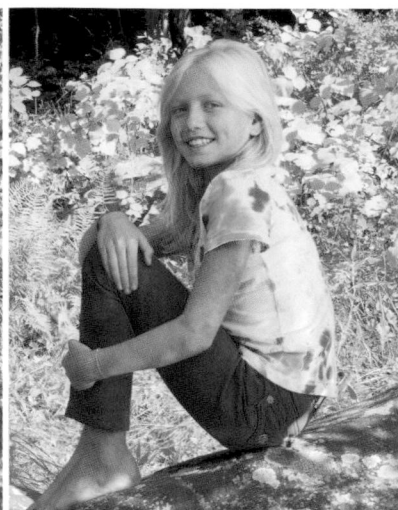 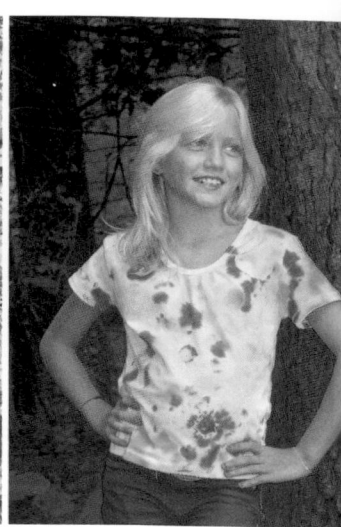

More on Increasing the Light

The +/- control on your camera is actually one of the most useful tools on a compact camera. You use it to fine-tune your exposures. But it's important to know that it can't always do the job of getting you a good exposure. That's why we're continuing to explore this topic.

The girl's face in the picture on the left is too dark, due to the brighter background. Using the +/- control to increase the exposure would make her face lighter, as illustrated by the picture in the middle. But that also increases the brightness of the background, making it look even more overexposed than it is.

A better choice in this case would be to find a place in the shade to shoot, as illustrated by the picture on the right.

Contrast and Outdoor People Pictures

High contrast is a killer for people pictures, because it creates strong and unflattering shadows on a subject's face, as illustrated by the top left picture. We can reduce and even eliminate those shadows with a little photo know-how. Here it is:

Top right: I used a reflector, held opposite to the position of the sun, to fill in the shadows.

Bottom left: I used a diffuser, held between the sun and the subject to reduce the contrast range. (See next page for diffuser-positioning tips.)

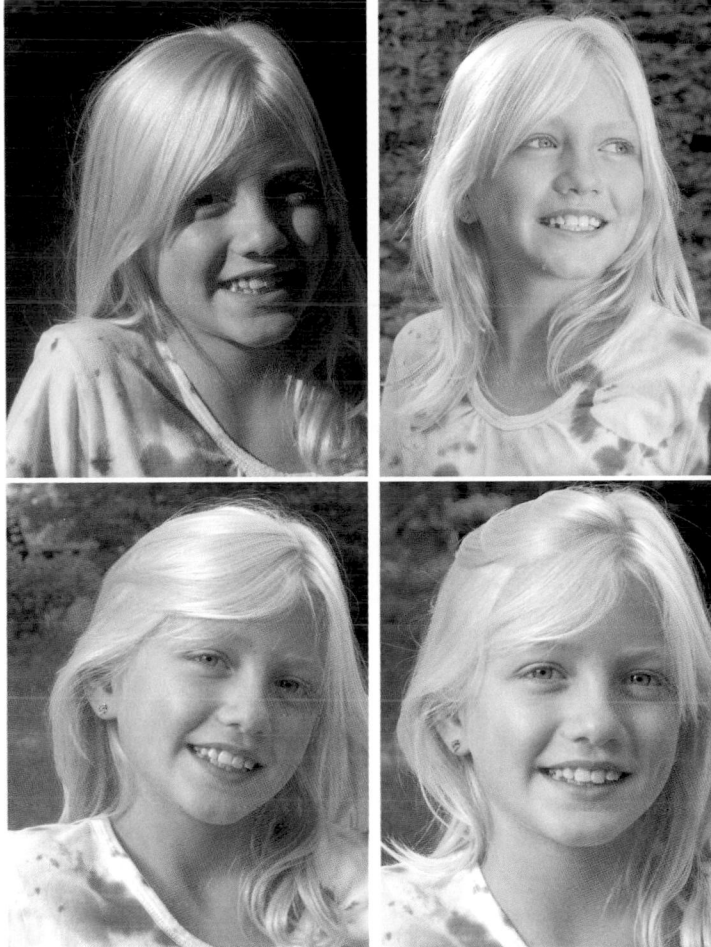

Bottom right: I used a diffuser, held between the sun and the subject, and activated my camera's built-in flash.

When photographing people, pay very careful attention the shadows on your subject's face. If it's sunny and you don't have the accessories mentioned above, try to position the subject in the shade, and make sure the background is in the shade, too.

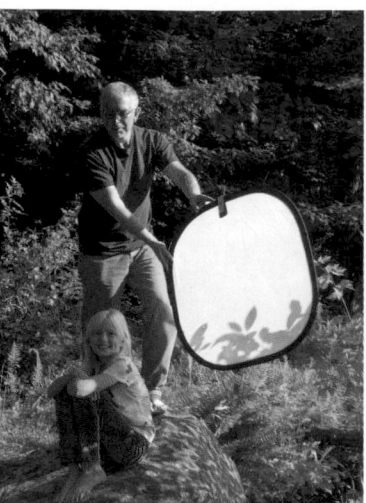 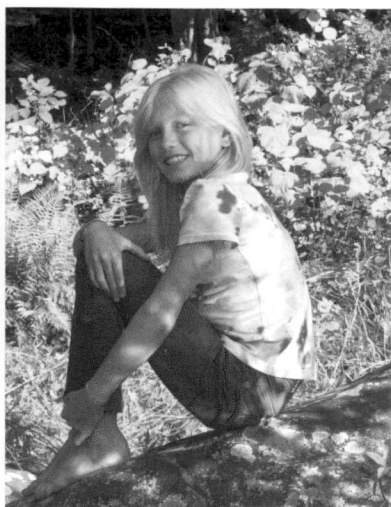 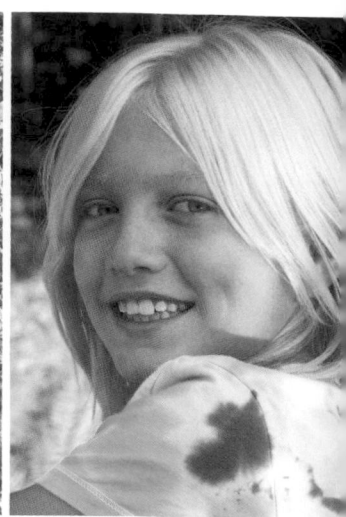

Diffuser in Action

Here's a look at a diffuser in action.

In the left picture, you see my friend holding a diffuser between the sun and his daughter. Notice the strong contrast range in the scene.

In the middle picture, you'll notice that some sunlight is falling on the girl's face, creating weird and unflattering shadows. What's more, the background is too bright and the girl's face is too dark.

In the picture on the right, the diffuser eliminates the shadows and contrast on the girl's face.

A reflector, held on the opposite side of the girl's face would have filled in the shadows caused by the strong directional sunlight.

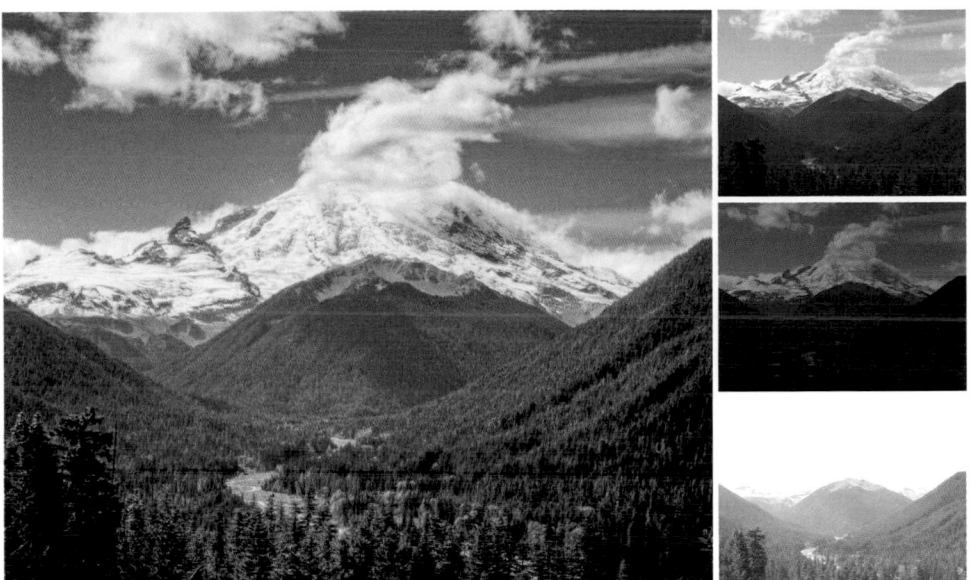

Contrast in Scenic Pictures

Unless you shoot a scenic picture on a heavily overcast day and don't include too much of the sky in your frame, you are going to get a picture with a lot of contrast, as I did here when photographing Mt. Rainier in Washington. Shadows will be dark and highlights may be washed out.

With a compact camera, the fastest and easiest way to get a natural-looking image is to shoot for an HDR (high dynamic range) image. Sure, you could greatly improve the image in Photoshop Elements (or the image editing program that came with your camera), but you'd spend a fair amount of time on the computer working on the image.

Here's the basic idea for creating an HDR image. Set your camera on a tripod and take three exposures (at the same aperture): one at the 0 EV setting, one at the +2 EV setting, and one at the -2 EV setting—as illustrated by the images you see on the bottom row. Then, using an HDR-imaging program like Photomatic Pro (www.hdrsoft.com), combine the images into a single image that captures all the different brightness levels in the scene, as illustrated by the top image.

I converted my color HDR image to a black-and-white image in Photoshop Elements using the Black-and-White filter in Nik Software's Color Efex Pro, a plug-in that's available at Nik Software (www.niksoftware.com). I made the black-and-white conversion to encourage you to play around with black-and-white when taking and making landscape images.

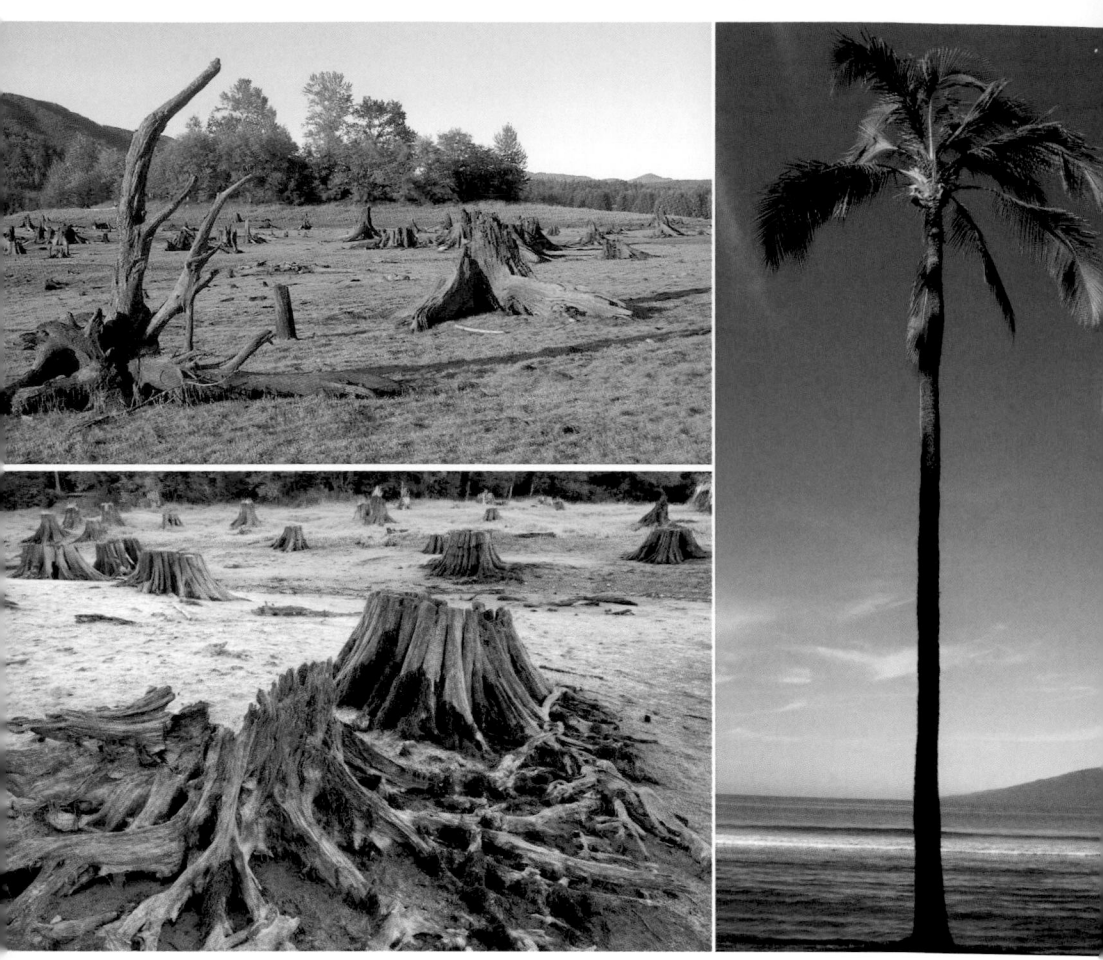

The Color of Light

Light has color, and its hues and intensity vary throughout a given day. From the type of warm light that we get after sunrise and before sunset (top) to the cool light that comes before and after those hours (bottom) and around midday (right), seeing the color light and responding well to it is part of being a serious photographer.

Most people prefer pictures with warm light, which is one of the reasons that sunset and sunrise pictures are appealing. You can control the color of light simply by shooting at different times of the day. You can also control the color of light by adjusting your white balance. This is covered in more detail, beginning on page 101.

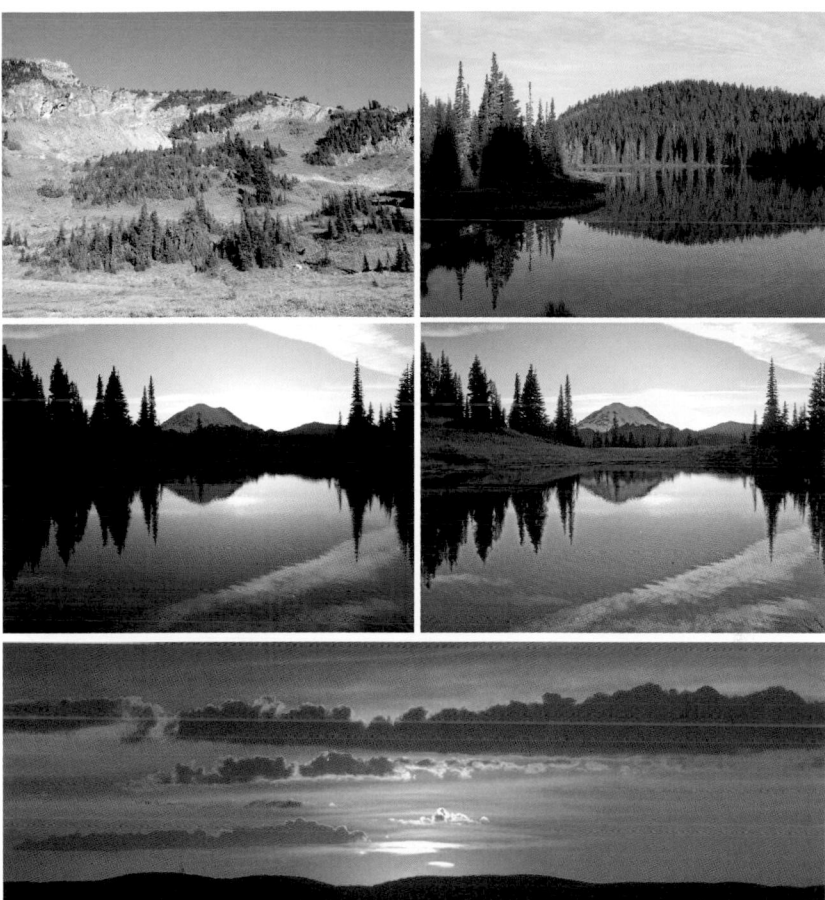

The Direction of Light

Part of seeing the light is considering its direction, and that applies to all subjects. Here are a few examples of different types of lighting in landscape photography.

Top left: front lighting

Top right: side lighting

Middle left: back lighting (not good if there is little detail in the sky)

Middle right: back lighting enhanced in Photoshop Elements by opening up the shadows and using the Shadows/Highlights adjustment … and a contrast boost

Bottom: Ahhhhh! Nice backlighting with lots of color and detail in the sky

Before you take a landscape picture, notice the direction of light, and envision the way the light will be recorded by your camera.

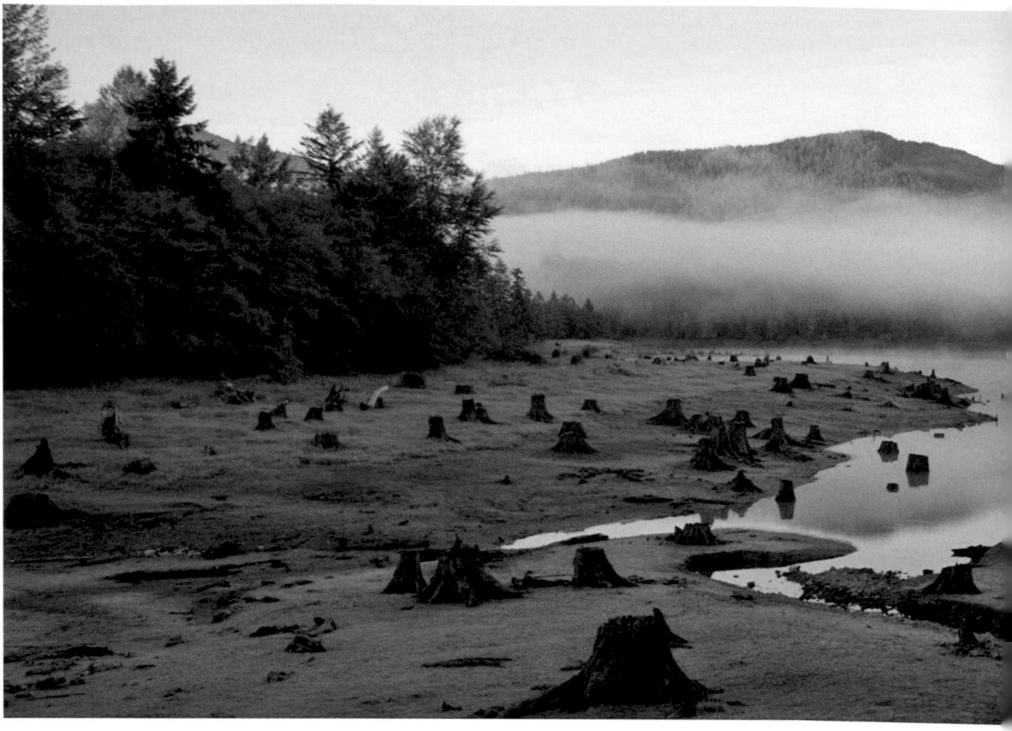

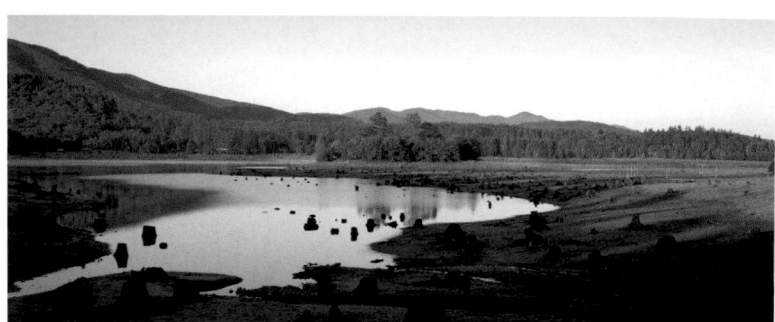

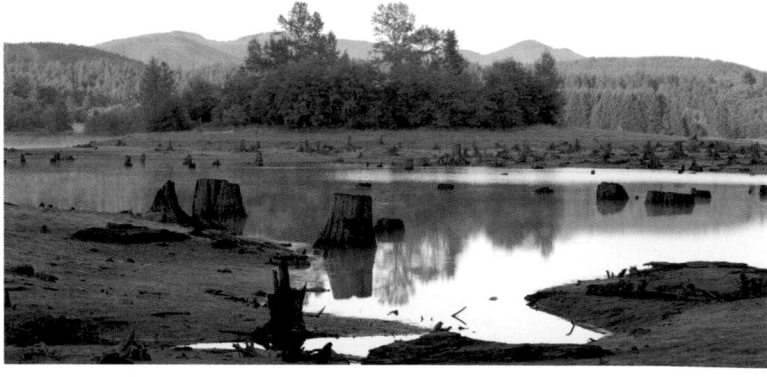

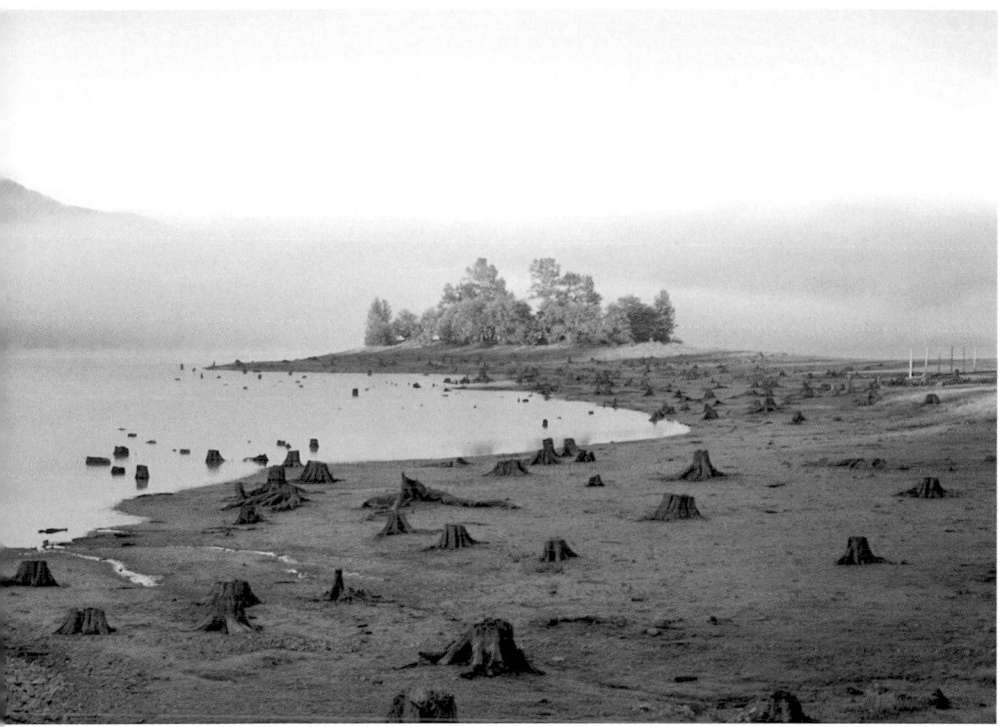

The Quality of Light

These three pictures, all taken in the same location and cropped, illustrate why the quality of light is so important.

In the top image, the quality of light is simply fantastic. It's created by the morning fog and the rising sun. Talk about the luck of being in the right place at the right time!

The middle picture, taken at after sunrise, has a nice quality, but it's not as nice as the top image because the fog is missing.

The bottom picture is boring due to the poor quality of light. It was taken just before sunrise on a clear day.

Want great light quality in your pictures? Shoot in the early morning and late afternoon, and pray for fog, mist or clouds.

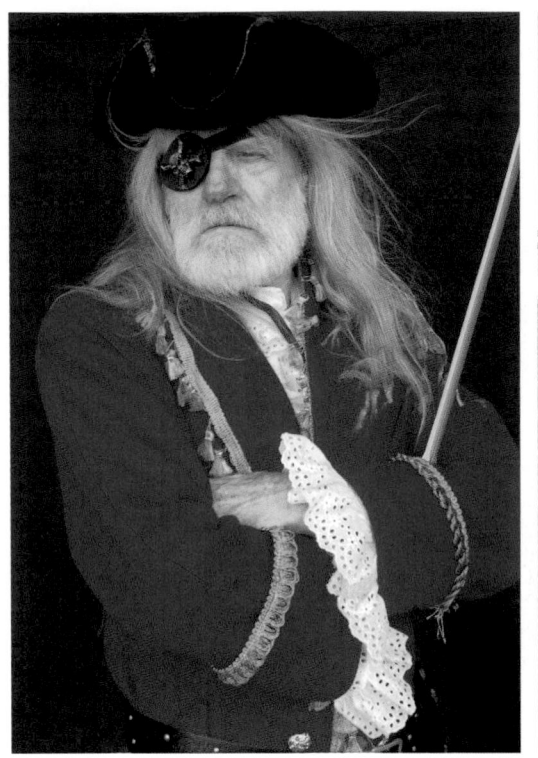
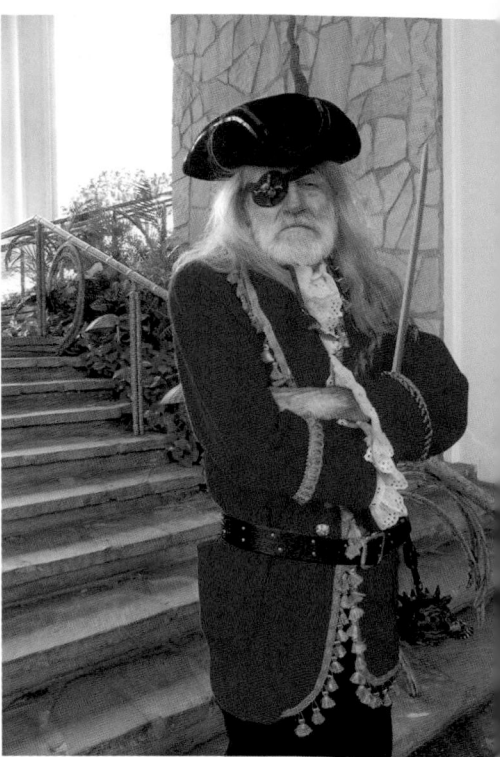

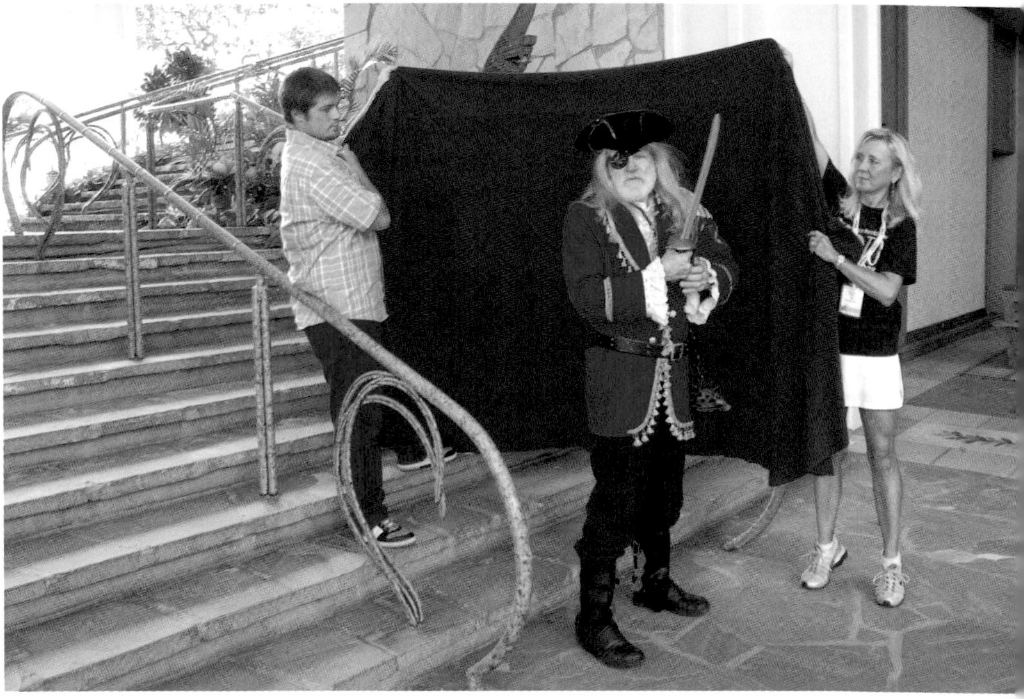

Finding the Light: Part I

Finding good light is an important part of being a good photographer. To find light, we need to look for the light. This requires being aware of the direction of light, the color of light, the quality of light and the contrast range in the scene.

While teaching a workshop at the Maui Photo Festival & Workshops at the Hyatt Regency Hotel, I found some nice, soft light for a natural-light portrait in the Festival's reception area. The light was indeed nice; it came from a large, open-air space (maybe 60 feet wide by 20 feet high) at the end of an expansive hallway. The light was low in contrast, making an automatic exposure easy as pie. The problem: The background for a portrait that I wanted to take was boring and distracting.

No problem actually. I had two of the festival's volunteers grab a tablecloth off one of the tables and hold it behind my subject, Zane Matthias, one of the directors of the festival. He was dressed like a pirate for one of the photo shoots.

I found the light and I liked the light. Even so, as you'll see on the next page, I found an even nicer light—in the same area, earlier in the day on the following day of the festival.

My point of showing you the pictures on this spread and asking you to compare them is to make you see that even when you find nice light, it's good to go back to the same location at different times of the day and look for better light. You just may find it.

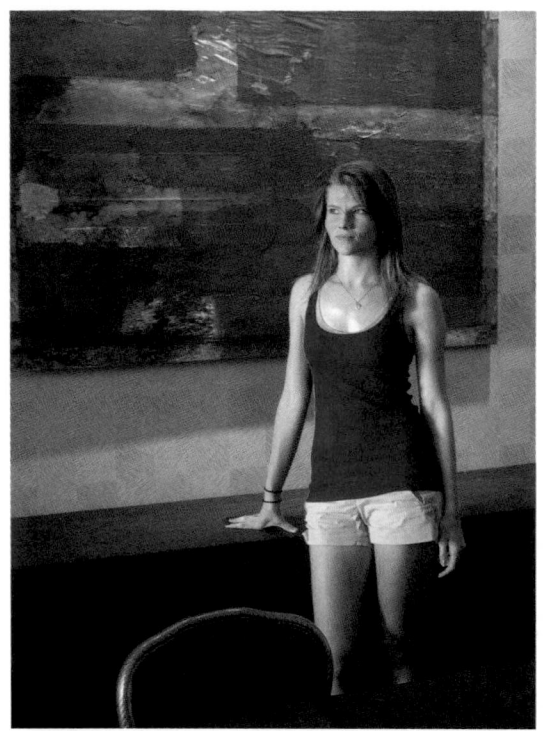

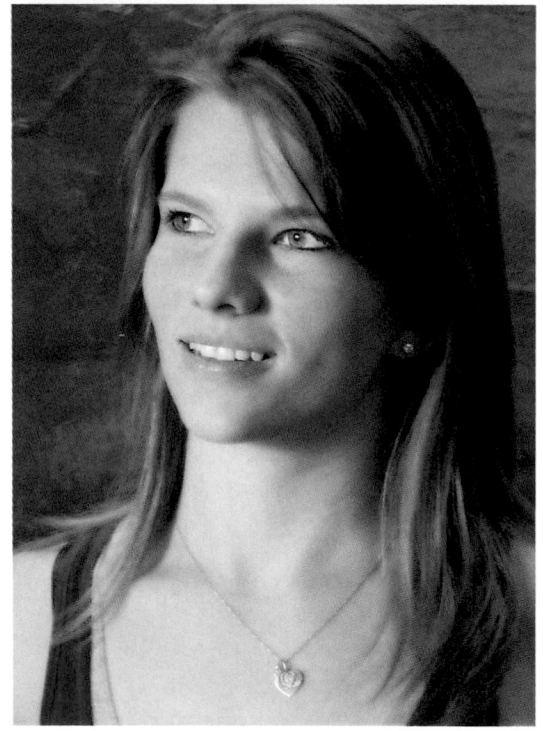

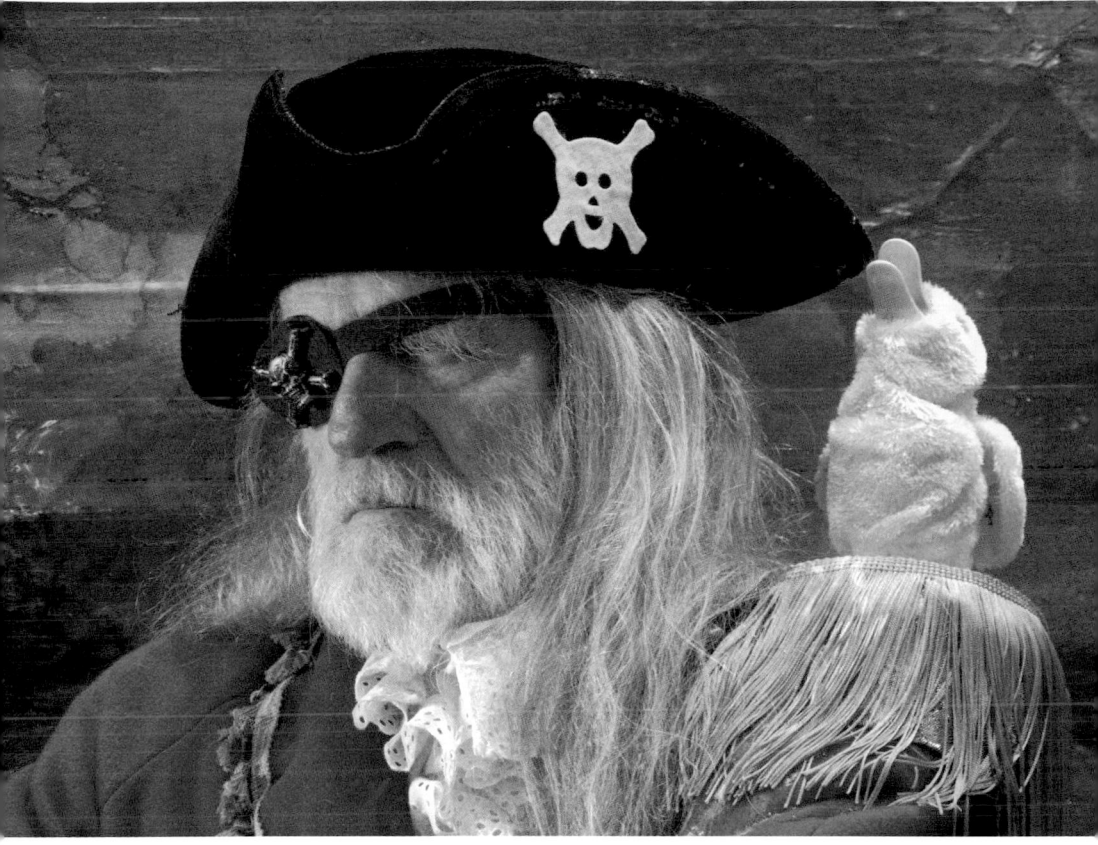

Finding the Light: Part II

Always be looking for light.

As you read on the previous page, I found nice light in the reception area of a hotel. The picture on the previous page was taken around noon. The pictures on this page were taken earlier on the following day, when a stronger, more direct light was streaming into the area from the rising sun.

Notice how there is more contrast in this scene, and how the pictures don't look as flat as those on the previous page. See how the shadows here add a sense of depth to the pictures.

All the photographs on this spread were taken in the Av (aperture priority) mode. If your camera does not have an Av mode, choose the P or Green mode. To preserve the highlights in these pictures, I set my exposure compensation to – 1/3.

The background here is a painting that was already hanging on the wall. In addition to looking for the light, always be on the lookout for nice backgrounds, too.

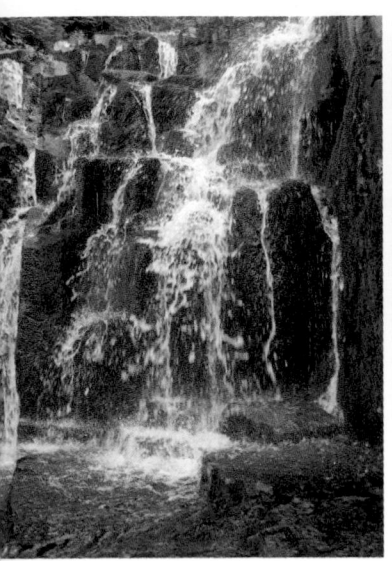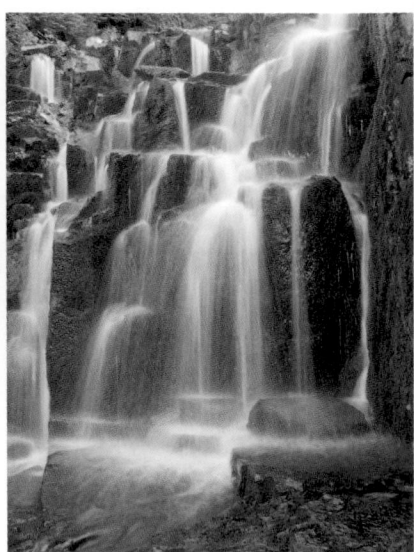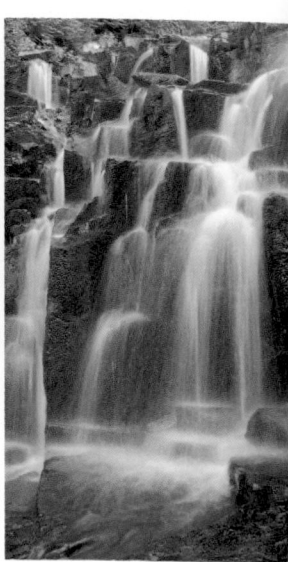

Controlling the Movement of Light

Yes, when light reflects off a moving subject, such as water, it too moves. Control that movement easily by adjusting the shutter speed.

For the picture on the left, I set the camera to a high shutter speed, 1/500 of a second. Yuch. For the picture in the middle, I set the shutter speed to 1.5 seconds. A much more pleasing effect, I think. If your camera does not offer shutter speed control, you may not be able to get a shot like the one on the right.

When using slow shutter speeds, you'll need a tripod. It's also a good idea to use the camera's self-timer to prevent camera shake, which may occur when you press the shutter release button.

Speaking of controlling, this picture was shot in the shade. There was not a lot of color in the scene. Presto chango! With a bit of a boost in saturation, the picture on the right takes on beautiful color.

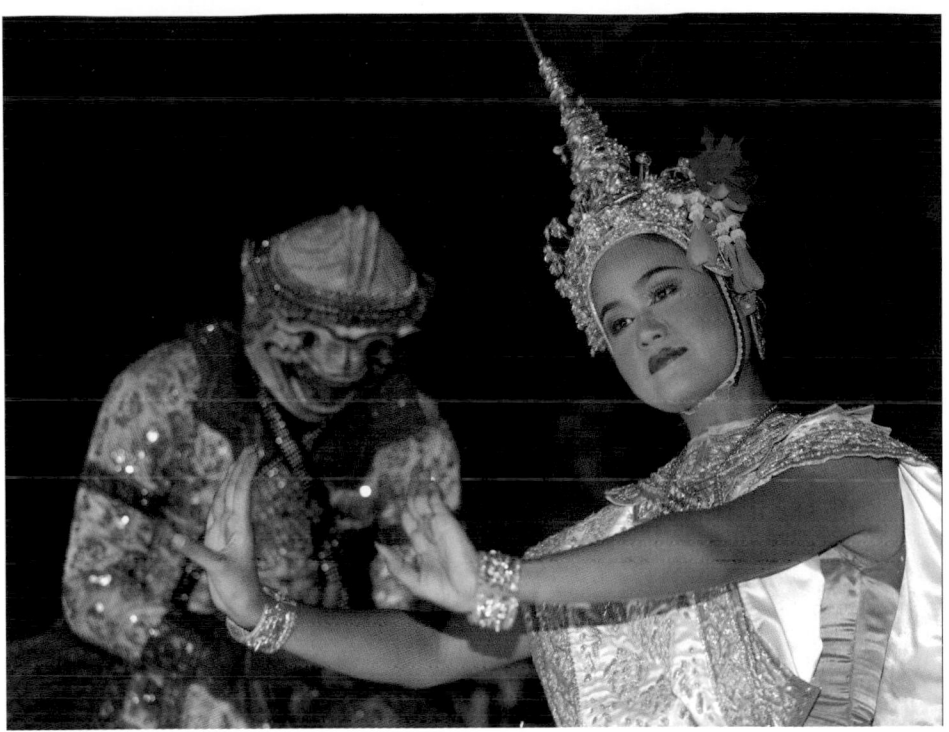

Part V

Understanding ISO

The ISO setting on a compact camera is one of the most important settings. This setting can affect the sharpness of your pictures as well as depth of field and image quality. I say *can* rather than *does* because lighting conditions come into play with image quality, too.

In this chapter we'll take a look at this all-important and often overlooked camera setting.

For now, just know that when you set the ISO, you are basically (not technically) changing the camera sensor's sensitivity to light. As the ISO increases, so does the sensor's sensitivity. So you might think that a high ISO setting is always best.

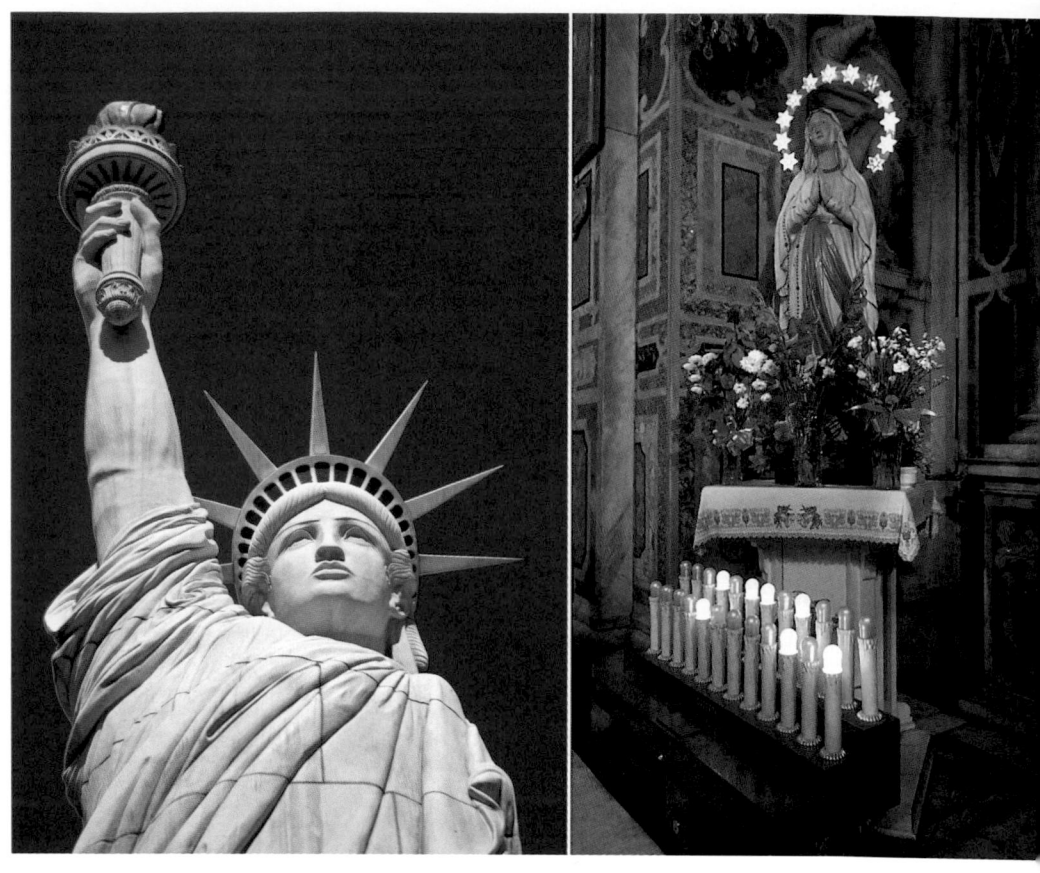

Bright Light and Low Light Settings

My basic ISO rule is to always use the lowest possible practical ISO setting for the existing lighting conditions. In bright light, I shoot at ISO 100. In low light, I start with an ISO setting of 200. If that low-light setting does not let me shoot at a fast enough shutter speed for a sharp shot, I boost the ISO to 400. If that does not work, I use a tripod to steady my camera during a long exposure.

Above ISO 400, images from most compact cameras, including mine, get a bit grainy. The higher the ISO, the more grain (digital noise) you get in your pictures.

As mentioned earlier, digital noise shows up mostly in the shadow areas. So, when checking your images on your computer, zoom into the shadow areas and look for noise. You can remove noise in the digital darkroom, but it's best to shoot for the cleanest possible shot and avoid that extra work on the computer.

Note that not all compact cameras offer ISO settings.

Digital Noise Degrades Image Quality

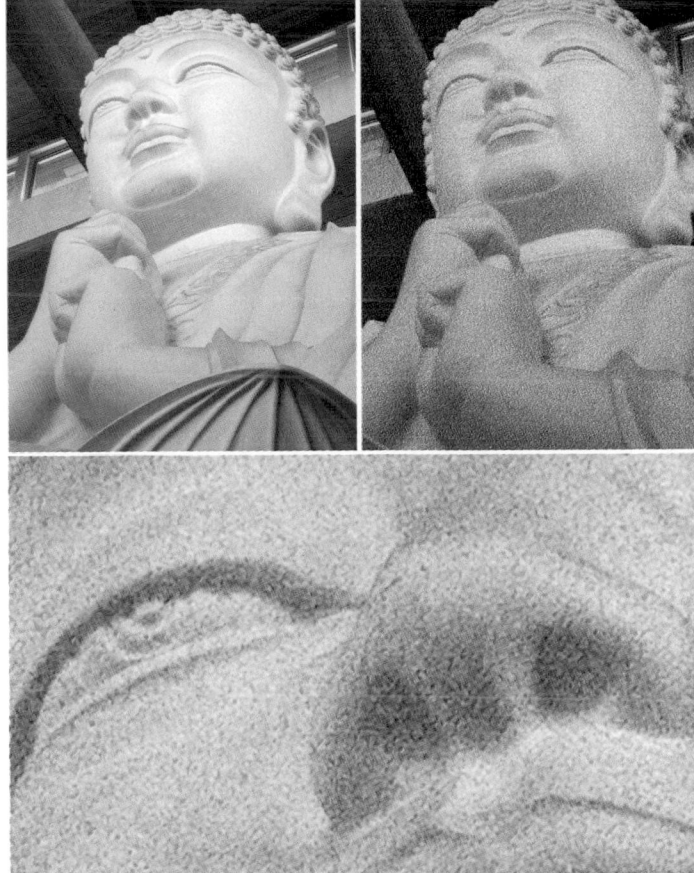

As I mentioned on the previous page, digital noise shows up mostly in the shadow areas. But it's also evident in bright areas of an image.

The picture on the top left was taken at ISO 100. It's a nice clean shot. The picture on the top right was taken at ISO 800.

The noise shows up in two forms: luminance noise (what we call *grain*) and chroma noise (strange color patters that detract from image quality).

Check the bottom image. It is an enlarged section of the top right image. Up close, it's easy to see this nasty noise.

Keep in mind that you'll get more noise when shooting in low-light conditions and at longer shutter speeds.

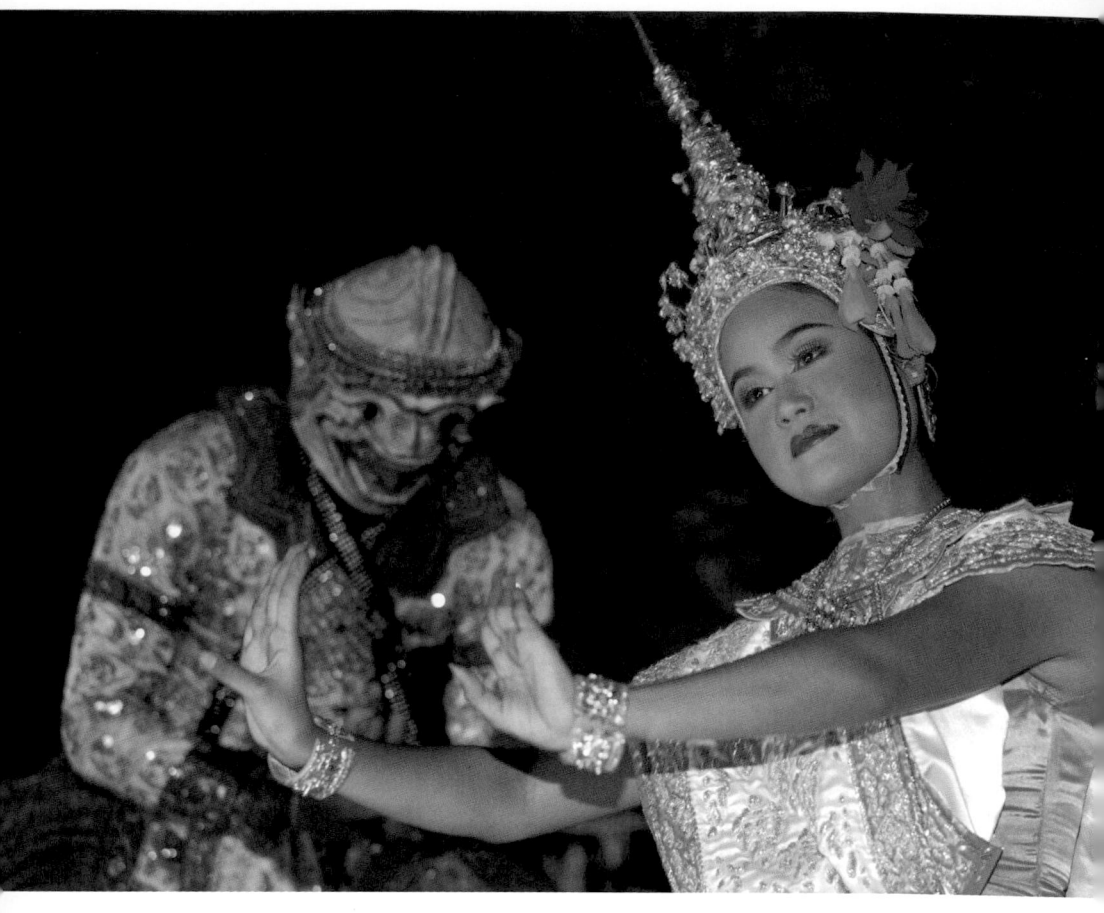

Set Higher ISO to Stop Action

As ISO gets higher, the shutter speed at which you can shoot gets faster. The faster your shutter speed, the better your chance of stopping action. That said, you still need to be aware of digital noise when lighting conditions are normal.

A shutter speed of 1/500 of a second can stop most action. On a sunny day, you may be able to shoot at ISO 200 for an action-stopping photograph. If not, boost your ISO.

Think you'll get too much noise? Remember this: A noisy picture is better than a blurry picture. However (and this is a joke), one blurry picture is a mistake; 20 blurry pictures is a style.

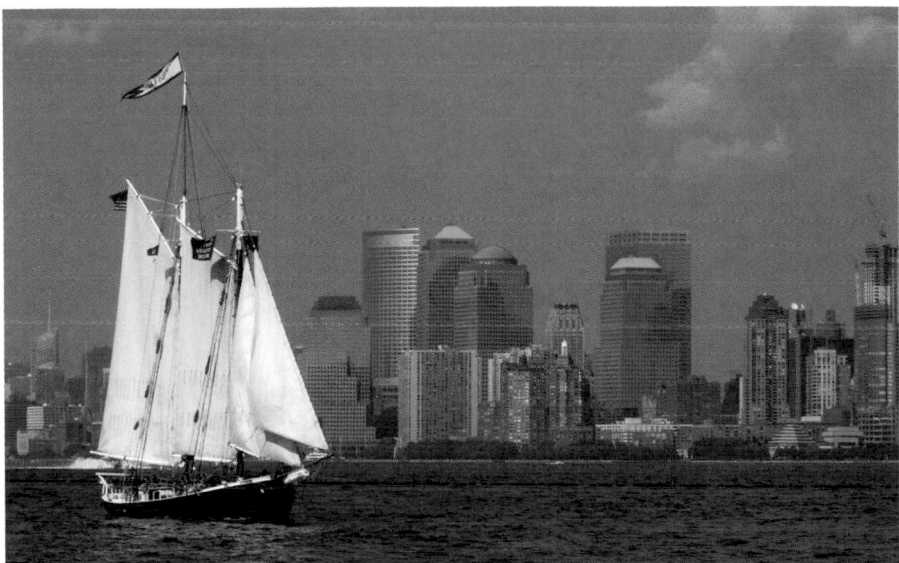

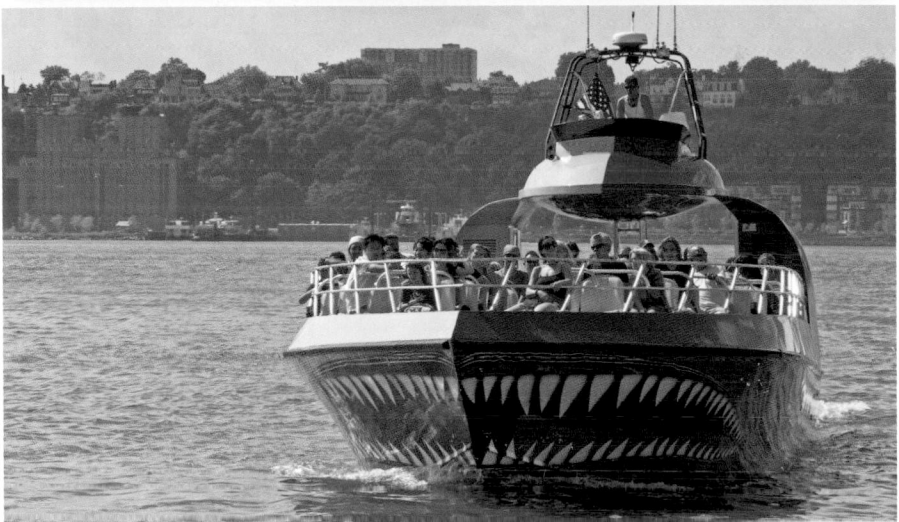

Increase ISO to Stop Your Movement

When *you* are moving fast (or bouncing around as I was while riding the "Beast" in New York City), you probably want to choose a higher-than-usual ISO setting. This will allow you to shoot at a fast shutter speed and avoid creating a blurry shot from your movement.

While bouncing around on the Beast, I took the top shot with my ISO set at 200. This gave me a shutter speed of 1/500 of a second. This is a good shutter speed to choose when you want to stop action.

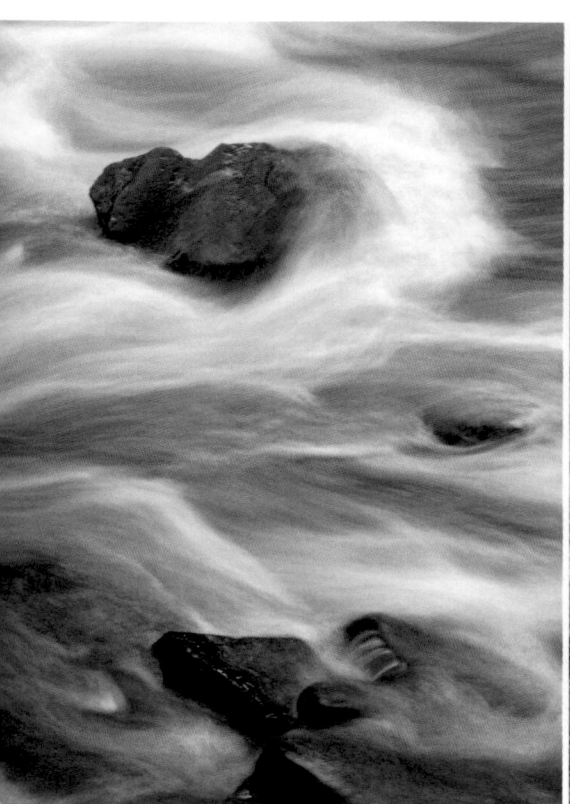 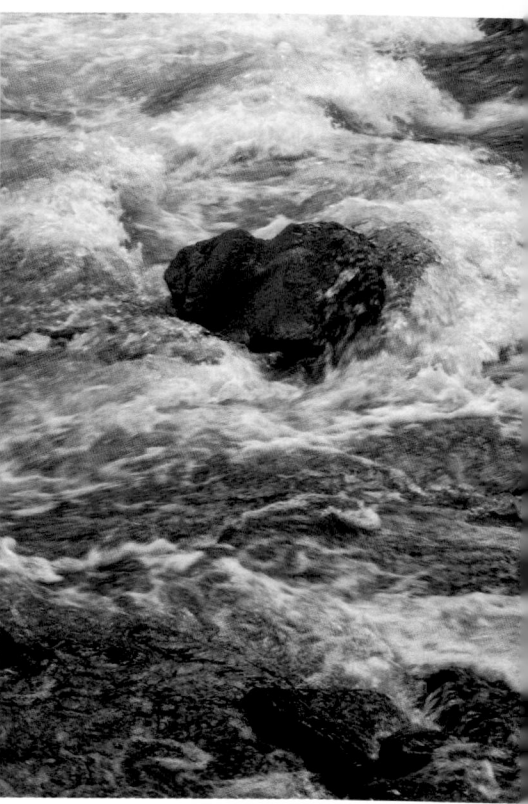

Lower ISO to Blur Subject Movement

When you want to blur movement, choose a low ISO setting. A low ISO lets you shoot at slow shutter speeds.

I took the left shot with my camera set to ISO 100, which gave me a shutter speed of one second (my camera was on a tripod). The picture on the right was taken with the camera set to ISO 400, which gave me a shutter speed of 1/1500 of a second. Yuch.

Some cameras have built-in ND (neutral density) filters that let you shoot at a slow shutter speed in all lighting conditions. If you don't get a slow enough shutter speed by choosing the lower ISO, check your camera's menu for an ND filter and choose it. Just remember to reset the ND filter to "Off" when you finish your long-exposure shot.

Note that not all compact cameras offer manual shutter speed control.

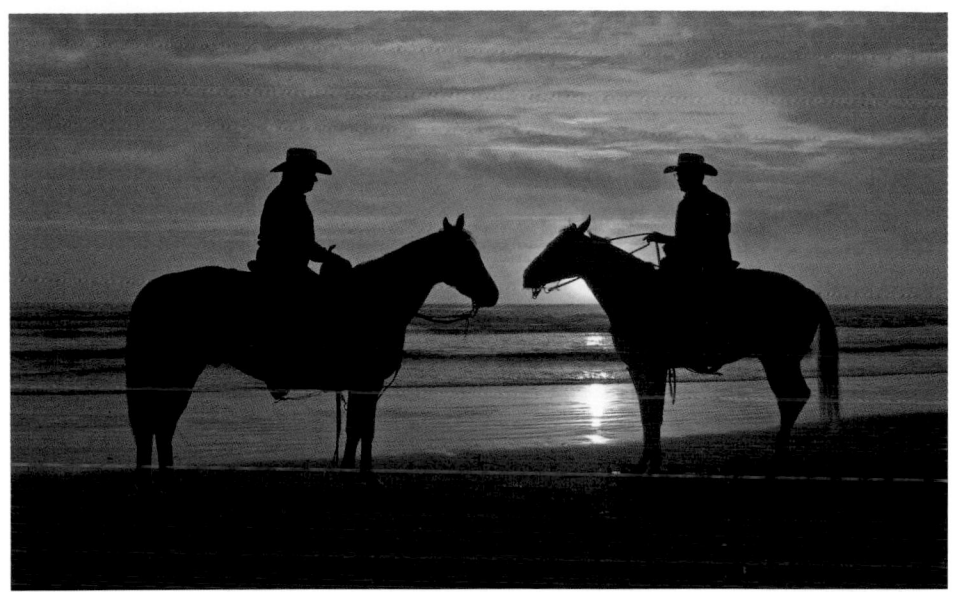

Part VI

Get the Best Image Quality: RAW and JPEG

This one is a no-brainer. When you set the Image Quality on your camera, you are, that's right, determining the quality of your image.

Sounds simple, right? Well, basically it is. But there are times when you don't necessarily have to choose the highest quality setting to get the best image quality. This applies to particular situations and uses.

Basically, you have two choices: RAW and JPEG.

RAW captures all the detail in an image, so it's more forgiving. Your exposure can be a bit "off" and you might be able to get a good image with a bit of digital darkroom work.

Conversely, when you shoot JPEG files, the image file is compressed and you lose some image quality in the compressing and uncompressing process. As you will read, this may or may not be noticeable.

By the end of this chapter, you'll know which image quality setting is best for you, depending on your shooting situation and how you'll use your images.

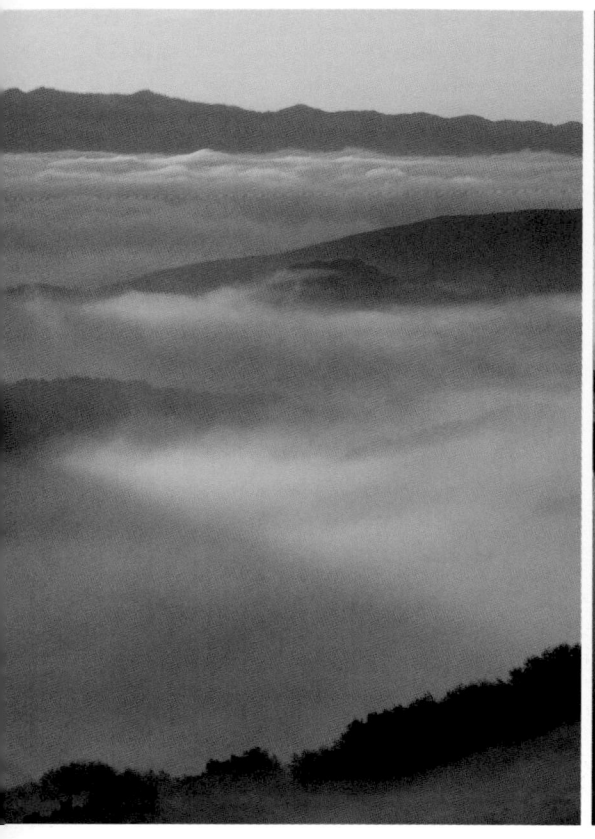
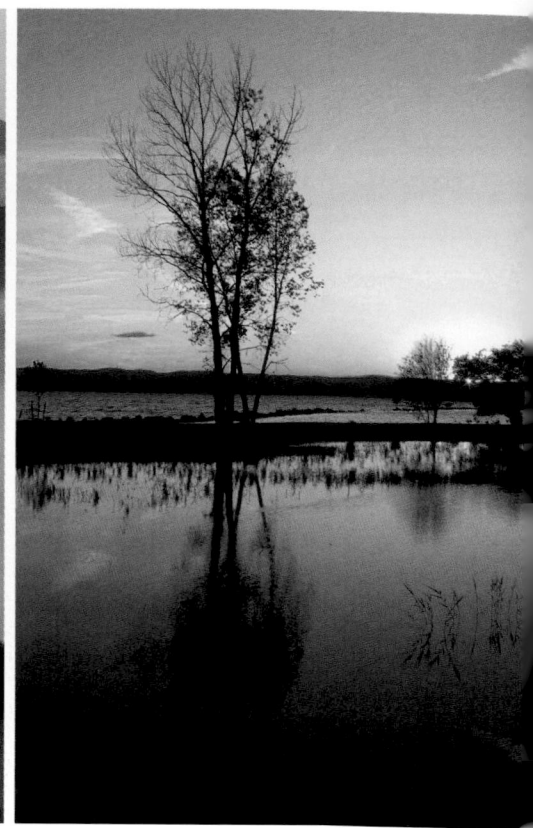

When RAW Rules

Do you like to see fine details in your images … and subtle changes in tone and color? Do you like to shoot scenes with a nice contrast range? Want the best quality image?

If you answered yes to all of the above, then you want to shoot RAW files.

The two scenes pictured on this page have a lot of color, contrast and detail; and all of it was recorded to the max with RAW files.

As I mentioned in the chapter opener, some of that detail would have been lost if I had shot JPEG files.

RAW files take up more space on a memory card and hard drive. They also take longer to process. Worth the space and wait? You be the judge; but my advice is better safe than sorry. Shoot RAW when it's feasible.

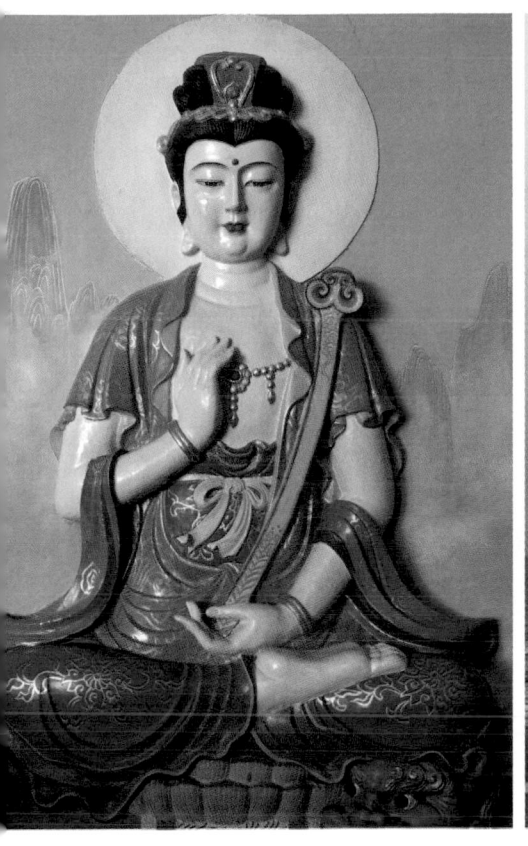

When JPEGs are Okay

Rick "RAW Rules" Sammon actually says that JPEGs are okay in certain situations and for a certain type of image.

These two scenes don't have a lot of contrast, unlike the pictures on the previous page. When the contrast (difference between the bright and dark areas of a scene) is low, you will likely get the same results with a JPEG as you do with a RAW file.

If you are only shooting pictures for fun or emailing … or maybe posting to a fun web site, then JPEGs may be okay.

If you're not sure, then remember what I said on the previous page: *Better safe than sorry.* Shoot RAW if and when you can.

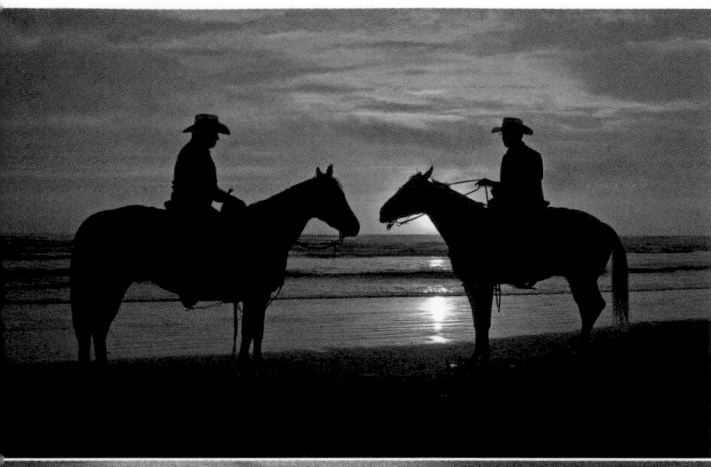

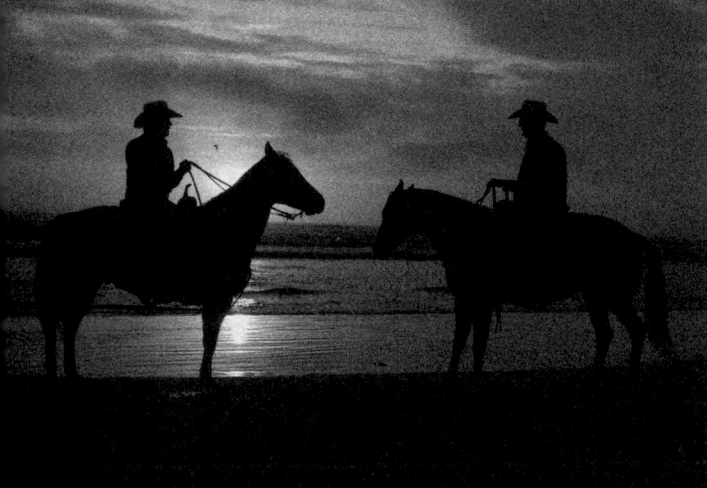

Settings for JPEG Image Quality/ Compression

Compact cameras have different JPEG quality settings. They range from Low to High/Best. The amount of compression, (also from Low to High/ Best), is another choice on some cameras.

My advice for serious shooters is to choose the High/Best settings. It'll mean you're using the maximum number of pixels and a low compression rate, which will result in the best possible image.

The top picture here was shot at ISO 100. The bottom picture was shot at ISO 800.

Sure, if you just want a picture for fun, choose a lower setting to spare memory card space. Just keep in mind that if you ever want to make a big print, you may be sorry that you chose such a low image-quality setting.

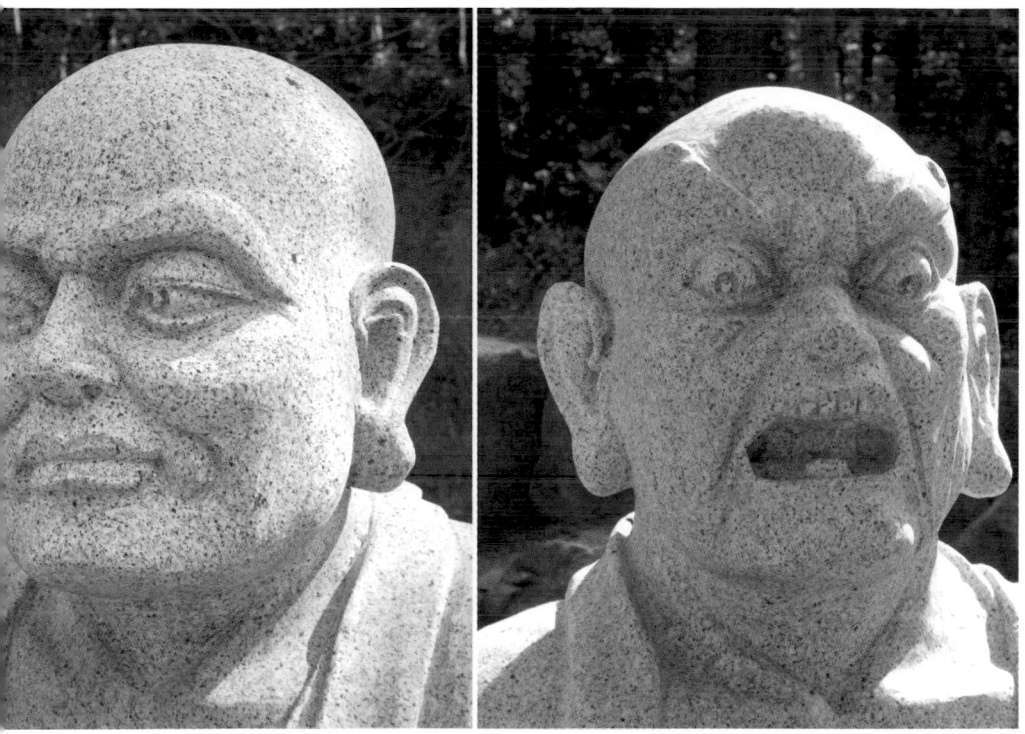

The Importance of Seeing the Light

How many times do you think I can talk about the importance of seeing the light in one book? The answer is very, very often; it is so very important.

The opening pictures for this chapter had a lot of contrast, which is why RAW ruled for those images.

These two pictures show the difference between a scene with little contrast (left) and a lot of contrast (right). The contrast range is so great in the picture on the right that even a RAW file could not preserve (via a rescue in the digital darkroom) the highlight area on the head and side of the statue. In situations like this, it's important to remember this tip: You either have to control the light with a diffuser, reflector or a flash—or deal with the fact that the picture may just not be there.

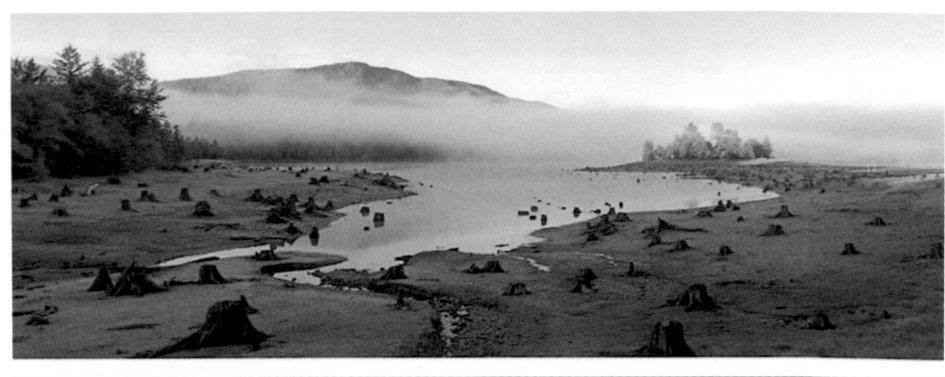

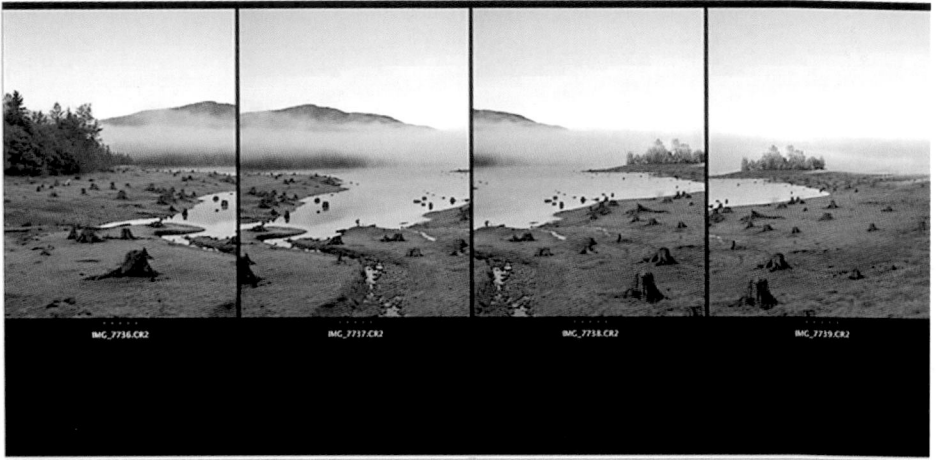

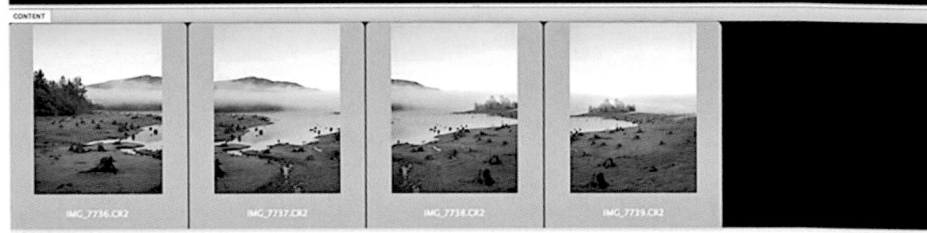

RAW Really Rules with Panoramas

In Chapter IV on Light, you saw an image that looks similar to the top image you see here. That image was a single shot. The top on this page is a panorama that I created with the four pictures in the screen grab, using Photoshop Element's Photomerge feature.

As you can see, my pictures are RAW files; it's identified by the CR (Camera RAW) designation. RAW rules, especially in panoramas ... because the light level and contrast range often change during the shoot. It creates a very nice photograph, don't you think?

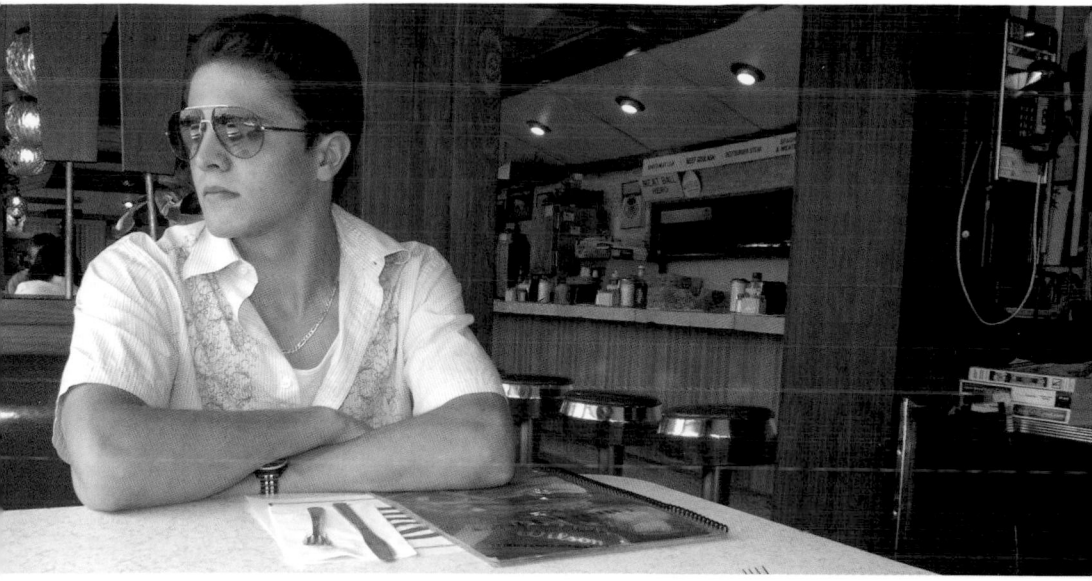

Part VII

A Case for White Balance

In the days of film, there were different types of films and color-correction filters for shooting under various lighting conditions. There was sunny, tungsten, Fluorescent and so on. With the right film film/filter combination, a photographer could achieve perfect color … or desired color.

Similarly, when you set the white balance on your camera, you are telling the camera that you want white to appear as white. When that happens, all the other colors in a scene should be correctly recorded.

In this chapter we'll explore white balance—a setting that you really should use even if you shoot RAW files. Find more on RAW files and white balance at the end of this chapter. Please note that not all cameras offer these options.

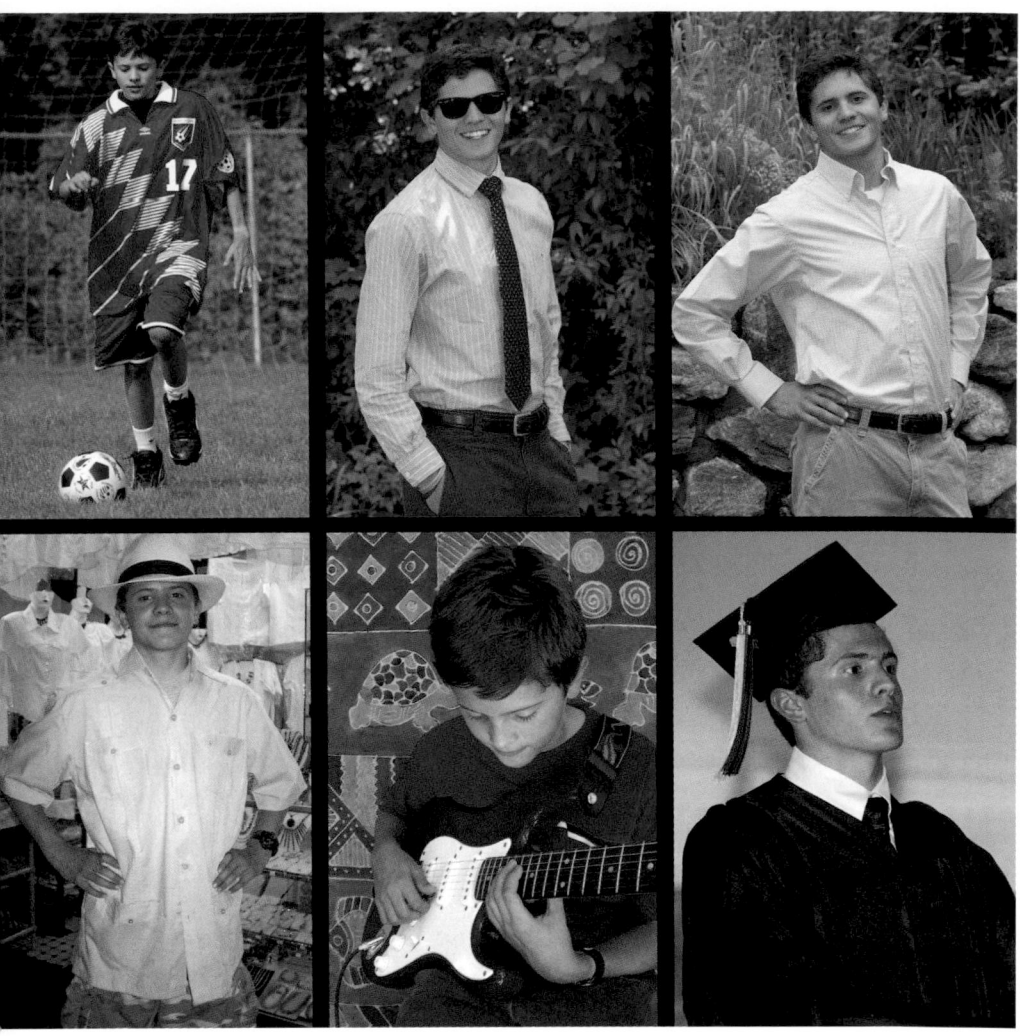

Individual White Balance Settings

Take the time (maybe a few seconds) to set the white balance and you'll get accurate colors in most lighting situations. Here you see (left to right, from top) the effects of choosing the following white balance settings: Daylight (Sunny), Shade, Overcast, Fluorescent, Tungsten and Flash.

"What about Manual/Custom White Balance?" you ask. Well, say you are an advertising photographer and one hundred percent accurate color is required. I'd use the Manual/Custom white balance settings, which requires you to take a reading off a piece of white material and then do a Manual/Custom white balance setup. My guess is that you're not a pro photographer, so forget about the Manual/Custom setting.

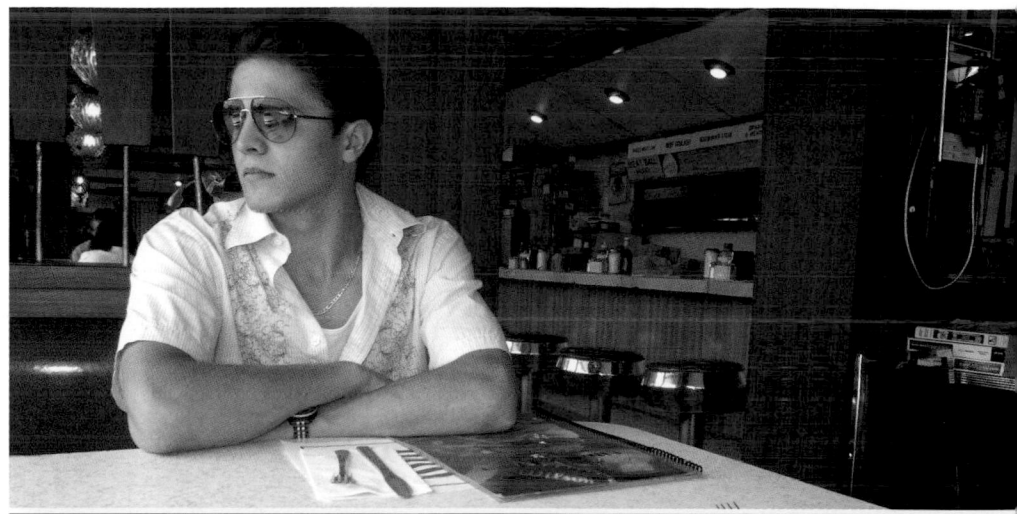

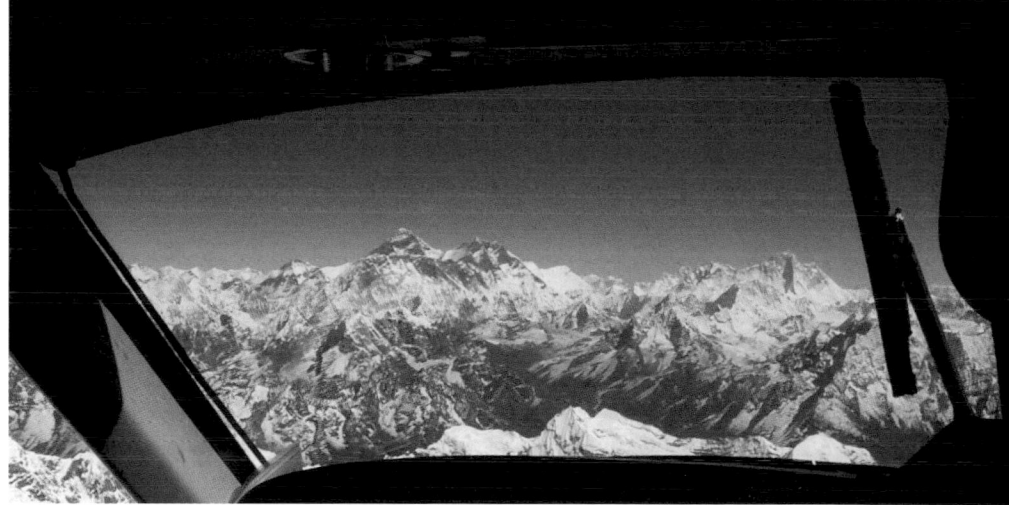

Auto White Balance

Now you are probably asking, "What about Auto white balance?"

Well, there is actually a time when I use auto white balance, and when you probably want to use it, too. When light levels are mixed or when you are not sure about the color of light, Auto can do a good job.

In the photo on the left, both daylight and tungsten light illuminated my son. In the above photograph, I was shooting through a tinted window at an altitude at which the color of daylight is different from the color at sea level. I used the Auto white balance setting for both pictures.

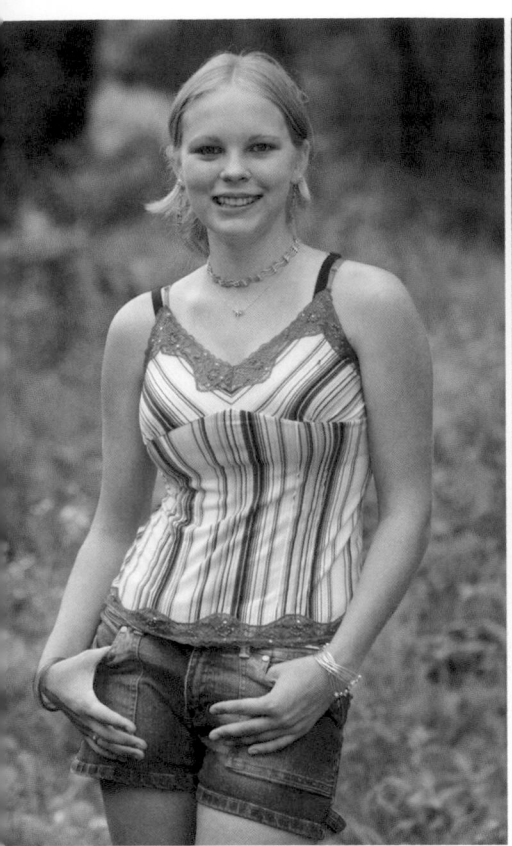 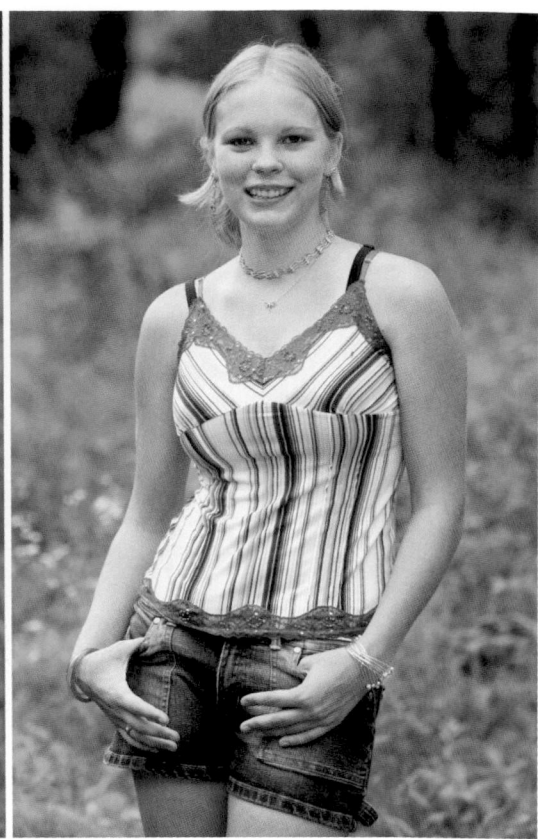

When White Balance Goes Wrong

If you are not convinced that setting the white balance is important, check out these photographs. The picture on the left shows the effect (created in Photoshop) of what would happen if the white balance were set to Fluorescent for an outdoor shot. The picture on the right was taken at the correct white balance setting, which was Shade.

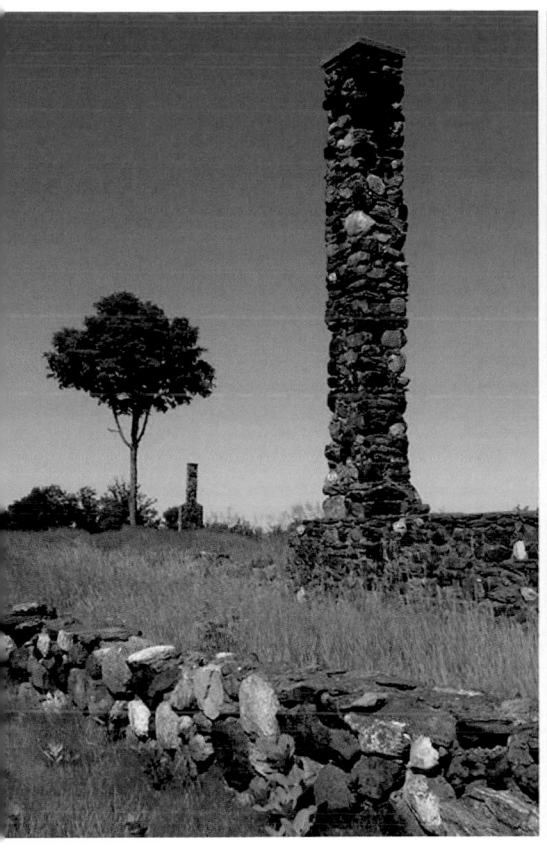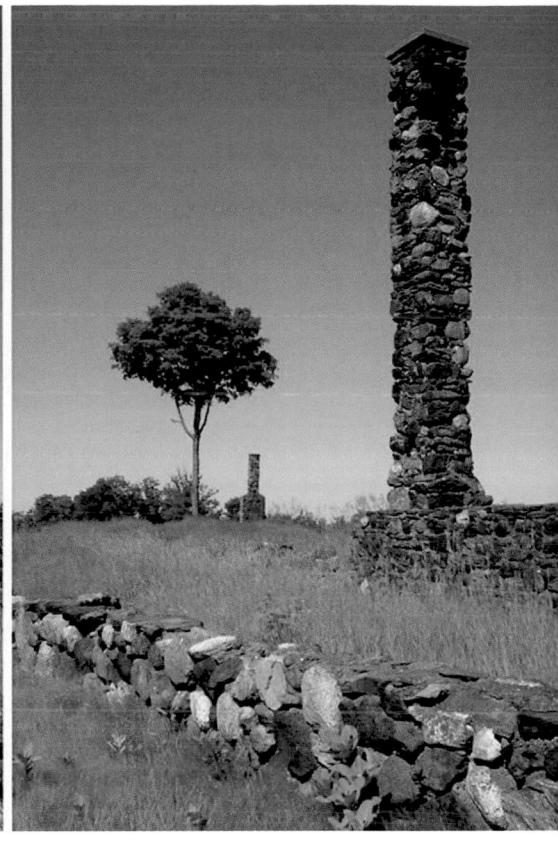

When the Wrong White Balance Can Actually be Right

On the previous page you saw the negative effect of choosing the wrong white balance. Pretty yucky color! There are times, however, when the "wrong" white balance can actually be okay ... or even preferred over the "correct" white balance setting. Here is an example.

When it comes to landscape photography, "warm" pictures—that is, pictures with deeper shades of red, orange and yellow—are often preferred to "cool" pictures, those with a blue tint.

When shooting on sunny day with the white balance set to Sunny, pictures will look a bit cool. For a warmer look, set the white balance to Shade. That is what I did to create the warmer picture you see here on the right.

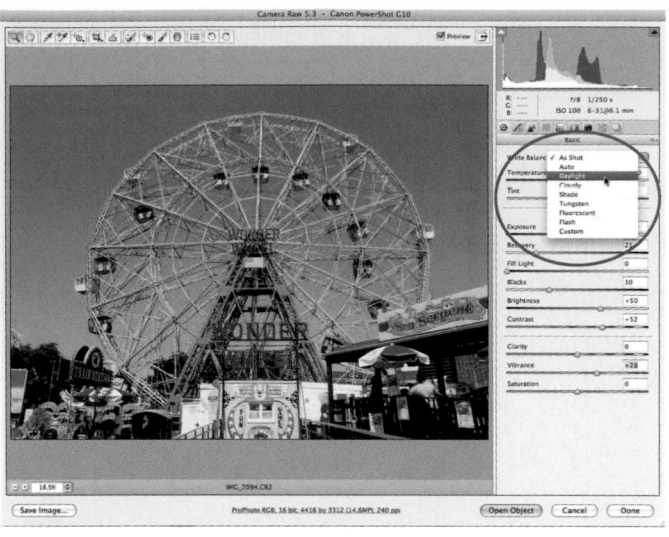

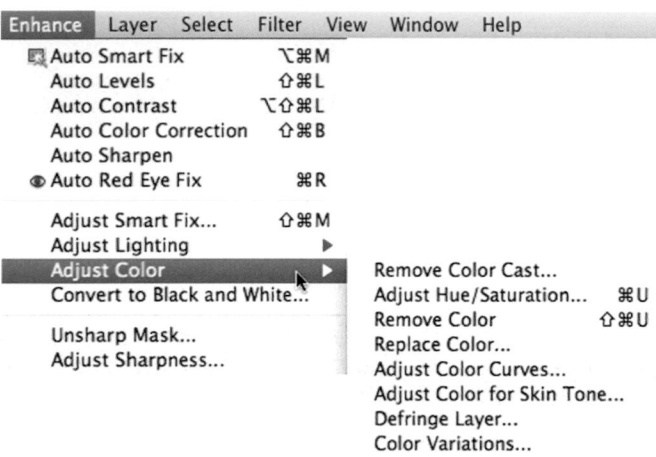

Correcting White Balance in Camera RAW

One of the advantages of shooting RAW files is that if you make a mistake when choosing the white balance, you can quickly and easily change it in the Adobe Camera RAW program.

You can also adjust colors in Photoshop Elements, but it's faster, easier and more accurate in ACR. So, if you're looking for a more sophisticated workflow and understand image-editing processes well, definitely go RAW when you can.

In newer versions of ACR, it is also possible to adjust the white balance of JPEG images. You can open any image file with this program and adjust the white balance manually. How cool is that?!

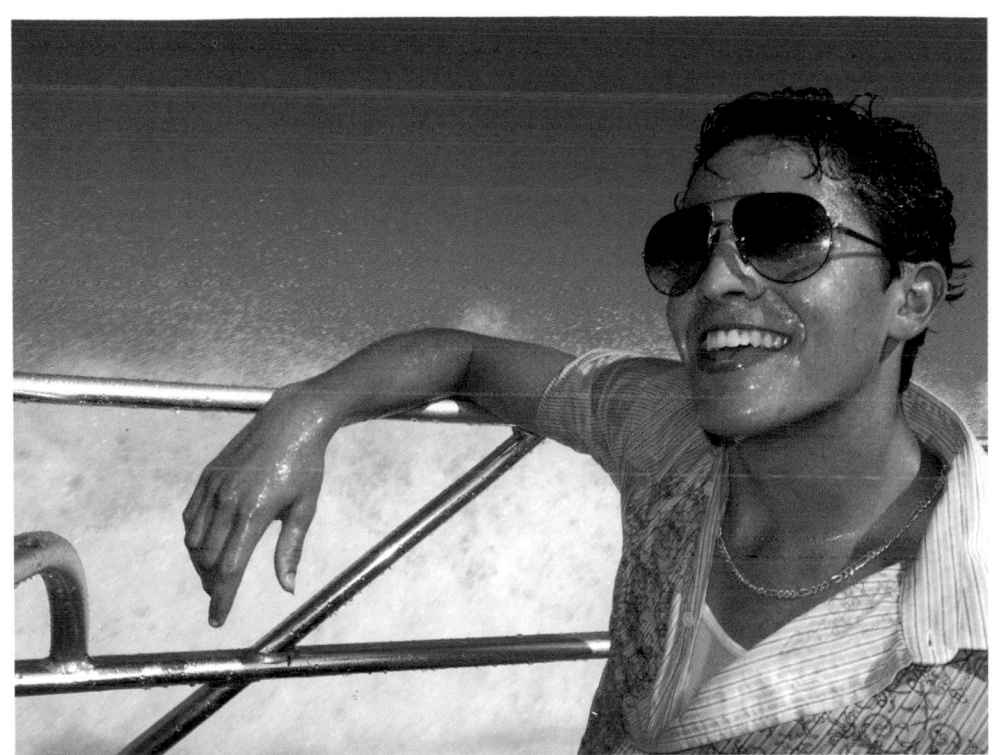

Part VIII

Flash Settings: On, Off and Partial

One of the coolest and most advanced features in a compact camera (believe it or not) is the built in flash. Because the flash offers automatic exposure, you get good exposures indoors and out—in many cases.

When the flash exposure is a bit off (over- or underexposing your subject), many compact cameras let you increase or decrease the flash output via the camera's menu.

If you need more flash power, and when you want to be more creative with flash photography, you can add an accessory flash.

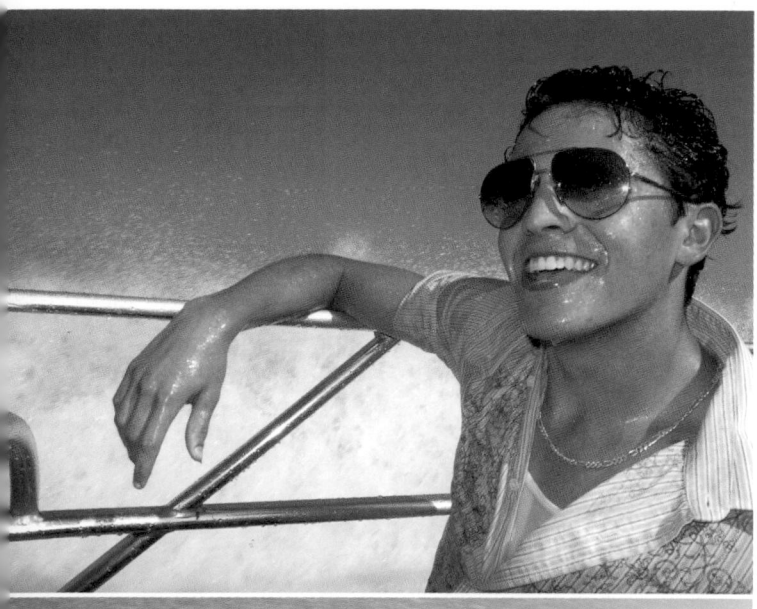

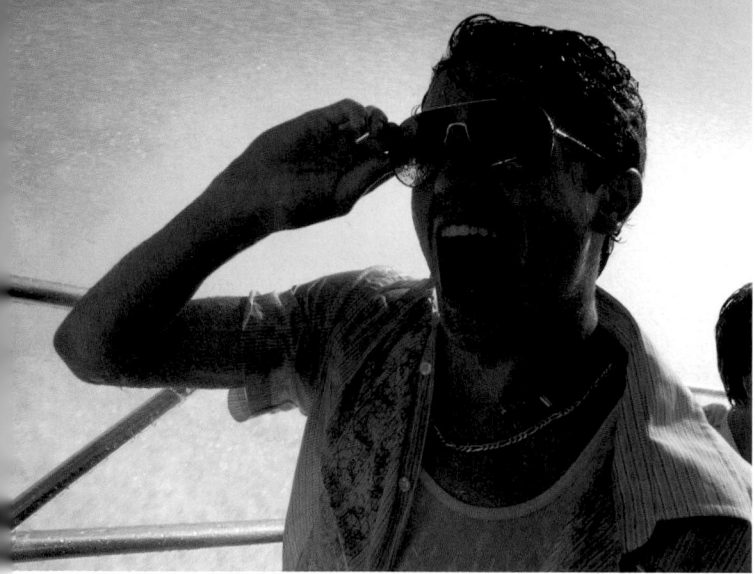

Sunny Day Flash Shots

I'll start off this chapter with a set of pictures that illustrates the effectiveness of using a flash in perhaps an unlikely situation: outdoors on a sunny day.

The top shot is the flash shot. The bottom shot is the non-flash shot.

As you can see, a benefit of using a flash is to fill in shadows caused by backlighting (in this case). It also can provide top lighting or side lighting.

To use the flash in your camera in bright light, take it off the Auto mode and set it to the Always Fire mode. At this setting, the flash fires even in bright light conditions to help you get the shot you envision.

Fill Flash Outdoors in the Shade

Pictures taken in the shade can also benefit from using a flash, because background light is often brighter than the light falling on the subject.

The top picture here is the flash shot. The bottom picture is the natural-light shot.

Using a flash in the shade has another benefit. When sunlight filters through leaves, it adds a greenish tint to the subject, making blond hair and skin look greenish.

The flash, overpowering the natural light, can bring out the true color of your subject. What's more, it can also make your picture look sharper, because the flash increases the contrast in a scene.

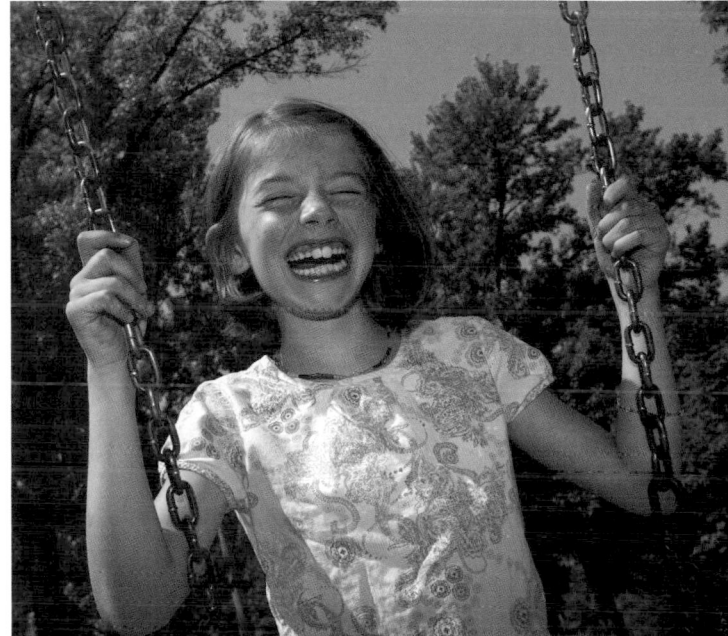

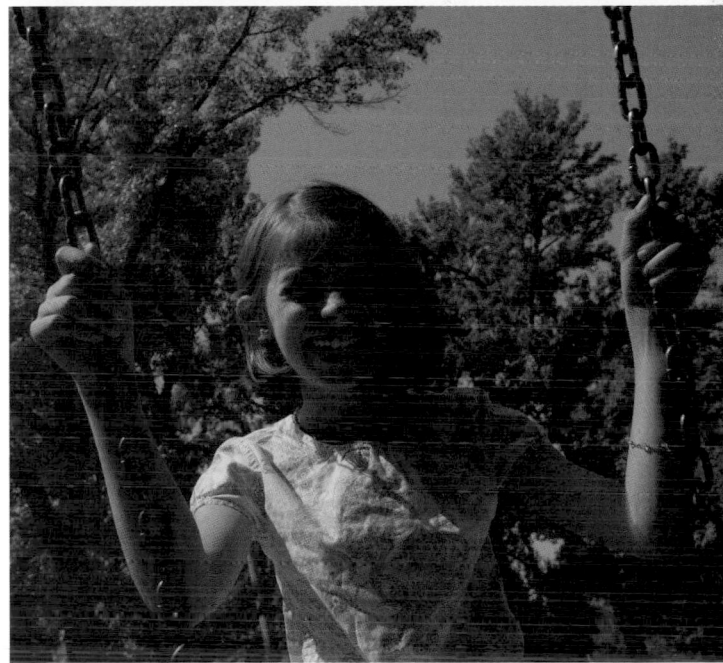

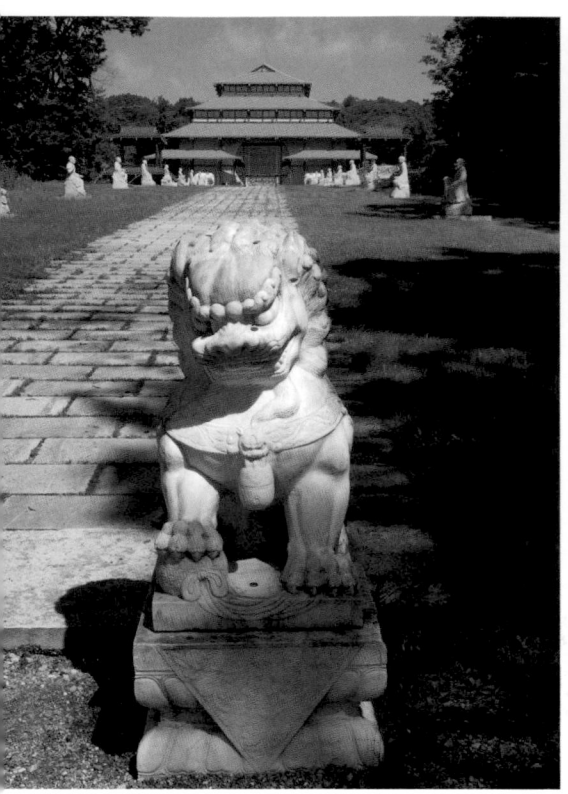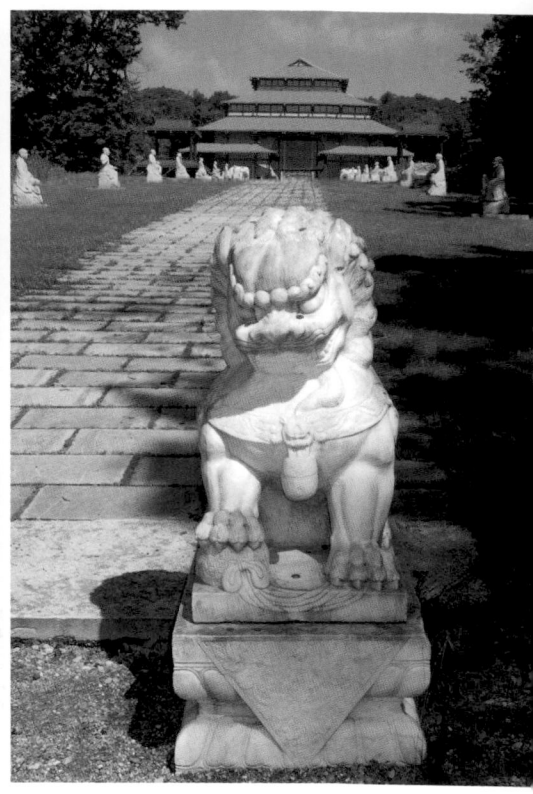

Add Just a Touch of Flash

Some cameras let you adjust the flash output over and under the Auto setting with +/- controls. If you take a shot and your subject is overexposed, reduce the flash output starting at −1/2. Continue to adjust the flash output until you have the desired result.

Similarly, if your subject looks took dark, increase the flash output starting at −1/2. Continue to adjust the flash output until you have the desired result.

The picture on the left is the natural-light shot. The picture on the right is the flash shot. I reduced the flash output by −1 to add just a touch of light. As you can see, some of the shadows on the statue are still visible in the flash shot.

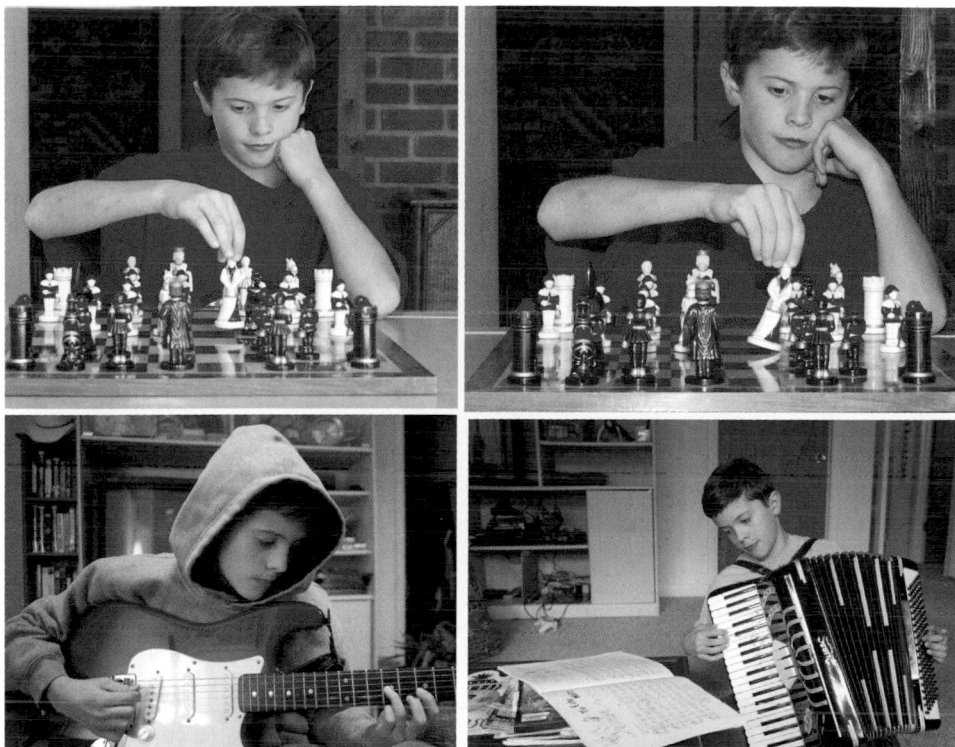

When Flash May Not Be Good

Here are two examples of when you might think you need flash, but probably don't really want to use it—because it might ruin the mood of the picture.

The natural-light pictures are on the left. The flash shots are on the right. Which ones do you like best?

My message: Use your flash wisely … and creatively.

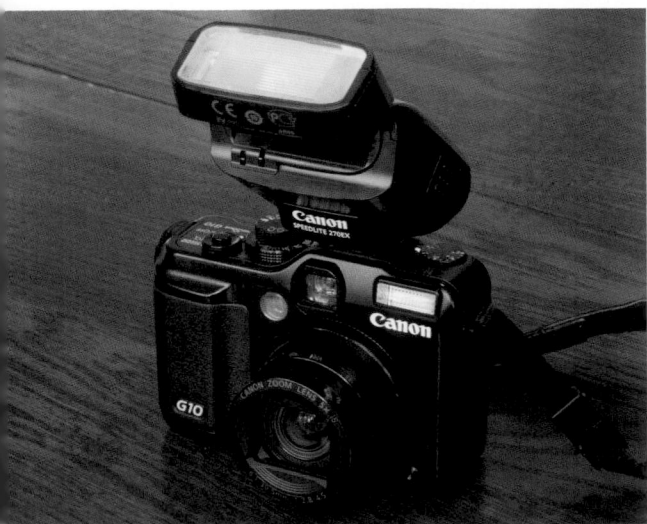

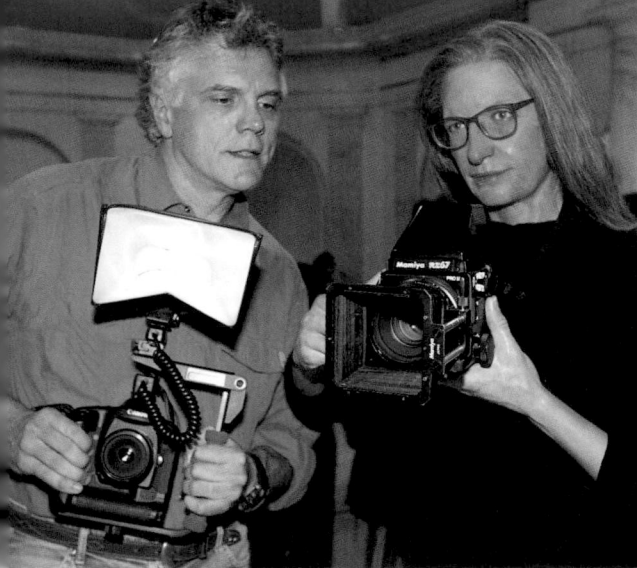

Adding an Accessory Flash

Serious compact camera shooters may want to invest in an accessory flash. Check to make sure your compact camera has a flash hot-shoe, which holds the flash.

An accessory flash not only has much more power (goes a greater distance) than a built-in flash, but some models offer swivel heads for directing (bouncing) the flash light off a ceiling or a wall.

The advantage of bouncing light off a larger surface is twofold:

One, it increases the size of the light source, which can help when taking pictures at the wide-angle setting (or using wide-angle adapters) on zoom lenses.

Two, it softens the light for a softer and more flattering effect.

My wife, Susan, took the picture of me with Annie Leibovitz at Madam Tussaud's Wax Museum in New York City using a flash with a swivel head. Notice that there are no harsh and unflattering shadows in the picture.

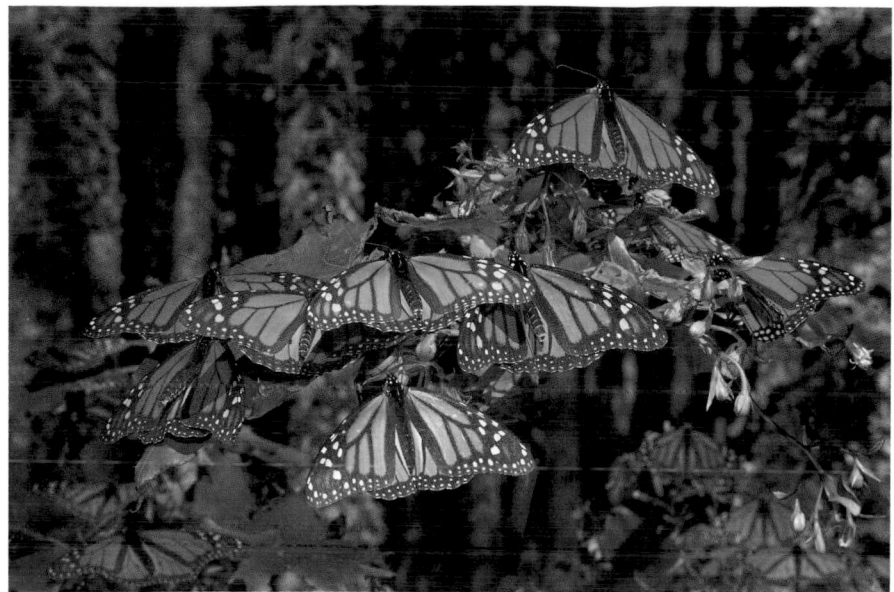

Part IX

The Zoom Lens Advantage

Way before zoom lenses were invented, photographers were zooming. They zoomed with their feet!

Today, we can still zoom with our feet—by moving toward or away from a subject to make the subject appear larger or smaller, respectively. However, the zoom lens on a compact camera offers the advantage of not having to move!

There are other benefits to using a zoom lens with the aperture control on your camera. In this chapter we'll take a look at the built-in zoom and what it can do for you.

Also remember that you can add accessory lenses—telephoto and wide-angle—to some compact cameras. But I don't recommend using them because they can degrade the image. What's more, I don't recommend the digital zoom feature in a compact camera for the same reason. Rather, take full advantage of the optical zoom … and your feet.

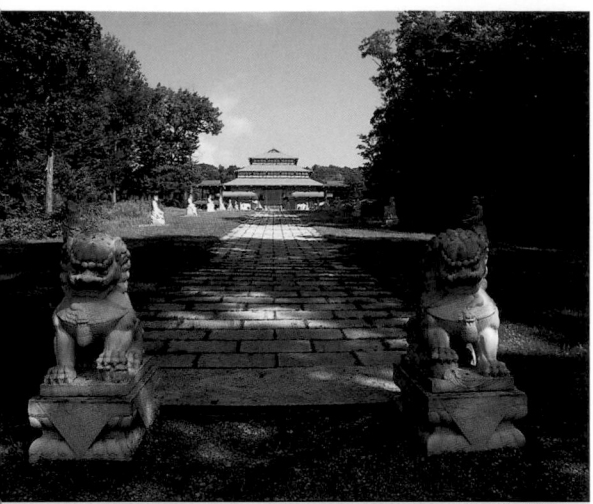

Closer or Wider, It's Your Choice

When you are composing your picture, carefully think about the elements in the scene and ask yourself if each component adds to or takes away from the picture you are trying to make.

Remember, there is a big difference between taking a picture and *making* a picture.

Here you see three shots that were taken with my Canon G10. From top to bottom: widest setting, middle setting and maximum setting.

I like all three pictures, because each shows a slightly different view of the Buddhist temple. However, the top two are my favorites, because they have a greater send of depth than the bottom picture.

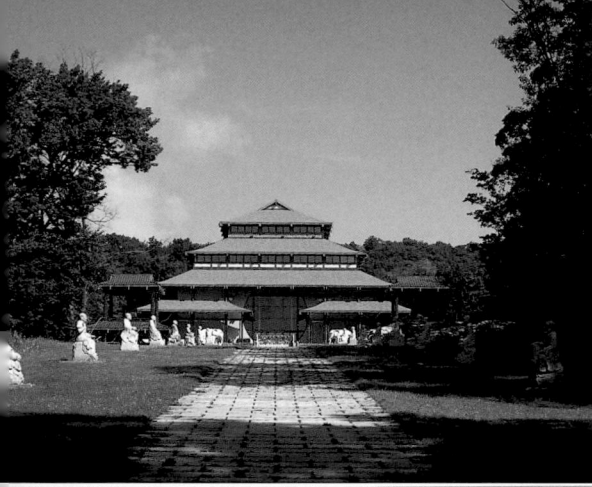

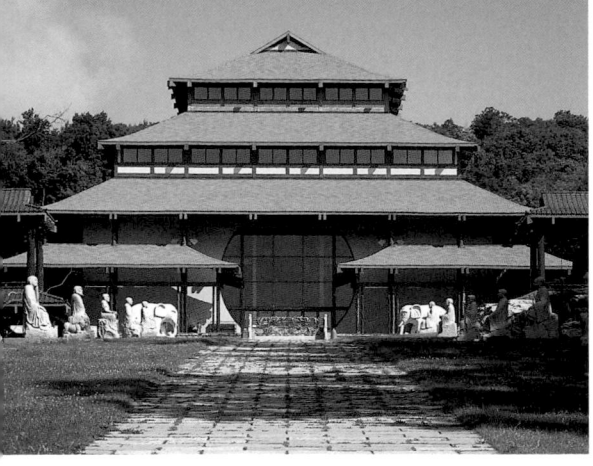

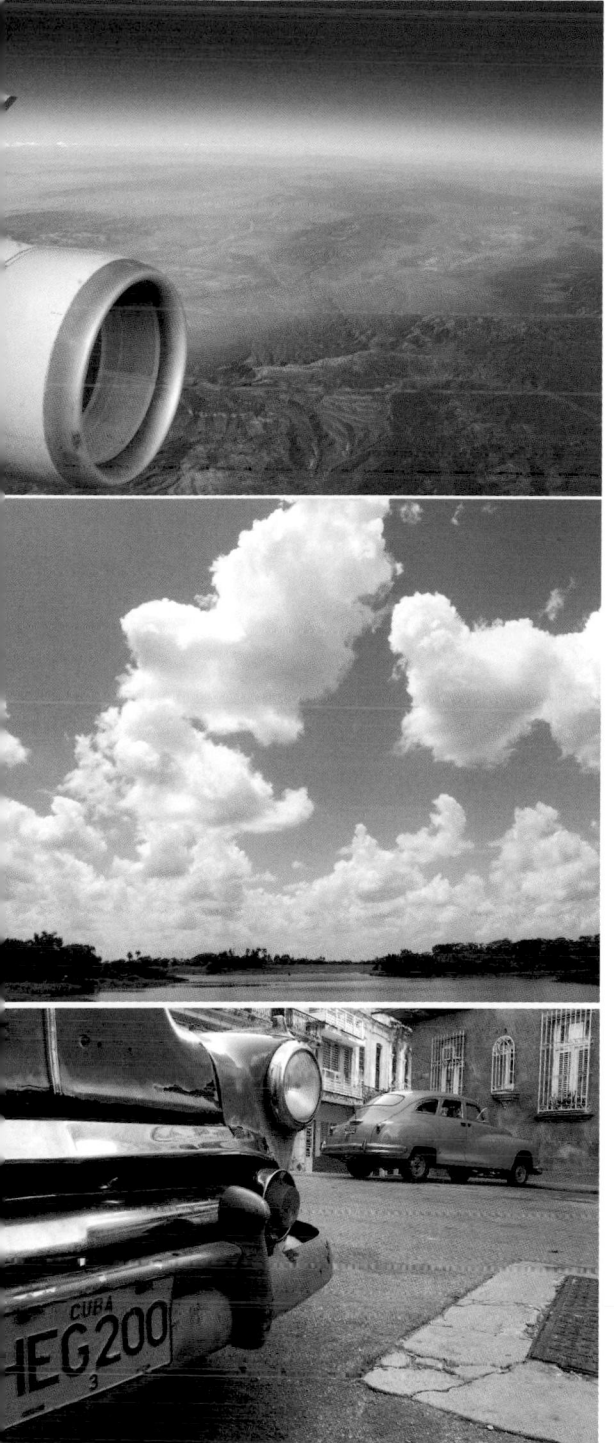

Compose Creatively

For my professional SLR picture taking, I use zoom lenses 99 percent of the time. I love zoom lenses because they let me compose creatively in-camera. I get to include what I want to capture in the frame and exclude what I don't.

Here are three examples of creative in-camera cropping.

When making the top photograph, I composed the scene with the jet engine off to the side, following the rule, "Dead Center is Deadly."

When making the middle photograph, I followed the rule, "Don't place the horizon line in the center of the frame."

When making the bottom photograph, I followed the rule, "Use a foreground element to create a sense of depth in an image."

See, when photographing, you get to decide what rule(s) you want to follow—and which ones you're going to ignore. Nice change from your school days, eh?

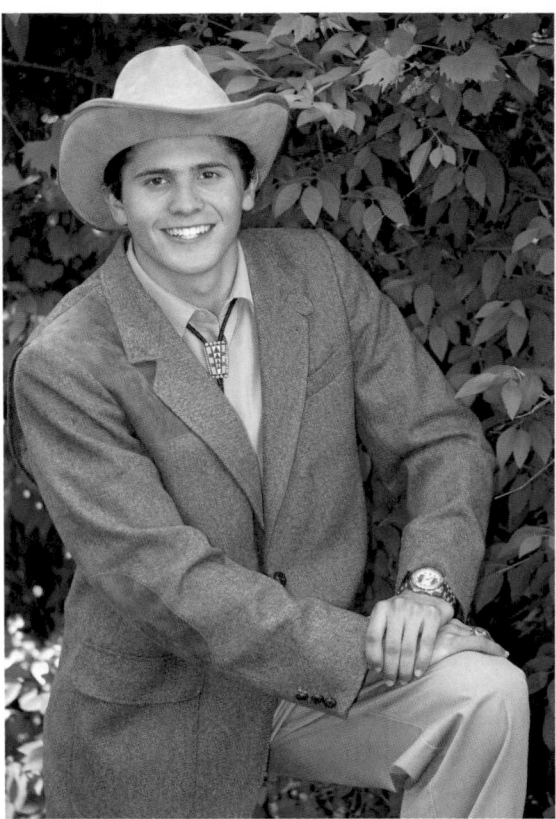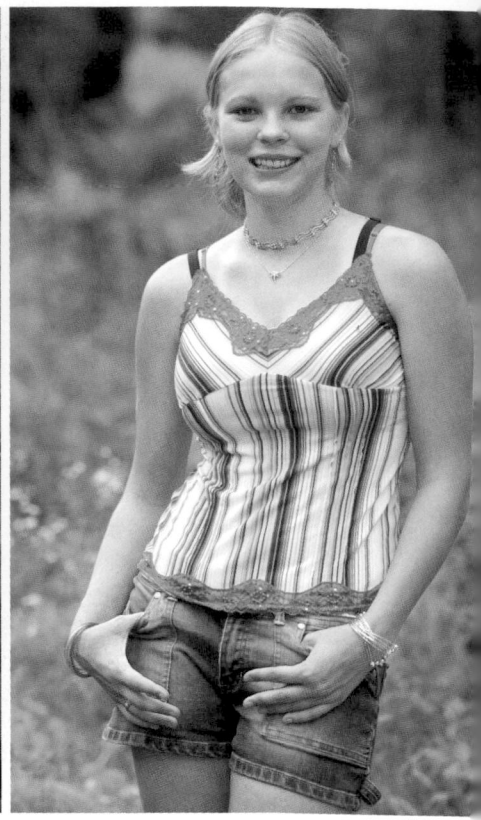

Blur the Background

One of the main advantages of compact cameras is that, due to the small image sensor size, they offer good depth-of-field—this is the term for describing the area in front of and behind the subject that is in focus. In fact, folks who move up to an SLR sometimes complain about the lack of depth-of-field (the area in front of and behind the subject that is in focus).

Even at f/8 you might get everything in the scene in focus, which actually may not be your goal all the time.

To blur the background, as illustrated in the picture on the right, use the longest zoom lens setting, set the aperture at its widest setting (lowest f/number) and stand as close as practically possible to the subject.

The picture on the right shows the effect of using a telephoto setting on a zoom lens when the aperture is set to its widest setting. The picture on the left shows the effect of using a wider zoom lens setting and a smaller aperture. More of the background is in focus.

Blur the Background by Changing Position

Here's a set of pictures that illustrates another way to blur the background.

When making the top picture, I stood relatively close to the subject and set the smallest aperture on my camera, f/8.

When making the bottom picture, I stood back several feet and set the widest aperture on my camera, f/2.8.

Notice how the statue of the elephant in the background (well, the entire background actually) is much softer in the bottom picture.

To create that effect, I stood back several feet from the statue and zoomed in so that the head was roughly the same size as the elephant. This is also a benefit of using a longer focal length; it "flattens" an image.

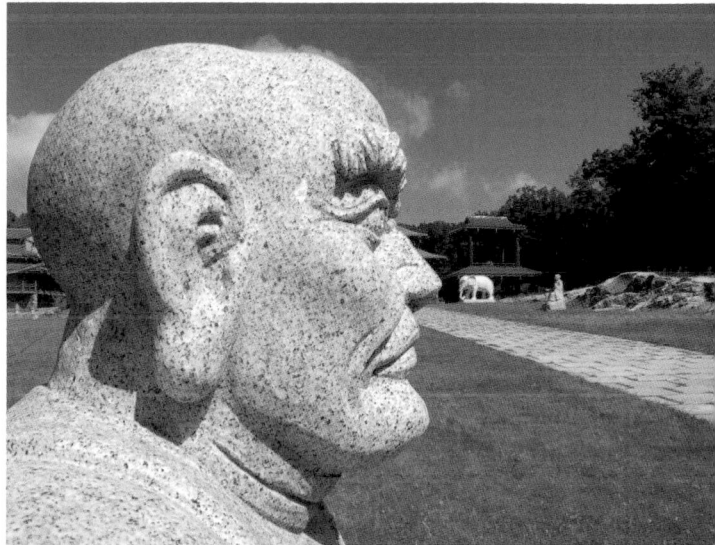

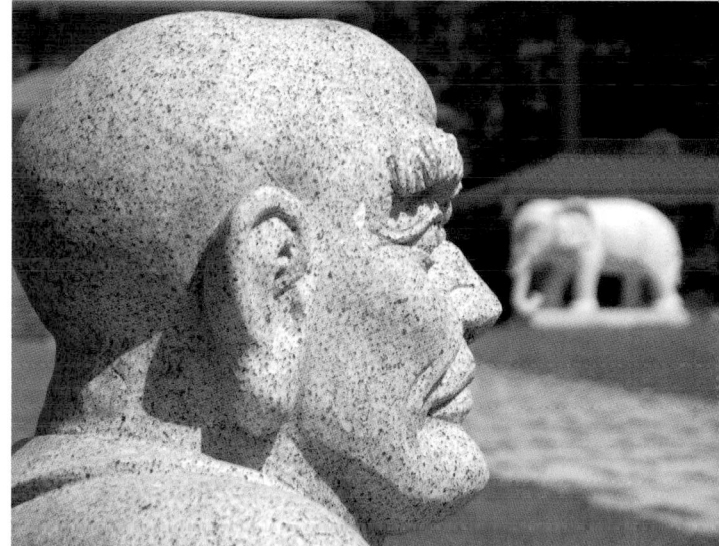

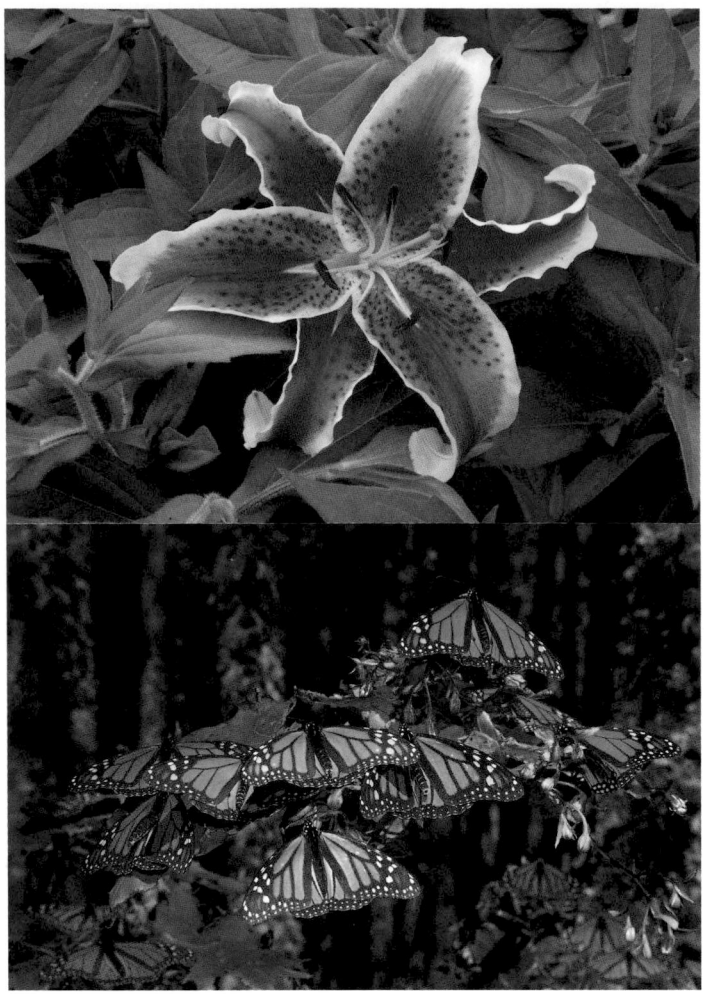

Cool Close-Ups

You can take cool close-ups with compact cameras, too. If your camera has a close-up mode, choose it.

If not, shoot at the widest setting on your zoom lens for maximum depth-of-field, as illustrated in the top picture.

To blur the background, use the technique mentioned on the previous page. That's what I did for my photograph of several monarch butterflies resting on a bush.

I took that picture in Mexico at the over-wintering site of the famous monarch migration. I have lots of shots that I took with my SLR, but I took this shot while I was having lunch. It was just a fun shot, but it has turned out to be one of my favorites.

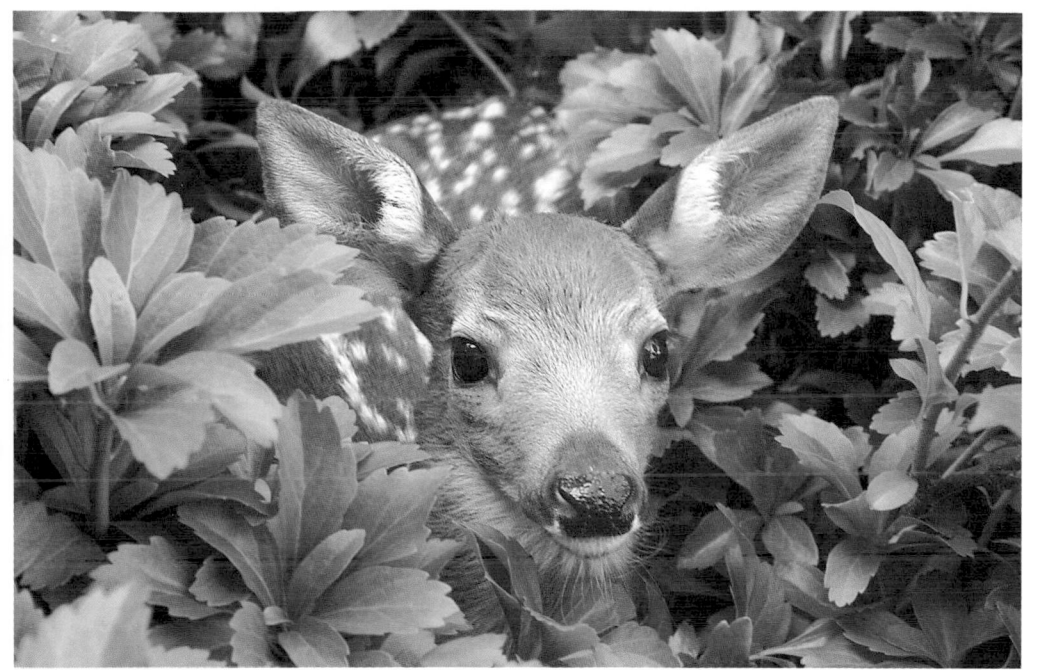

Part X

Setting the Mode

Like professional-grade cameras, many compact cameras offer a range of settings and adjustment options for photographers to use in different situations.

There's always the trusty automatic mode, but when you want to get more creative—and show some real shooting know-how— here are some things to consider. In this chapter, we explore the auto modes as well as tips for using the exposure, metering, focus and drive modes. C'mon. This will be fun.

Fully Automatic Picture/Exposure Modes

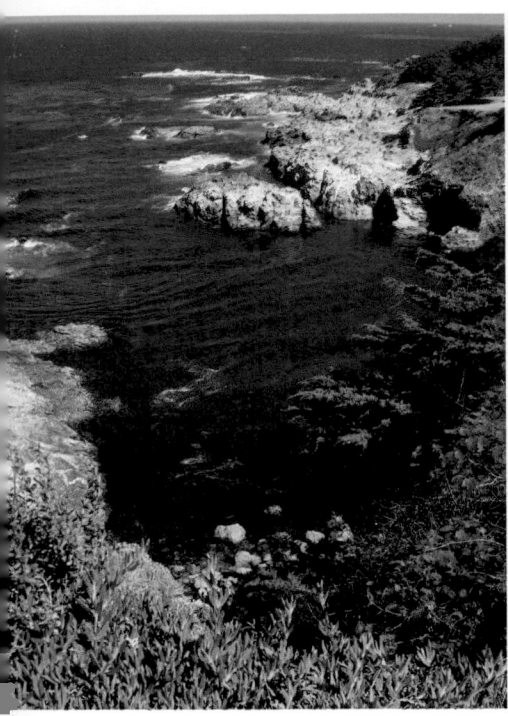
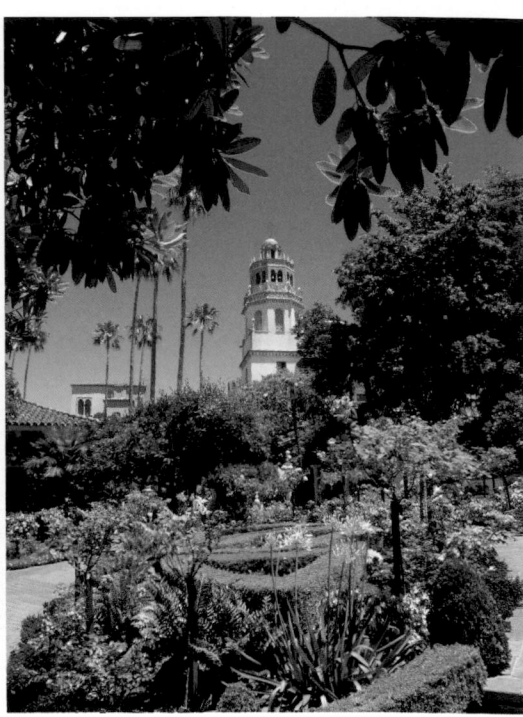

As photographers, we like to take portraits, landscapes, cityscapes and close-ups—serious shots and fun ones. We like still life photography and we like to capture sports and wildlife action. We shoot day and night.

Sometimes, we take our time and make careful camera adjustments. But sometimes, we simply want to point and shoot. That's when it's really nice to use fully automatic picture/exposure modes.

In this section we'll look at automatic picture/exposure modes that are available on most compact cameras. By doing some of the "thinking" for us, these modes help photographers get good shots at a moment's notice by, in most cases, simply pointing and shooting. What could be easier and more fun?

Let's go.

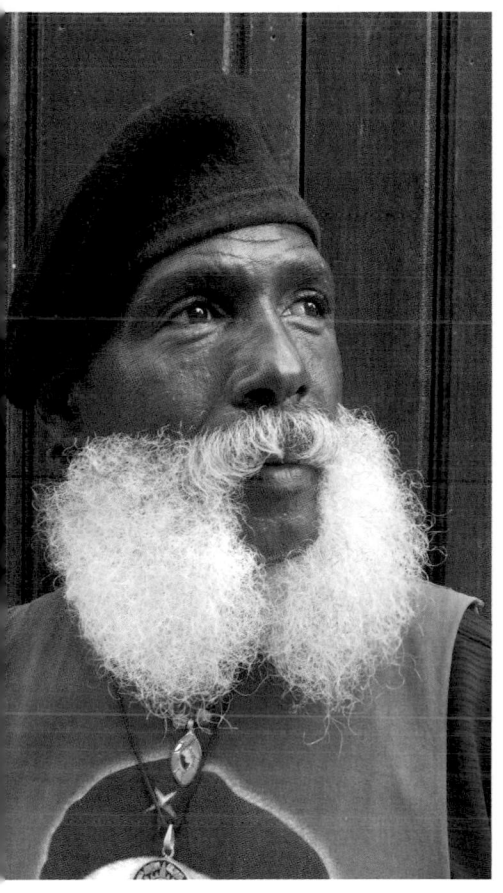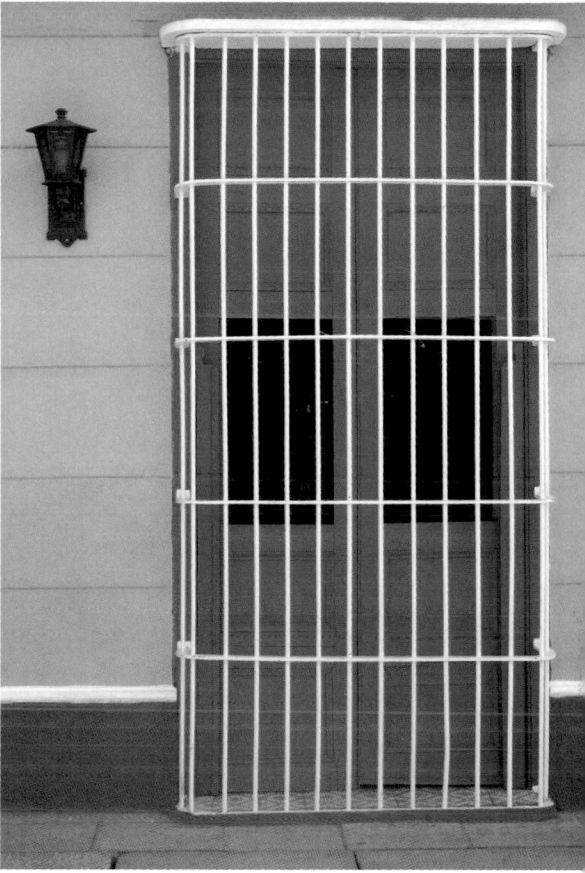

Full Auto Mode

Designed for fast point-and-shoot photography, the Full Auto mode is rather amazing. When set to Full Auto, the camera sets the shutter speed and f-stop. You take the picture. It's that simple.

This mode is a good choice when there is not a lot of contrast (that is, difference between the shadows and highlights) in a scene, as was the case in these two pictures in Cuba.

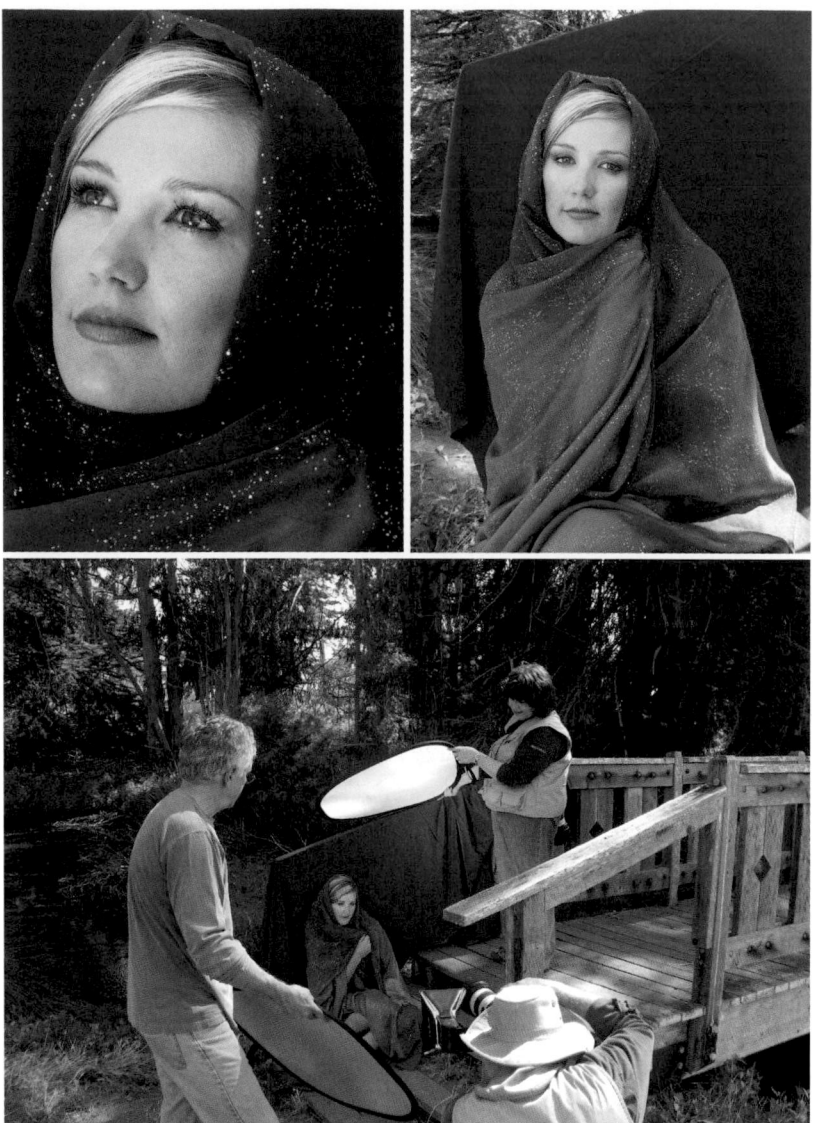

Portrait Mode

Use the Portrait mode for taking portraits, such as this one I took of a model during one of my California workshops. At this setting, the camera automatically sets an appropriate f-stop to slightly blur the background. This helps your subject stand out in the scene.

Just for fun, I included two behind-the-scenes pictures on this page, so you can see what goes into making a picture.

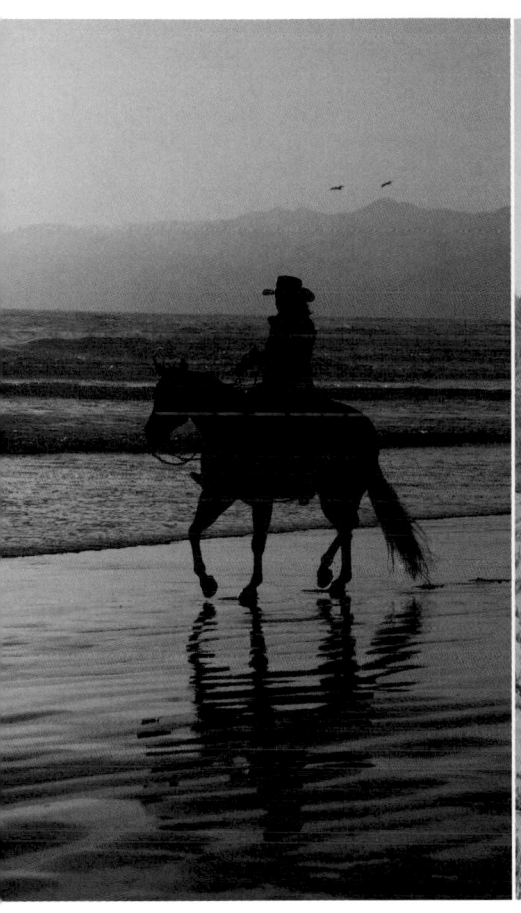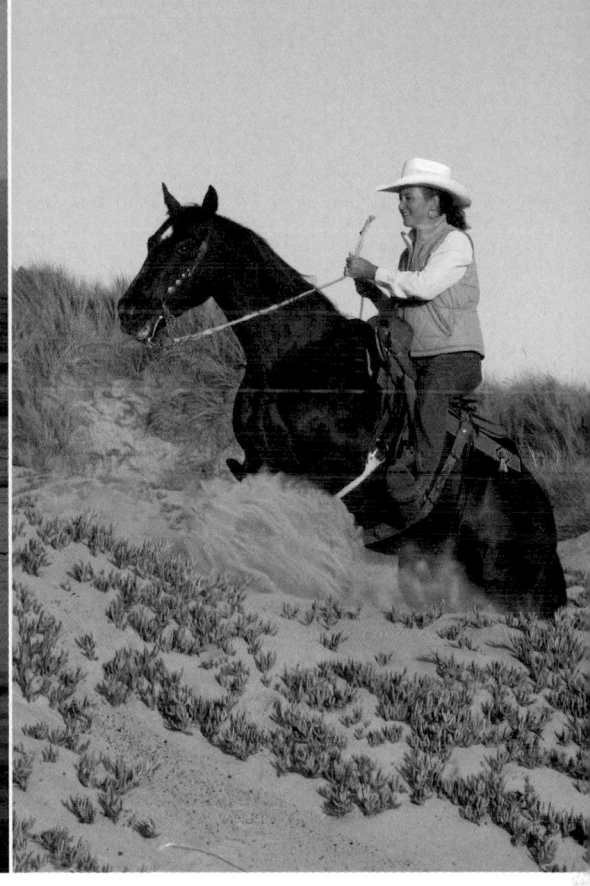

Sports Mode

The Sports mode is designed for action photography—and not only sports action. In this mode, the camera automatically sets a higher shutter speed to stop the subject's movement.

On some compact cameras, focus tracking, which constantly keeps a moving subject in focus until the exact moment of exposure, is automatically activated.

When you simply want to stop action for your image, this mode will deliver good results in most outdoor, bright-light situations. That's why I chose the Sports mode for these two pictures that I took in Los Osos, California.

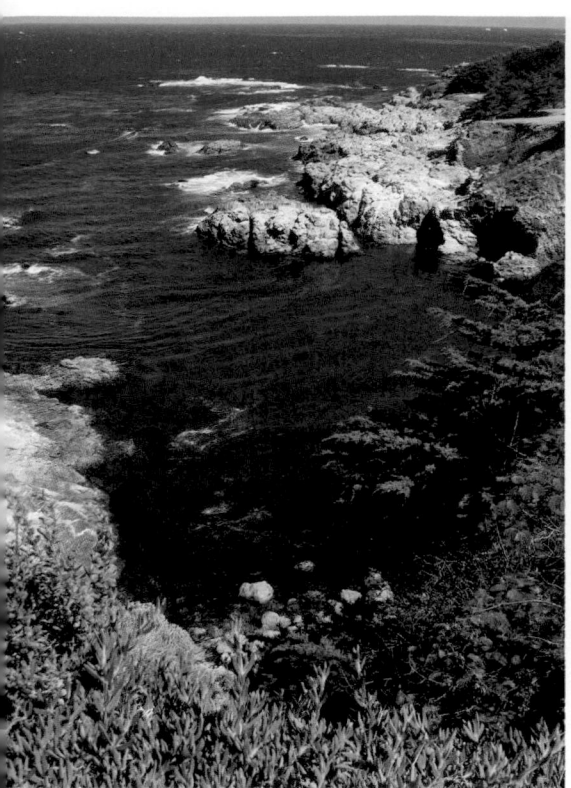 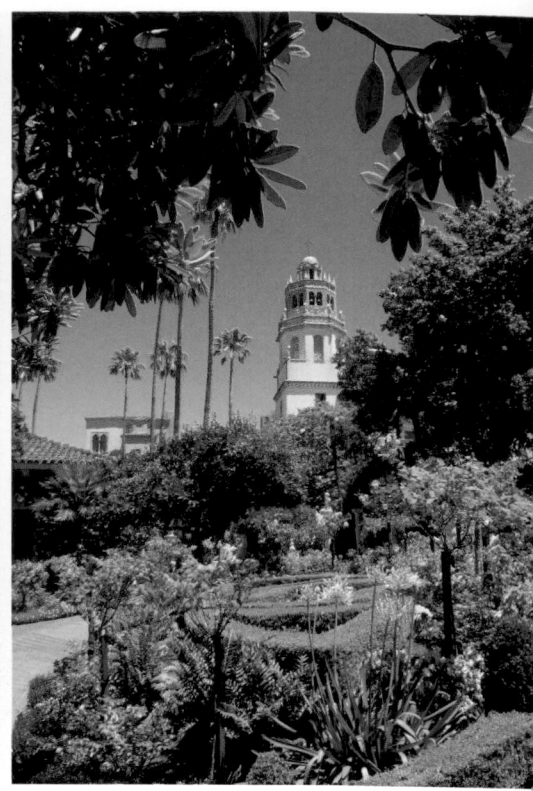

Landscape Mode

In landscape photography (as well as in cityscape and seascape photography), you usually want most of the scene to appear in sharp focus—because that's how you see it with your eyes. In the Landscape mode, a compact camera sets a small aperture to produce good depth-of-field. Notice how all the elements in both these scenes are in sharp focus.

The picture on the left was taken in Big Sur, California. The picture on the right was taken at Hearst Castle, also in California.

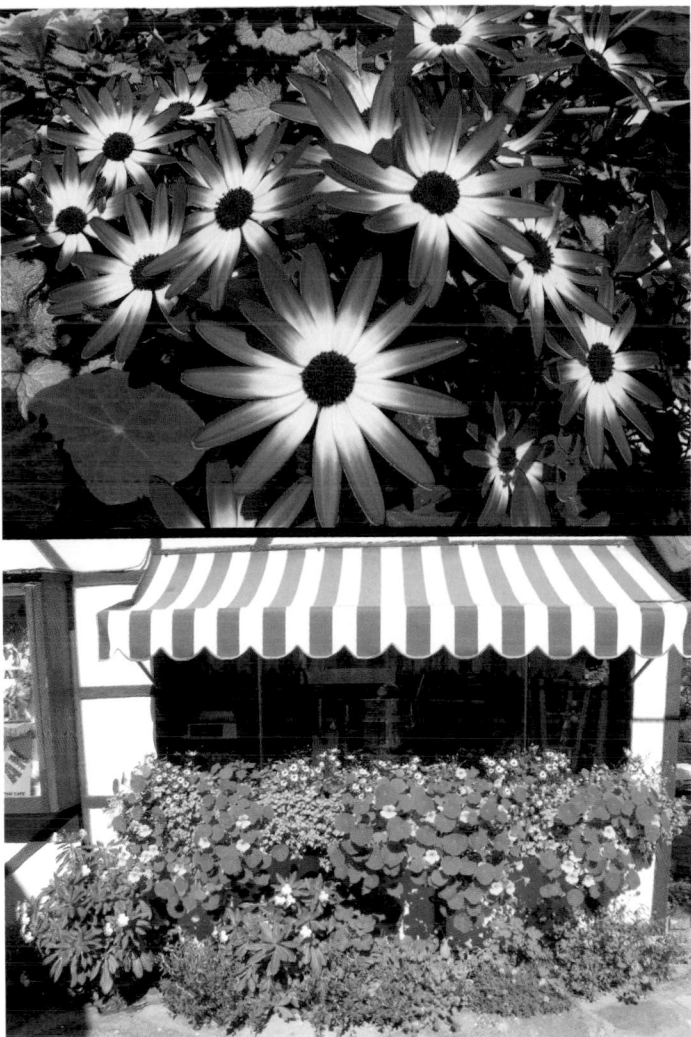

Close-up Mode

Close-up photographs need to capture fine detail with good depth-of-field. To help you get a sharp shot in the Close-up mode, the built-in flash in a compact camera automatically pops up (or you can activate an accessory flash) to illuminate the subject. A compact camera in Close up mode also sets a small f-stop for good depth-of-field.

Here, too, I offer a behind-the-scenes picture—this time to illustrate that it's always a good idea to look for pictures, even when there seems to be none.

This cute little shop is in Carmel, California.

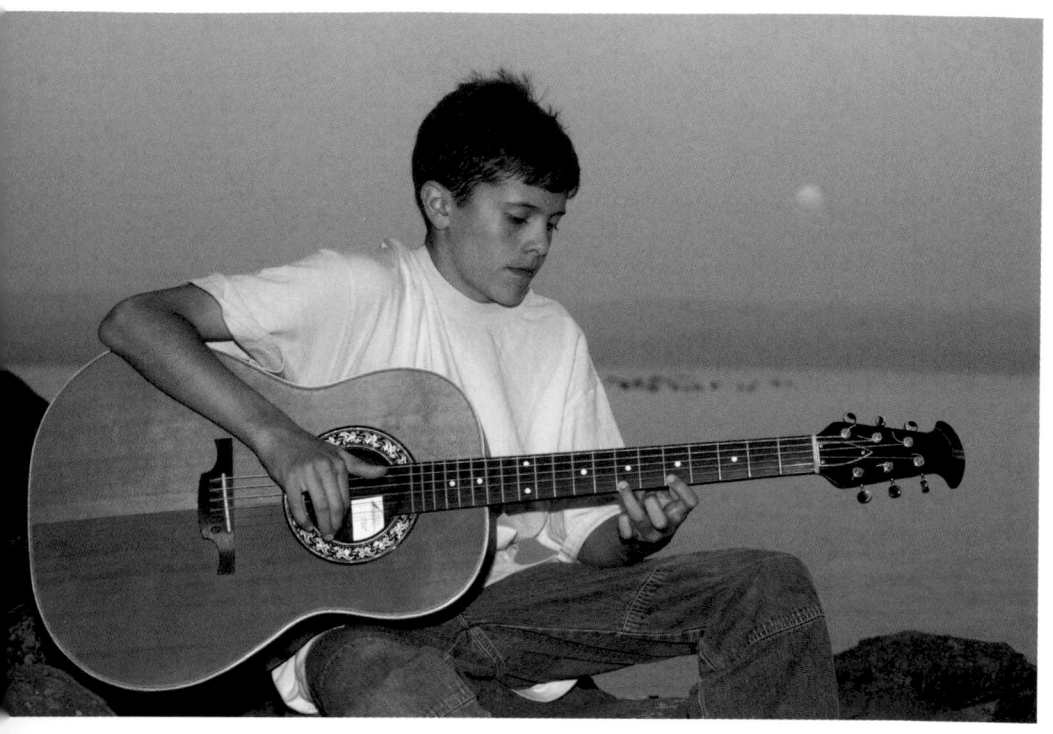

Night Portrait Mode

Want to use background lights as a backdrop for a portrait at night? Then set your camera to the Night Portrait mode. Here, a slow shutter speed is selected to capture the background lights, and the built-in flash automatically pops up (or you can activate an accessory flash) to light your subject.

This mode is useful when you want to get a good exposure of both the subject and an illuminated background. It's the mode I used for this picture of my son playing his guitar on the banks of the Hudson River.

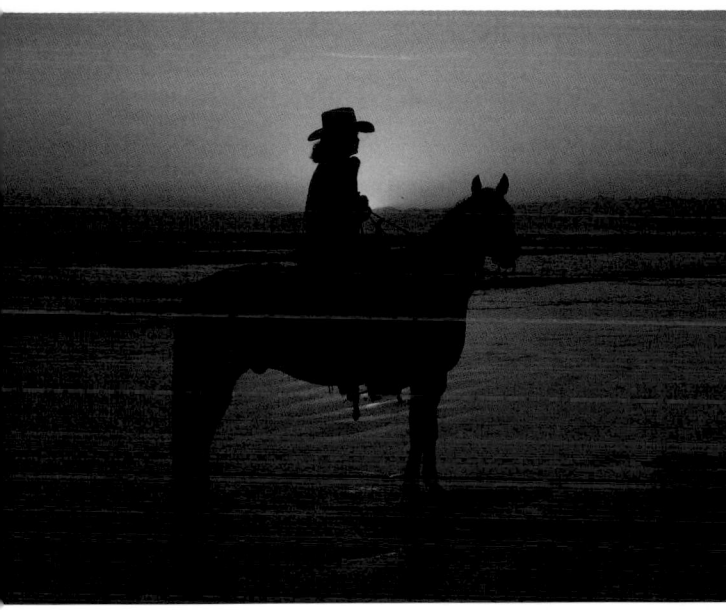
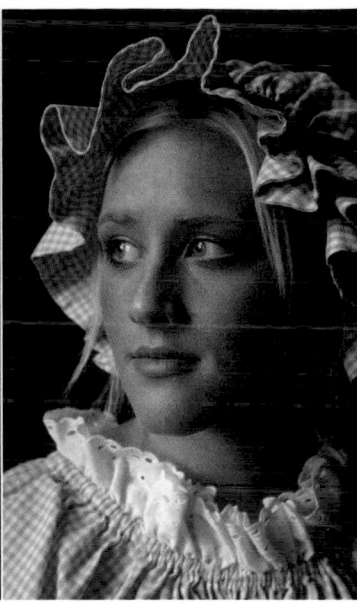

Flash-Off Mode

Indoors and outdoors, there are times when you don't want to illuminate a subject in low-light conditions with a flash. These are times when you want a more natural look in a picture.

In such cases, use the Flash-Off mode. Be careful to hold your camera steady though. In very low light, you'll need a tripod to minimize camera shake, which can cause a blurry picture.

When you are taking pictures outdoors in low light, you can use the Flash-Off mode to prevent the built-in flash from firing and illuminating foreground subjects.

I photographed this horse and rider on the beach in Los Osos, California. I photographed the young woman during one of my workshops in Vermont.

Choose your automatic mode carefully. If you do, you can get some great shots while the camera does the exposure "thinking" for you!

Creative Exposure Modes

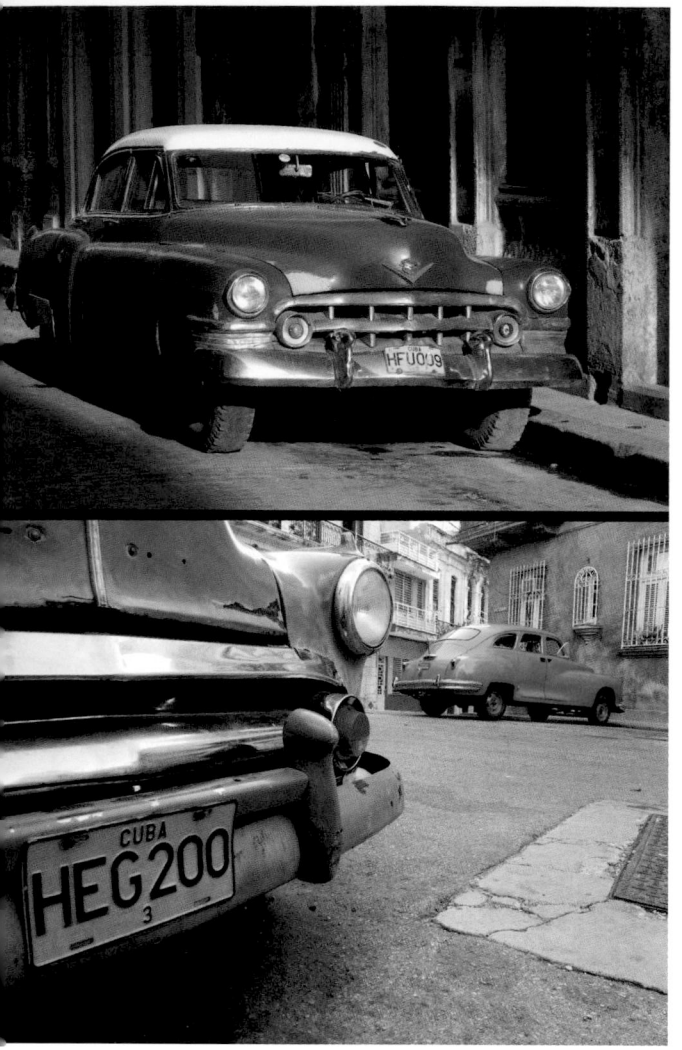

In the previous section, we explored fully automatic picture/exposure modes. Those modes are designed for situations in which you want the camera to make f-stop and shutter speed decisions for you. Right, those modes don't offer any creative control, except when it comes to choosing a subject and composing a picture.

So let's take a look now at creative exposure modes. Except for the Manual mode, creative exposure modes are automatic, but not fully automatic. You can still take control and be creative.

Check 'em out.

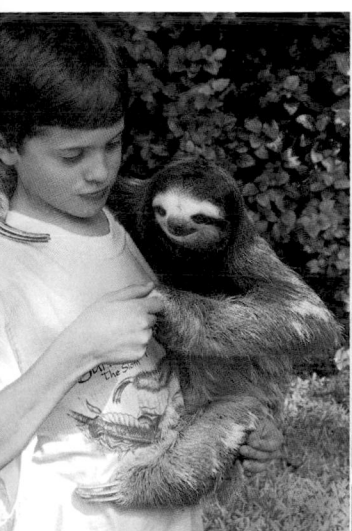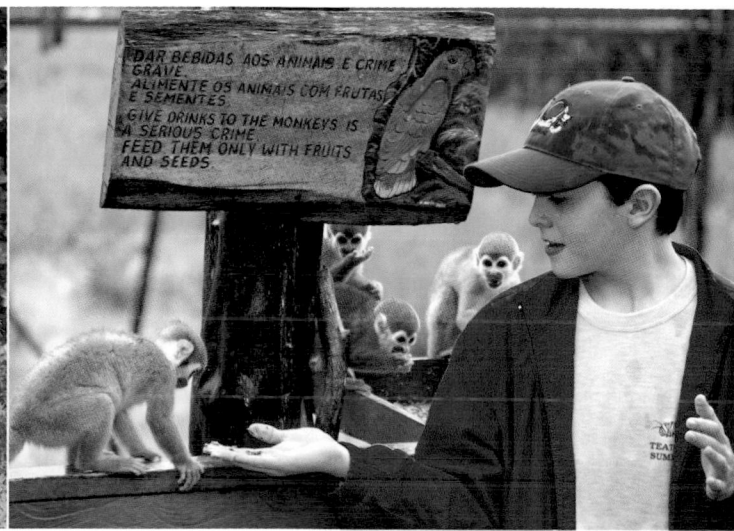

Program Mode

When set to the Program mode, your camera sets the shutter speed and f-stop for a correct exposure of the scene. However, at a moment's notice, you can change that combination to a slower/faster shutter speed or to wider/smaller f-stop. That's because the Program mode is what's called an adjustable program mode, meaning you can make adjustments in your shutter speed/f-stop choice while you are shooting.

So, if you want the background or foreground to be more or less in focus, or if you want to blur or "freeze" the subject, you can make an adjustment quickly and easily by turning a wheel or by pressing a button that adjusts the f-stop and shutter accordingly—without changing the exposure.

I used the Program mode when I took these two pictures of my son, Marco.

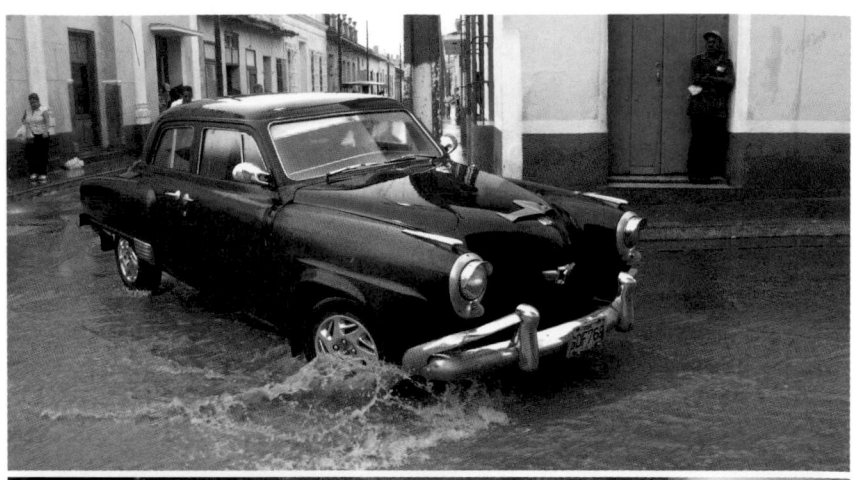

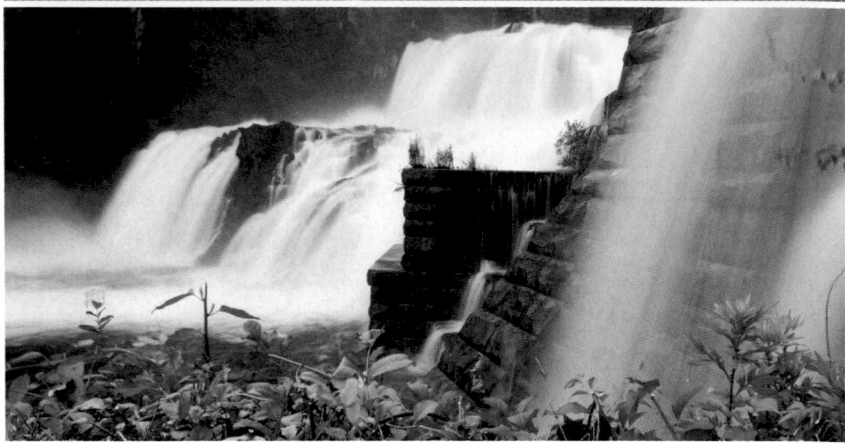

Shutter-Priority (Tv) Mode

If precisely controlling motion in a picture is your objective, set your camera to the Shutter Priority mode. Use fast shutter speeds (usually above 1/250 of a second) to "freeze" action and slow shutter speeds (usually below 1/30 of a second) to blur action.

I "froze" the action in this Cuban rainy-day scene by setting the shutter speed to 1/250 second. I blurred the action in this waterfall photograph by setting the shutter speed at 1/30 second.

The beauty of this mode is that even if the light level changes, the shutter speed stays set, because the camera automatically selects the appropriate f-stop for a correct exposure. If there is not enough light for a proper exposure, you'll get a warning on your camera (or in the viewfinder). This warning could be a blinking light or a flashing f/stop or shutter speed. If that happens, you'll need to boost your ISO, use a tripod or activate the camera's flash.

Aperture-Priority (Av) Mode

When it's important to precisely control depth-of-field (the area in focus in front of and behind a subject), use the Aperture Priority mode.

The beauty of this mode is that even if the light level changes, the f-stop stays set—because the camera automatically selects the appropriate shutter speed for a correct exposure.

Set a small aperture (f/8 or so) for maximum depth-of-field, as illustrated in this picture that I took at the Hearst Castle. To blur the background, as I did for this picture of my son, set a wide aperture (f/4.5 or so).

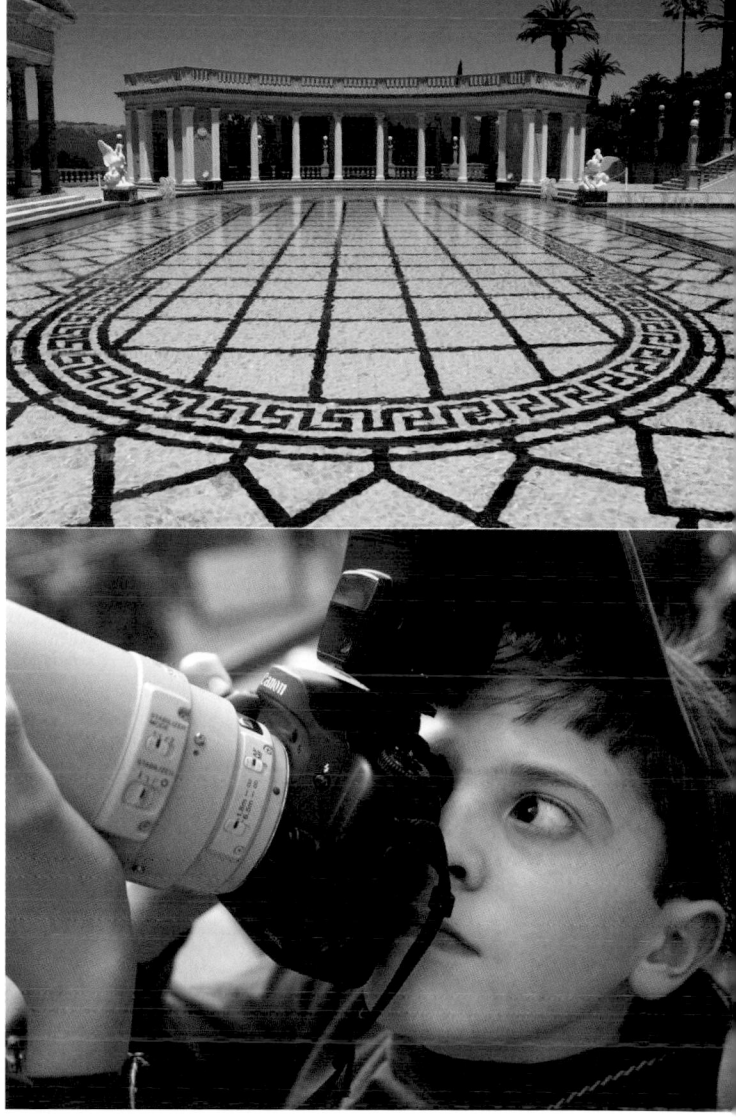

If there is not enough light for a proper exposure, you'll get a warning on your camera (or in the viewfinder). This warning could be a blinking light or a flashing f/stop or shutter speed. If that happens, you'll need to boost your ISO, use a tripod or activate the camera's flash.

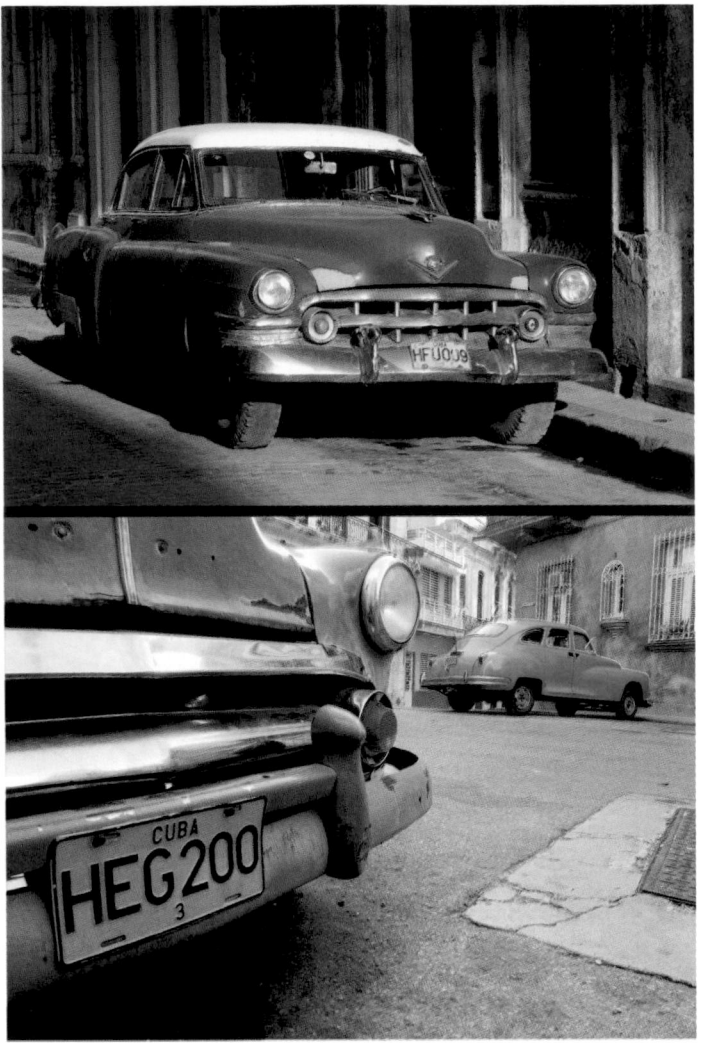

Manual Exposure (M) Mode

For total control over exposure, especially in tricky lighting situations that can fool a camera's exposure meter, choose the Manual Exposure mode.

In this mode, you separately set both the shutter speed and f-stop for a slightly darker or lighter picture (or background). You can also change the settings to control the degree of subject movement—as well as subject movement vs. the background movement, and vice versa.

I took these two pictures in Cuba early one morning with my camera set on the Manual mode, because I wanted total control over the images.

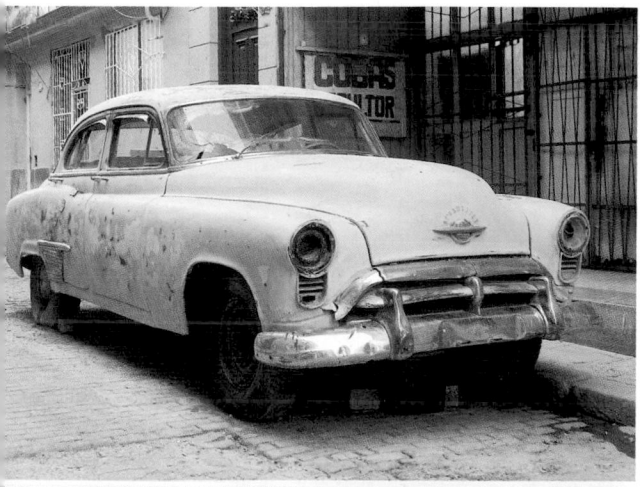

Exposure Bracketing

Higher-end compact cameras offer a safety exposure feature (in the Program, Tv and Av modes) called Exposure Bracketing.

With either a dial or menu settings, you can change the exposure value (EV) from 0 (the recommended setting) to over (+) and under (−) that setting—sometimes in half stops, sometimes in full stops. Some cameras let you bracket your exposures up to two stops over the 0 settings, while other offers a three-stop exposure compensation range.

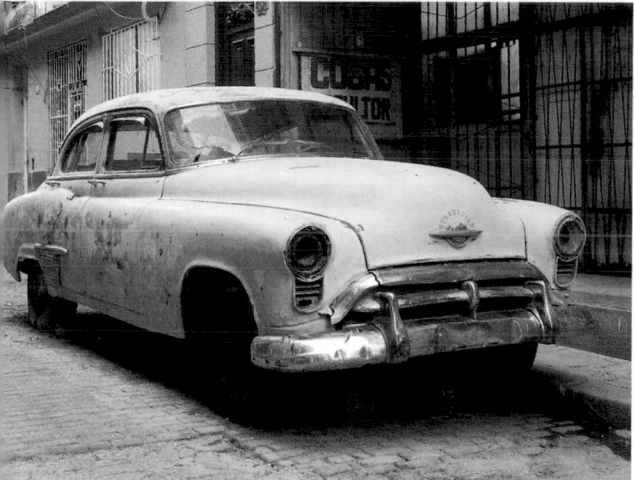

When you are not sure about the correct exposure, it's a good idea to bracket.

Here is an example of taking pictures at the recommended setting (center), one stop over that setting (top) and one stop under that setting (bottom).

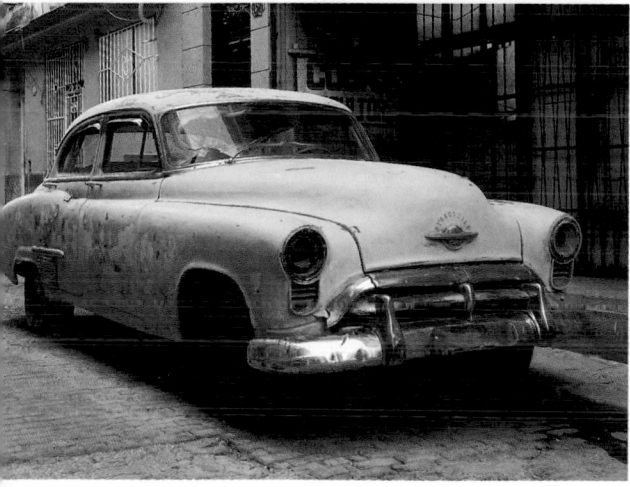

Metering Modes

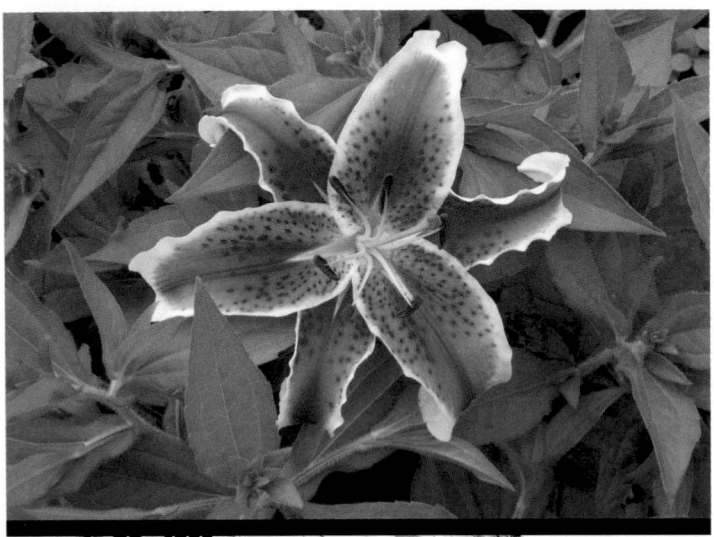

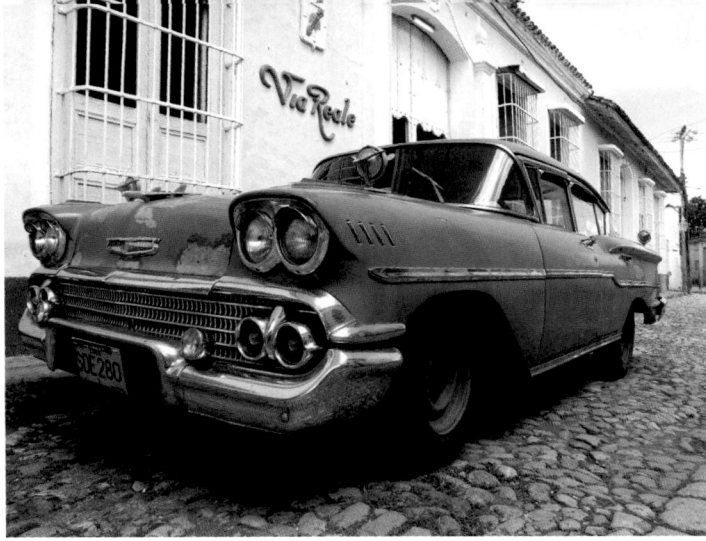

Most high-end compact cameras offer different types of metering modes. They may have different names on different camera brands, but they are basically all the same.

Each metering mode has its advantages. If you know which mode to choose in a particular lighting situation, you'll have a good chance of getting a perfect exposure.

This section provides an overview of the different metering modes.

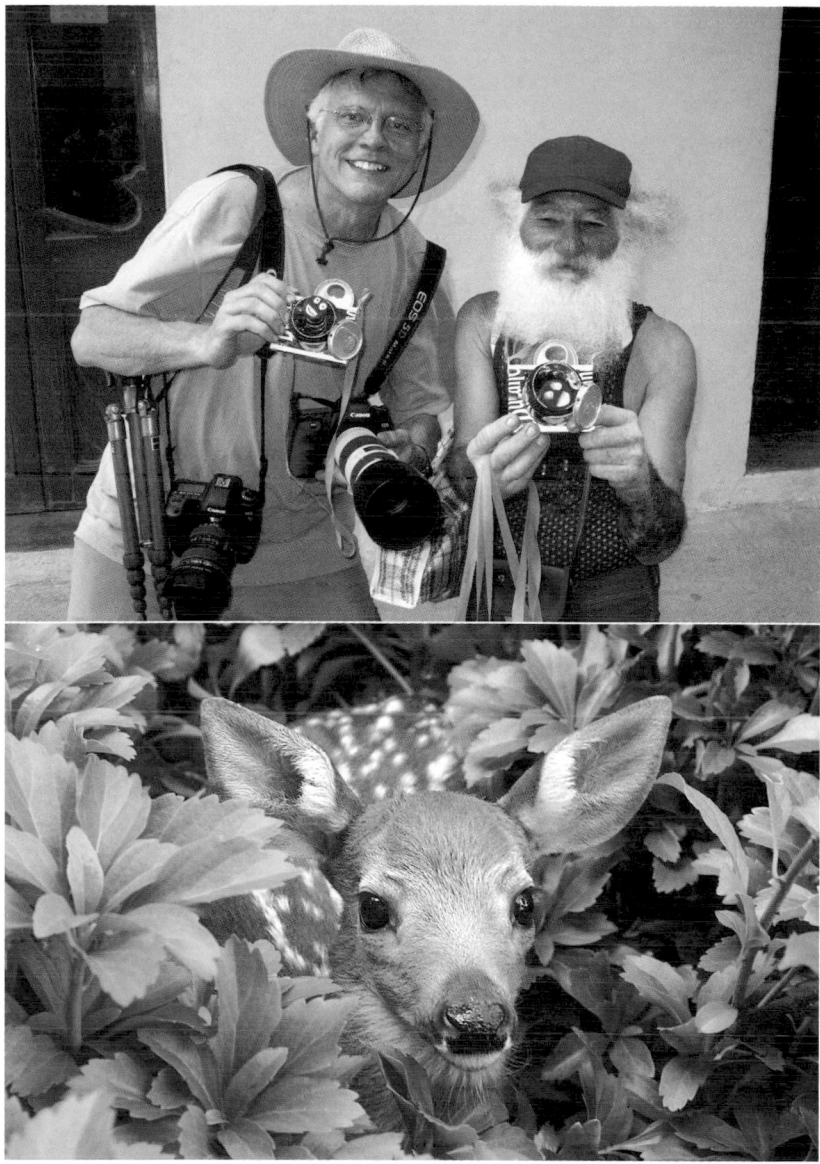

Average

An average metering mode—known usually as *evaluative metering*—measures the brightness level of the entire scene. This is a good choice in many situations, because it evaluates the different areas of a scene and selects the best exposure.

It is ideally suited for quick shooting, when there is not a lot of contrast in the scene, as illustrated by this picture of me on location and the one of deer in our backyard.

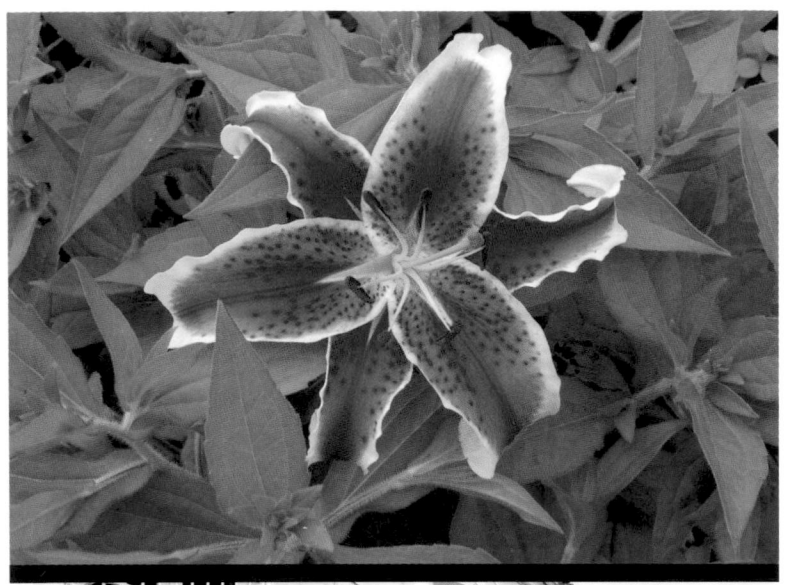

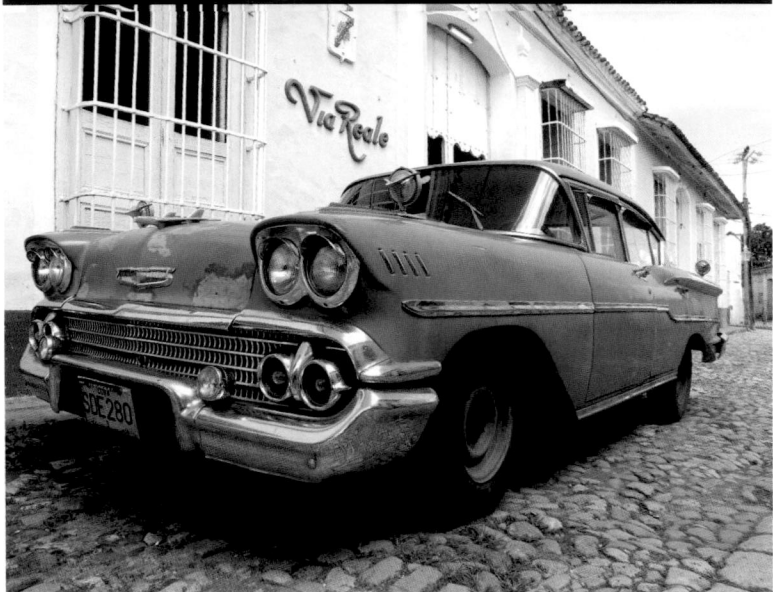

Center-weighted Average Metering

Center-weighted Average Metering gives special emphasis to the center of the frame, but it also covers the surrounding area. This is a good metering mode to select when the surrounding area is only slightly darker or lighter than the center.

I used this mode for this picture of a flower in my backyard and of a car in Trinidad, Cuba.

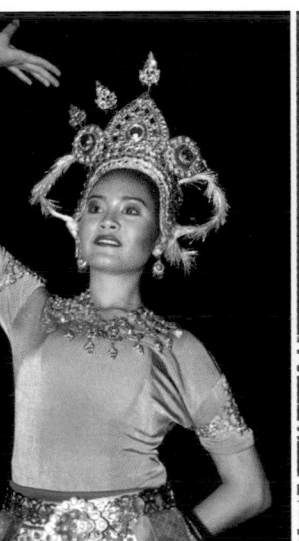 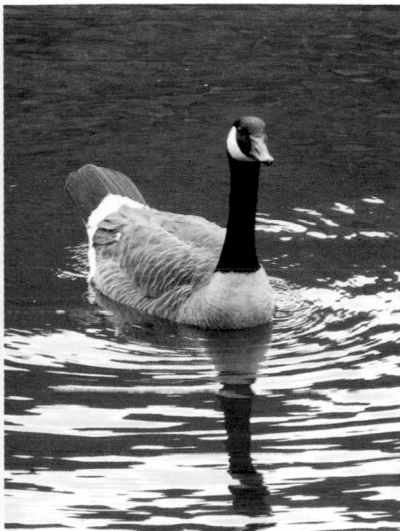 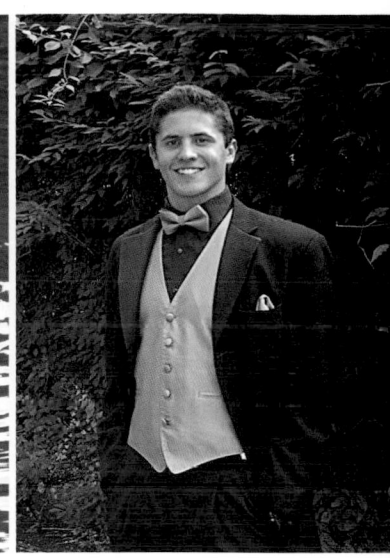

Spot Metering

Spot Metering measures only a small area in the center of the frame. When you have a select area of a picture and don't want other areas of the scene to affect your exposure, this mode is the way to go.

The size of the spot varies from camera to camera. High-end cameras usually have a smaller spot than entry-level cameras.

Focus Modes

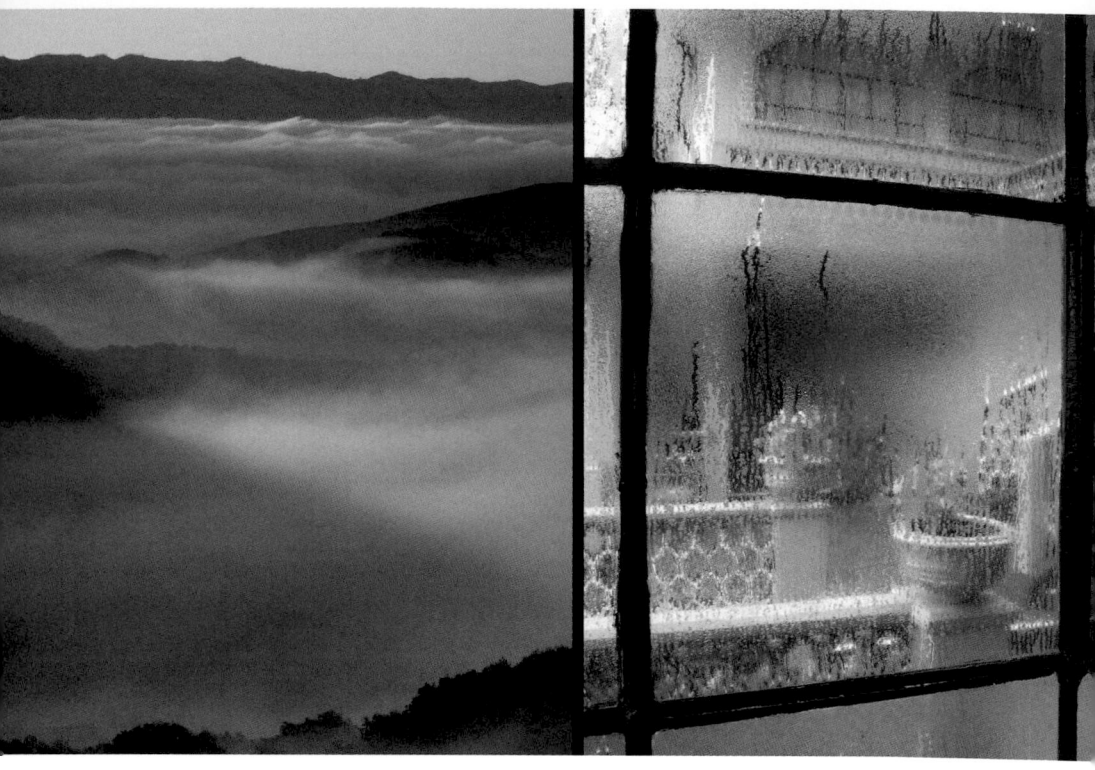

Just because you have an auto focus camera does not mean that the camera knows where to focus or what you intend to make the main subject of your photograph.

In this section, we'll explore the different focus modes. Understanding these tools will help you get sharp shots each and every time.

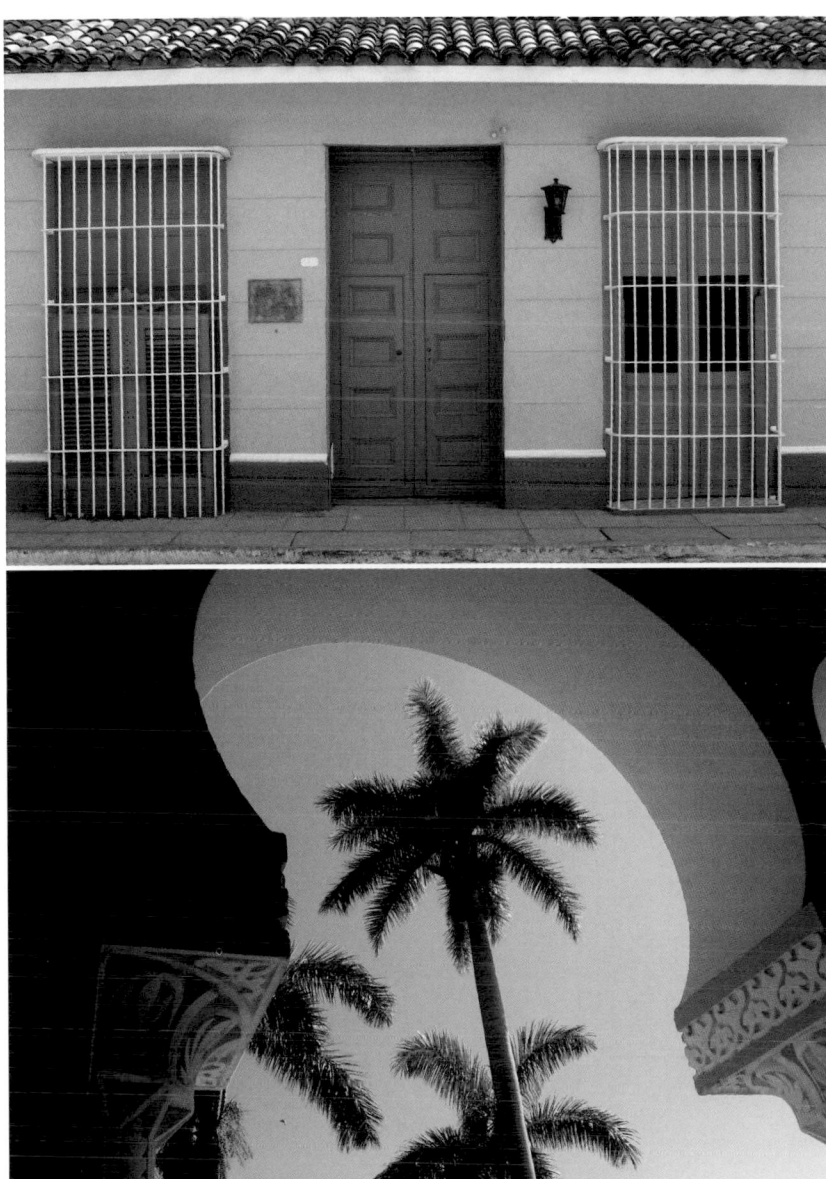

One-Shot

The one-shot focus mode is the one to use when a subject is not moving. Basically, if the subject is not moving and you are not moving, it's virtually impossible to take an out-of-focus picture (if your shutter speed is high enough to prevent camera shake). Just make sure that the focus point selection is over your subject. More info on that on the next page.

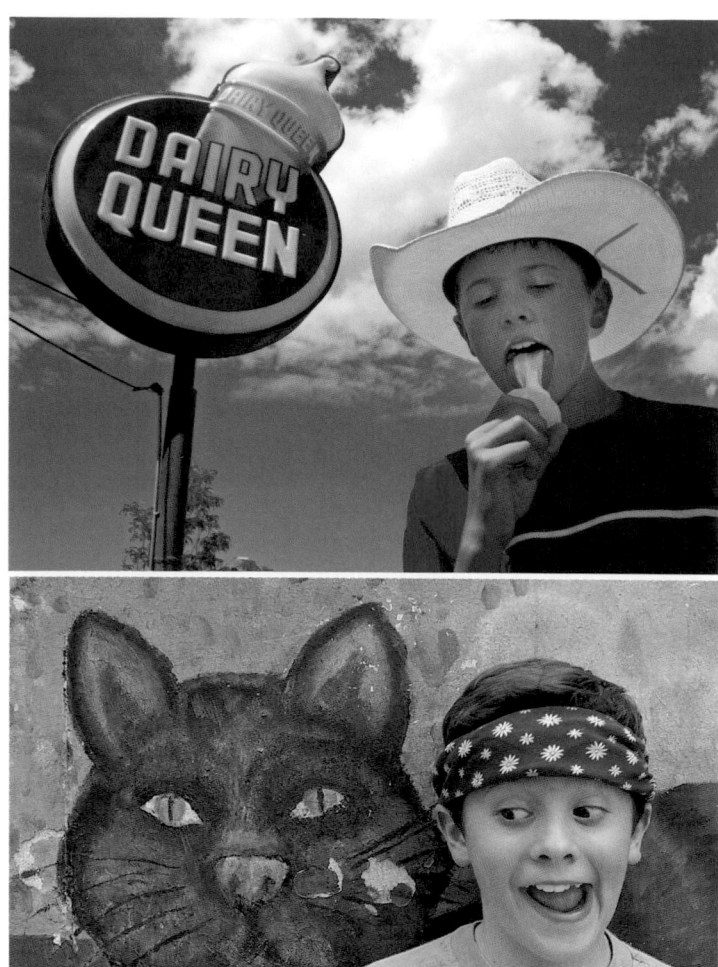

Focus Lock

When a subject is off center, you want to use the focus lock feature on your camera. Here's how it works.

Frame the subject and place the center focus point over the subject. Press the shutter release button down half way. That locks in the focus. Keep your finger on the button. Now, recompose your shot and press the shutter release button down all the way.

Focus lock is one of the coolest features of auto focus cameras, because it offers creative auto focusing.

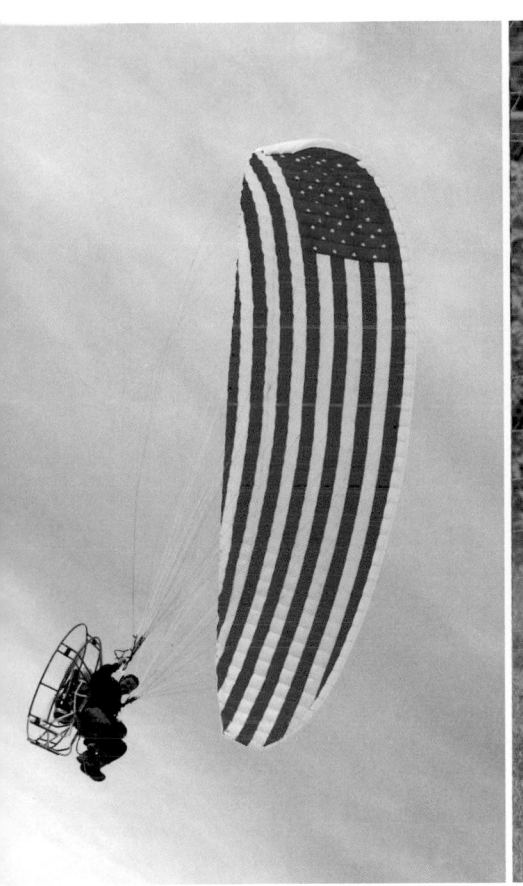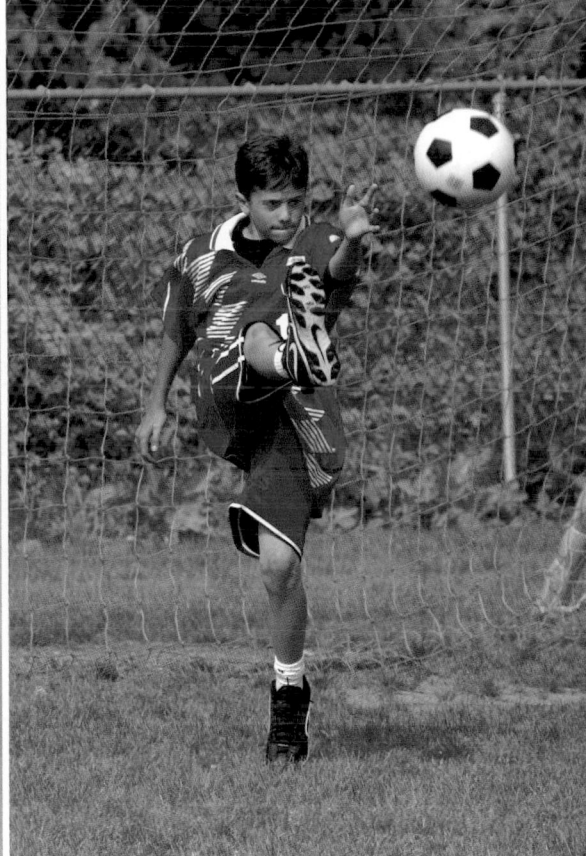

Focusing Tracking

Not all compact cameras have the feature called focus tracking or *AI servo focus*, but if you plan to photograph action, look for it when choosing a camera.

When the camera is set to focus tracking, the AF system tracks a moving subject when you press the shutter release button half way. For action, sports and wildlife photography, this feature greatly increases your chances of getting a sharp shot.

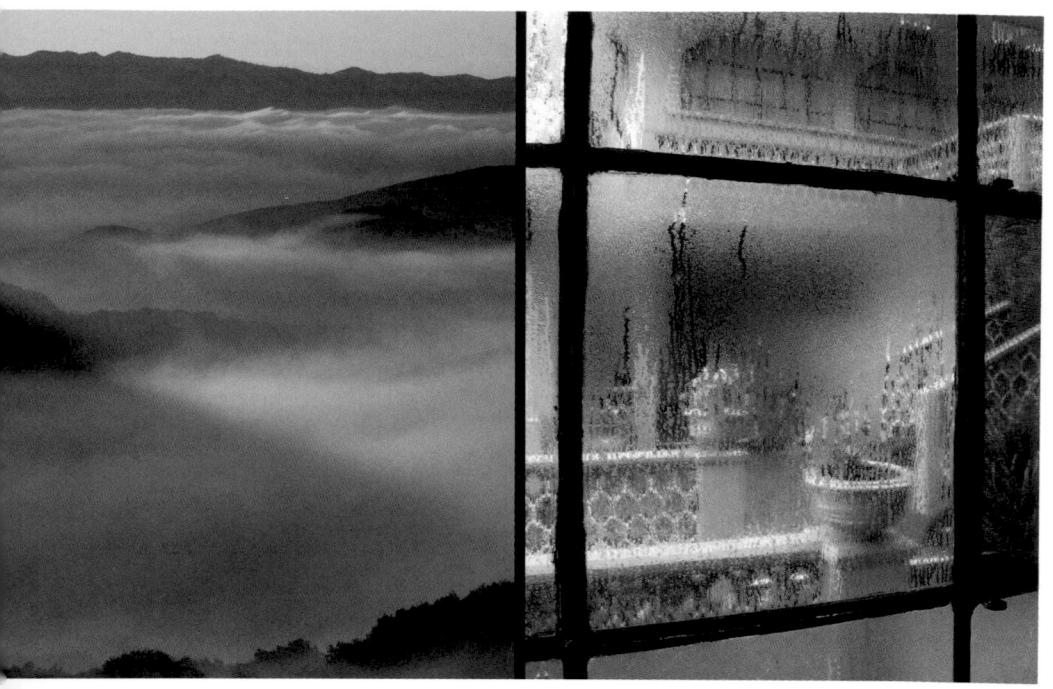

Manual

Auto focus cameras use contrast to focus. When there is no or low contrast, the camera may not focus, preventing you from taking a picture. That's when you want to choose the manual focus mode.

Manual focus is also the mode to use when shooting through glass or other foreground objects that you don't want in focus.

When using the manual mode, be sure to check your focus by zooming in on the image on your camera's LCD monitor.

Drive Modes

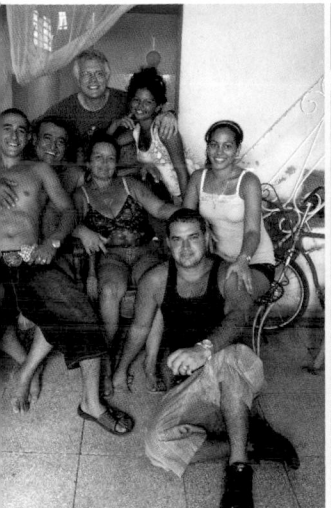
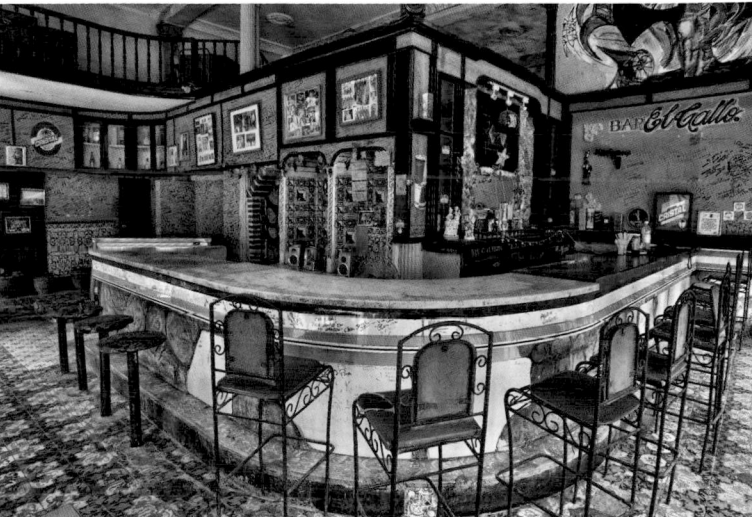

Most compact cameras have three drive modes. These determine how many pictures are taken and when they are taken as you press the shutter release button. These three modes are single frame advance, rapid frame advance and self-timer.

This is fairly basic stuff, but I thought I'd give "newbies" a look at when to use each mode.

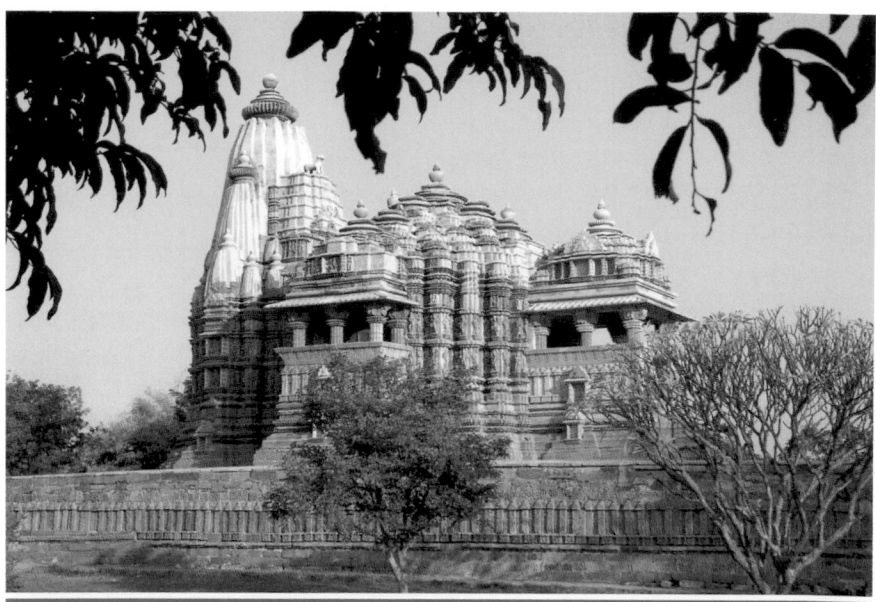

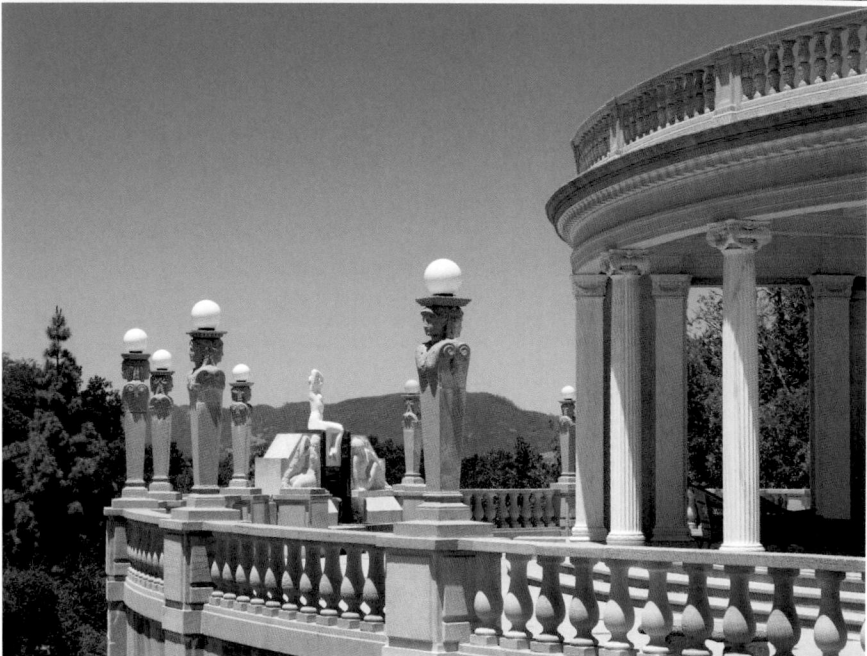

Single Frame Advance

When a subject is not moving and when you don't plan to take a sequence of photographs, single frame advance is a good choice – because you don't need several pictures to capture the action.

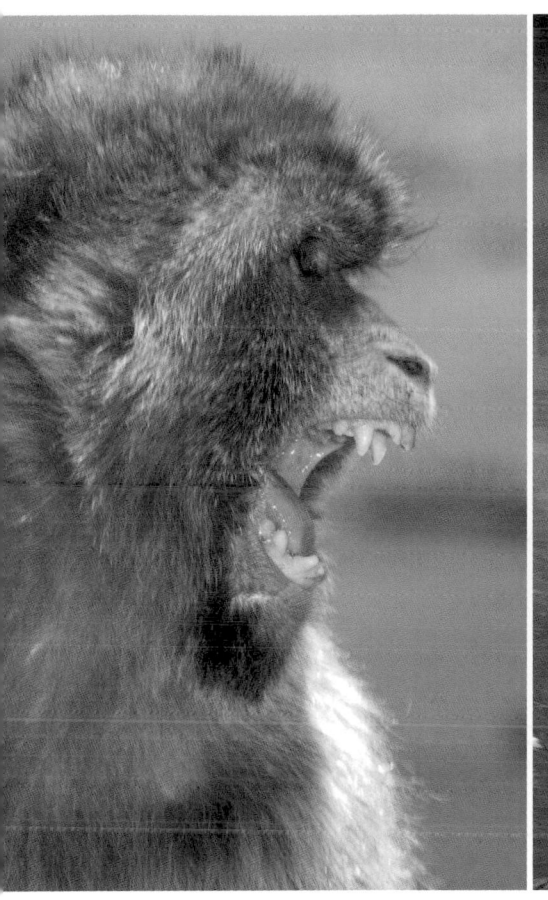 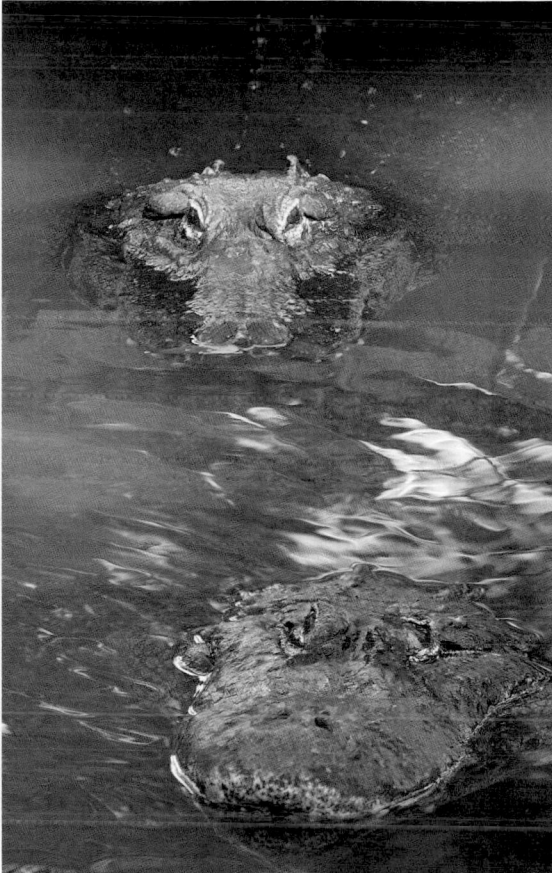

Rapid Frame Advance

When a subject is moving and when you plan to shoot an action sequence, choose the rapid frame advance mode. That way, you'll get several pictures in rapid sequence, ensuring that you capture the action.

The higher the price of the camera, the faster the frame-per-second advance—in most cases.

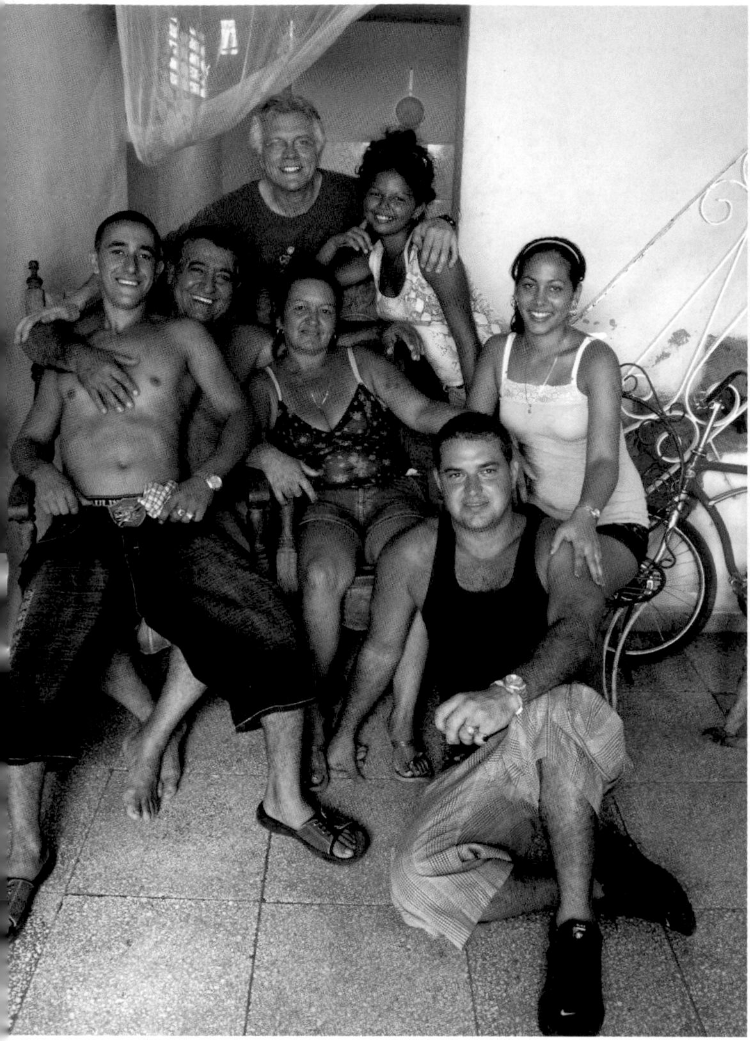

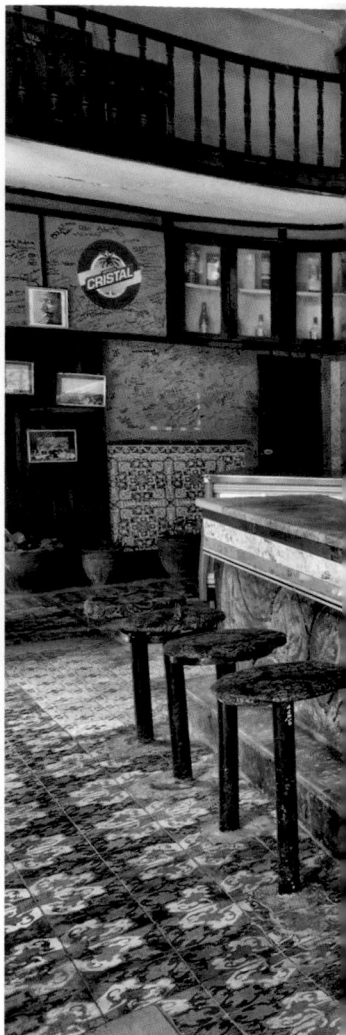

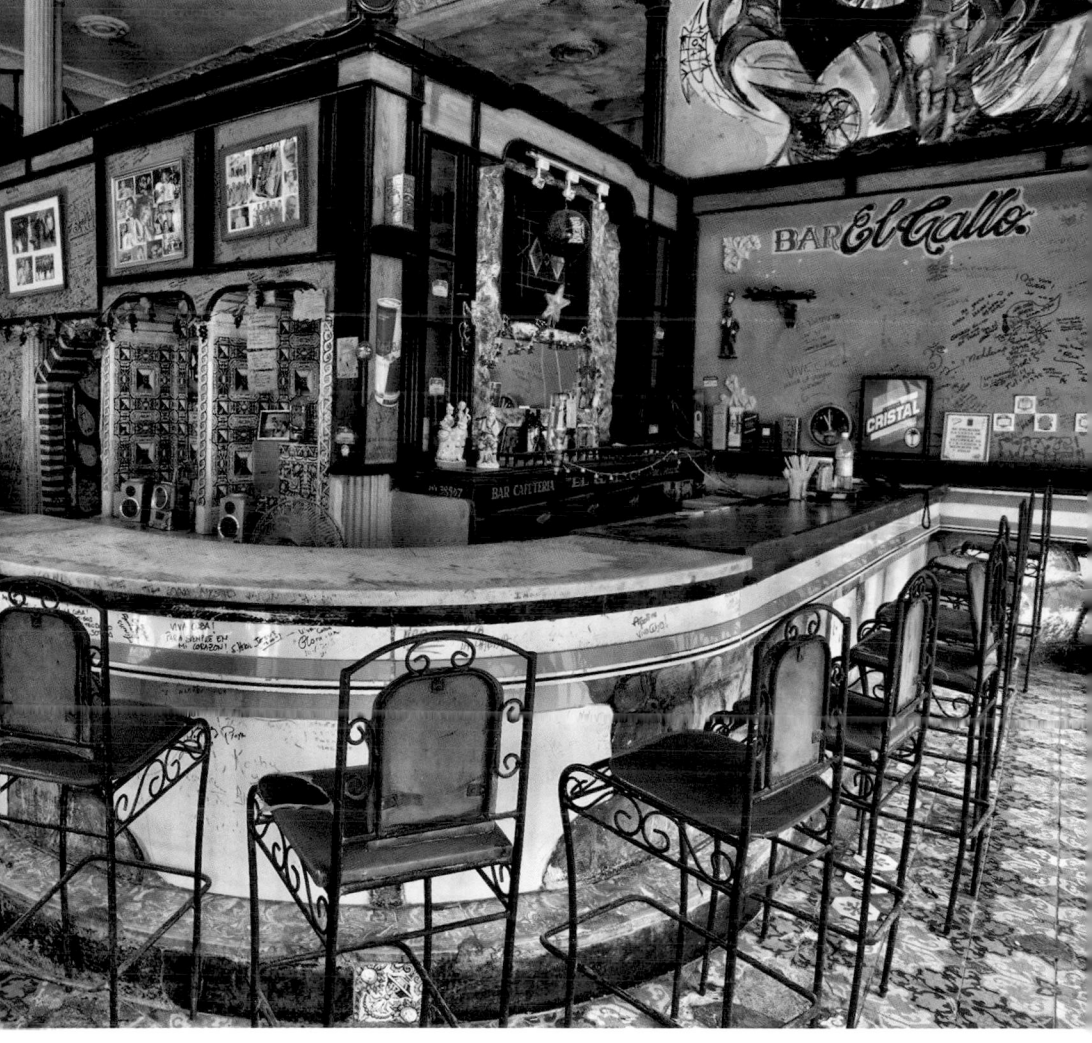

Self-Timer

The self-timer was originally designed so that the photographer could get into the photograph. It's still used for that. But, it's also a good idea to use the self-timer when shooting at slow shutter speed—even when your camera is on a tripod.

By not pressing down on the shutter release button, you increase your chances of getting a sharp shot. This is because pressing the shutter release button often shakes the camera ... just a bit.

If you are into HDR (high dynamic range) photography, you'll also want to use the self-time to avoid camera shake during long exposures.

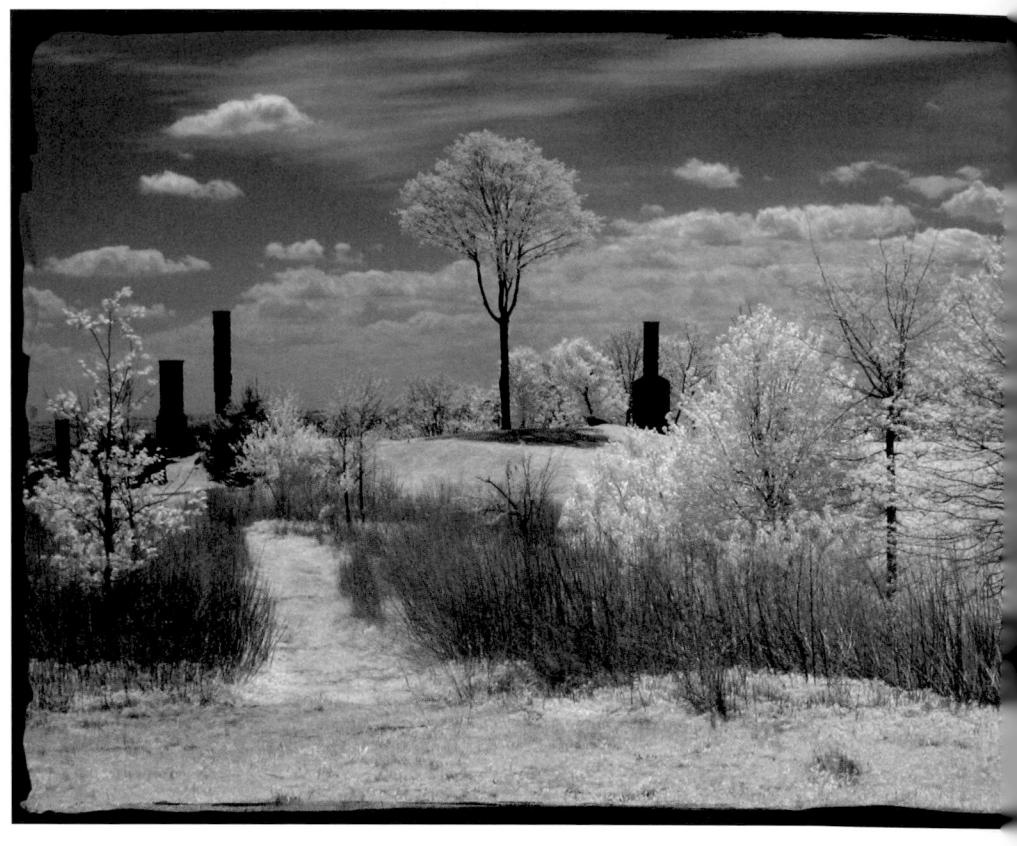

Part XI

The Wonders of Infrared Imaging

Digital infrared photography opens up a whole new world of creativity—even for photographers who already have a creative bent. And today, it's easier than ever to jump into the world of IR imaging with a compact camera.

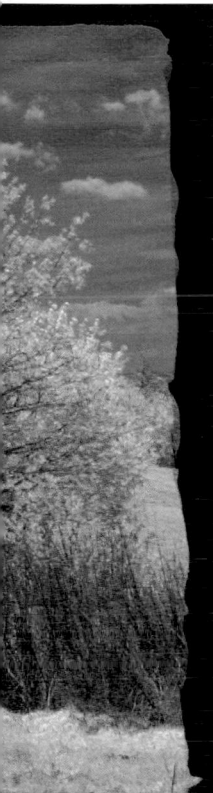

LifePixel (www.lifepixel.com) converts many Canon and Nikon cameras to IR-only cameras. The image on the left was taken with my LifePixel-converted Canon SD-800 compact camera. It's enhanced a bit in Photoshop Elements.

IR images look creative and artistic because some of the reality is removed from the scene. Removing color is the first step in removing the reality. Then comes the real fun: green foliage turned white, making it look as though the landscape is covered with a thin coat of snow or ice ... or perhaps even vanilla frosting!

Play around with adjustments and filters in Photoshop Elements, or cxpcriment with Plug-ins, and you'll have even more creative options. Add a digital frame, as I did here using a Brush frame from OnOne Software's Photo Frame Pro 3 (www.ononesoftware.com), and your pictures look even more artistic.

The creative possibilities attainable in the digital darkroom are endless. In this chapter I'll offer just a few examples of IR photography with an IR-only camera.

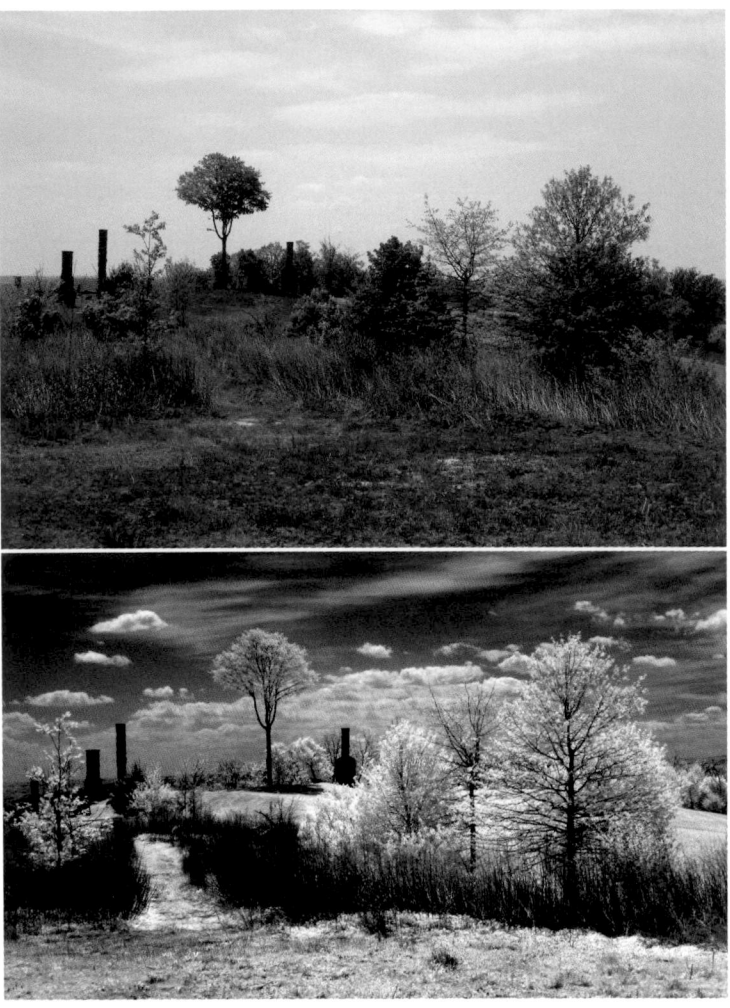

From Drab to Fab

I took the top picture with my non-IR camera. Pretty drab, don't you think?

I took the bottom image with my IR-converted cameras. Kinda cool, no?

When choosing an IR-conversion type, think about the kind of pictures you think you'll like to take: color, vivid color, black-and-white, etc. The bottom picture shows the effect of the black-and-white conversion (again, in-camera). It's the same image that opens this chapter.

For that image, I changed the color of the sky (and the overall tone of the image) from grey to blue using the Gradual Blue filter in niksoftware's ColorEfexPro (www.niksoftware.com).

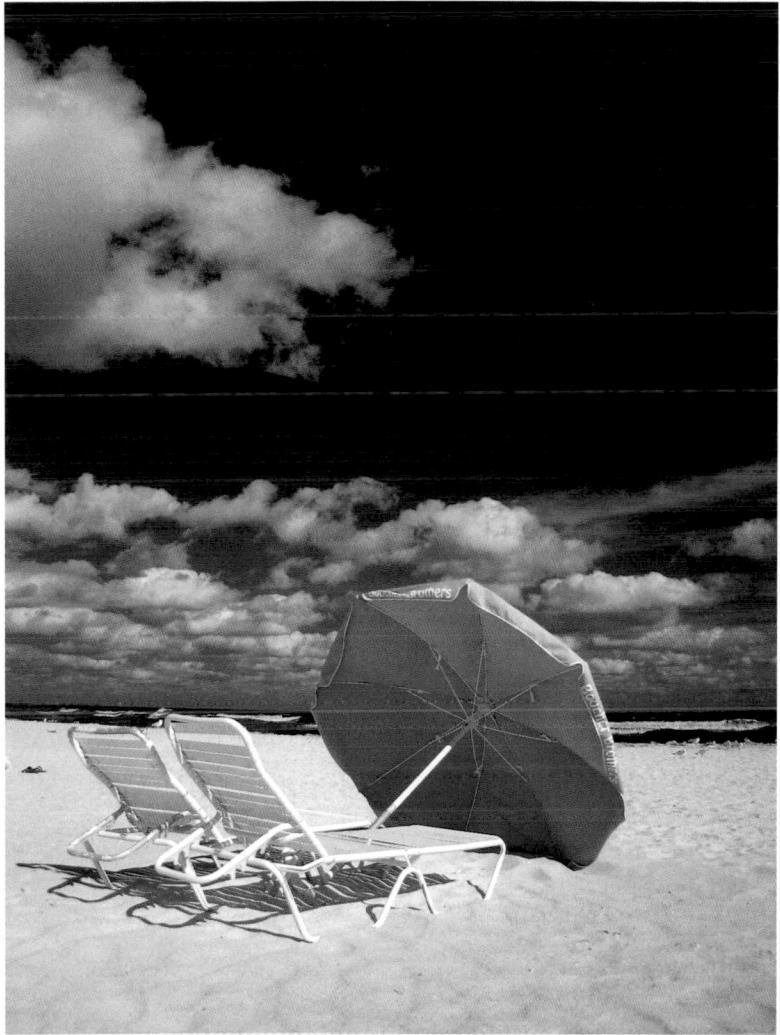

Black-and-White IR

Back in the film days, photographers used black-and-white IR film to create dramatic images with a black sky and white clouds. Today, we can do that much easier with an IR-converted camera.

This is another image taken with my IR-converted SD 800 camera. Notice how IR provides vivid contrast to a scene. The white clouds pop out against a darker-then-seen sky.

If you like this kind of effect, you may want to choose the black-and-white conversion option. Or, you could choose a color conversion and then remove the color in Photoshop Elements.

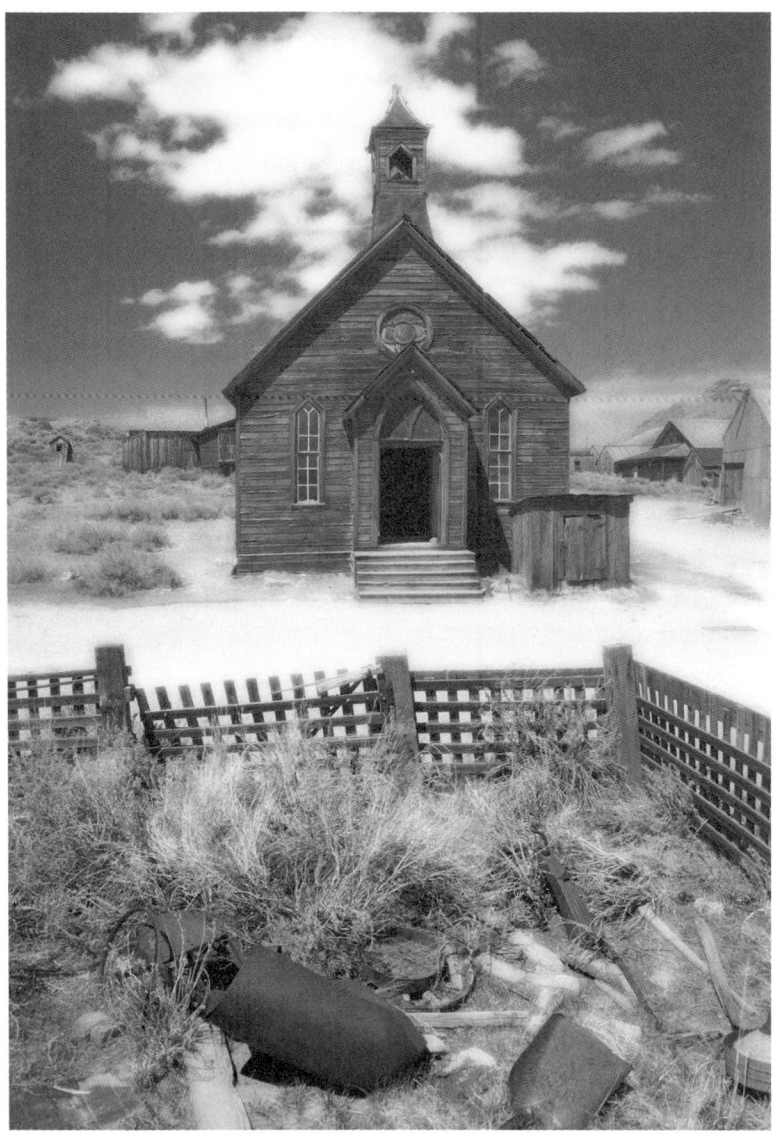

Have Fun with Filters, Too!

As with virtually every image you take (color and IR), you really are never finished working (and playing) with an image in Photoshop Elements. Elements' built-in filters, such as the Diffuse Glow filter—used here on a picture shot at Bodie State Historical Park in California—can further help you create an artistic image. Plug-ins can be fun, too.

My advice: Work and play to your heart's content.

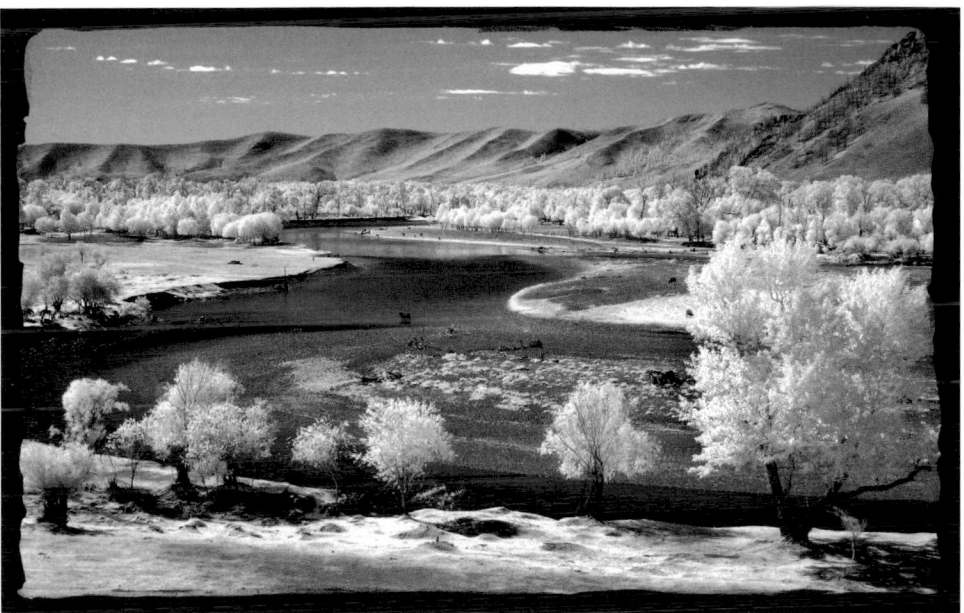

Seeing in IR

After you get into IR photography, you'll start to see in IR. That is, you'll see in your mind's eye the white foliage and dark sky and other potential IR effects. With that seeing power, you'll begin to see scenes that will look great in IR—not all scenes do.

This is one of my favorite IR images. I took it in Mongolia with my IR-converted Canon SD800 camera. When I saw all the trees, the winding river and cloud-filled sky, I knew it was a perfect scene for IR photography. I did not even photograph the scene with my color camera.

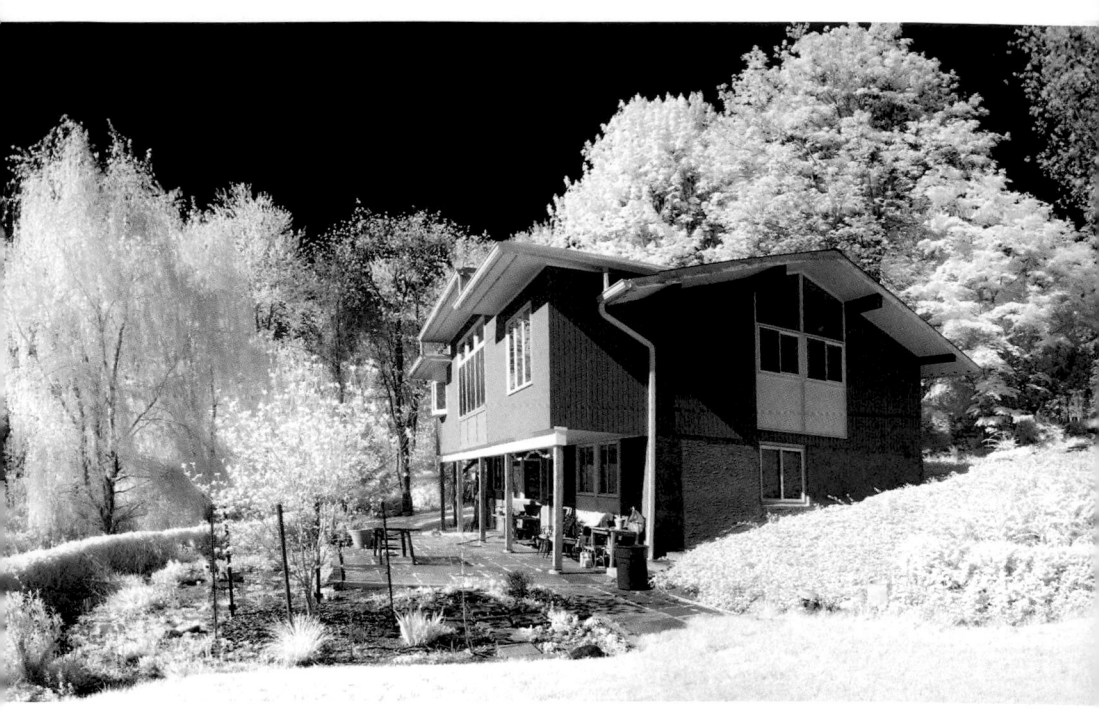

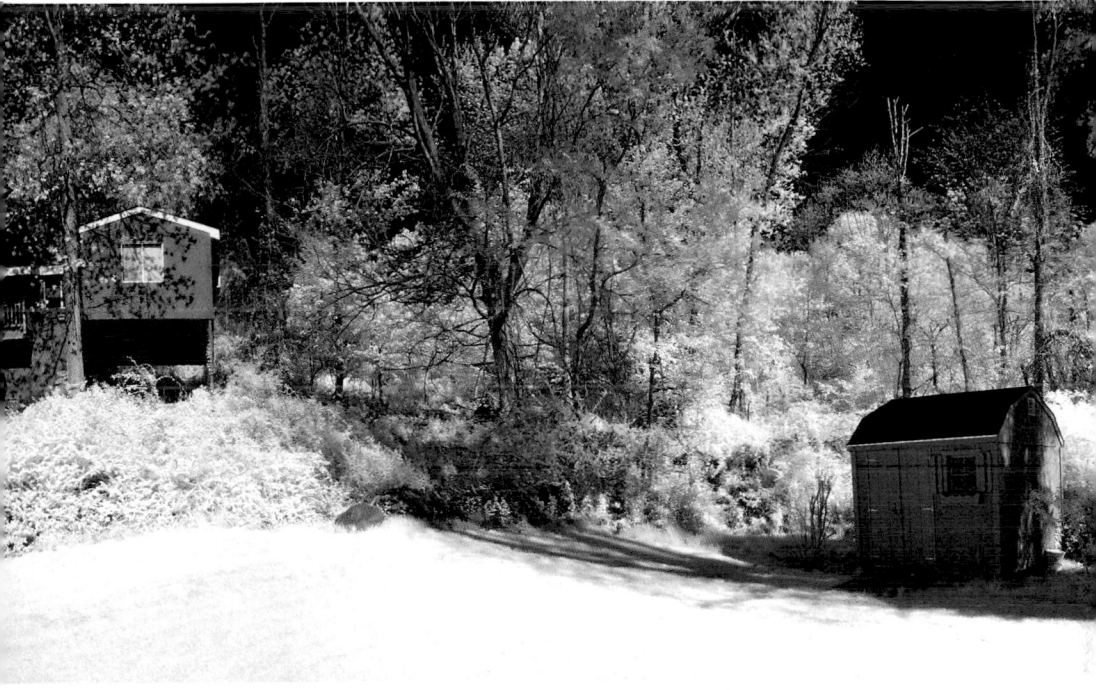

Panos in IR

Coming up is a chapter on shooting panoramas. After reading it, try shooing an infrared panorama for some extra IR fun and creativity.

If you are in a creative slump, or just want to have more fun with your photography, get into IR photography.

Get a discount on a camera conversion at litepixel.com by using this code upon checkout: ricksammon.

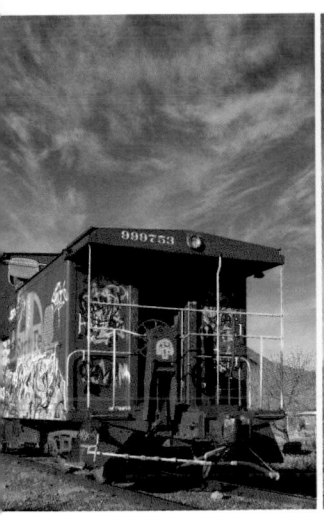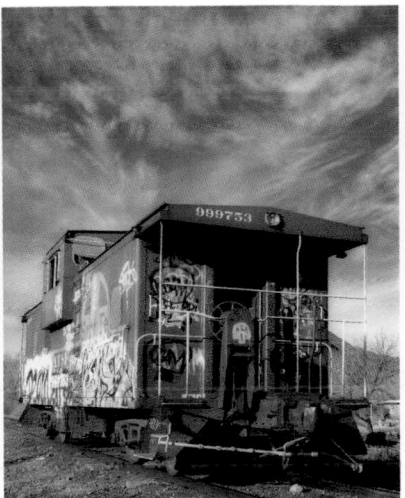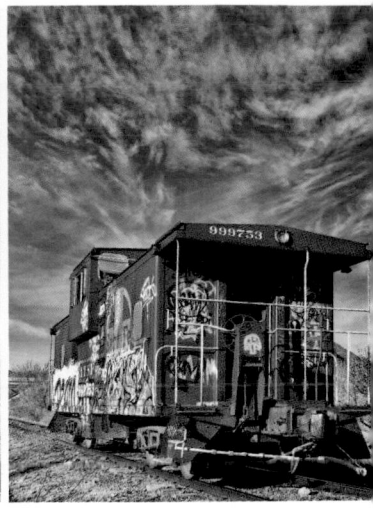

Part XII

Photoshop Elements Confessions

Yes, once again I must confess. I used Photoshop Elements to enhance virtually all of the pictures in this book, even if the enhancement was as simple as cropping the image or boosting the contrast just a smidge.

Overall though, enhancing pictures from compact cameras is fast, easy and fun. And it's often necessary, simply because the images that compact cameras produce can't match the image quality you get from a digital SLR. This is mostly due to the smaller image sensor on compact cameras.

Here is another confession: I actually did use Photoshop Elements—and not Photoshop CS4, its bigger (and much more expensive) brother—to enhance the pictures in this book. Photoshop Elements is actually a very powerful image-editing program, as you'll see.

On the following pages you'll find my top 21 Photoshop Elements enhancements for compact camera images. They also apply to digital SLR images.

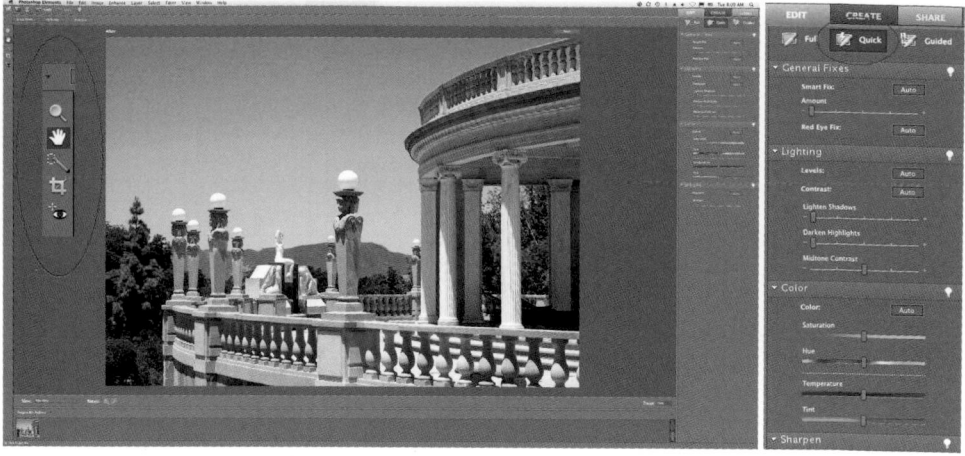

#1: Quick Look at the Quick Mode

We'll take a just a quick look at the Quick Mode, because my guess is that you'll be working (and playing) in the Full Mode, as this offers much more creative control over your images than the wimpy Quick Mode. Two main reasons you'll probably have limited use for Quick Mode:

First, the Tool Bar (magnified and inserted here)—located on the left side of the Quick Mode window—has only a few tools:

- The Zoom Tool lets you zoom in and out of an image.

- The Hand Tool lets you move elements around in an image.

- The Selection Tool helps you select elements in an image for individual enhancements.

- The Crop Tool is designed to let you easily crop (trim) an image.

- The Red Eye Tool lets you fix the dreaded red-eye effect that is often caused when taking flash pictures indoors in low-light situations.

Second, your controls (magnified and enlarged on the right side of this image) are also limited. But worse than that, when you use these controls, you are likely making adjustments directly to your image file. This is something that you really don't want to do, because you might accidentally save the image and lose your original file ... forever. If you do use the Quick Mode, make sure you are working on a copy of your original image.

All that said, if you are brand new to Elements, play around with this mode, but promise yourself to move on to the Full Mode soon. Promise!!

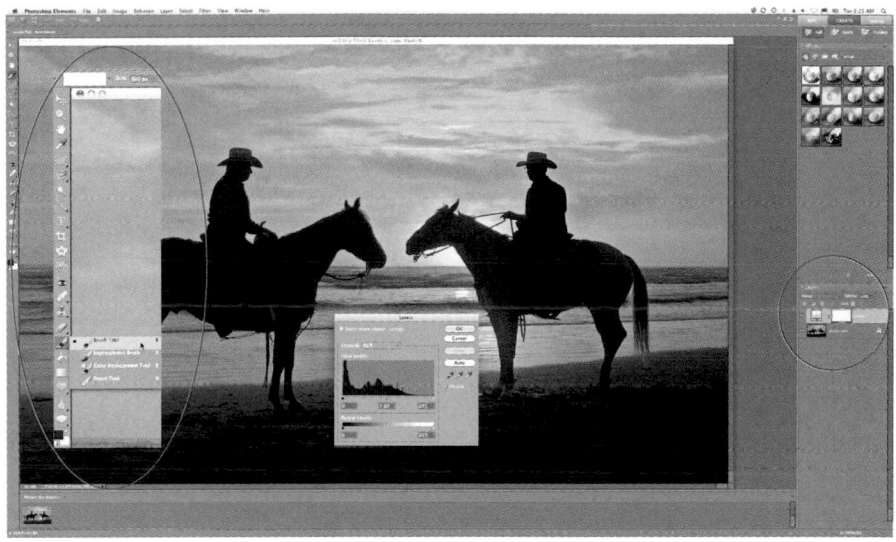

#2: The Full Mode is Full-Featured

Welcome. You are about to take full advantage of the power of Photoshop Elements, which actually includes many of the same features found in Photoshop CS.

The Tool Bar (magnified and inserted here) has all the tools you need to enhance your images. When you click on some of these tools, you get a "fly out" menu with other tools.

For example, when you click on the Brush tool (covered in more detail in a few pages), you can access the Impressionist Brush. This lets you add artistic effects to an image as you move the brush around your image. The Brush tool option also includes the Color Replacement Brush, which lets you quickly and easily replace colors in an image, and the Pencil tool, which is used like a pencil on your images.

Entire books could be written about the use of each tool available in Photoshop Elements, so I want to focus on taking pictures. My advice: Play with the tools. You'll quickly see what each one does.

The best feature of the Full Mode is that you can use Adjustment Layers. See the circled area on the right of the screen grab. Learn more about adjustment layers in the Love Those Adjustment Layers section of this chapter. For now, the concept is that you should make your adjustments on a different layer—not on your original image. The benefit is that you can ditch the adjustment layer if you don't like it … even after you save your file. That is, *if* you save your file as a TIFF or Photoshop File.

This is important: If you save your files as a JPEG, your layers will be automatically flattened and lost. If saved as a TIFF or Photoshop file, you can go back and fine-tune your adjustment on that layer after saving. How cool is that?

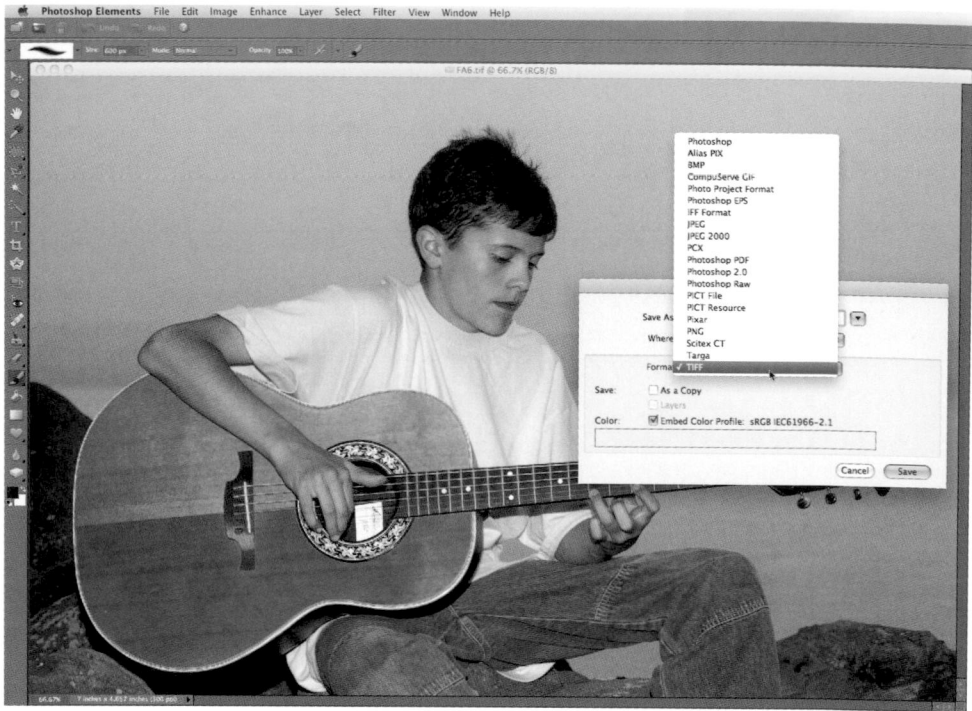

#3: Save a Copy

On the previous page I mentioned the importance of saving your pictures as TIFF files or Photoshop files. To save a file, go to File > Save As and then choose the file format you want for your saved image. TIFF and Photoshop files are larger than JPEG files, but I suggest you make the space and save all your pictures in one of these formats. Use JPEGs only for emailing and for posting images on web sites and blogs.

Again, TIFF and Photoshop files preserve your adjustment layers. When you save an image as a JPEG file, the file is flattened and you lose your layers—forever.

You'll find more on image files in the Resize the Right Way section of this chapter. And as promised, more info on adjustments layers is coming.

#4: Crop Creatively

"Crop my pictures and you're a dead man." That was the title of one of my articles for which I received dozens of e-mails from photographers agreeing with the concept.

Cropping is a very, very personal thing. You crop to add impact to an image and to trim out unwanted areas ... or to simply make a picture more to your liking.

In Elements, you crop with the Crop tool, circled on the Tool Bar in this screen grab. You simply click on the

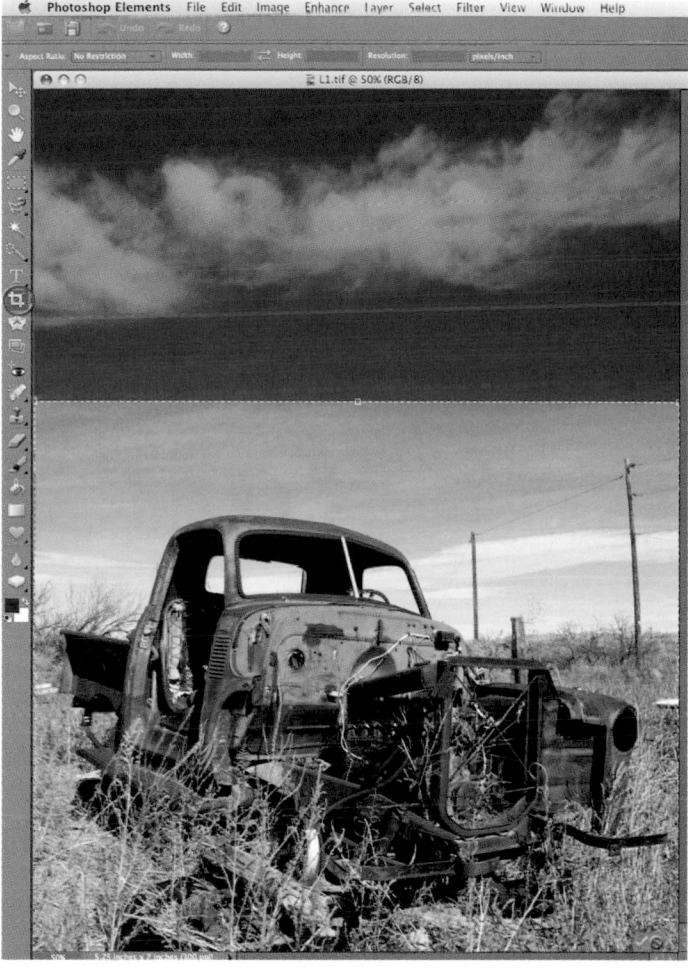

Crop tool and move the crop icon into the image. Click where you want to begin to crop and then drag the crop icon to where you want to end your crop.

Here's a trick. Hold down the Space Bar when you are dragging the crop icon and you can easily move your crop area around the image. When you release your mouse and select your cropped area, the other part of the image is darkened.

So remember, crop creatively ... and try to see pictures within a picture.

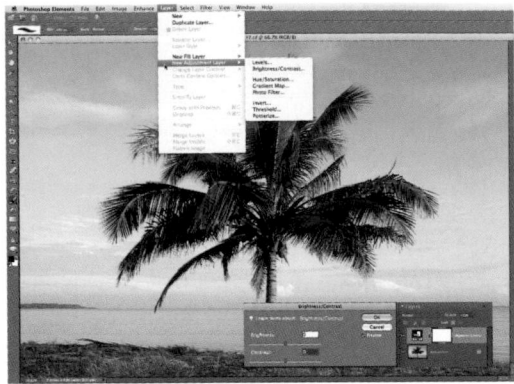

#5: Love Those Adjustment Layers

Okay. This is a very important section. Why? Because you really need to make all possible adjustments on Adjustment Layers, rather than directly on the original image.

In The Full Mode is Full-Featured section of this chapter, I mention the importance of using Adjustment Layers. To create an Adjustment Layer, go to Layer > New Adjustment Layer and then click on the type of layer you want to create: Levels, Brightness/Contrast, etc.

Another reason to use Adjustment Layers: You can paint in and paint out your adjustments quickly and easily. It's called masking, and here's how to do it.

When you create an Adjustment Layer, you automatically create what's called a Layer Mask, the white box shown in the Layer's window in this screen grab. A Layer Mask lets you mask out (paint out) an adjustment, which allows you to apply an adjustment selectively.

After you apply your adjustment, click the Layer Mask to activate it. Now, on the bottom of the Tool Bar, click black foreground color box (default setting). Next, click the Brush tool on the Tool Bar. See the Touch of a Brush section of this chapter.

Now, when you click in the image and move your brush over an area, you "paint out" the adjustment. In an image like this one, you may want to increase the contrast of the grass and not the sky, or vice versa.

If you are going through the process and not masking out your effect, then you have not set the foreground color to black.

Here's another cool thing about the Layer Mask. If you make a mistake and paint out in the wrong area, all you have to do is press the X key, which switches the foreground color to white. Then, just brush over that area of the image again.

Master Adjustment Layers and Layer Masks and you'll be able to make professional-quality enhancements with this basic image-editing program.

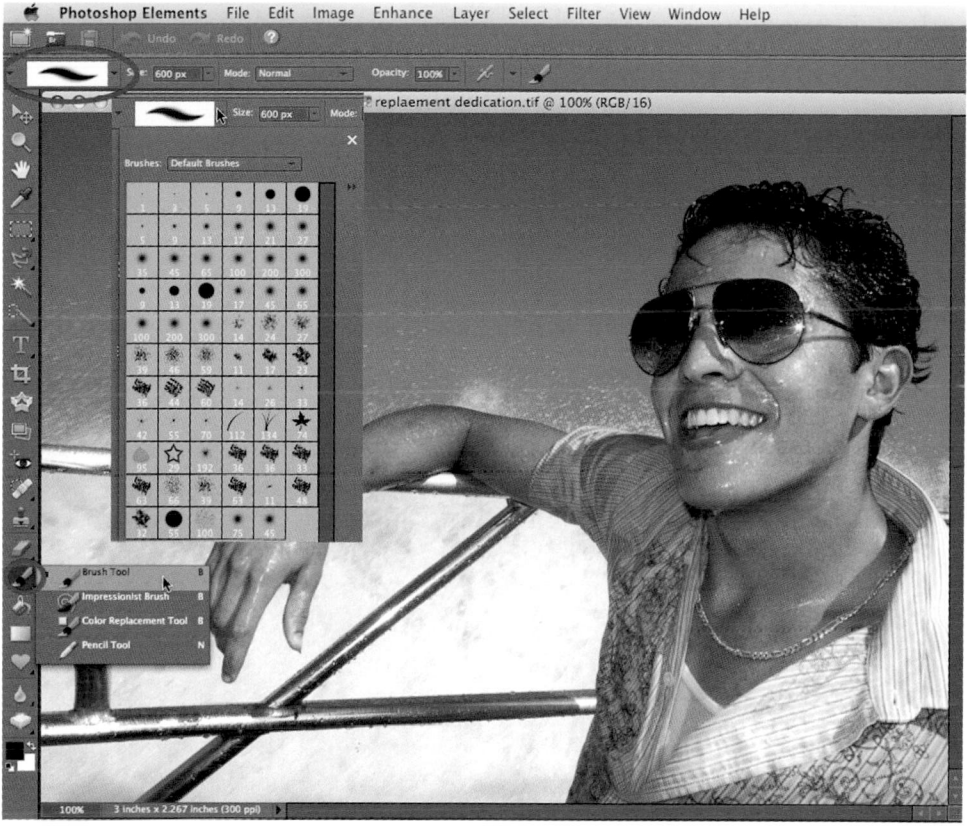

#6: The Touch of a Brush

The brush size and style you select is very important. You first select a brush by clicking on the Brush tool in the Tool Bar. Next, click on the small fly-out arrow at the top of the Elements window to choose a size and style.

When working on your images, you have the choice of either a hard edge brush or a soft edge brush. I use soft edge brushes 90 percent of the time because the effect on an image is less noticeable than that of a hard edge brush.

Here's a cool tip: You can change the size of the brush by using the bracket keys on your keyboard. The right bracket key makes the brush larger; the left bracket makes it smaller.

Nested in the Brush tool is the Impressionist Brush. Choose a small size brush to paint in an impressionist art effect on your picture. Note that I said small size brush; that is the key to creating the artistic effect.

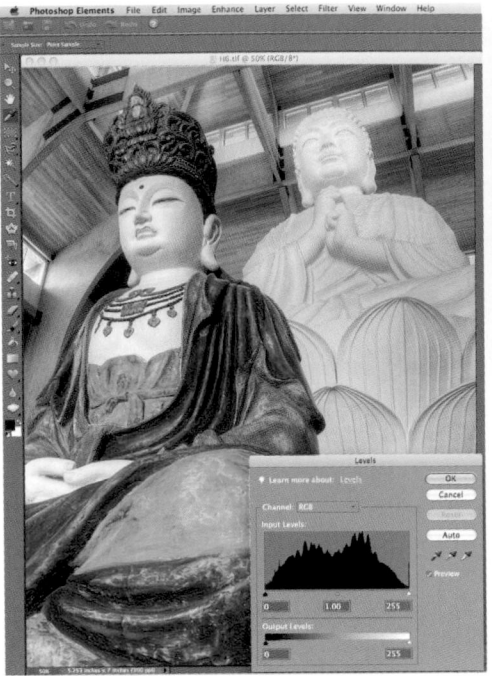
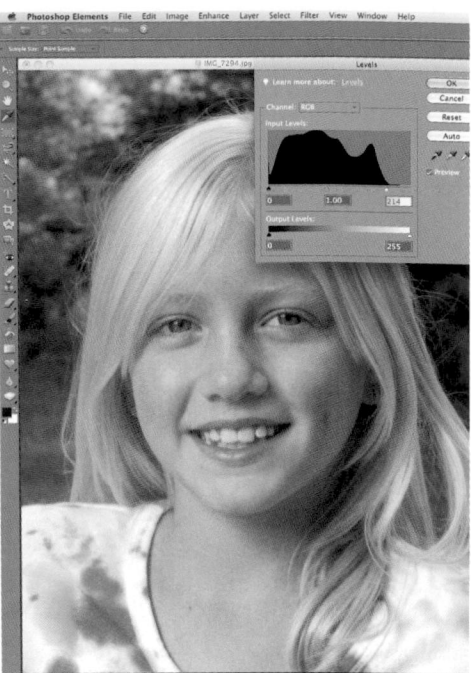

#7: A Look at Levels

Levels is the adjustment that you'll probably use most, because it's here where you, with a click or two of your mouse, adjust the brightness, contrast and color of an image. Here's the basic concept.

When you create a Levels Adjustment layer, you get the Levels window. Here you see a histogram of the image. The histogram shows the distribution of the brightness levels in the image. Shadow areas are on the right; mid-tones are in the middle; and highlights are at the right of the "mountain range."

You adjust the Levels (expanding out the brightness range) of the image by clicking on the small triangles at the bottom of the histogram and moving them to a position just inside of the mountain range.

The image on the left does not need any Levels adjustment. The histogram shows an even distribution of the brightness levels in the scene.

The image on the right lacks some highlights, shown by the mountain range not reaching the right side of the histogram. As you can see, I moved the highlight slider to a point just inside the mountain range and thereby brightened the entire image.

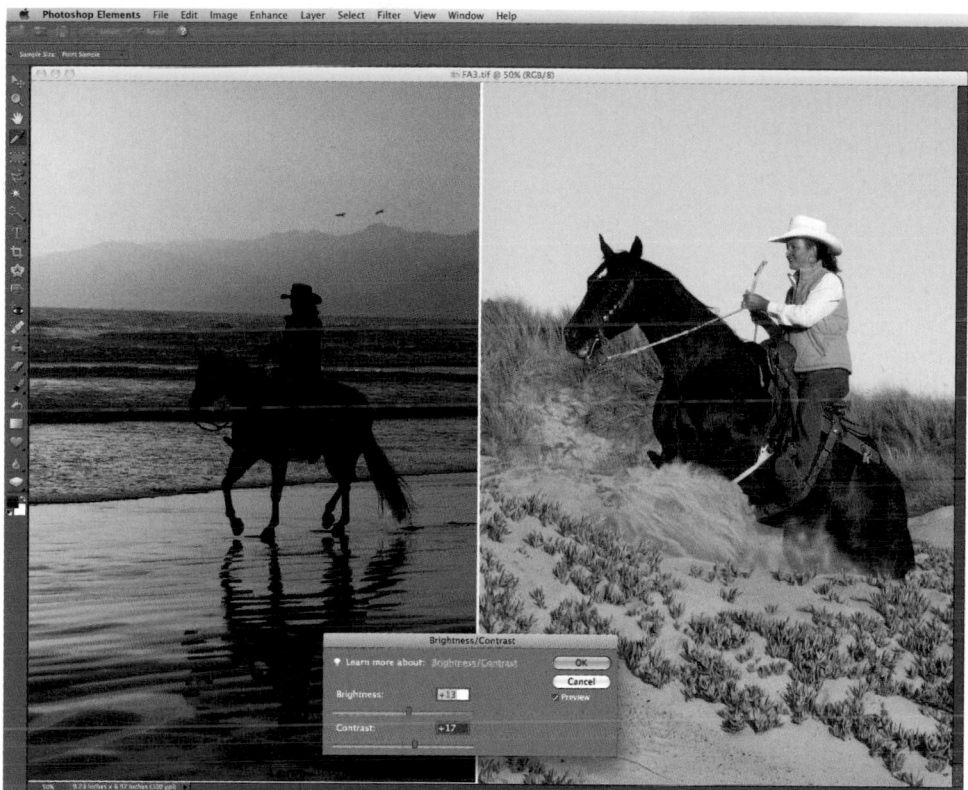

#8: Brightness/Contrast Basics

Most pictures taken with compact cameras can use a boost in contrast. At least that is what I've found.

When you create a Brightness/Contrast Adjustment Layer, you get a dialog box with two sliders: one for Brightness and one for Contrast. Forget about the Brightness control here; boost the brightness with Levels. For contrast, you can boost it with Levels, too, but you may want to boost it with the Brightness/Contrast adjustment because it's easier to use.

At first, you'll love boosting the contrast, because a boost in contrast makes a picture "pop." It's a nice trick for improving most pictures, especially sunset pictures. However, if you overdo it, you'll lose detail in bright areas, such as the hat this cowgirl is wearing.

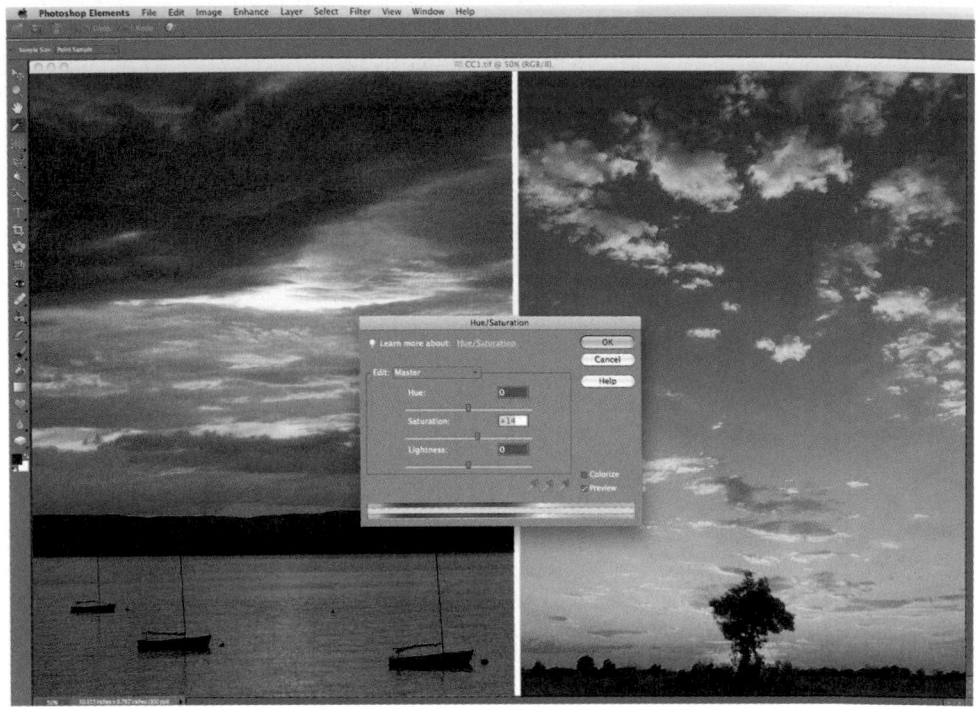

#9: See What Hue/Saturation Can Do For You

Hue refers to the depth of color in an image. My guess is that you'll never use this tool, unless you want to change the overall look of an image. On the other hand, my guess is that you'll have a blast with Saturation.

When you create a Hue/Saturation Adjustment Layer, you get the Hue/Saturation window. Move the Saturation slider to the right to increase the saturation of an image. This will increase the intensity of the colors. Move the slider to the left and you de-saturate the image. Move it all the way to the left and you get a black-and-white image.

Be careful when adjusting the saturation of an image. Too much saturation can make a picture look fake, as illustrated by the picture on the left. Used correctly, and it can improve a picture, as illustrated by the picture on the right.

Forget about Lightness here; use Levels for that.

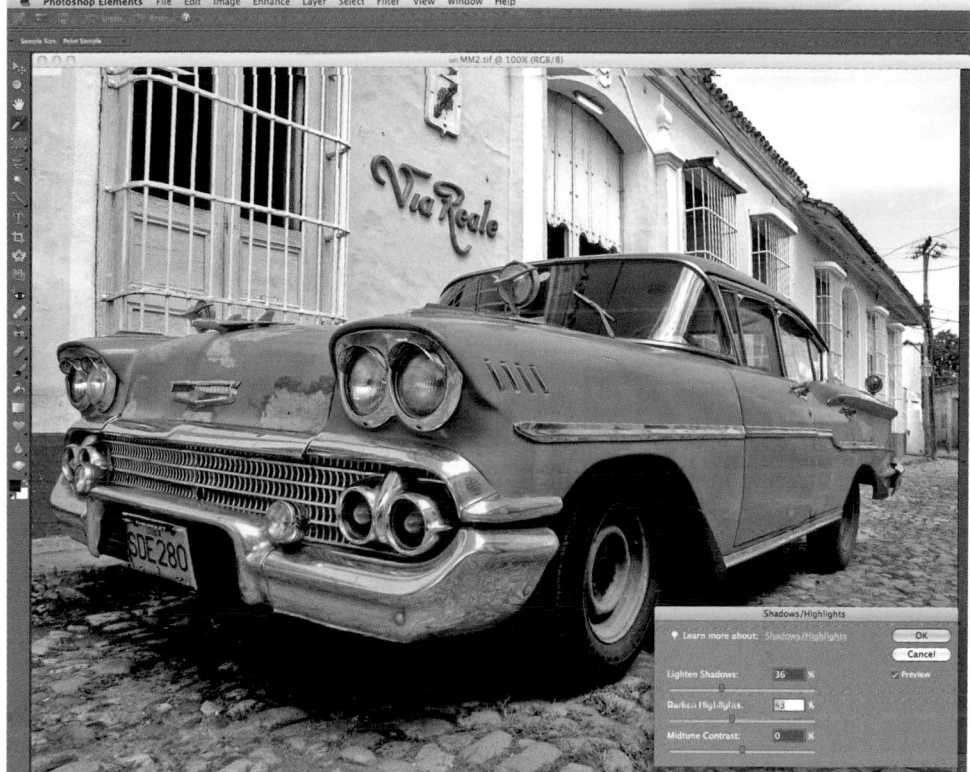

#10: The Super Shadow/Highlight Control

The Shadow/Highlight control is not available as an Adjustment Layer. Still, it's worth using. Just remember to use it on a copy of your original image.

Go to Enhance > Adjust Lighting > Shadows/Highlights. When you do that, you get a window in which you can, more or less, open up the shadows and tone down the highlights of an image independently.

This is actually a very cool feature, even though it's not available as an Adjustment Layer. Play around with it and you'll find it quite useful.

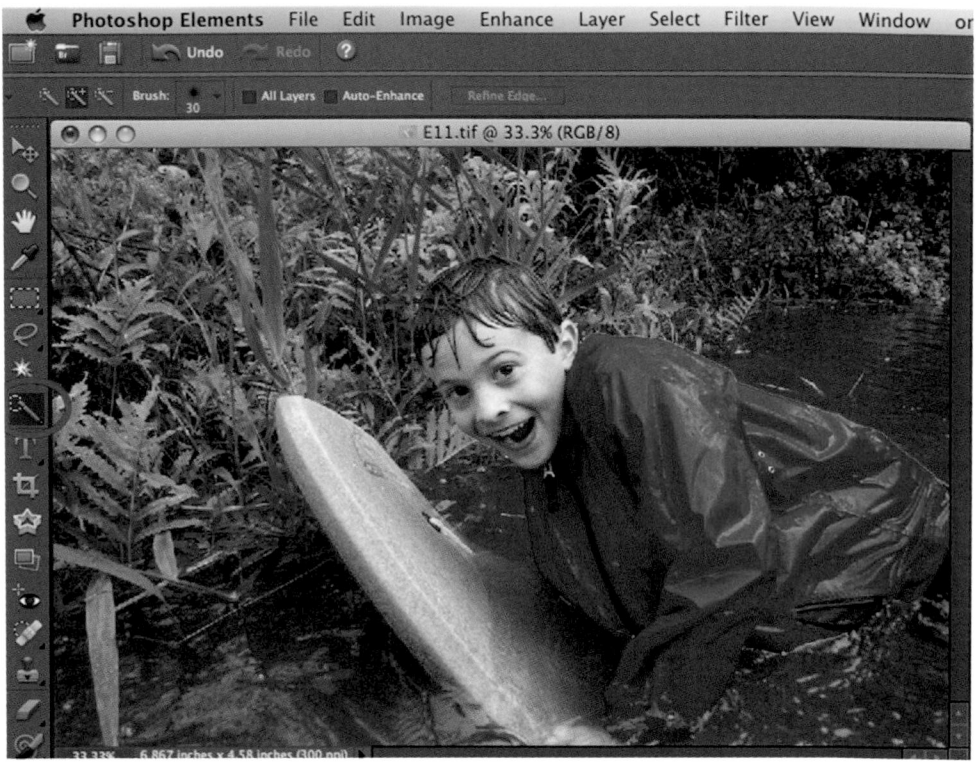

#11 : Select Your Selections Carefully

Within Elements, you can select a specific area of a picture on which you want to work. After you select an area, you can apply many adjustments and enhancements to only that area.

You select an area by choosing a Selection tool on the Tool Bar. In the fly-out menu, choose whether you want to use the Selection tool or the Quick Selection tool. Both tools select areas based on color.

For this image, I chose the Quick Selection tool (as I often do because it does a good and quick job). I used the tool to select the area around my son and his wakeboard by moving the brush over that area. Once selected, I went to Hue/Saturation and de-saturated only that area, the selected area of the image.

Here's a tip: If you accidentally select an area of an image that you don't want to select, hold down the Options key and move your brush over that area. That process will de-select that area of the image.

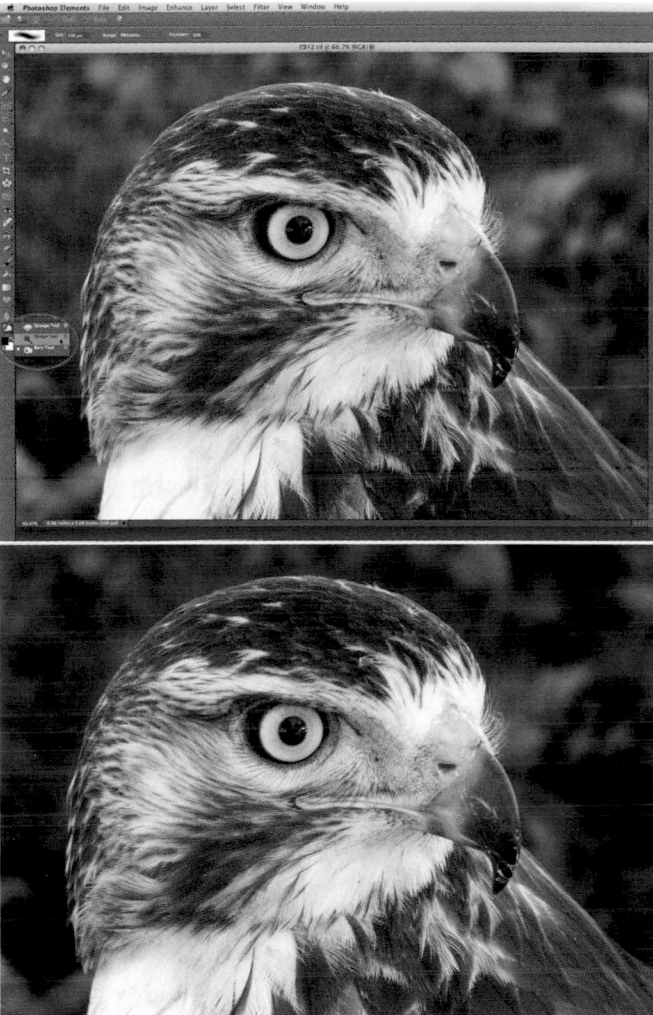

#12: Do It with the Dodge/Burn/Sponge Tool

The Dodge/Burn/Sponge tools are nested together on the Tool Bar. The Dodge tool lets you lighten an area of an image using a brush. The Burn tool lets you darken an area the same way, and the Sponge tool lets you saturate or de-saturate an area also using a brush. When you select the Sponge tool, you choose to de-saturate or saturate the image by clicking on the Mode icon at the top of the Elements window.

Compare the top image to the bottom image. You'll see that the area around our fine-feathered friend is darker in the bottom image. That's because I used the Burn tool on the area, selecting a soft edge brush and "painting" over that area to draw more attention to the main subject in the frame.

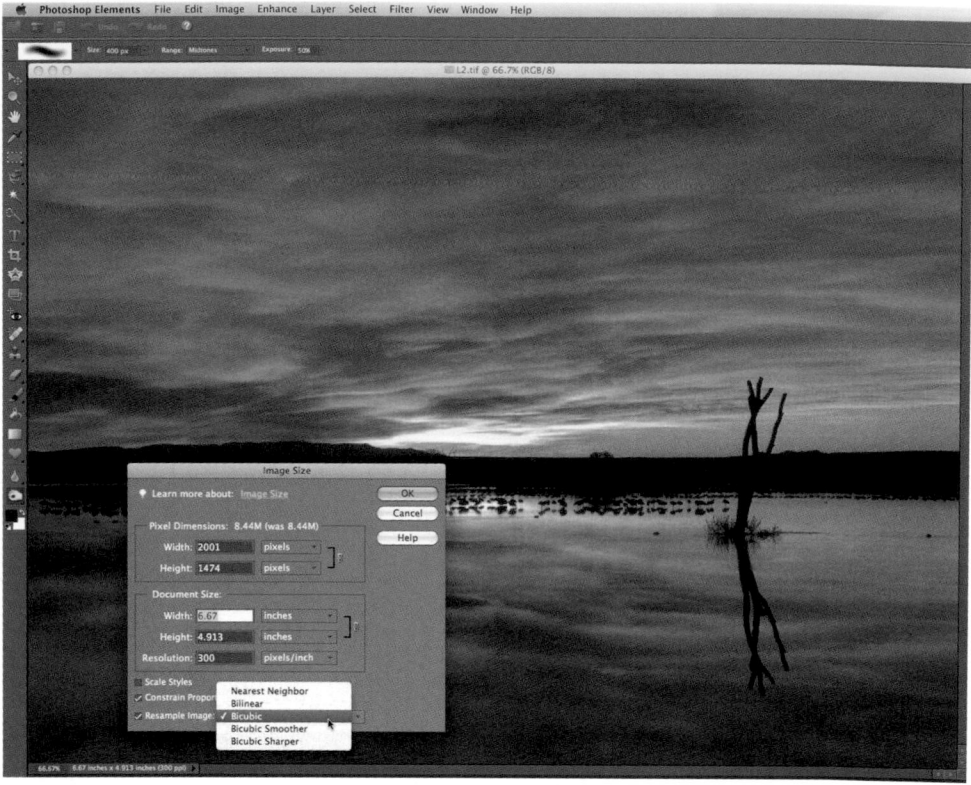

#13: Resize the Right Way

In Elements, it's easy to upsize or downsize an image by typing in a new numbers in the Image Size document window. However, you need to use the appropriate resizing method if you want your image to look good.

Go to Image > Resize > Image Size. In the Image Size window, you can increase or decrease the size of your image, but be sure to choose the correct Resample Image method. When you want to increase the image size, say for a larger print, choose Bicubic Smoother. When you want to decrease the image size, perhaps for a web site, choose Bicubic Sharper.

Tip: When you upsize an image, increase the image by only ten percent at a time. In other words, upsize the image by ten percent and save. Do that until you reach the desired image size.

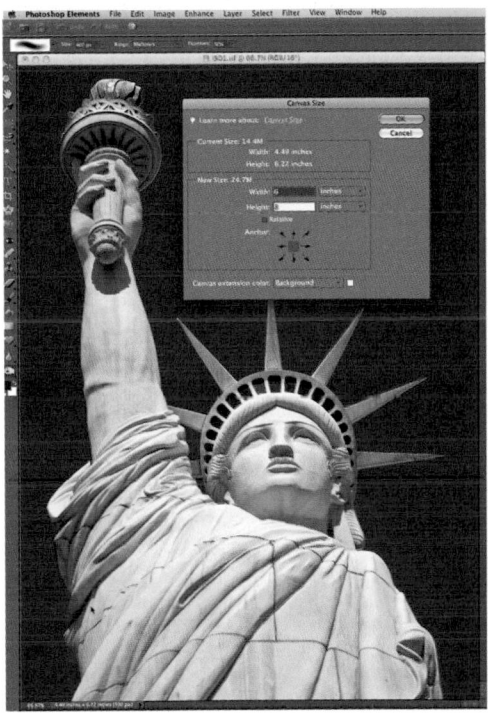 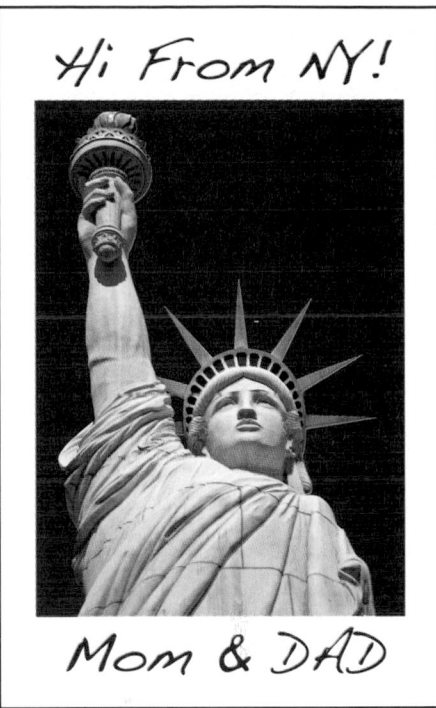

#14: Check-Out Canvas Size

Canvas Size is different from Image Size. When you change the Canvas Size, you change the size of the area around your image. This gives you extra space to work and play.

Go to Image > Resize > Image Size. If you leave the Anchor box at its default setting (center box is darkened) and type in a new Width and Height, the Canvas Size will increase.

You can also increase the Canvas size in different directions by clicking on the arrows in the Canvas Size window. Click on the top right arrow, for instance, add an inch to the Width and Height, and your image will have a blank area to the right and bottom of the original image. Note that the foreground color is the color of your canvas.

In this example, I left the Anchor box at its default (center) setting. I added two inches to the Height and a quarter inch to the Width. In the new canvas area, I used the Type tool to create an electronic postcard.

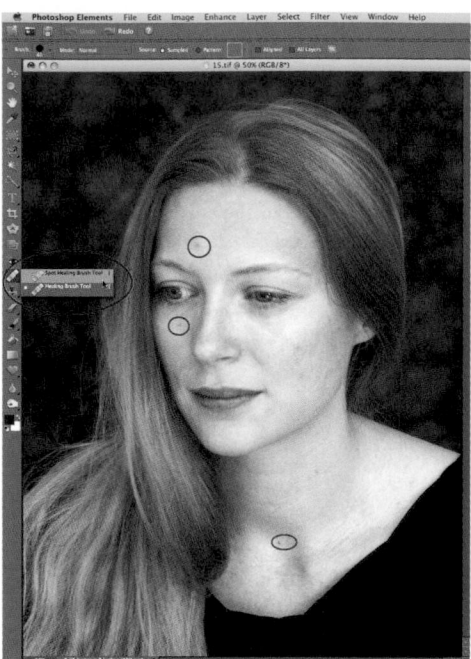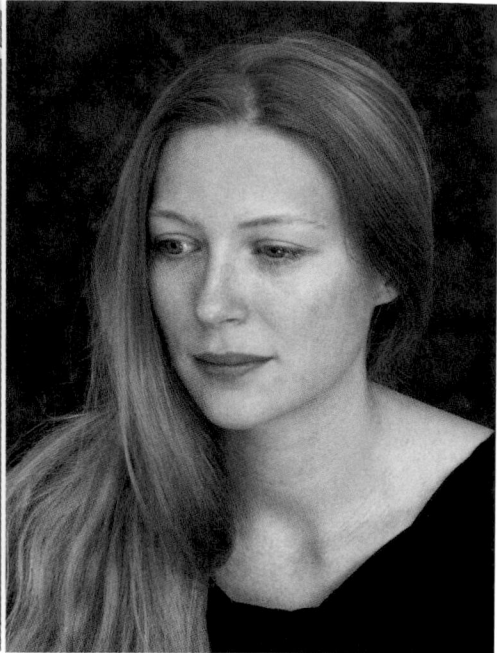

#15: Heal with the Spot Healing Brush

You'll find the Spot Healing Brush in the Tool Bar. It's a cool tool for retouching blemishes in an instant. All you do is select it, choose a brush size (approximating the size of the blemish), and click over the blemish. It's that easy. I suggest using a soft edge brush for a smooth and even effect.

Nested with the Spot Healing Brush is the Healing Brush. It does basically the same thing as the Spot Healing Brush, but it is a bit more difficult to use. In exchange for the effort, you get more control over your fix. You use the Healing Brush like the Clone Stamp Tool, which is covered on the next page.

As noted at the beginning of this chapter, these two images look differently because the screen grab (left) is a lower quality than the original image.

#16: Copy and Fix with the Clone Stamp Tool

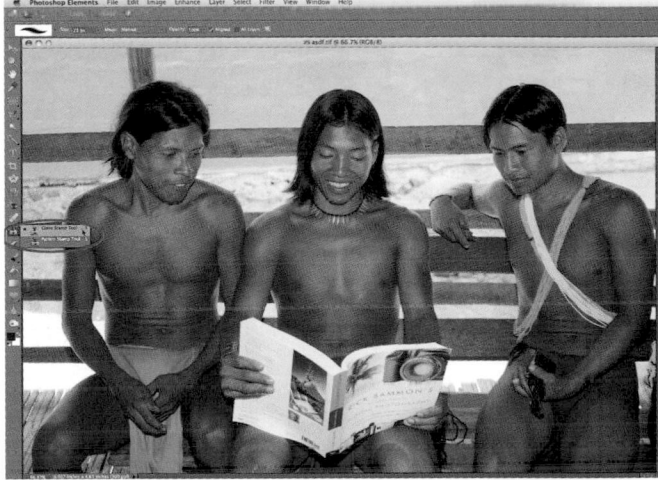

The idea of the Clone Stamp tool, found on the Tool Bar, is to copy and paste one area of an image over another.

It's the technique I used on the bottom image to remove the pole that looks as though it is growing out of the man's head on the left. I copied the blue background and pasted it over the pole, which erased the pole from the image. Here's the technique.

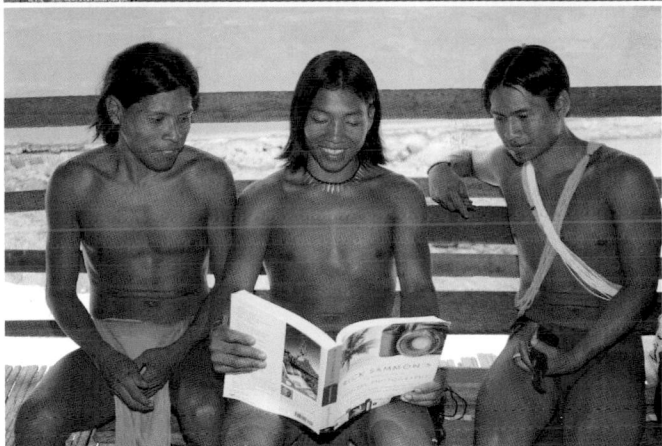

Select the Clone Stamp tool. Hold down the Option/Alt key and click on the area you want to copy and paste. Release the Option/Alt key.

Now, move your cursor over the area you want to hide or fix. Click and move your brush over that area. (I suggest using a soft edge brush.)

In an instant, you can remove unwanted elements (including people) from an image.

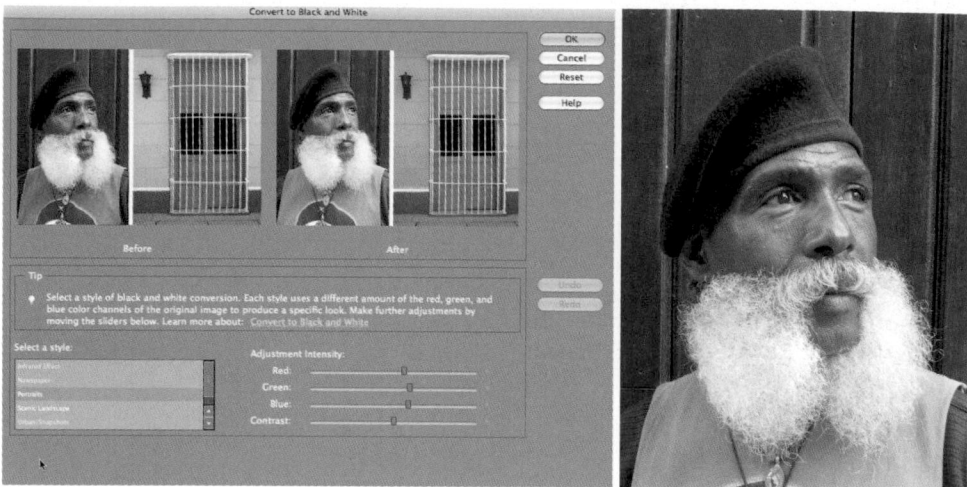

#17: Wow 'em with Black-and-White Images

When you remove the color from a scene, you remove some of the reality. When you remove some of the reality, a picture can look more artistic.

Go to Enhance > Convert to Black & White. You could simply click OK, but I think you will have fun experimenting with the different options. Select a style, using, for example, Portrait for portraits, Scenic Landscape for landscapes and so on.

Also play around with the Adjustment Intensity sliders. The colors here simulate the colors of the filters that photographers used to use when taking black-and-white pictures. They can make a big difference on an image, and they have a different effect on different types of pictures.

Don't forget to play around with the Contrast slider, too. Some black-and-white effects can be enhanced with a bit of a contrast boots; others look fine just the way they are. Experiment and see what happens.

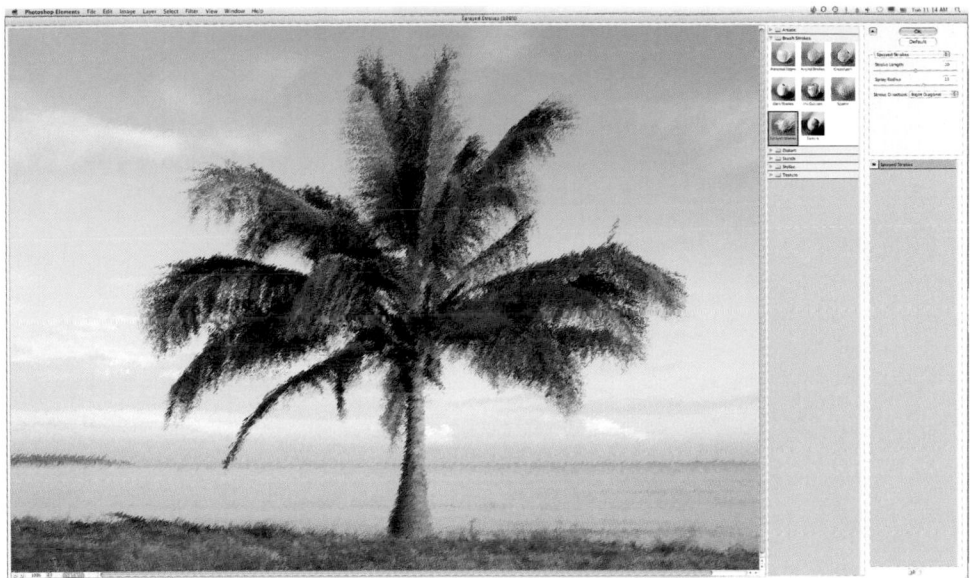

#18: Have Fun with Effects

You can have a lot of added fun in Photoshop Elements when you play around with all the built-in effects. They are located on the right side of the main window … if you have selected the Full Mode.

Click on Effects and then click on the different icons to get that effect. Here I used the Sprayed Strokes effect (at the default setting) on a shot I took of a palm tree. You can get other versions (intensity settings) of the same effect by playing around with the sliders.

Clicking on the icons on the word Effect brings up other effects: Filters, Layer Styles, Photo Effects and All. You can scroll through the effects by using the scroll bar on the right side of the window.

Have fun with this one. Let your imagination go wild.

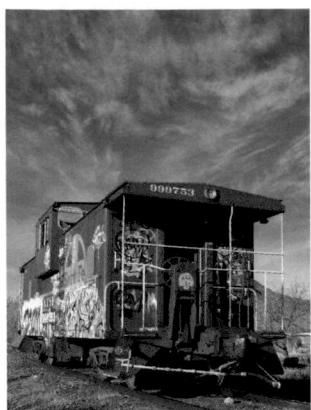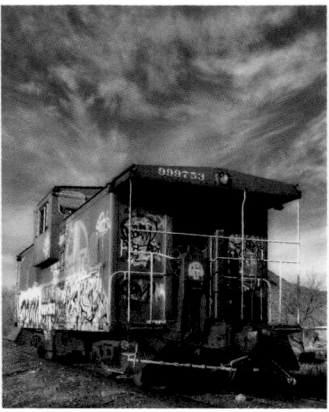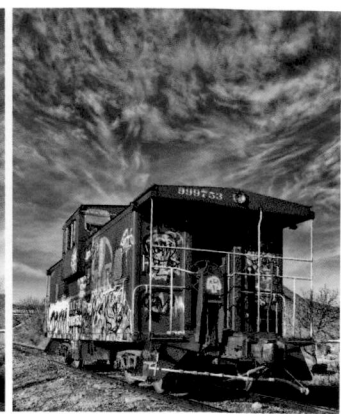

#19: Play With Plug-ins

Plug-ins expand the capability of Photoshop Elements and broaden your creative horizons. Basically, they do a lot of things to an image behind the scene with just a click of a mouse. They are available on a CD or via a download from the Internet.

Hundreds of plug-ins are available. I actually have a web site devoted entirely to using plug-ins. It is called the Plug-In Experience; the address is www.pluginexperience.com. Visit the Plug-In Experience to find web sites for the plug-ins I mention below. The site also offers some nice discounts on various plug-ins.

Here are some examples of plug-ins, from left to right: original image, Nik Software's Color Efex Pro/Duplex and Topaz Adjust/Spicify.

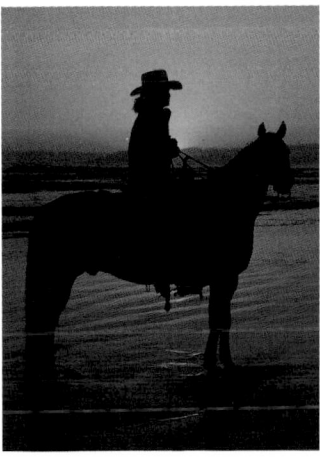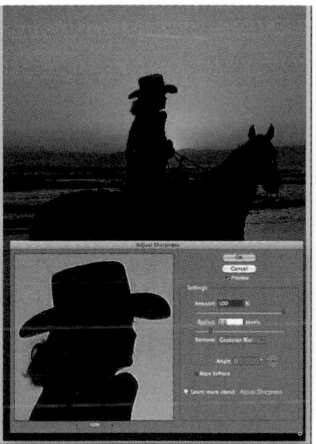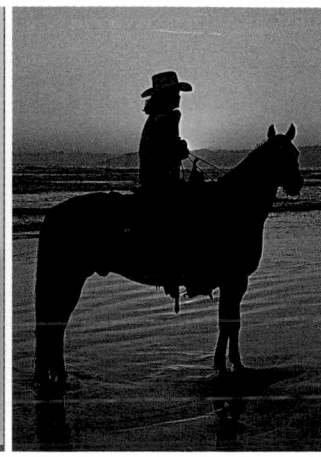

#20: Sharpen as the Final Step

You always want to sharpen as a final step, because other things you do, such as adjusting Levels and Contrast, will affect the sharpness of your image. The last thing you want is an over-sharpened image, shown here on the right. This image was sharpened 500 percent. The image on the left was sharpened 90 percent.

For most of your images, simply go to Enhance Image > Adjust Sharpness. Move the amount slider to the right to sharpen the image. I moved it too far to the right for the picture on the right to illustrate what happens when you over-sharpen an image: you get halos around the edges of subjects and you increase the digital noise in the image. Yuck!

There is no exact formula for sharpening. Just keep in mind that you can't sharpen an out-of-focus picture, and you want to sharpen as a final step. Just use your eye and common sense. If your picture looks pixilated, you have over-sharpened your image.

What about the Radius slider? Well, it adjusts the radius to be sharpened around the pixels. Just leave it at the default setting. That's my recommendation anyway for newbies to Photoshop Elements.

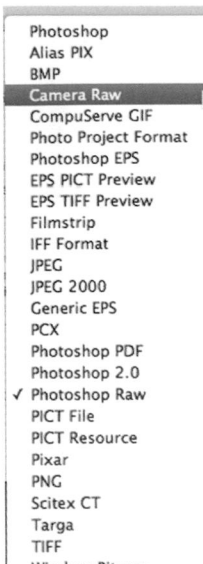
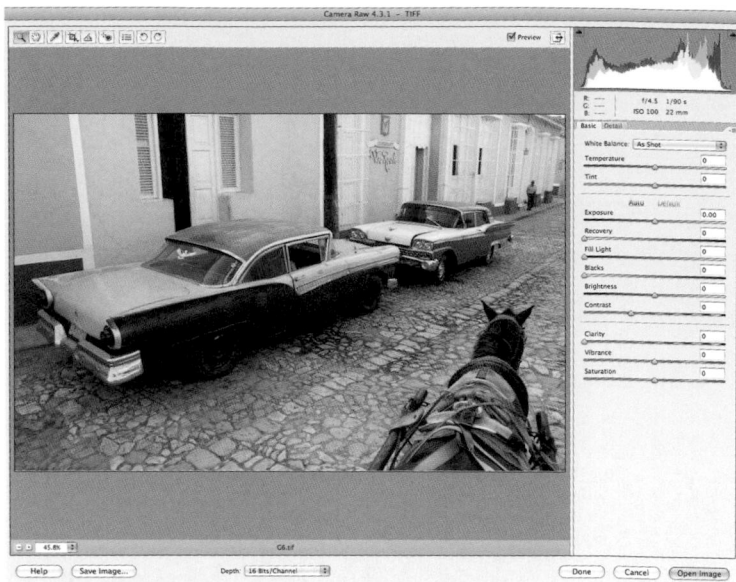

#21: Reward of RAW Files

They don't call me Rick "RAW Rules" Sammon for nothing.

I mostly shoot in RAW and enhance my pictures in Adobe Camera RAW—the window you see on the right. In that window, you have total control over your image with very powerful controls. These controls include Recover, which helps to recover overexposed highlights, and Fill Light, which helps to fill in dark shadows.

I know this is the last section in this chapter, but you really should start your enhancements here first. I saved it for last because I did not want to scare you away from the start with talk about RAW.

Shooting RAW files is an option for photographers who want to take their photography/ photo editing to the next level. It rules!

But here is some good news. Even if you shoot JPEGs, you can use Adobe Camera RAW to enhance your images. Go to File > Open and then choose Camera RAW as the file type. When you open your JPEG image, you'll be in the Camera RAW window.

Entire books have been written on Camera RAW. There is that much to know. For now, because I only have one page, my advice is to click on everything and move each slider to see what each does. You'll be amazed at the enhancement power that is available at your fingertips!

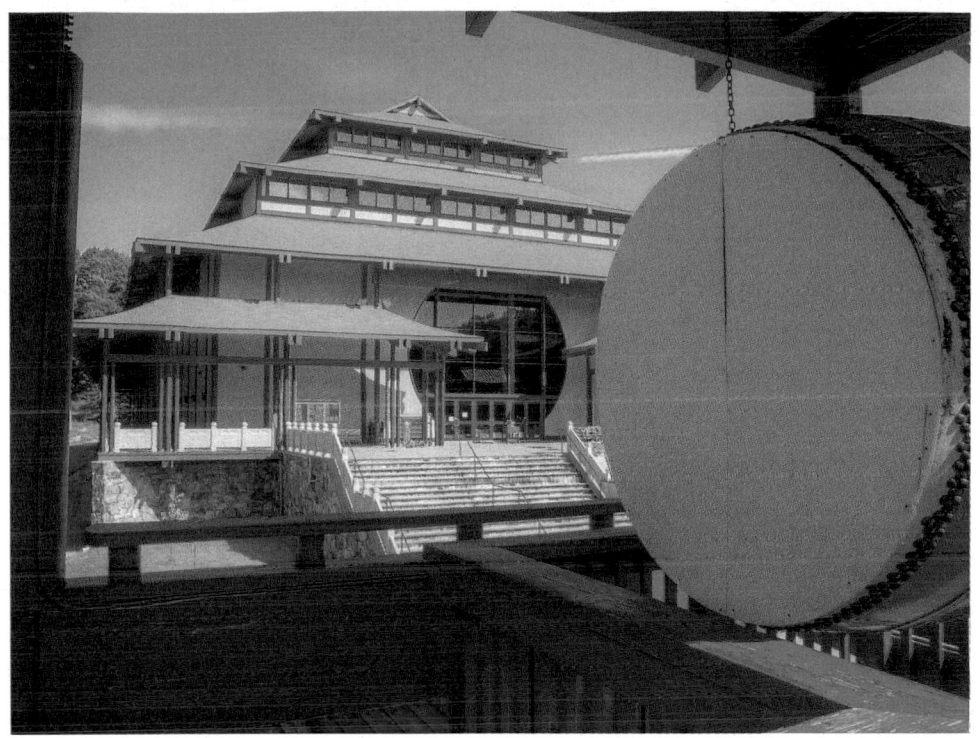

Part XIII

Expand Your Vision with HDR Imaging

The image you see here of a Buddhist temple near my home in Westchester, New York, is actually the end result of combining three photographs of the same scene and processing them digitally. It took about five minutes to create one high dynamic range (HDR) image with a bit of a Levels adjustment in Photoshop Elements.

HDR photography captures a much wider, that's right, *dynamic range*, than a straight out-of-the camera-image. What's more, HDR images tend to look more artistic and creative than straight shots … in my opinion anyway.

I use Photomatix Pro (www.hdrsoft.com), which is one of several HDR imaging programs, to create my HDR images.

Let's start the HDR fun!

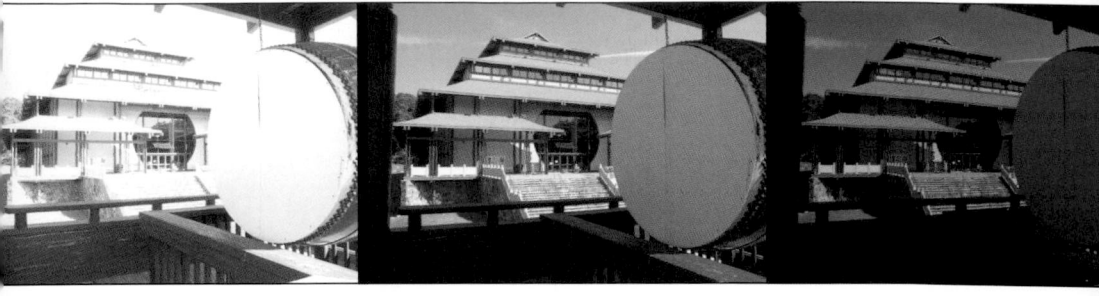

Take at Least Three Shots

Here are the three photographs that I took of the scene. One was taken at the 0 exposure compensation. This means that I took the image at the camera-recommended exposure setting. Then I took two additional exposures: one at +2 and one at the −2 exposure compensation setting.

Covering that wide of an exposure range, I was sure to capture both the highlight (sky) and shadow (rock) details that I wanted to see in my final image.

The +/− bracketing technique that I used for my temple image is not set in stone for all HDR images. Sometimes you need to take more individual exposures that cover stops over and stops under the "correct" exposure. This is the case when you are photographing in very high-contrast situations. Sometimes, when there is not a wide contrast range, only one-stop bracketing is needed.

What you don't want is too few exposures. In my exploration of HDR photography, I have taken up to nine exposures at half-stop increments to capture all the detail in a scene.

Speaking of taking the actual pictures, I suggest using a tripod and your camera's self-timer or a cable release (and maybe even locking up the camera's mirror) for a steady shot.

In addition, you must leave your aperture constant for a pano set. This means shooting in the Aperture Priority Mode (as I do) or in the Manual mode.

Generate HDR

The first step to generating an HDR image in Photomatix is to click on the Generate HDR button, which brings up this menu.

Be sure to click Align Source Images (just in case there is any movement in your images), Reduce chromatic noise (nasty color bands around bright/dark edges) and Reduce noise (for a clean image). Keep in mind that the more boxes you check, the longer it will take to generate your HDR image.

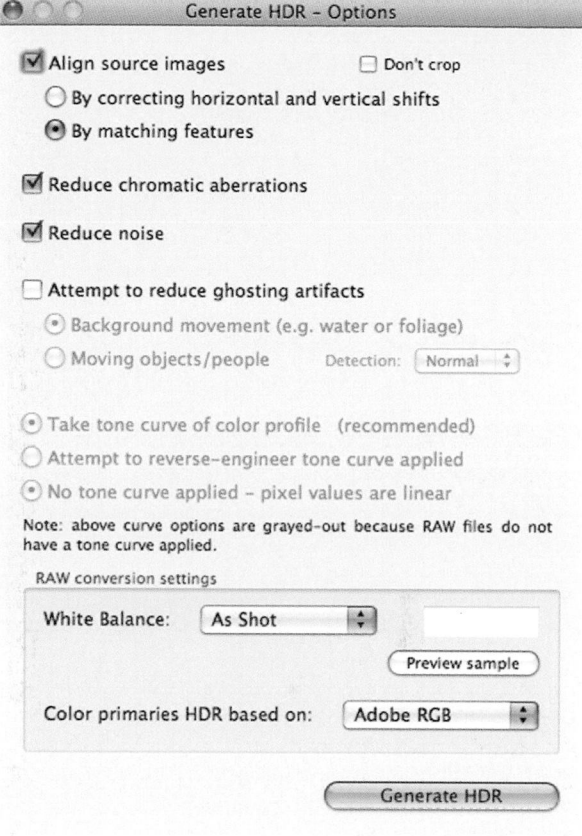

Now, click Generate HDR. After you click Generate HDR and wait a minute or two, you will get a window that displays your HDR image. It will look weird, because your monitor can't display all the tones in the HDR image. Don't panic. Simply click Tone Mapping to go to the next window, which is described on the following page.

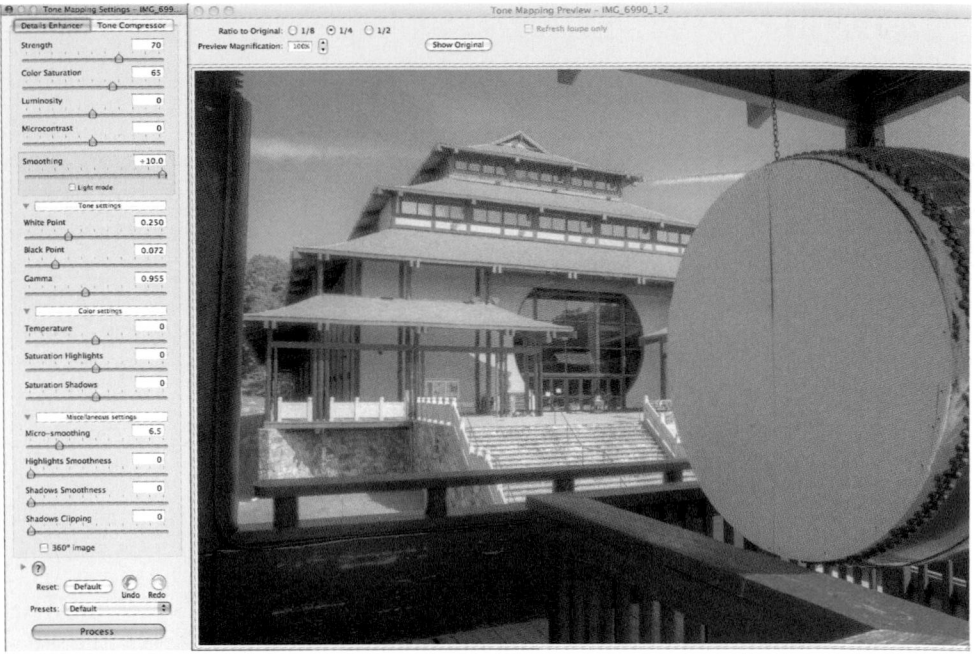

Do It with Details Enhancer

After you click Generate HDR, you have two major options. You can use Tone Compressor and Details Enhancer. Both have names that describe what they do.

Basically, I leave Tone Compressor alone, because Photomatix does a great job of compressing the tones. I go straight to Details Enhancer.

My advice is to play—and I mean *play*—with the sliders to see the effect each has on an image.

A quick tip: The more you boost the Strength, Color Saturation and Luminosity in the Details Enhancer, the more artistic and creative your image will appear; reduce these settings for a more natural look.

And here is one final tip: Each time you play with an HDR image, press the Default button. That'll bring Photomatix back to its default settings. If you don't, whatever effect you created last will be applied to your new image.

The Fun Never Stops

Here is a look at (from top to bottom): Original image take at the 0 EV setting, the Photomatix HDR image, and Photoshop plus Topaz Adjust enhancement.

See! The fun never stops in the digital darkroom!

Topaz Adjust is not a true HDR plug-in; but it can, indeed, expand the dynamic range of an image … even a single image.

Speaking of single images, if you drag a single RAW file onto the Photomatix icon on your desktop, Photomatix will generate a Pseudo HDR from that single file. Like Topaz, it's a not a true HDR image, but it sure has a wider dynamic range than your original file … created magically!

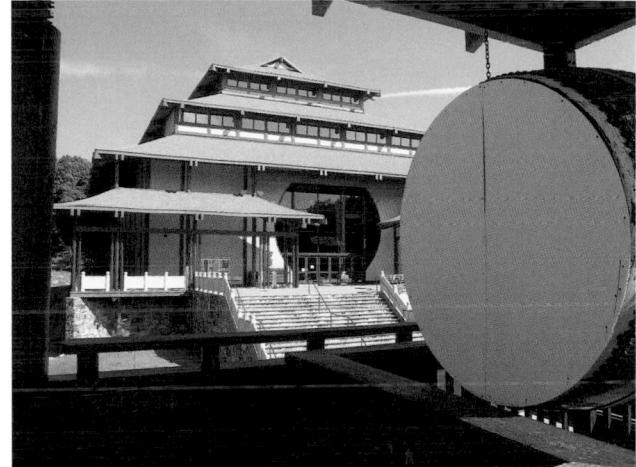

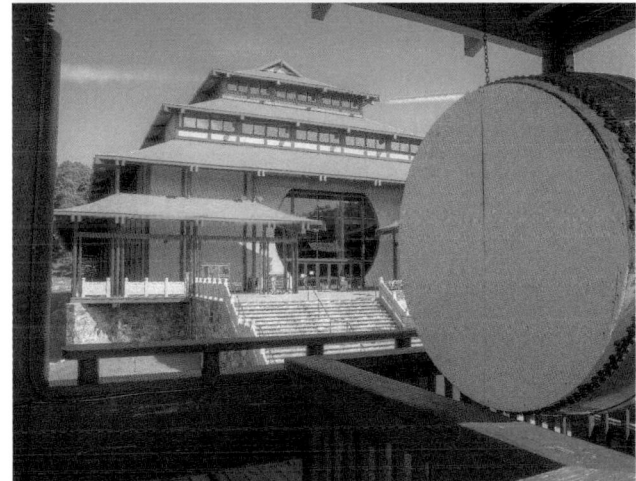

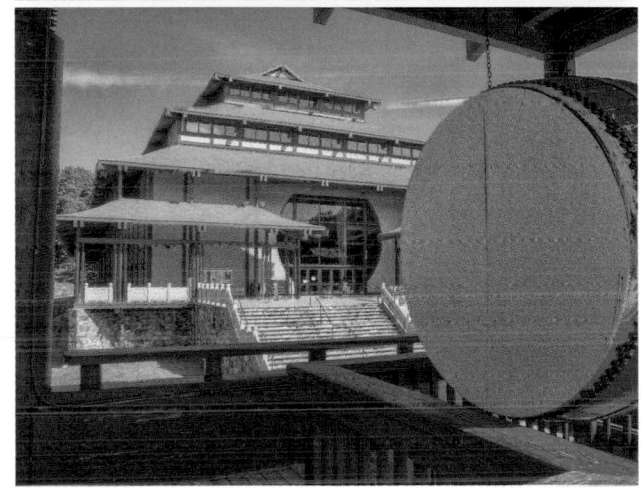

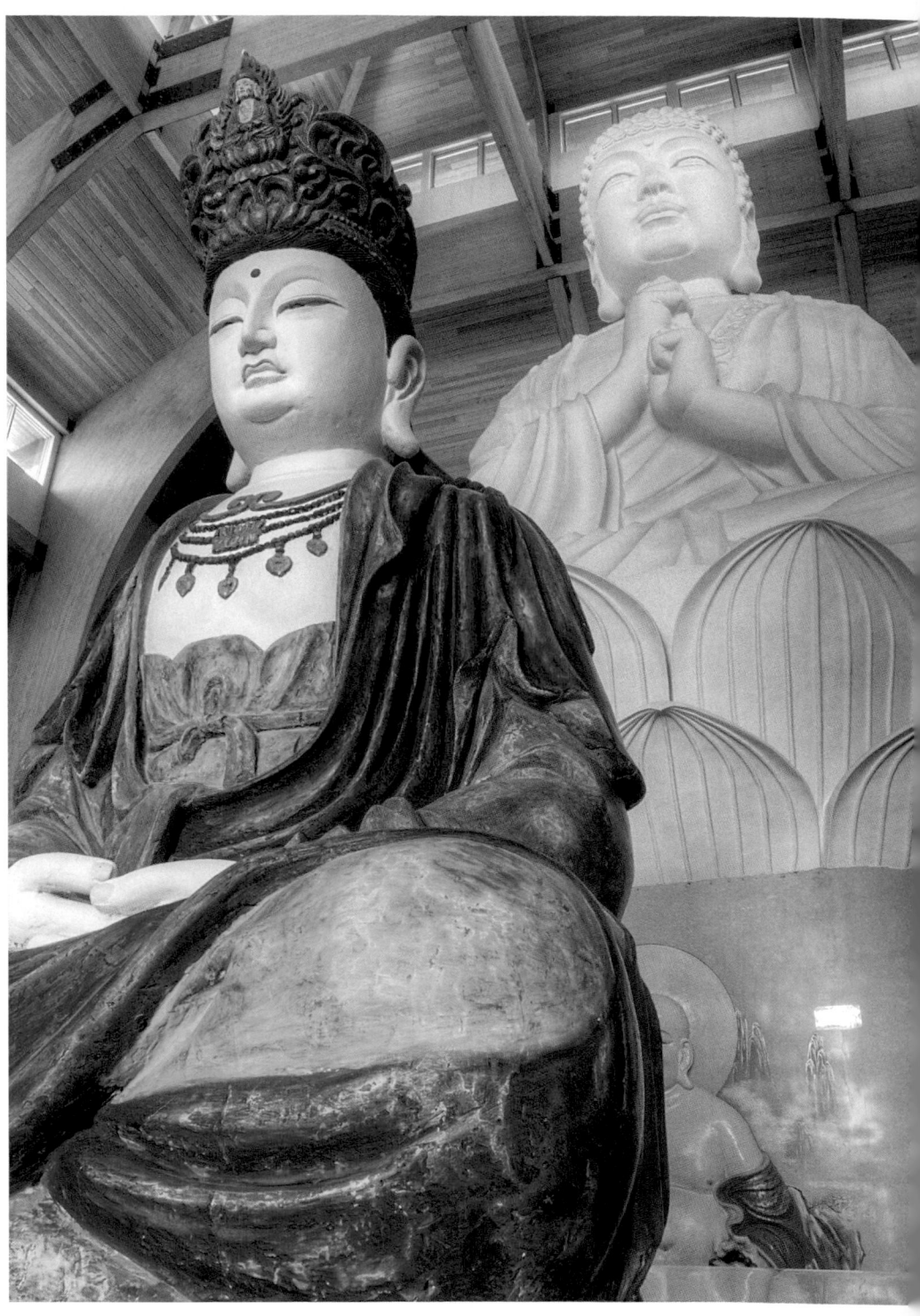

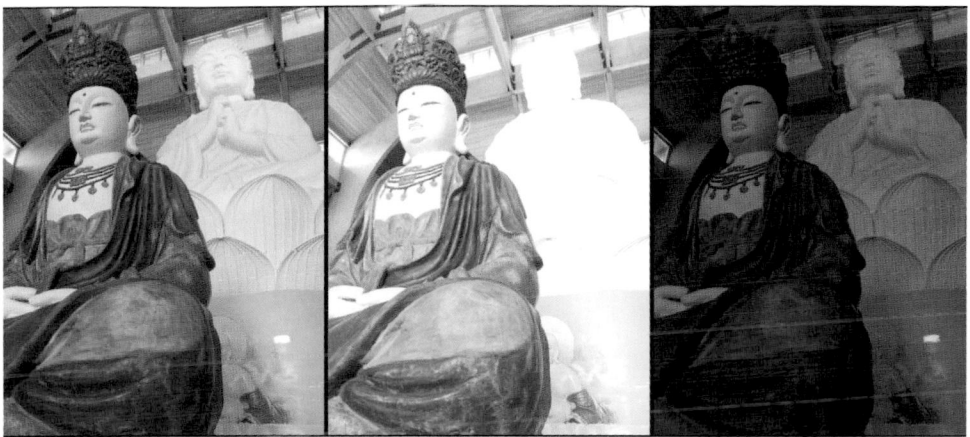

Take HDR Inside, Too

Here is one of my favorite indoor HDR images. It was created in Photomatix using three images. One was taken with no exposure compensation; one was taken at two stops over the recommended exposure setting; and one was taken at two stops under the recommended exposure setting.

What's amazing to me is that the widows in the background are not overexposed and the shadow areas are not blocked up. Now that's cool.

Get a discount on Photomatic on the hdrsoft.com web site by using this code upon checkout: ricksammon.

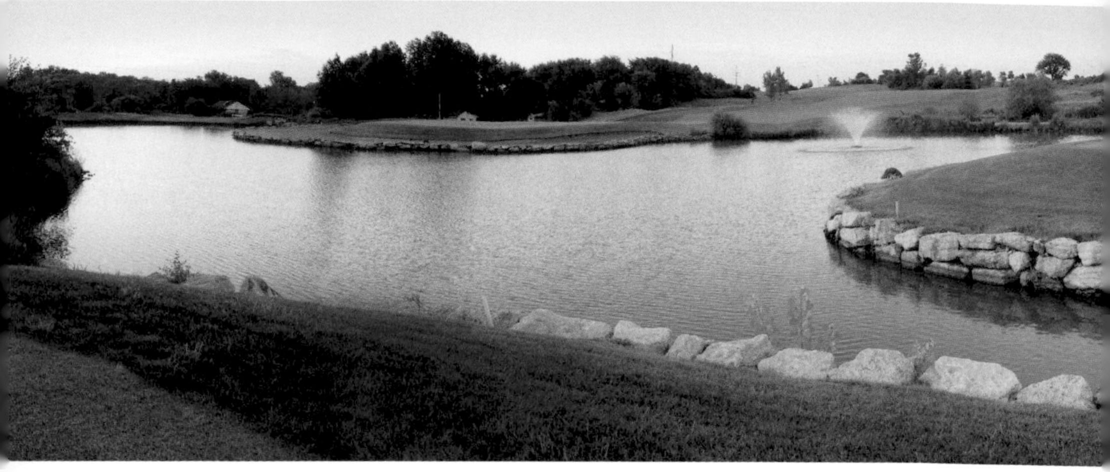

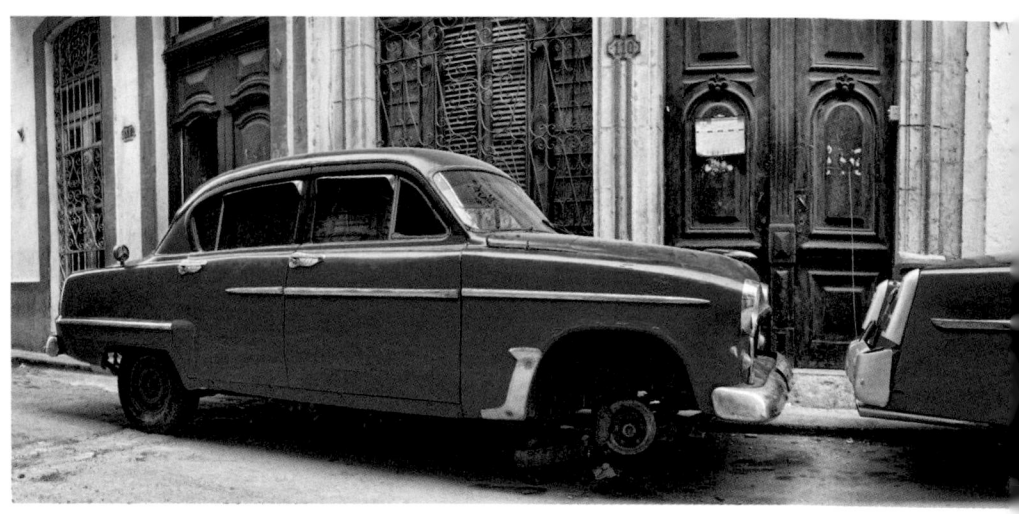

Part XIV

Shooting Panoramas

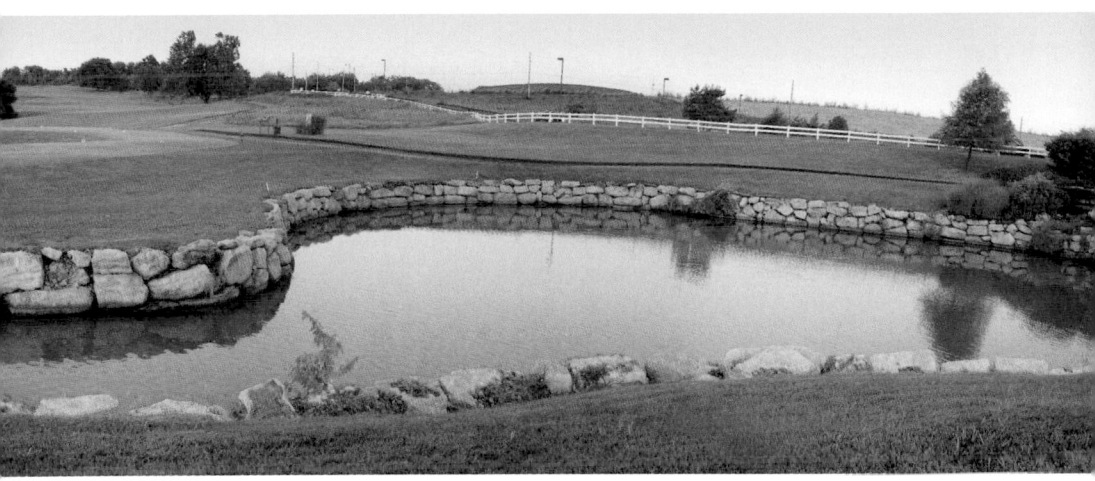

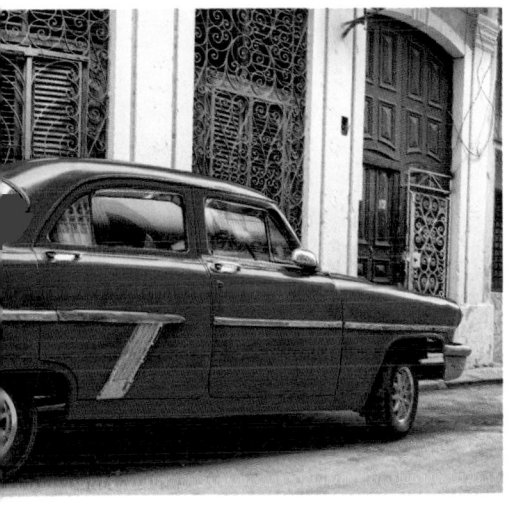

Creating panoramas in Photoshop Elements 7 and 8 is a ton of fun—not to mention an enjoyable creative process.

In this chapter you'll find some guidelines for creating panos, which, by the way, has never been easier ... thanks to the new Photomerge feature in Photoshop Elements. It's a much-improved version of earlier Photomerge features in Elements.

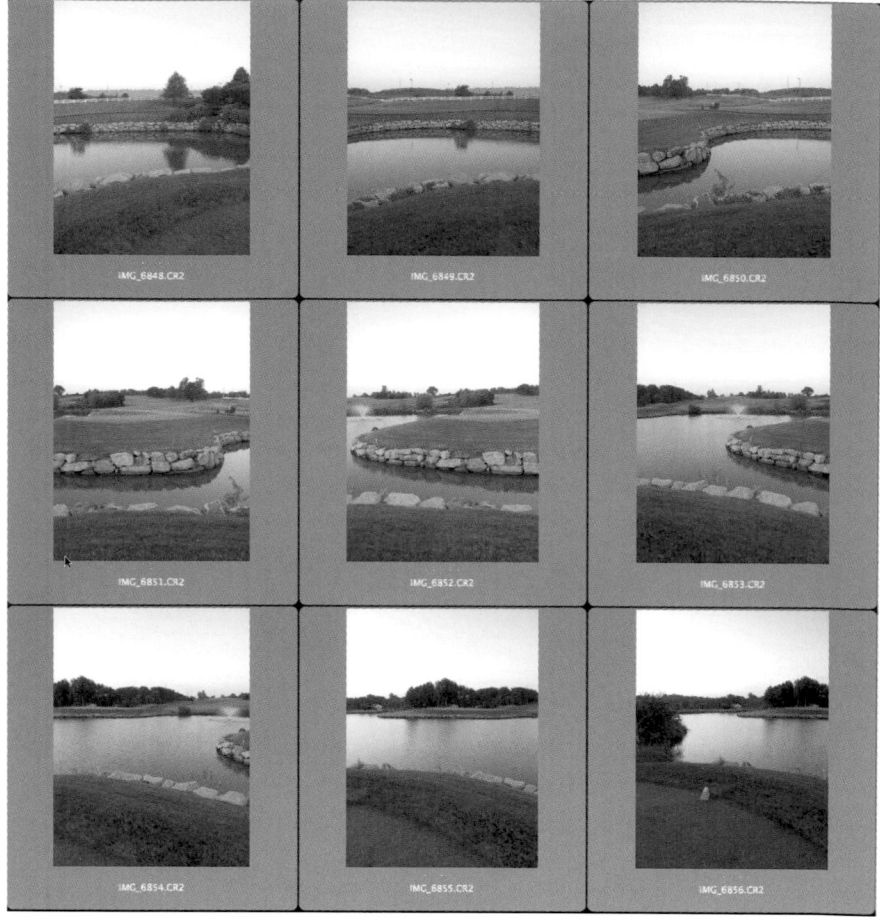

Getting Started

The first step is to take the pictures for your panoramas.

When shooting for a pano, overlap your images by at least one-third. This Adobe Bridge screen grab shows that I actually overlapped my images by a bit more than that. Better safe than sorry, I say.

Also, it's best to set your camera on the Manual exposure mode (so that the exposures match up). It's also wise to use a tripod. Better yet, use a tripod with a panorama head, so that your exposures are level.

That said, I hand-held my camera and had it set on the aperture priority mode for both of the panos you saw the beginning of this chapter. Why? Because I did not have my trusty tripod with me, and I figured a less than perfect pano is better than no pano at all!

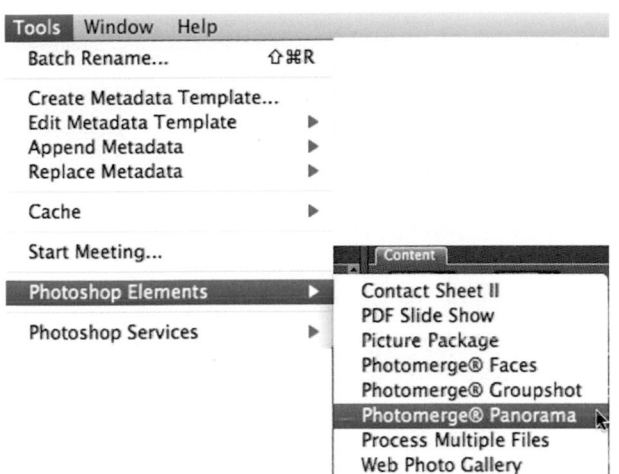

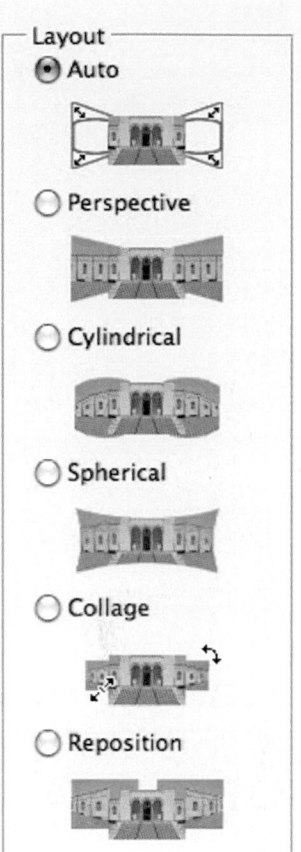

Pano from Adobe Bridge

First select your set of images for the pano in Adobe Bridge, which comes pre-packaged with Elements. Then go to Photoshop Elements > Photoshop Panorama.

After your images are selected, select a Layout; Auto works in most cases. Then press OK and wait. The larger the files, the longer your wait. It's good to know this because you may want to downsize your pano files and do a test before you get to work on your serious large-file pano.

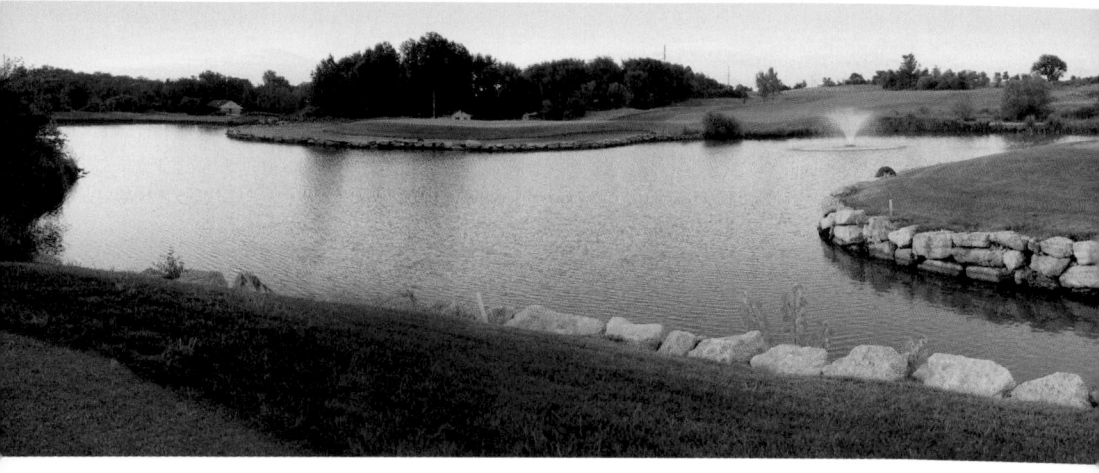

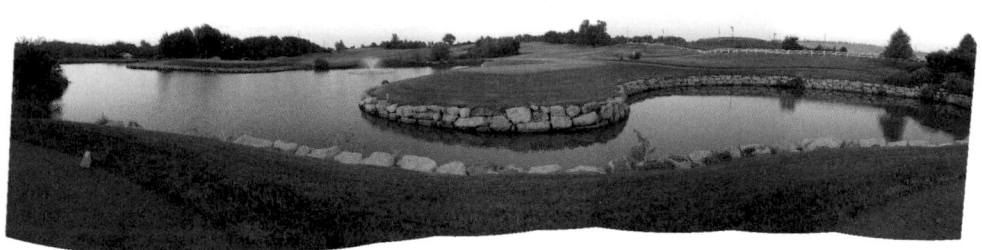

Shoot Verticals

You'll notice that I took vertical shots for my horizontal panorama of the golf course. That's because shooting verticals, as I did (rather than horizontals) minimizes the bow-tie effect, which refers to images that are cut off at the top and bottom of the frame. The bow-tie effect is often associated with panos. You can avoid it by leaving extra space above and below the important part of your image—right, which you can accomplish by shooting verticals.

Here, I lost very little image area, relatively speaking. But as you will see, I cropped the image much tighter for my final pano.

When your pano is created, you'll lose some picture area at the top, bottom and sides of the frame, as illustrated by this screen grab. With that in mind, when you are composing pictures for a pano, leave some extra space around your main image area. That will help to ensure that you'll not lose important areas of the scene. Here, too, better safe than sorry. Leave more room than you think you'll need.

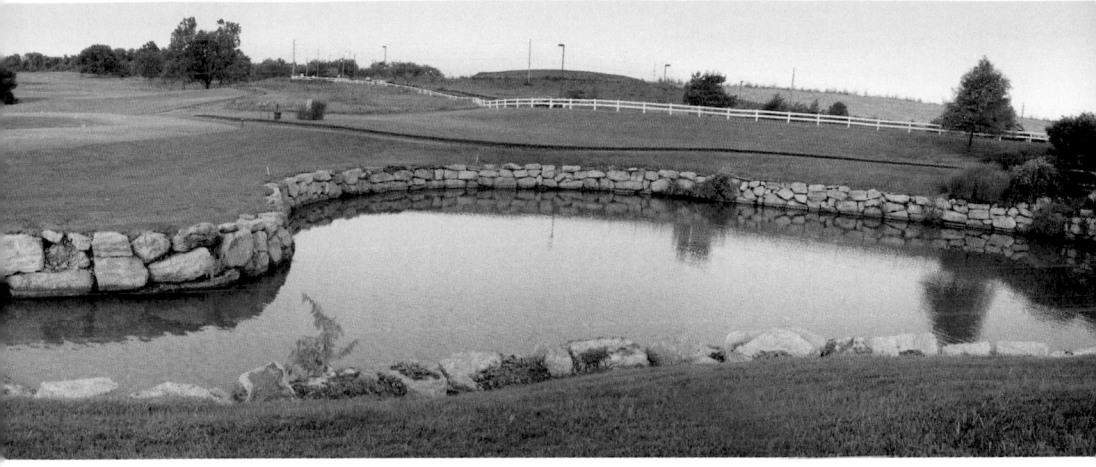

More Fun Awaits You

After your pano is created, you can still have more fun in the digital darkroom.
Here, you can enhance the color, contrast and sharpness of the scene in
Photoshop Elements.

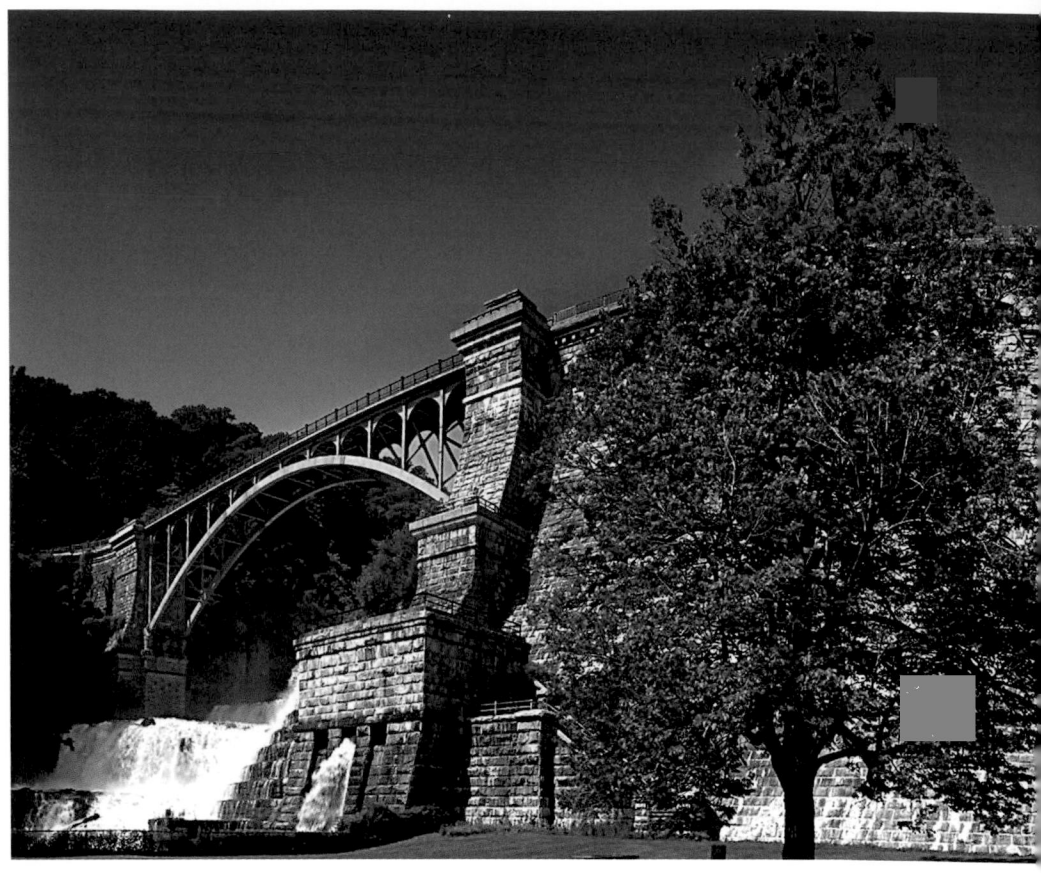

Expect Surprises, Too

This image of the New Croton Dam in Croton-on-Hudson, New York, is one example of the way-cool surprises that await you in the world of panorama photography. After selecting the Auto Layout and then pressing OK, I was very pleasantly surprised at the apparent curvature of the dam.

Yes, friends, the dam really is straight, as illustrated by one of the pictures from my pano series. This effect was created by photographing from a position so close to the dam. To avoid the curvature, I could have stood further way ... if a parking lot filled with cars had not been in my way!

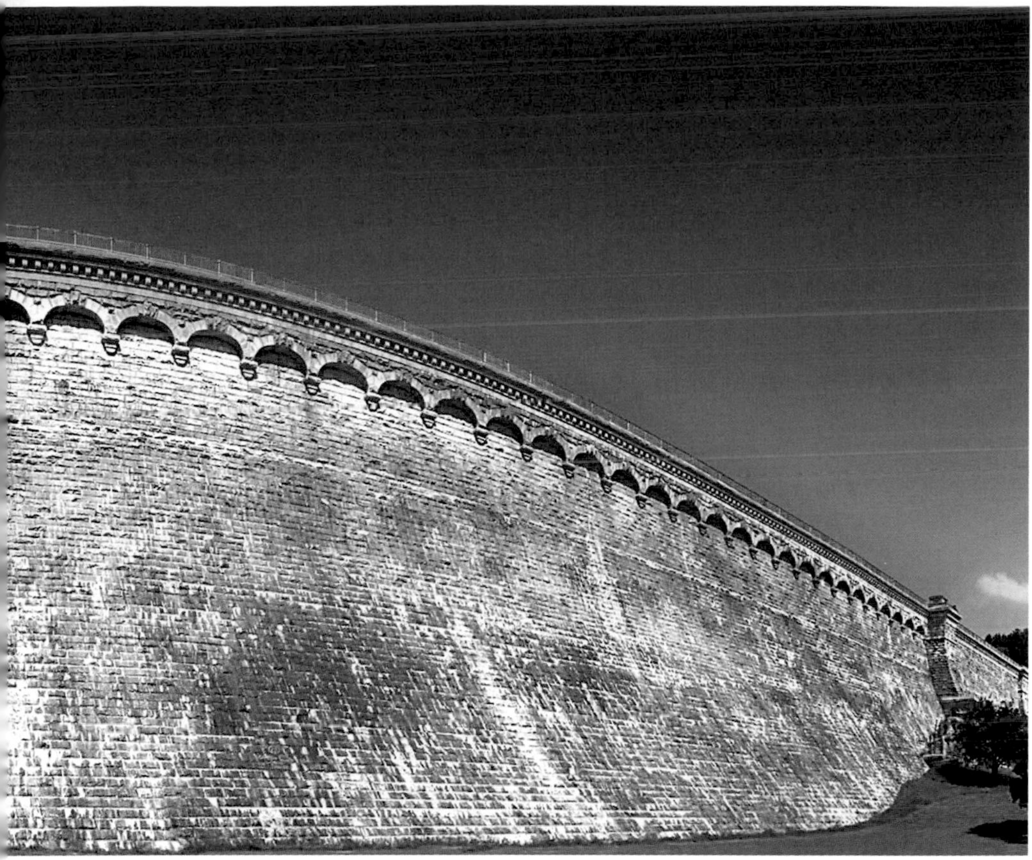

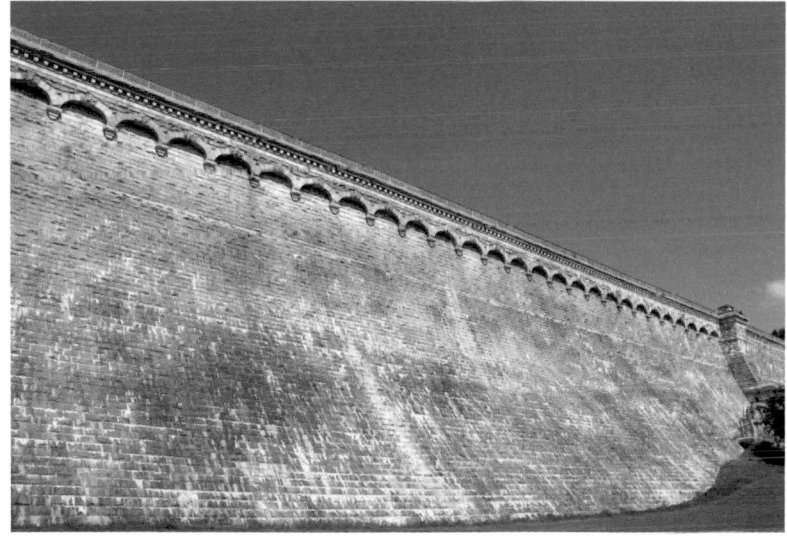

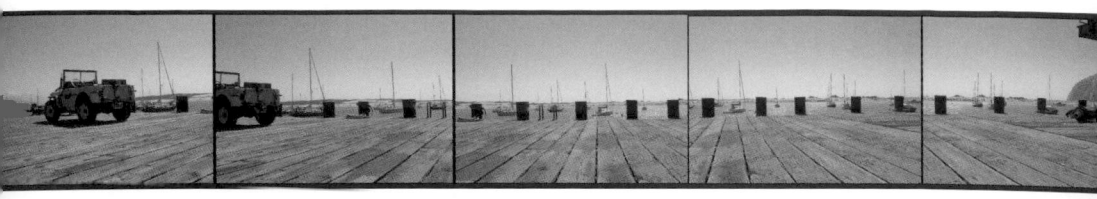

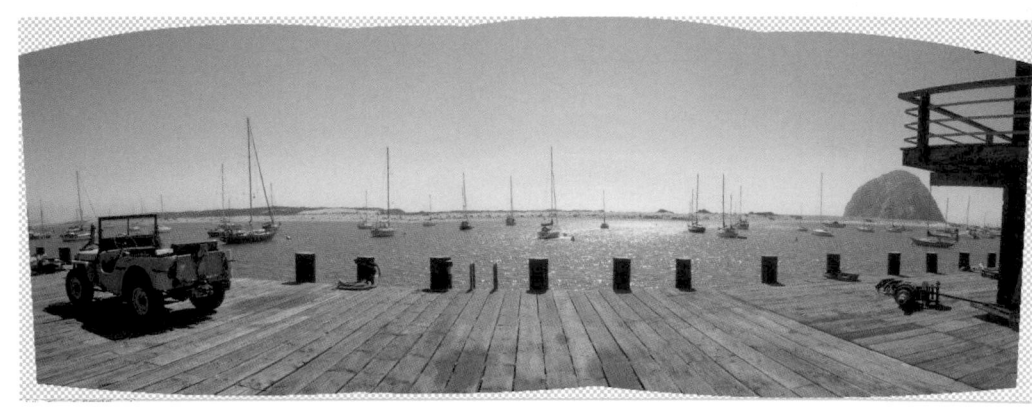

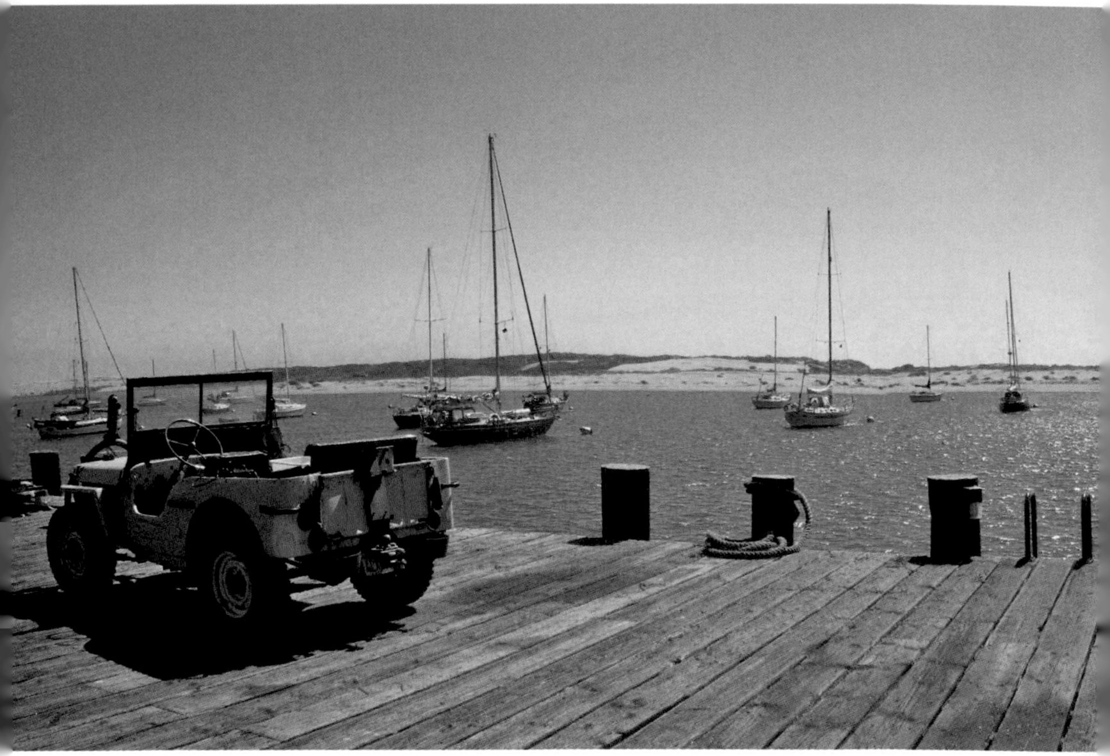

A Truly Amazing Match

At the beginning of this chapter, I mentioned that the new Photomerge is much improved over previous versions. Well, here is an example.

Check out the images from which I made the panorama you see here. Notice how the lines on the dock are at different angles in each picture. Yes, Photomerge lined them up almost perfectly. Now that is truly amazing.

Okay, I said, "almost perfectly." I am sure all you keen-eye image-makers noticed some imperfections in the stitching process on the dock. So is Photomerge perfect? No. Is it fun? Yes!

Have fun with panos and reveal the wide view!

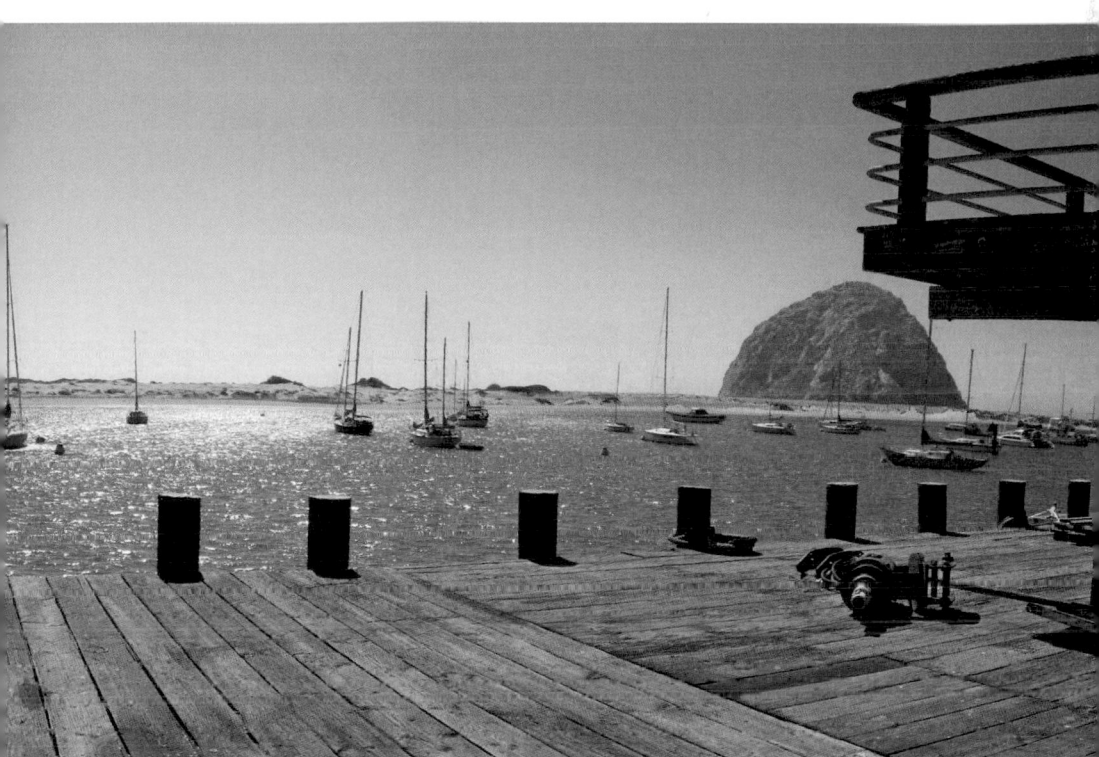

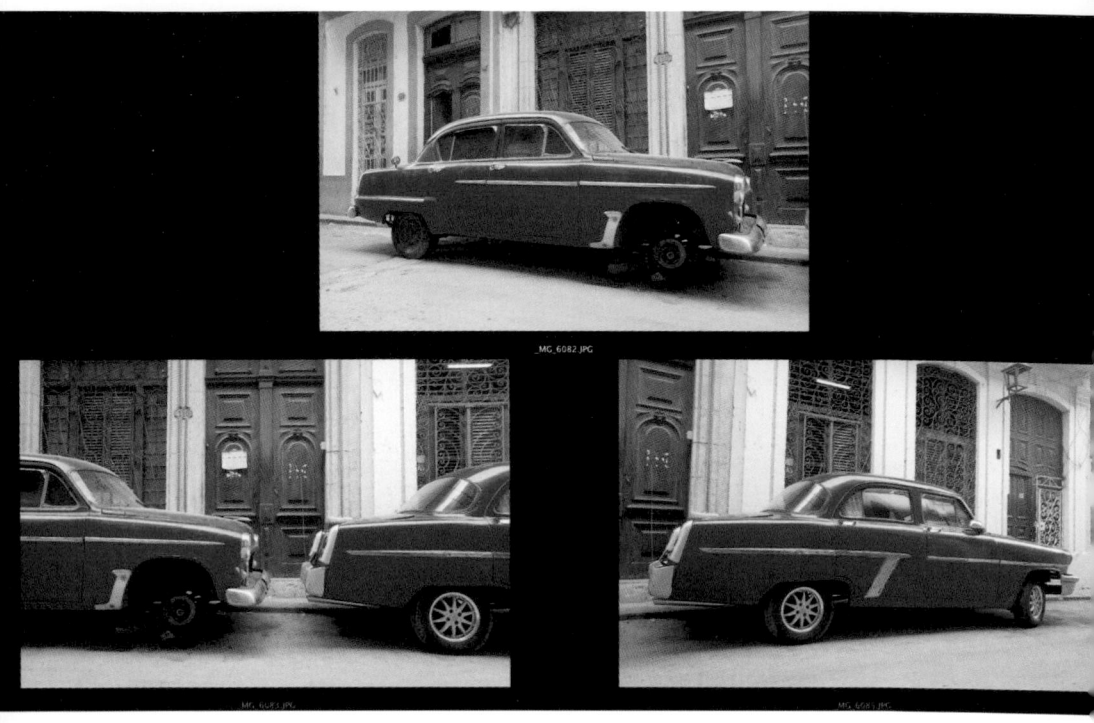

Shooting Panos in a Tight Spot

Panoramas are usually associated with sweeping landscapes, seascapes and cityscapes … and even golf courses. However, you can use pano technique in relatively tight places, too. Think: narrow street. That's the setting for one of my favorite panos from a trip to Cuba. Cool, no?

The next time you are in a tight spot, try a pano! As always, you need to start by taking a series of shots. Basic guidelines are covered on page 186.

Here are the three shots I took of this cool car in Cuba to create the pano on the chapter intro page.

Experiment with Layouts

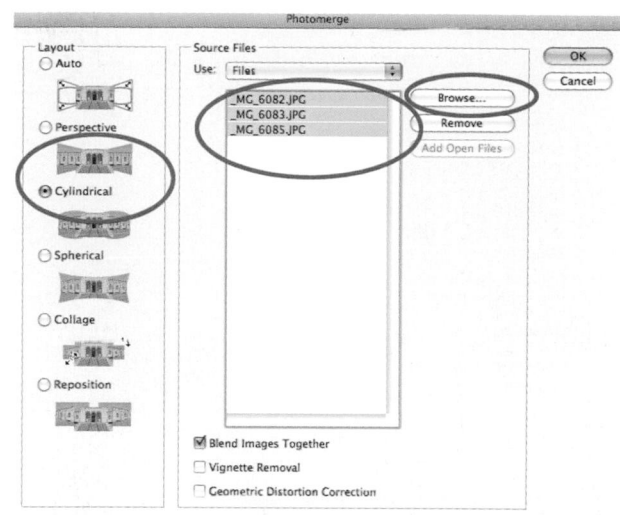

As I mentioned, don't get discouraged if your first pano is out-of-whack when it comes to alignment. You may need to select a different Layout. For example, Cylindrical produced the best pano for my set of images; it's show here.

As illustrated, Perspective produced a very wacky and unacceptable image.

After your images and Layout are selected, all you need to do is press OK and wait. The larger the files, the longer your wait. It's good to keep this in mind because you may want to downsize your pano files and experiment with different Layouts before you commit to waiting out your large-file pano.

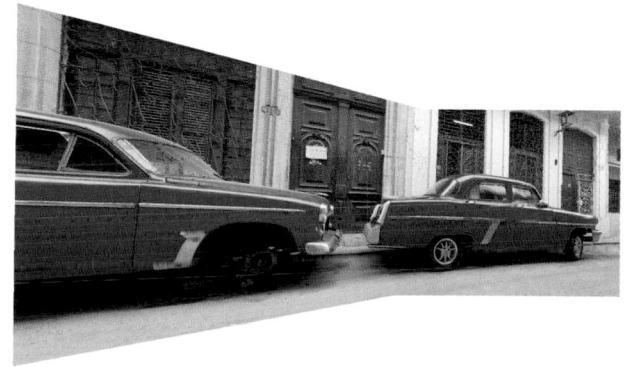

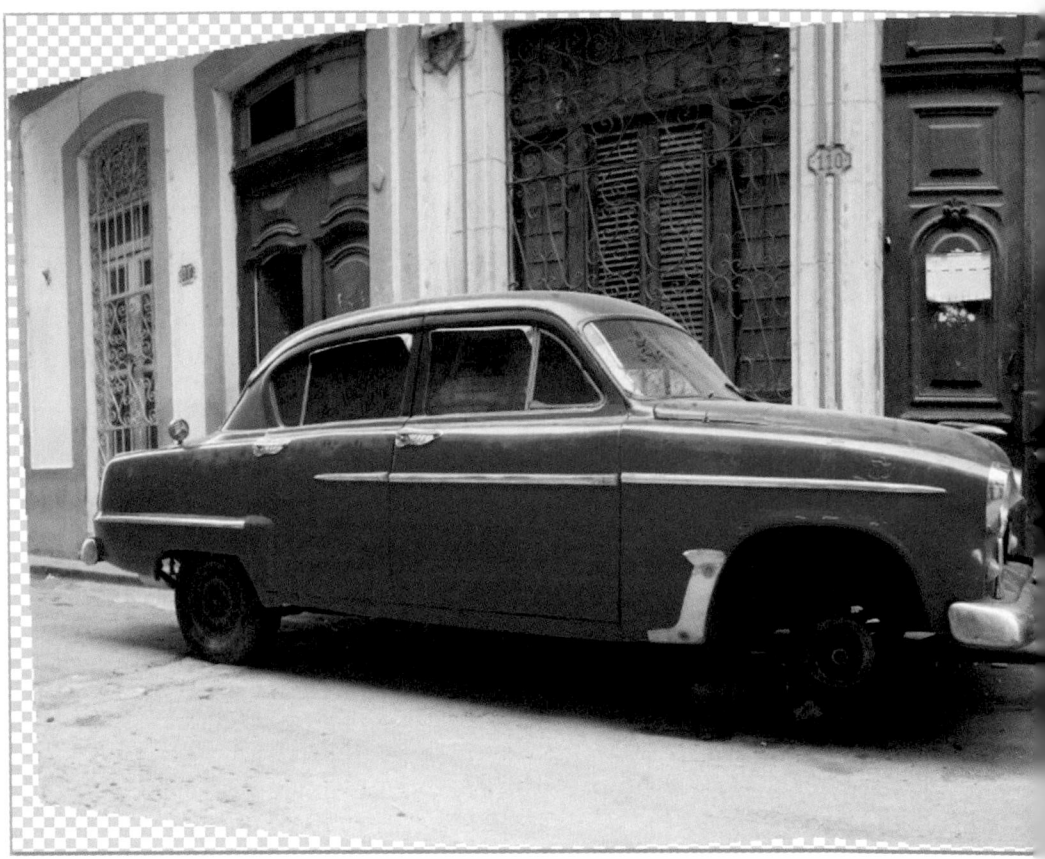

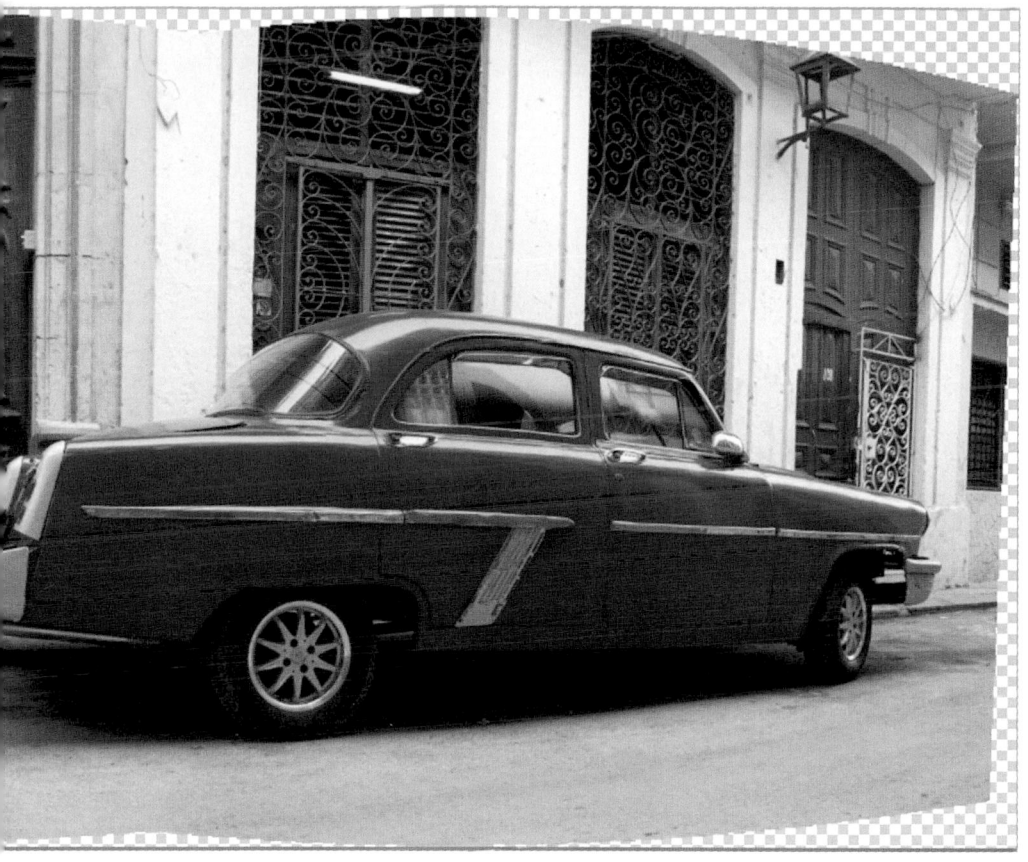

Expect to Crop

When your pano is created, you'll lose some picture area at the top, bottom and sides of the frame, as illustrated by this screen grab. With that in mind, when you are composing pictures for a panorama, leave extra space around your main image area. That will help you avoid losing important areas of the scene. Here, too, better safe than sorry. Leave more room than you think you'll need.

My final tip: Have fun with panos ... and experiment!

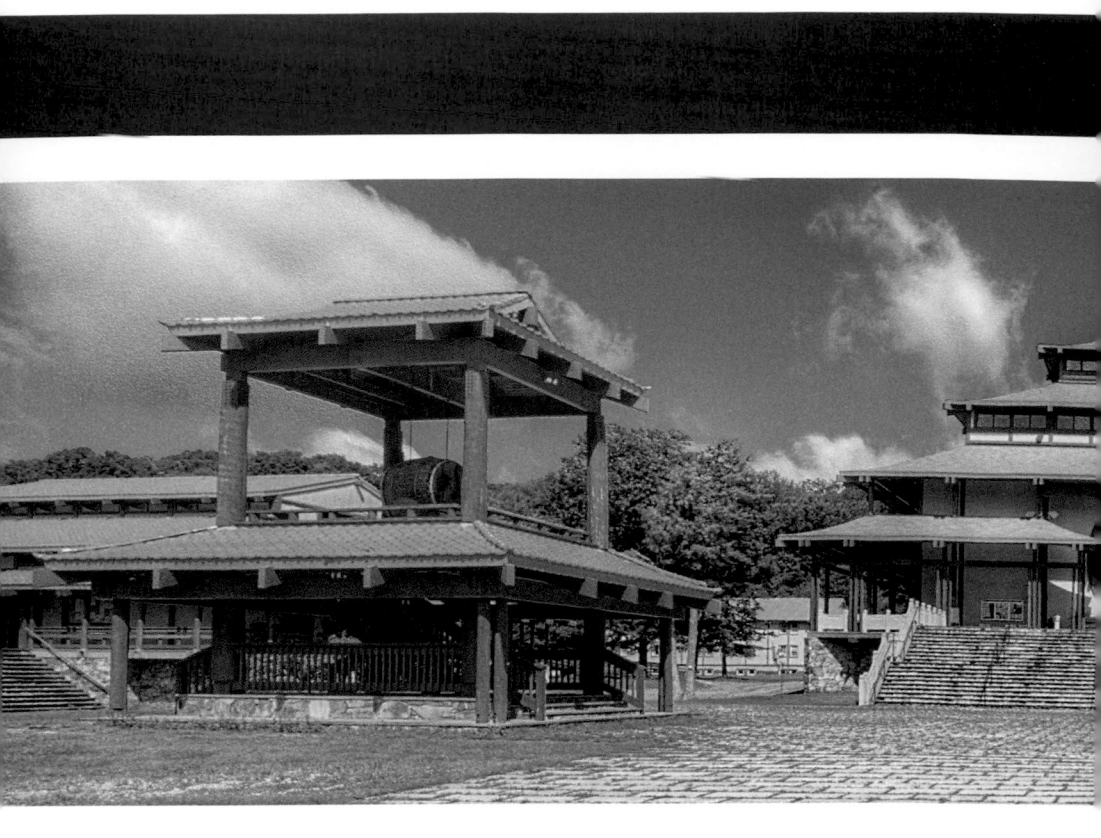

Part XV

HDR + Panos = Way-Cool Imaging Fun

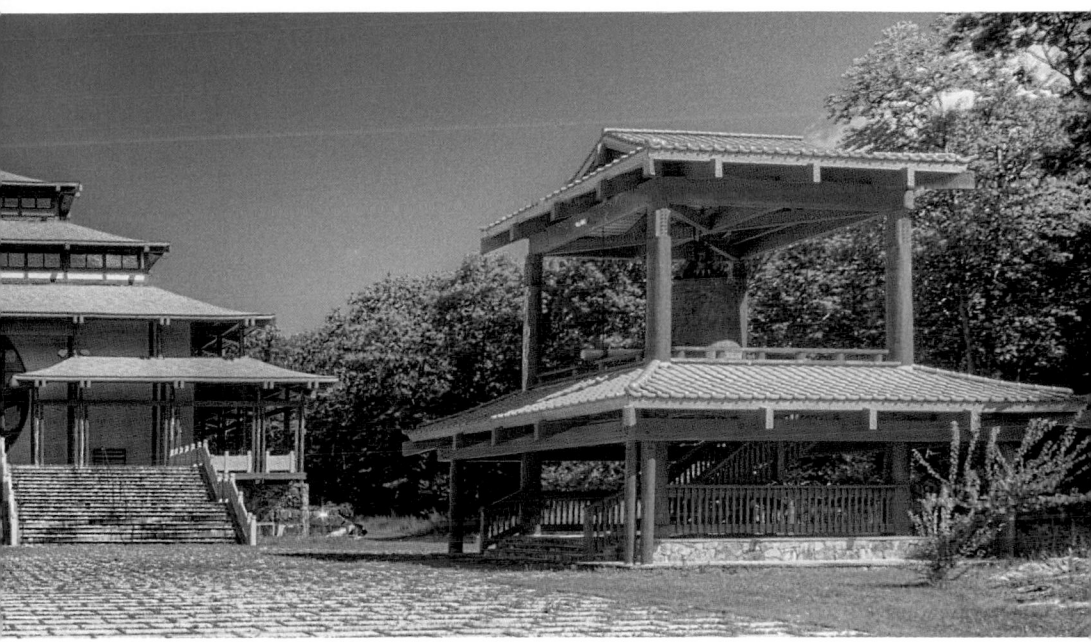

We've talked about HDR imaging and shooting panoramas. Now, in this chapter we'll take a look at how to combine these techniques to get some way-cool images.

What? You think this technique is too advanced for a compact camera owner? No so!

Sure, creating an HDR pano will take more time than pointing and shooting with a compact camera, but I teach this technique to beginner students—and they love it! Plus, the results are definitely worth the extra effort.

You'll need a camera with manual exposure control … and a tripod. If you take the time, or should I say *make* the time, you can create beautiful panos like this one. Go for it!

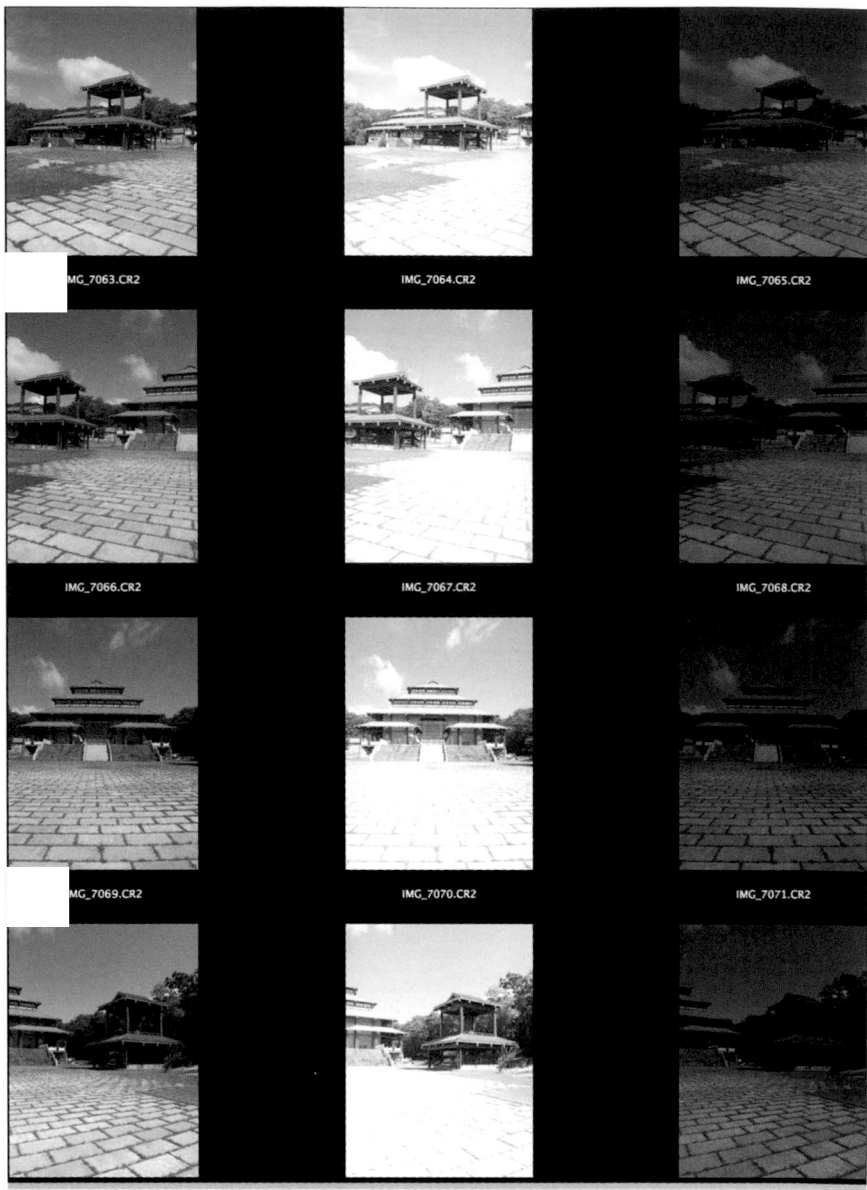

Shooting for an HDR Pano

The first step in creating an HDR pano is to take HDR images for each section of your panorama. Here is a screen grab that shows what I did for my HDR pano. Each horizontal row shows three images for each section of my four-section final image.

My exposures, from left to right: O EV, +2 EV and –2 EV.

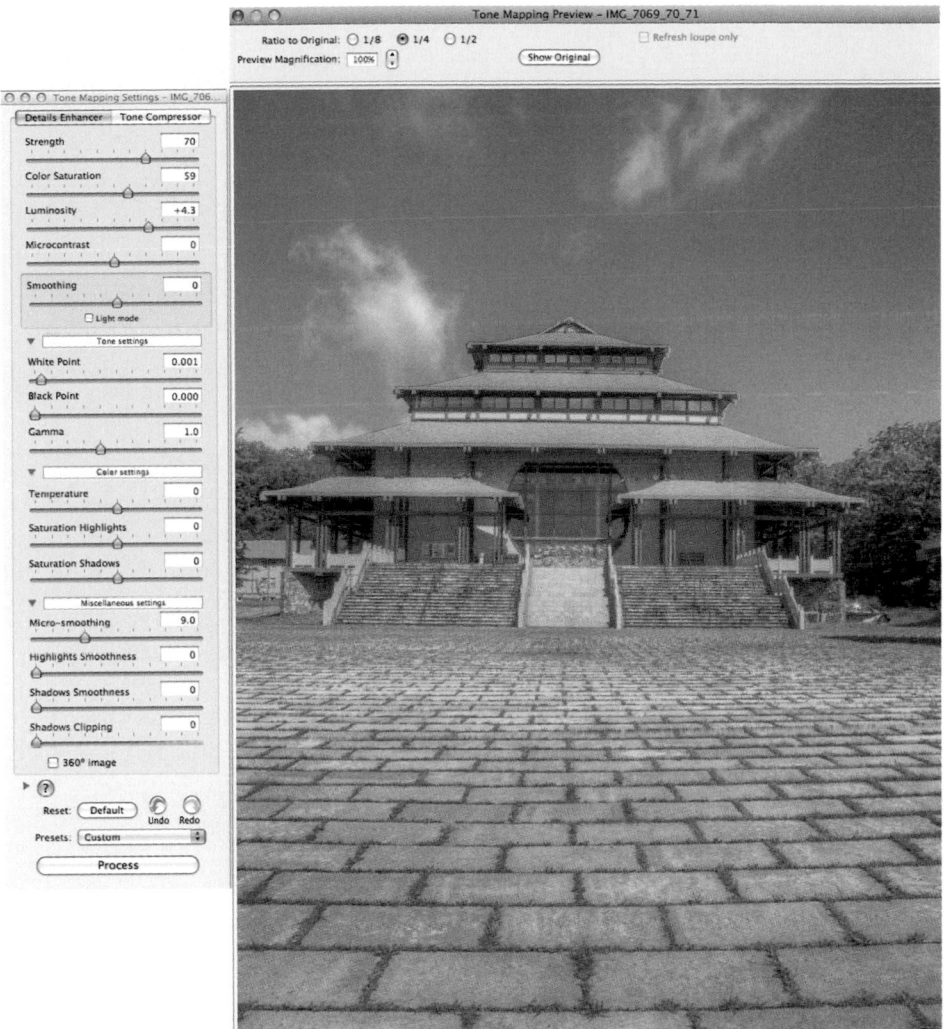

Generate an HDR Image for Each Set of Images

The next step is to create an HDR image from each set of three images in Photomatix. For my pano, I did not play with any of the Tone Compressor or Details Enhancer sliders. If I had, I would have had to apply all the same settings to all my HDR images in this set. I decided that it would be better to make a global enhancement after my HDR images were merged into my pano.

Enter Photoshop Elements

After you have processed all your HDR images, it's time to make your pano in Photoshop Elements.

Mostly likely, after going through the Photomerge steps mentioned in the Shooting Panoramas chapter and pressing OK, you'll get a bow-tie looking image, like this. That's the nature of Photomerge panos, as I mentioned before.

Also as noted earlier, if you shoot verticals, as I did, rather than horizontals, your bow-tie effect will be less and, if you leave extra space above and below the important part of your image, you probably will not lose important parts of your main subject when applying the bow-tie crop.

Play in Photoshop Elements

The final steps are to crop your image and then apply any desired digital enhancements to your image. Here I increased the saturation and contrast to make the image pop.

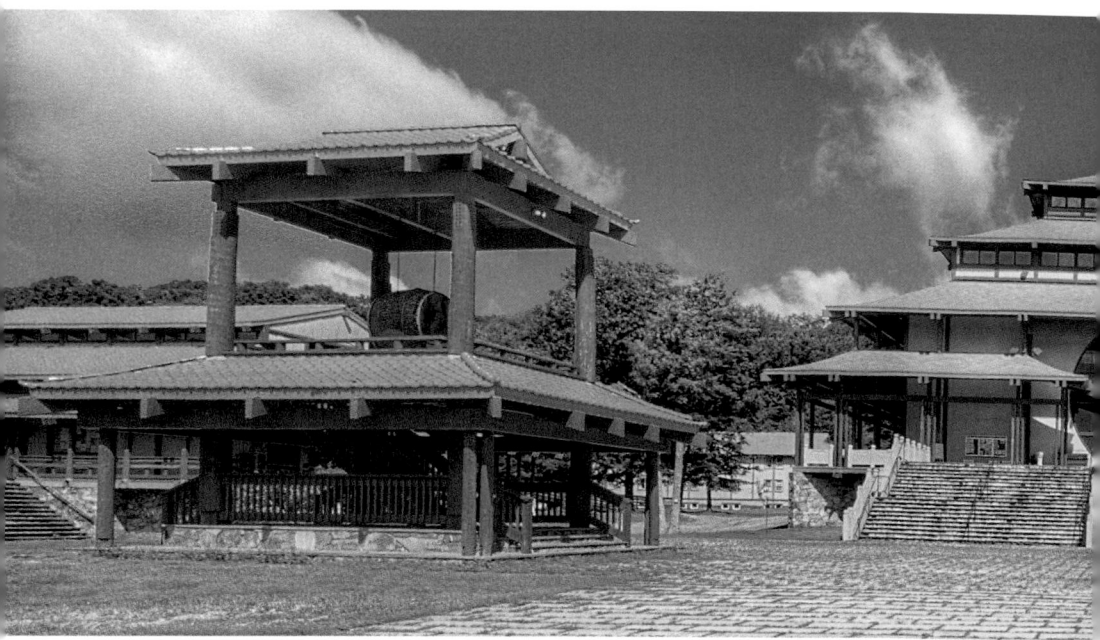

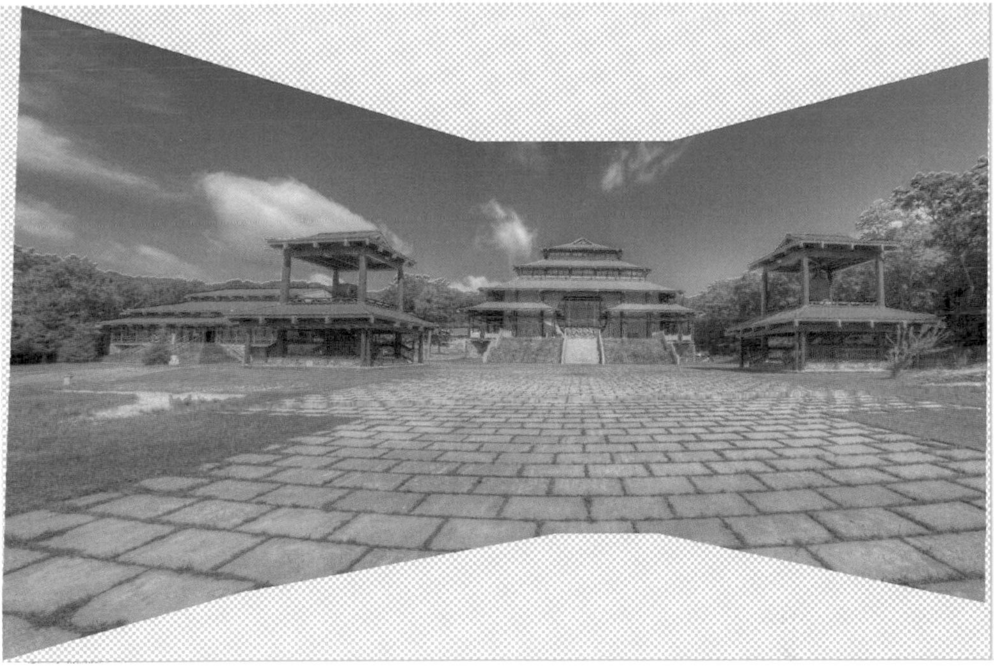

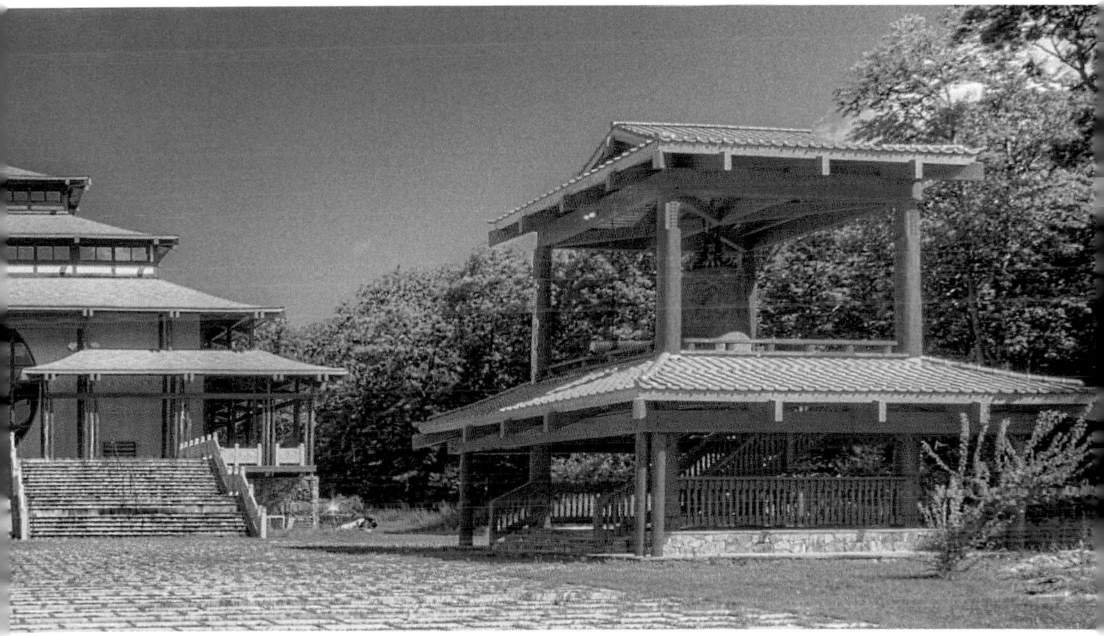

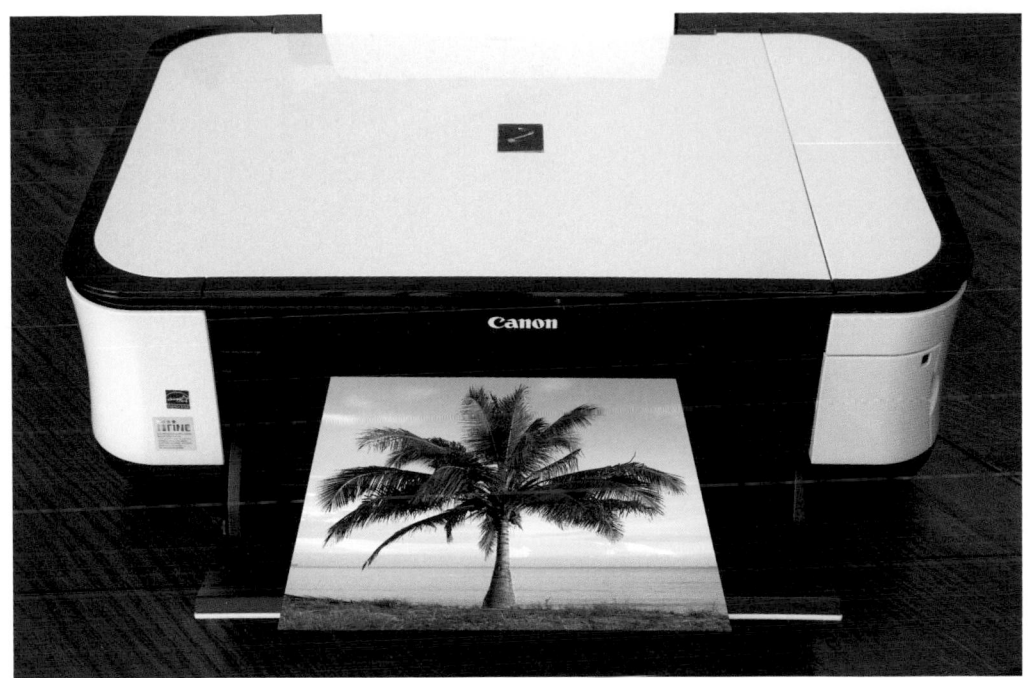

Part XVI

Make a Better Print

Today's cameras and printers make it possible to create truly excellent prints that will rival any traditional photo print. Almost every inkjet printer on the market will give you photo-quality printing. Yet some photographers are frustrated by not being able to get a great print.

This chapter, written by my good friend Rob Sheppard and illustrated with my images, offers a quick look at how you can make a good print.

I say *quick* because printing is an art form. Entire books have been written on the subject. My favorite: *301 Inkjet Tips and Techniques* by Andrew Darlow.

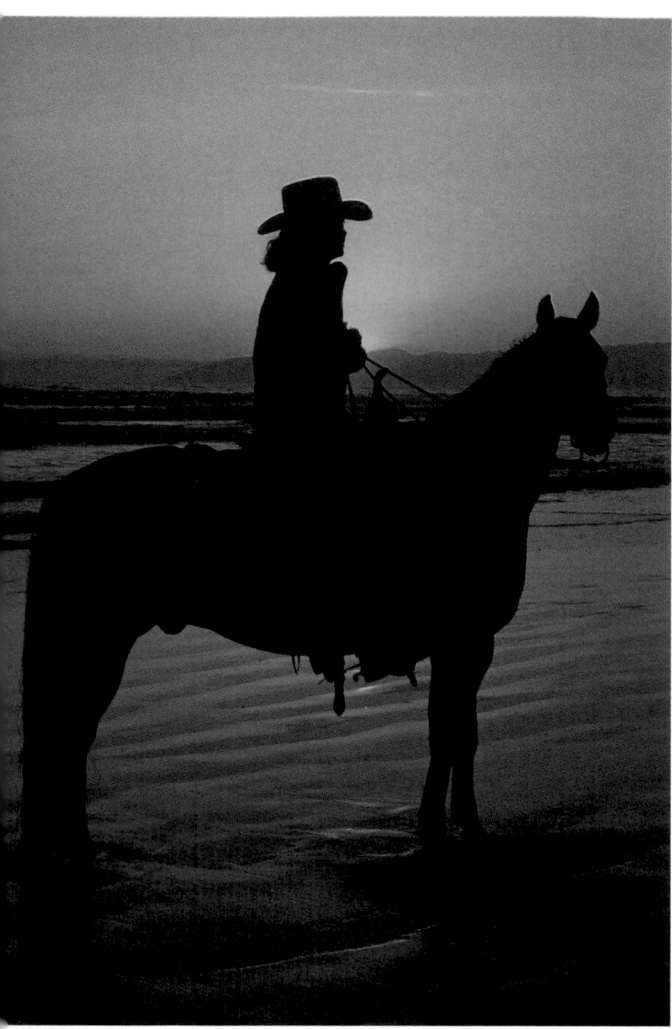

Shoot It Right

To get a good print, you really have to start right from the beginning ... when you first take a picture.

What I'm saying is that if the picture isn't sharp from the start, it cannot be sharp in the print. Similarly, if parts of the picture are overexposed, then no amount of work will make them look right in the print.

To get a good image for printing, it is important that you pay attention to sharpness, exposure and noise when you're shooting. Use a fast enough shutter speed to stop movement in your picture. If you don't, then any camera movement will likely cause blurring. Use a tripod or brace the camera when shutter speeds get slow; anything under 1/60 second can be suspect.

Noise is like grain from the days of film. It looks like a sand texture over your photograph. Underexposure and high ISO settings will increase your grain, and this will show up in your print. Keep noise to a minimum by using the lowest possible ISO and watching your exposure.

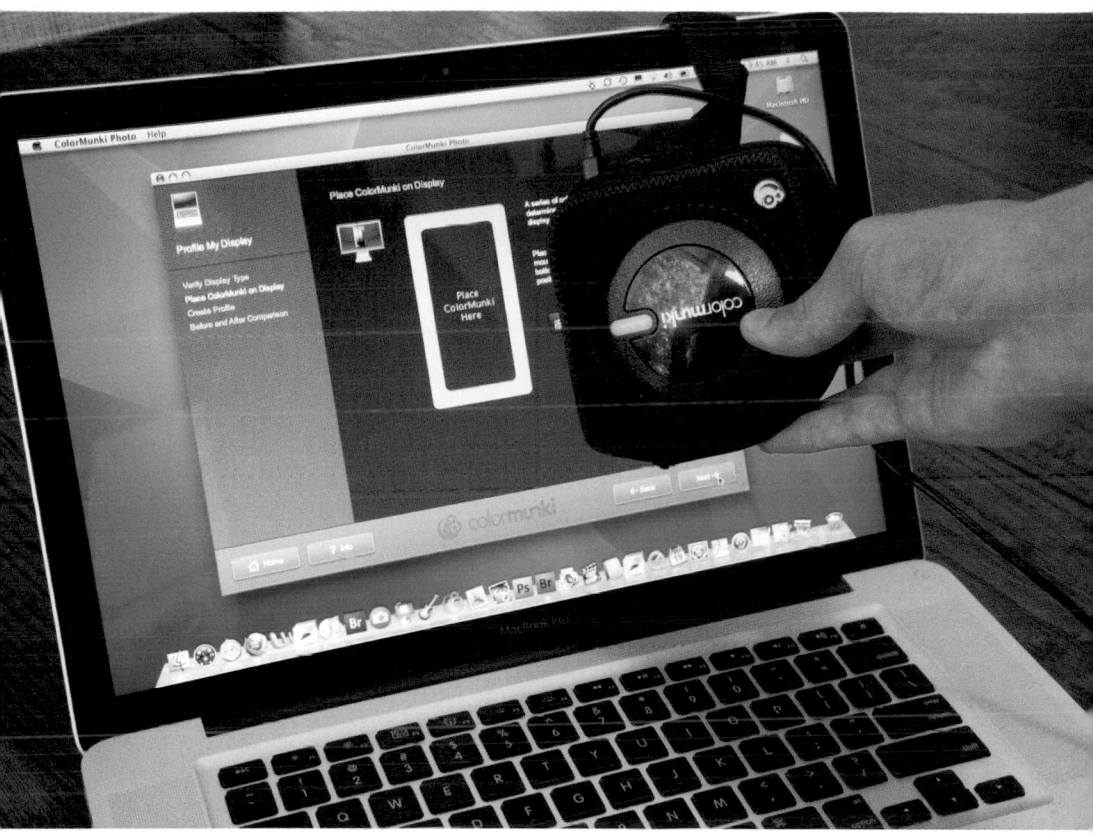

Calibrate Your Monitor

A calibrated monitor will not guarantee that you'll get a good print, but it will give you predictable, consistent results so you are *more likely* to get a good print. Calibration tools are readily available at a variety of prices, and any of them will—at minimum—help you get started in creating a consistent work environment on your monitor.

Here is an image of Rick's calibration device, the Colormunki, which he uses to calibrate his laptop and desktop computers as well as his printers and digital projector.

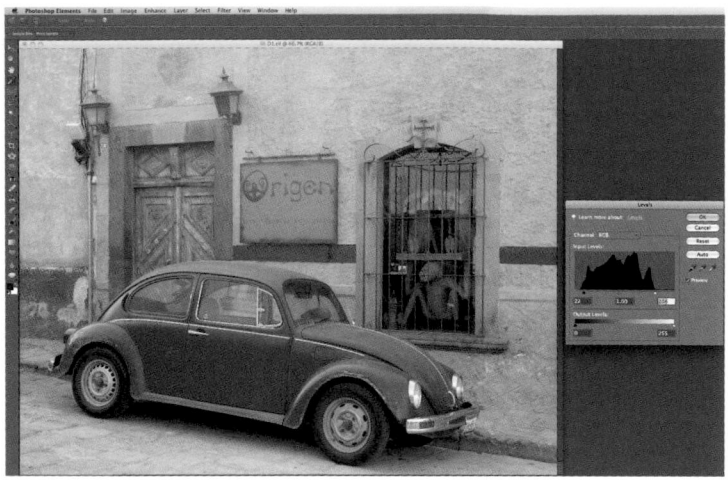

Adjust Your Photo

Your camera is designed to give you good pictures, but it isn't necessarily designed to give you image files for the best prints. There are a few things that you need to check on your images to make sure that you are getting a good image file for printing.

First, crop and rotate the picture as needed. It is easy to correct crooked horizons and remove problems along the edges of your picture. Don't print a crooked picture; people will notice.

Check your blacks and whites. Many prints look a bit weak, and people think it's because the colors aren't right, so they increase color saturation. Then they find it doesn't work. Almost all digital files need to have the blacks and whites checked to be sure they are adequate for printing.

The best way to do this is to use Levels adjustments or something similar that allows you to actually see the blacks or dark parts of your picture. In Photoshop Elements and similar programs, you can hold down the Alt or Option key as you adjust the black side of Levels, and you will see a black threshold screen. How much you need to adjust is subjective, but usually you need some. Do the same with the white side; but here, you want to keep whites barely showing.

Next, check your mid-tones. This is where you really affect the overall exposure correction in the computer, and this will definitely affect the look of a print. You can do this with Levels or a Tone Curve. It can be especially important to brighten dark tones.

Now adjust color. Check your color balance to be sure you have no color casts that might adversely affect your print. Then look at individual colors to see if there are any corrections that need to be made to their hue or saturation. It is usually best to adjust individual colors and saturation rather than doing an overall adjustment.

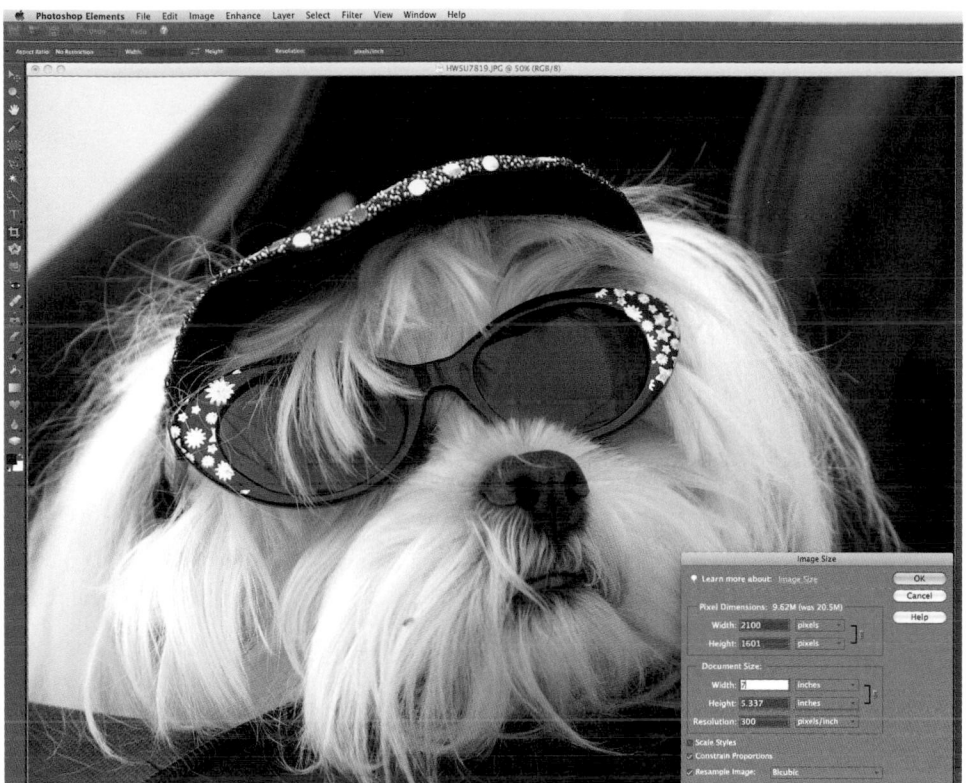

Size your Photo for Printing

In Photoshop Elements, you need to set the image size of the print you want to make. Go to Image > Resize > Image Size. In that window, set the Width and Height of the image. For making high-quality prints, you want to set the Resolution to 300. When you want to email a photo or use a picture for a web site, set the Resolution to 100.

When you upsize (make a larger image), set Bicubic to Smoother. When you downsize an image (make it smaller), set Bicubic to Sharper. Please keep in mind that these are general guidelines for the beginner printer.

Again, printing is an art form. Check out *301 Inkjet Tips and Techniques* by Andrew Darlow for more on this topic. It's the book I mentioned at the beginning of this chapter.

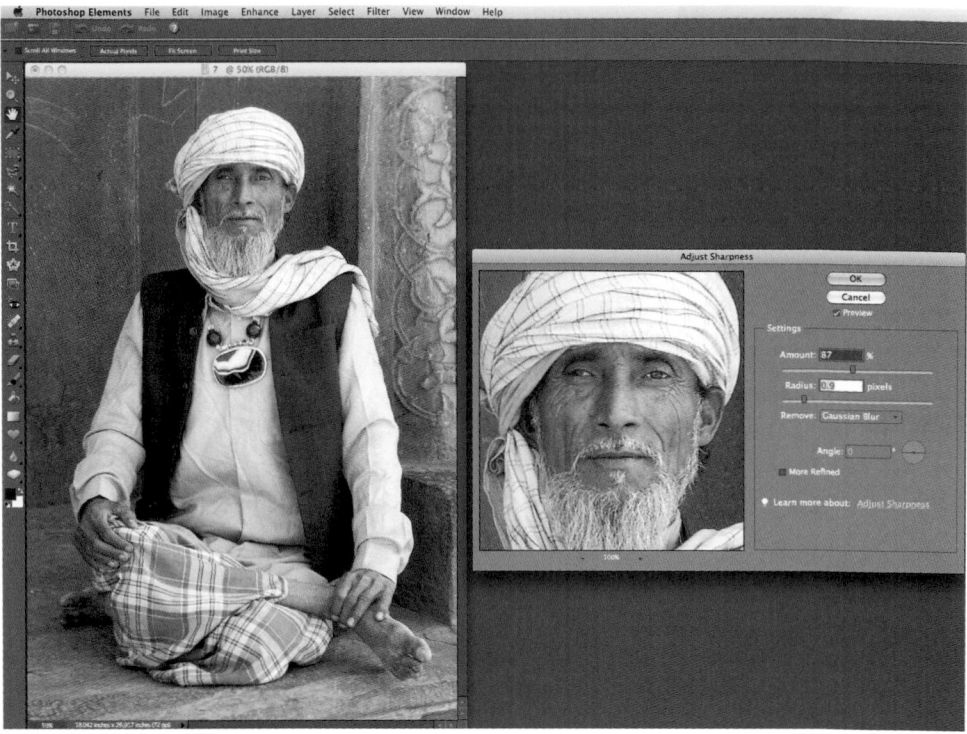

Sharpen your Photo

If you are shooting JPEG files, then your camera will sharpen your photo to some degree. If you are shooting RAW, no sharpening is applied to your image in-camera.

Nevertheless, most photos will need some sharpening for printing. JPEGs require a little less because, as I just mentioned, this type of photo file has already been sharpened in-camera.

There are many formulas for good sharpening. They all work, but they differ in order to address different needs for different subject matter. Sharpen a picture appropriately for the subject.

That is, keep in mind that detailed landscapes and buildings can handle more sharpening than a portrait. You will also find that you may need to sharpen differently for a glossy print versus a matte print. Use your artistic eye to figure out what works best for your images.

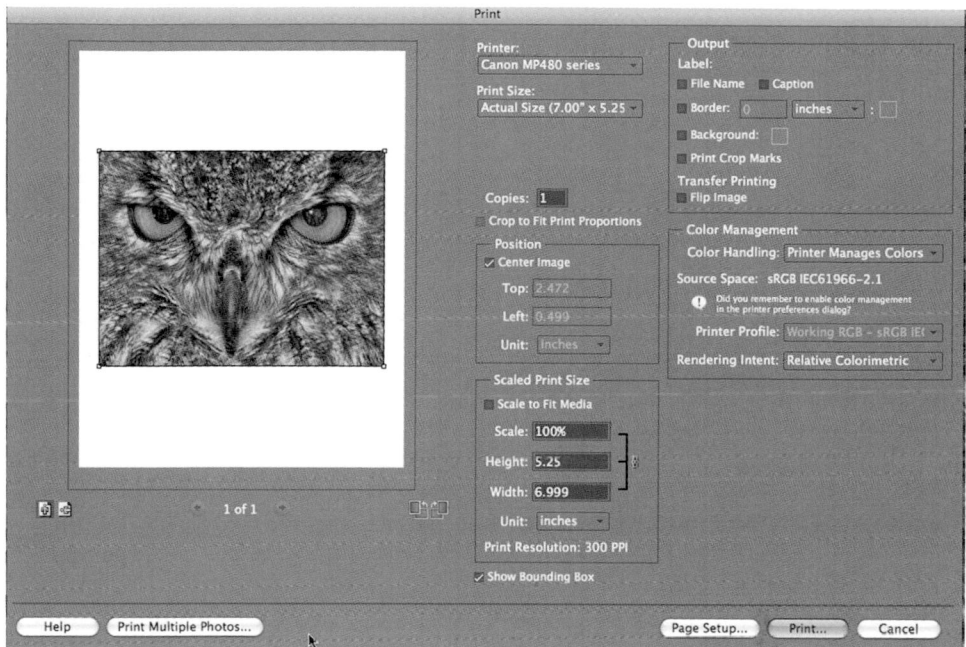

Working with the Printer

You must tell your printer how to deal with the file that's coming from the computer. This is called *setting the printer driver*. It's here that you tell the printer what is going on: what type of paper you put in it, the quality of the photo your want printed (top-quality, etc.), color or grayscale printing, and so on. Printer manufactures make printer drivers for different papers and so do paper manufacturers. Pick the right profile for the best results.

If you mess up here, your print will be messed up, so take your time and set these settings very carefully.

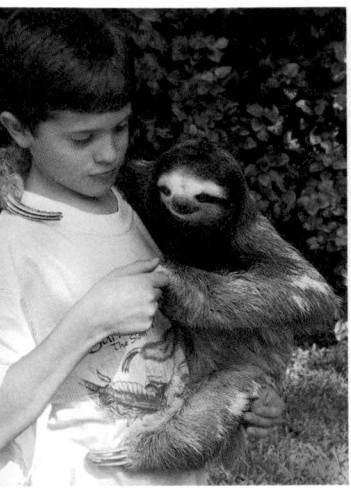 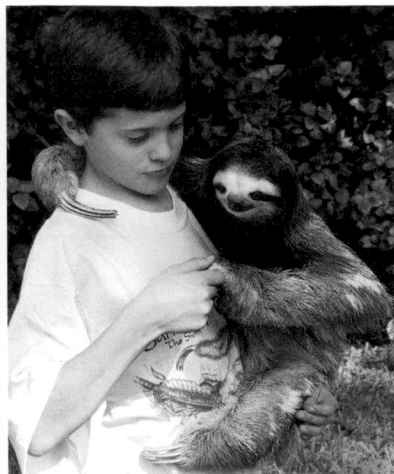 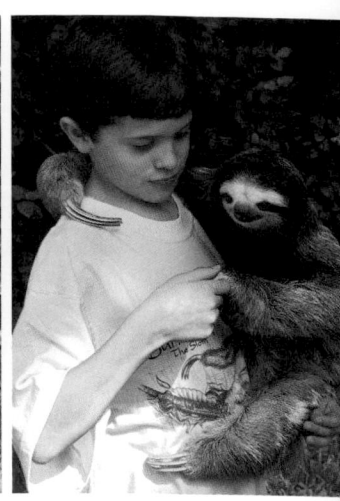

Test Your Print

Manufacturers of digital photo gear have promoted their products to imply that the process is so perfect that all you have to do is follow a few simple instructions and you'll get a perfect print. That's not necessarily true.

Even if you get your print to match the monitor, that doesn't necessarily mean it's a great print. A monitor is not a print and a print is not a monitor.

It is important to consider your first print a test print. If it looks great, then fine; you're done. However, if it doesn't look perfect, don't despair. Look at it and decide what needs to be done. Then try making some adjustments to the picture and reprinting.

If you don't set up your monitor and don't tell your printer what's going on, you will most likely get an off-color, too light or too dark, or muddy print—or all of the above.

For example, the center picture here has good color and brightness. The picture on the left is too red, and the picture on the right is too green and too dark. See what happens if you skip important printing setup steps?! It ain't pretty.

P.S. From Rick:

Check out Rob's web site: www.robsheppardphoto.com

And don't miss his blogs: www.photodigitary.com and www.seeingcreation.com

Index

X

X key, and Layer Mask, 162

Z

0 exposure compensation setting, 180

zoom
  blurring background, 116, 117
  built-in, 26
  capabilities, compact camera, 26
  close-ups, 54, 118
  composing with, 114–115
  digital, 26
  overview, 113
  range, 26

Zoom Tool, Photoshop Elements, 158